a special gift

---
presented to:

---
from:

---
date:

You are a hiding place for me;
You, Lord, preserve me from trouble,
You surround me with songs and shouts of deliverance.

—Psalm 32:7, Amplified

{ Sanctuary }

The Women's Devotional Series

To order, call **1-800-765-6955.**
Visit us at **www.reviewandherald.com**
for more information on other Review and Herald® products.

{ Sanctuary }

finding *sanctuary for the soul*
in the presence of God

ardis stenbakken, editor

REVIEW AND HERALD® PUBLISHING ASSOCIATION
Since 1861 | www.reviewandherald.com

This book was
Edited by Jeannette R. Johnson
Copyedited by James Hoffer
Designed by Patricia Wegh
Cover photos © 2009 iStockphoto
Typeset: Minion 10.5/13.5

PRINTED IN U.S.A.

13 12 11 10 09   5 4 3 2 1

Library of Congress Cataloging-in-Publication Data
Sanctuary : a daily devotional for women by women / edited by Ardis Dick Stenbakken.
    p. cm.
    1. Seventh-day Adventist women—Prayers and devotions. 2. Devotional calendars—
Seventh-day Adventists. I. Stenbakken, Ardis Dick.
    BV4844.S26 2009
    242'.643—dc22
                                2009013197

ISBN 978-0-8280-2472-3

There is an aspect of this book that is unique.

None of these contributors has been paid—they have shared freely so that all profits go to scholarships for women. As this book goes to press, 1,458 scholarships have been given to women in 105 countries.

For more current information, or to contribute to these scholarships, please go to http://adventistwomensministries.org/index.php?id=60. In this way, you too can provide a sanctuary, a safe haven for others.

Girl, God Is Good

To whom will you liken me that we may be compared?
Isa. 46:5, NIV.

ONE JANUARY 1 a friend and I decided to fast and pray during the coming year. The spirit impressed me that we should pray for our families, friends, and campus family, so we joyfully embraced the idea. That first morning we set out on a long walk to an area that we felt that we would be surrounded by only trees and the beauty of nature—the sky, the pleasant sound of birds, and, from time to time, the sound of rain in the distance.

Sometime after we began our prayer session, a dark cloud rolled in, and we again heard the rain at a distance. My friend suggested that we begin a praise session, so we began to sing praise choruses and asked God to send the rain away. He did! And the same thing happened the second time we met for our prayer time. However, when we heard the rain the third time, it seemed to be coming from both directions. Because of our earlier experience, we decided to have another praise session. We sang song after song, but the rain continued to come closer and closer. We began to praise God more, but the rain would not go away. Right there, we decided that we would not leave. It looked as though we were going to get wet anyway, so we asked God to prevent us from getting wet, because we were not leaving until we had prayed for everyone on our list. By that time we both had only our family members to lift in prayer.

We continued in prayer. Name by name, we presented our family members to God while the showers became heavier. We had now gotten off the ground and stood praying. Our sleeping bags were wet, our bedsheets were soaking wet, our hair was damp, but our clothes and feet felt dry. We finished our prayers and left. Not even wanting to talk about the miracle, we were silent until we were on our way back to the dorm. I then exclaimed, "Girl, you see how God is good? This year we just need to challenge God more!"

But right there the Spirit corrected me, and I said, "Sorry, girl! This year we need to challenge *ourselves* to *trust* God more! He is willing and ready to do all things on our behalf."

We laughed in appreciation for what God had revealed, because now we knew what God wanted us to do that year: to challenge ourselves to trust Him more.

Don't you want to take that challenge too?

Nadine A. Joseph

New Resolutions Every Morning

It is of the Lord's mercies that we are not consumed, because his compassions fail not.
They are new every morning: great is thy faithfulness.
Lam. 3:22, 23.

ON THE FOURTH PAGE of the first newspaper of the year were pictures of seven individuals who had been asked: "What is your New Year's resolution?" As I read each one I thought about what the real basis for their declaration might have been.

One youth said, "I want to find a successful career in my field of education." (Was this like Solomon's prayer for wisdom or for personal and/or professional gain and prestige?) A young father said, "I want to spend more time with my wife and family." (Was he aware of having to give an answer one day to the question "Where is the flock that was given thee, thy beautiful flock?" [Jer. 13:20].) Three women made resolutions related to health issues: two wanted to lose a few pounds; the other said she wanted to quit smoking. (Had they learned that their bodies are the temple of God and wanted to purify them for Him? [1 Cor. 3:16].)

Another respondent vowed she wouldn't go to garage sales anymore. She said she didn't need any more junk. She didn't say what she would do with the money saved from this compulsive buying. Maybe she was considering supporting a worthy charity or mission project.

Then there was the man who said, "I never make New Year's resolutions, because then I don't end up breaking them!"

I wondered how I would have answered the question "What is your New Year's resolution?" What would I want the readers of the newspaper to know about my personal resolutions? What really matters? What areas of my life need changing, and which would make an impact on me, as well as those who read my resolutions?

I noted that the resolutions made by those pictured in the newspaper reflected the physical, social, and intellectual aspects of their lives—but none touched on their spiritual lives. None pledged to have a closer walk with God, or to ease the burdens of humankind.

Why wait for the new year to make resolutions for living a better life, for dropping a bad habit, or brightening the day for some less fortunate soul? Let's make commitments every morning to our God who provides for us 24/7/365.

Edith Fitch

Thank God for Our House

But my God shall supply all your need.
Phil. 4:19.

EVER SINCE WAYNE AND I got married, one of our plans was to buy our own house. When I became pregnant with our first child, it became apparent that the studio apartment we rented didn't have enough space. We tried contacting the various housing developers whose numbers we saw posted on billboards, but to no avail. I asked God if He was going to allow the year 2003 to finish before we got our house.

As 2004 began, the Lord inspired me to start thanking Him for our house. I obeyed His command, and one week later He began opening doors for us to realize our goal. We were able to access funds to make the down payment on a house that was being advertised on television. Before the year ended—on December 13, to be exact—we moved into our own house!

The God we serve is an awesome God! Without a doubt again He is concerned about our every need and is willing and able to supply them all. The song tells us that "His eye is on the sparrow, and I know He watches me." But He not only makes provisions for us here on this sin-sick earth—He has something better in store.

John 14:1-3 tells us of our heavenly home, which the Lord has gone to prepare for us. He says that we should not be troubled but trust Him. Why? Because He has gone to prepare a place for us, and when everything is ready He will come and get us to be with Him forever. If we accept His promise, we will inherit all He has gone to prepare for us.

Revelation 21 gives us a vivid picture of what heaven will be like. Imagine the beauty! I have the privilege of seeing the beauty of some mansions here on earth on TV, and there are not words enough to describe them. Just imagine what Jesus has in store for us!

The Word of God further states that we "will build houses and dwell in them" in the earth made new (Isa. 65:21, 22, NIV). What a wonderful provision our God has made for us, and one day, if we remain faithful, we shall possess our inheritance.

Thank You, Lord, for our house: the one we live in now—and the one You have promised to each of us.

Thamer Cassandra Smikle

It's Your Turn Now

Give all your cares to the Lord and He will give you strength.
Ps. 55:22, NLV.

AUBREY COMES AT LEAST once a week to spend the day with us. It's a great privilege to have a whole day to spend with such a bright little granddaughter. We all have fun!

This year we had a bountiful harvest from our peach tree, and I looked for ways to use peaches. One day I suggested to Aubrey that we make small peach pies. We could enjoy some of them and share others with neighbors. Aubrey was enthusiastic. So we started to gather and mix the ingredients. (When she helps me cook, as soon as we get even a few ingredients together she wants to start tasting. She discovered that pie dough ingredients are not the most tasty.) And then the fun began—rolling out the dough. I make a really easy oil piecrust, but it must be rolled out between two sheets of wax paper. Aubrey, standing on her little stool, picked up the heavy rolling pin and began rolling out the first little piecrust. But it wasn't easy for someone who had just turned 4. Finally I asked her, "Do you want Grandma to help you?"

"Yes," she said with obvious relief. "We can take turns, and it's your turn."

And so we took turns. She would begin the rolling out process on each little piecrust, but when things got too out of shape (or Aubrey just got tired), it was my turn again.

I thought about that little exchange and its implications and wondered if I don't often do the same thing with God. I try my best to meet life's challenges by myself, but when they get too tough (or I mess things up beyond repair), I turn to God and tell Him that it's His turn. And I imply that when the tough part is past, I'll take over again.

So I have to ask myself: wouldn't it be so much better just to ask God to work *with* me, that we work together as a team, rather than taking turns? I was certainly ready and willing to help Aubrey, and I am sure God wants to help me as well. God promises that if we give Him our troubles, our cares, He will take care of us, He will give us the strength. The *Message* paraphrases today's text this way: "Pile your troubles on God's shoulders—he'll carry your load, he'll help you out." First Peter 5:7 (NIV) has a similar idea: "Cast all your anxiety on him because he cares for you."

How about you? Are you working with God, or are the two of you just taking turns?

Ardis Dick Stenbakken

Touch From the Master's Hand

He touched the man's ear and healed him.
Luke 22:51, NIV.

SHE SLIPPED QUIETLY into my cubicle and said softly, "I've come to stay with you. No one should go through a procedure like this by herself." Thoughts raced through my head: It's only a biopsy. I'm a strong person. She's the chief nurse—she must have plenty of other things to do today. But as Mary smiled and settled in next to my gurney, I was surprised to realize how very glad I was to have her there.

The outpatient surgery nurse finished the last of the required preliminaries, which included starting an IV in my right arm, and I was on my way to medical imaging. Mary stayed right beside me. *How interesting to experience firsthand what other patients go through,* I thought. *If everyone is as caring and competent toward them, no wonder our Adventist Health hospital receives such outstanding patient-satisfaction scores!*

The interventional radiologist approached me, needles in hand, and introduced himself. I took a deep breath and reminded myself to stay calm and centered. *I can do this.* Standing by my gurney, Mary crossed herself, good Catholic that she is, and asked, "Would you like me to hold your hand?" I hesitated. *I'm a big girl,* I thought. *Do I need someone to hold my hand? Do I even want someone to hold my hand?*

Perhaps sensing my indecision, Mary simply reached out, picked up my left hand, and enclosed it in both of hers. In that instant everything changed. Yes, I was still aware of the needles being thrust into my neck and the professional bustle around me, but my consciousness was now focused on the feel of my hand in hers. A sense of comfort, safety, camaraderie, and connectedness washed over me. Later I would read *The Heart's Code,* by Dr. Paul Pearsall, and realize that the energy generated by her caring heart was flowing through our clasped hands into mine. At the moment I was simply, humbly grateful that Mary had given me such a personal and transforming gift—one I hadn't even realized I needed, or wanted.

Back in recovery I mused, *What people must have felt when the Master touched them!* For the first time in my life I could hardly wait to feel the touch of Christ's hand on mine—in person.

Arlene Taylor

The Angry Snake

For the wages of sin is death, but the free gift of God is eternal life through Christ Jesus our Lord. Rom. 6:23, NLT.

SNAKES ARE DEFINITELY NOT my favorite creatures! Many are poisonous and offer nothing but sickness or death. Genesis 3 tells us that of all the animals that God had made, the flying serpent was the most beautiful and intelligent. This creature was used as a tool of Satan to deceive Eve, and because of this it was made lower than any of the animals, crawling on the ground and eating dust. Later in this chapter reference is made to Satan, who, like a striking serpent, would try to destroy all. But then came the most wonderful, lifesaving antivenin—our Savior, who sacrificed His own life to save those who love Him, thus utterly crushing the serpent forever.

In the wilderness, when God removed the restraints that He had placed on the poisonous snakes in the area, the complaining Israelites soon learned of snakebite and death (Num. 21). Their only hope was in lifting their eyes to a bronze serpent made by Moses as instructed of God. Those who trusted and looked were healed. Those who refused to do so died. God is always the giver of life. He is almighty, and Satan has no power over Him.

During 2006 my husband, Keith, and I traveled across northeastern Australia. We saw a number of snakes on the road and some very poisonous ones being shown at outback shows. One night while staying with friends in the mountains, I stepped out onto their veranda to go down the steps. There I discovered a large carpet snake, crawling along the handrail. Its long body was beautifully marked, and I knew that these snakes, if let alone, were mostly placid. However, I didn't wait long before calling for someone to come. Unfortunately, the family dog also arrived on the scene, and the snake became angry. It coiled and struck at the dog again and again, barely missing him.

Don't be deceived by the subtlety of Satan; he also turns to strike as an angry snake. But it won't be long before Jesus returns and destroys him forever.

It's only through Jesus that we are protected from the bite of sin. If you have been bitten, seek His forgiveness today and be healed. Pray to live victoriously over Satan, and be thankful for the gift of life and salvation.

Lyn Welk-Sandy

God Will Put His Angels in Charge of You

God will put his angels in charge of you to protect you wherever you go.
Ps. 91:11, TEV.

EARLY ONE SUNDAY MORNING I was leaving Michigan, where I'd been visiting my children and grandchildren, to return to my home in Tennessee. After my devotional time and breakfast, I packed my car and began my trip. It rained on and off most of the day. A heavy rainstorm, accompanied by thunder and lightning, hit as I traveled through Kentucky.

As I drove in the center lane, cars around me began slowing down. Suddenly a car in the fast lane sped down the road. It had barely passed me when it began to hydroplane, twisting and sliding, totally out of control. I applied my brakes carefully—I didn't want to lose control of my car—trying to slow down enough to avoid the out-of-control car. Then the car skidded into my lane sideways, scraped and damaged my front bumper, contined across the slow lane, went down into a ditch and up an incline, then turned around and headed back into the ditch, where it finally stopped.

A young couple stopped their car and ran back in the pouring rain to see if any of us involved in the accident were hurt. Thankfully, none of us were. Because this happened in a mountainous area, my cell phone wouldn't work, and I couldn't call for help. This kind couple, drenched through from the rain, were able to use their cell phone and called the highway patrol for assistance. They waited with me until an officer arrived. What good Samaritans!

After filling out the necessary accident forms, I was told I could continue with my trip. My car didn't have any damage that would prevent me from driving it. Unfortunately, the other car, which had five college students in it, had to be towed. How thankful I was for God's protection!

Later my friend Betty Chapin asked me what time the accident had occurred. I told her it had happened at 2:50 in the afternoon. She said she had been impressed to pray for me at that exact time. What a blessing to have friends praying for you!

My personal devotional time is part of my daily schedule before I leave home. As part of that, I want to be praying for friends—you never know when they may need it. Throughout the day I want God to put His angels in charge of me to protect me as He has promised. I hope you claim that promise today as well.

Patricia Mulraney Kovalski

Rose-colored Glasses

But we all, with open face beholding as in a glass the glory of the Lord, are changed into the same image from glory to glory even as by the Spirit of the Lord.
2 Cor. 3:18.

YEARS AGO JON CONLEE wrote a song titled "Rose-colored Glasses." One line says: "These rose-colored glasses that I'm looking through show only the beauty, 'cause they hide all the truth!" Did you know that there is Someone so in love with you that He has indeed put on rose-colored glasses through which to view you? That Someone knew you before you drew your first breath! He designed you, giving you your own individual DNA, and you are beautiful to Him! (Ps. 139). When you give Him your heart, there is so much excitement that all of heaven rejoices! Imagine your guardian angel doing cartwheels all the way to God's throne and excitedly saying to Jesus, "She did it! She gave her heart to You today!"

When we truly give our hearts to Jesus, we want to behold Him, we want to be like Him in all things, we long to have a closer relationship with Him. Things of this world begin to lose their appeal, and changes take place in our hearts. What shames our Lord shames us; what breaks His heart breaks our hearts, too. We begin looking at all people as valuable. No longer is the bag lady just a "bag lady"—she is a daughter of God, made in His image.

Tempers that once erupted more often than Yellowstone Park's Old Faithful begin to ebb. Though we seem to go forward two steps—and sometimes slide back 10—we're still making progress. The Word of God becomes to us a precious road map of life. We begin to thirst for God just as the doe in the dry scorching heat of summer thirsts for a spring of water so she can impart life to her fawn. His words are life to us, the Living Water, which we study for truth.

God looks at us through those rose-colored glasses, stained with the blood of His own precious Son, our Jesus. He sees in us what we are to become. He sees only the beauty, for the glasses hide the truth of our past. He looks at us, and He sees Jesus in us.

Our Father is asking you today: "Come to Me, My precious child; I have formed you; I knew all about you before you were even born! I will never forget you; 'I have blotted out, like a thick cloud, your transgressions' [Isa. 44:22, NKJV], and when I look through my rose-colored glasses—I see only the beauty in you!"

Karen Fettig

Experiencing God's Peace

You will keep in perfect peace [her] whose mind is steadfast, because [she] trusts in you.
Isa. 26:3, NIV.

IN A WORLD PUNCTUATED DAILY with terrorist attacks, rapes, murders, and every kind of violence and human misery, how is it possible to have peace? Our text shares the secret of peace amid the storms of life: trusting in God. I suppose it's possible for one's mind to be steadfast for other reasons—perhaps because they're stubborn and inflexible—but there's no peace in that kind of steadfastness. The steadfastness the text is referring to means to be unwavering, or loyal. When you determine to be loyal to God because you've learned to trust Him then He gives you peace—and more than that, perfect peace.

God doesn't ask us to trust Him blindly. In Psalm 34:8 (NIV) He invites us to "taste and see that the Lord is good." Our heavenly Father knows that we need to experience Him in a personal way in order to really know and trust Him.

When my son Brandon was 10 years old, he got his index finger caught in the gears of his bicycle, mashing it badly. He was always a squeamish kid who couldn't stand the sight of blood, but in the emergency room, while the doctor worked on his finger, I noticed that Brandon watched intently the entire time. When we got home, I asked him how he could stand to watch; the tip of the fractured bone was exposed and repulsive-looking to me. Brandon answered that he was afraid the doctor might decide to cut off his finger, or part of it, so he was watching to make sure that didn't happen! I had to smile at the unfounded fears of a child that only compounded his agony during his emergency room experience. He'd have had an easier time if he had trusted the person in charge, who was trained and knew exactly what to do.

But how often do we fail to turn to the One who not only knows exactly what to do but who always wants the very best for us, that which is for our eternal best good? He must shake His head when we fail to take advantage of the peace that comes from trusting Him. Paul tells us how to experience the peace of God: praying about everything (Phil. 4:6, 7). As we learn to commit *everything* to prayer, God, who is more than faithful, will surely grant us the peace that passes understanding.

Carla Baker

Oh! That Hurts!

A word aptly spoken is like apples of gold in settings of silver.
Prov. 25:11, NIV.

DURING A PATHFINDER FIELD TRIP my friend and I began skipping stones into the river. We collected as many as we could find, and soon we were each trying to outdistance the other. It was fun to watch the ripples race across the surface of the water. Perched on top of a rocky outcrop along the riverbank, we felt as if we were on top of the world—until an outraged cry rang through the air: "Oh! That hurts!"

We were having such fun that we hadn't noticed the rest of our friends making their way down to the river below. One of our stones had gone astray and struck a fellow Pathfinder, inflicting a painful wound to her head that required several stitches. We were filled with shame and remorse. Now, many years later, even though she has forgotten the pain, she still bears the scar.

I no longer throw stones, but if I'm not careful, I may say things that are even more hurtful than stones. It's easy to say things that cause embarrassment and inflict great pain. People seldom forget the hurtful barbs sent their way, especially when they come from friends and loved ones. Remember the old nursery rhyme "Sticks and stones may break my bones, but words will never hurt me"? It is more accurate to say that words *can* cause great harm. Sometimes the damage results in emotional scarring that remains for the rest of our lives.

Words have great power. Depending on how we choose to use them, words can destroy or heal. Kind words have the ability to uplift, inspire, encourage, and strengthen, creating endless joy and love for both us and the ones with whom we share them. In order to live a truly blessed life, we must throw out the negative words and speak only that which is good and true. As we do, ripples of joy will spread from us into the lives of others.

The Word of God says, "Reckless words pierce like a sword, but the tongue of the wise brings healing" (Prov. 12:18, NIV). As we invite the Holy Spirit to take control of our hearts, words both pure and lovely will flow from us to bless and uplift.

Father, please take control of our thoughts and feelings—and also our words. Help us to say words that only build and inspire rather than destroy. Amen.

Cordell Liebrandt

January 11

Let It Be!

The fear of the Lord leads to life: Then one rests content, untouched by trouble.
Prov. 19:23, NIV.

IT WAS PROBABLY the best job I've ever had—and the lowest paying. My uniform was a modest version of a formal tuxedo, with matching black hat bearing the words "Limo Driver." My official job was to drive senior citizens around town for personal appointments and shopping. But I had another reason for being there. I needed a lift! Although my husband's career was at its height, I found myself fighting thoughts that seemed to isolate me emotionally from those I loved. My thoughts were repetitive and confining: Poor me. This self-talk came freely and was increasingly addictive. From time to time I would imagine holding a pity party, complete with invitations, black balloons, songs, and games. On the outside, though, I was all smiles, especially at the retirement center. But before long my plastic smiles became real as I found others to center my thoughts on.

One individual at this active senior retirement center especially caught my eye. Even his name, King Gentry, set him apart. He was still quite independent, driving around town in his own car, escorting ladies to lunch, and being the life of the party at bingo. King Gentry was smart, too; he had a computer that he used regularly, writing to friends and family, or editing another one of his many poems for his book.

Recently I found one of Mr. Gentry's poems in my stationery box and finally took the time to read through it. It was just what I needed as a beginning retiree: "If we face eternity gracefully, Let it be./ Growing old with grace is hard to achieve./ Is it because we seem to think mostly Me,/ When we should think of a little more of We?/ If we love brother an' sister. Let it be./ And we believe life is made for all of We. . . . / If we live gracefully as we are, Let it be!/ May we share the gift of life more equally./ Only by the grace of God we live each day./ If we live well upon His grace, Let it be!"—King Gentry, July 21, 1999, Killeen, Texas.

I'll remember King's words: it's not just "me" but "we" walking down this road of life. I can survive—even thrive—if I reach out to others in friendship and love. Let it be!

Nancy Ann Neuharth Troyer

{ 18 }

Staying in Touch

Come near to God and he will come near to you.
James 4:8, NIV.

I RECENTLY TRAVELED several hours to see a family who had grown up across the street from where I had lived as a child. That family's siblings were near in age to my own brother and sister and me, and we have many happy memories and photographs of our times together. We had enjoyed sleepovers, camping and fishing trips, snow forts, boyfriends, girlfriends—countless hours were shared as children. As we now visited, we remembered those happy times fondly. It had been close to 30 years since we had seen each other, as we all now live in different states. Most of us have children and grandchildren to tell about, and in the short amount of time we had to visit we enjoyed catching up.

You would have thought that this would be a joyous occasion, right? Unfortunately, this get-together occurred because their father had died, and we were there to attend his memorial service. His family knew he had fallen asleep in Jesus, and they had the assurance of a heavenly reunion, but loss is never easy to bear—it cast a pall of sadness over the reunion. I was starkly reminded of the loss of my own father several years before.

Why is it that we lose touch with those we care about? How does it happen that they slowly drift away on a current of busy daily living? Before we know it, years have gone by, and we've lost a piece of our lives that we valued highly.

That can also happen to our relationship with God. If we are careless and let ourselves get too busy with our daily lives and don't keep in constant touch with God through daily devotions and time alone with Him, one day we wake up and realize that we don't have a close relationship with God anymore. We may even wonder why God doesn't seem close.

But the wonderful thing about God is that, unlike our human friends, it doesn't take a letter or an e-mail or a phone call—or even a funeral—to get back in touch. All we have to do is just whisper a prayer. Tell Him how you feel. Ask for His help and know that He will hear and answer. Make a firm resolve to do better at keeping in touch and know that God is always there, just waiting. There is joy in heaven over one sinner who renews a relationship.

Fauna Rankin Dean

Simple Things

What is the price of five sparrows—two copper coins? Yet God does not forget a single one of them.
Luke 12:6, NLT.

SOMETIMES WE THINK that God cares only about helping with our big problems, and we hesitate to ask Him for help with the simpler things. Our text tells us that God cares for the sparrows, and a recent experience showed me that He cares about even the smallest incidents in my life.

New neighbors recently moved from a nearby city to property adjoining our large acreage in the country. They are a devoted Christian couple, and we enjoyed getting to know them as they built their home and began to get settled. They brought their old dog with them, but since this dog is blind, they decided to get another dog to keep him company. Samson is a large dog with a deep-throated bark and sharp teeth that can look quite menacing. They assured us that Samson is harmless, but at times he has followed us a half mile or more up the road, barking all the way, as we traveled in our open golf cart. When we work where our properties adjoin, Samson seems to think we don't belong there and tries to chase us away. When his owners are home, one of them comes to get him, and that solves the problem for the moment.

One day we needed to do some work near the property line, and I knew the neighbors were probably not home. Since I didn't want to be bothered by Samson, I prayed that he would stay home. As usual, though, when he heard us coming, Samson started up the road toward us. But then he suddenly stopped just about at the property line. He kept on barking, but he didn't come any closer. At first I couldn't believe what I was seeing—then I realized that my prayer had been answered, and I sent a quiet "Thank You" up to heaven. The whole time we worked he barked, but it was as if an angel held him back from our property.

Several times since then we have worked nearby, and always we hear Samson barking, but he no longer comes near us. God not only answered my prayer that one time; He also sends His angel each time we work there.

Thank You, Father, for not only caring for the sparrows but also for the simple things in the lives of Your children.

Betty J. Adams

Nini and Mila

*The Lord appeared to us in the past, saying: "I have loved you
with an everlasting love; I have drawn you with loving-kindness."*
Jer. 31:3, NIV.

ON THE SMALL FARM on which I grew up, my father always liked to have animals around. For as long as I can remember we have always had pets in our home—dogs, cats, parakeets, monkeys, turtles, parrots, macaws, chickens, a bull calf, and even a billygoat.

After my sister Nini got married, she hated to be alone. During one period of time her husband was studying for his college entrance examinations, and he had classes almost all day. Her loneliness increased, so they decided to buy a little dog to keep her company.

One Friday afternoon the puppy search began. From time to time Nini called to tell me how things were going. At 4:30 p.m. my sister informed me she was buying a puppy. It was a little dog, a bichon frise breed, who soon received the name of Mila. I learned that this breed has the characteristic of being extremely docile. I went to her house, taking the camera, eager to see her new acquisition. As soon as I arrived I gathered the puppy in my arms—it was white, soft, and very small. How happy I was! That day was filled with joy.

The next day Nini's house seemed less empty to her. My sister had sleepy and mischievous company. At times Mila rested, seemingly exhausted, on the floor in the living room. If Nini had to get up and go to the kitchen, Mila trotted right behind her with heavy eyes. She wanted to be close by her new mistress.

On the day after they had purchased Mila, I woke up thinking about the little dog. What a lovely creature she was! Then, my thoughts turned to my spiritual life. I wanted to meet the little puppy on the very day my sister bought her. I didn't think about anything else all day. So I wondered, Do I get as excited each morning to know what God's will shall be for me that day? Am I paying attention to hear what God is saying to me? Do I go wherever God calls me, even when my eyes are heavy with sleep? Am I as faithful to God as Mila is to her owner?

It is my prayer that we may love, even as we are loved, with loving-kindness.

Iani Dias Lauer-Leite

A Father's Loving Care

Like as a father pitieth his children, so the Lord pitieth them that fear him.
For he knoweth our frame; he remembereth that we are dust.
Ps. 103:13, 14.

THERE WERE MANY ADJUSTMENTS to make during our first months in Penang, Malaysia. One was the poor electrical wiring in the buildings. Most homes weren't wired for clothes dryers, so our dryer would run for two minutes, overheat, and trip the breaker switch, meaning I had to flip the breaker and restart the dryer repeatedly. It could take a couple of hours to dry a load of clothes.

One day when I was down with a cold and feeling overwhelmed, I looked up into heaven and said, "Lord, couldn't You please send an angel to keep his finger on the breaker so I can just dry one load of clothes? I think I've just about had it."

I know what you're thinking—we're not supposed to tell God what to do, and you're right. But thankfully, "He remembers that we are dust" (Ps. 103:14, NIV), and He sometimes intervenes when life piles up too much. After praying, I flipped the breaker. To my amazed delight, the dryer stayed on for the whole load of clothes. "Thank You, Lord!" I exclaimed.

The next day I prayed again, and again that dryer, which had never stayed on longer than two minutes, stayed on till the clothes were dry. For three weeks the Lord kept the dryer on.

One day I shared this experience with a friend, rejoicing in God's provision. Satan then whispered, "Maybe it's a coincidence, since the dryer hasn't tripped the breaker for three weeks." I began to doubt, and later that day, while washing a load of clothes, the washer tripped the breaker—the washer had never done this before. This made me realize my mistake, and I begged God for forgiveness. How could I have listened to suggestions of doubt?

One week later an electrician came to rewire the laundry room. During that whole month the only time the breaker tripped was the day I doubted.

What a loving Father we have who stoops to meet our needs. How wonderful He is to patiently bring us the lessons we need to develop trust in Him. If He would answer a prayer of such minor significance to show that He cares, how much more will He satisfy our longing hearts when we seek after Him!

Teresa (Proctor) Hebard

With or Without Prayer

Peace I leave with you; my peace I give you. I do not give to you as the world gives.
Do not let your hearts be troubled and do not be afraid.
John 14:27, NIV.

A HEMORRHAGE FORCED US to admit our son to a hospital in São Paulo. After five days of suffering, the cause of bleeding was finally discovered—an artery had burst in the small intestine. Already weak, Wesley was not even able to get up; he was very concerned. His father and I didn't leave him alone for one moment; we suffered with him in the hospital hallways. Everything was being done, but we wanted the situation resolved quickly—we wanted the hemorrhage stopped! He received blood and was transferred to the intensive-care unit. Our son's health was in God's hands, and we knew that many church members were praying. His suffering right before our eyes hurt us, especially since there was nothing we could do.

I began to think, *Does this hospital have the resources to take care of his situation?* When I questioned the physician, he assured me that the hospital was well equipped; however, I didn't totally trust his response. My family, wanting to help us, had prepared for a transfer to another well-known hospital. The final decision for the transfer, though, would be mine.

I thought, *My sons were born in this hospital . . . I've had several surgeries here. In fact, in this hospital, everything is done with prayer.*

What a difficult decision! Take our son to a hospital with better resources but without prayer, or stay in this modest hospital where prayer was an integral part? How could I decide?

Frustrated, I thought, *How I would like for God to come down here now and tell me what to do! I do not want to make a mistake! God, I want Your will to be done!* At that moment I heard the voice of God talking to me: "Be still and know that I am God."

What peace I felt! I had no doubt my son was in God's hands, in the care of physicians who were qualified by Him. He would not be transferred! The doctor performed the surgery successfully the following day. Today my son is very healthy and has finished a graduate degree in law. He has a good job and is preparing for marriage. Most important, he is happy in Jesus.

Place your doubts, fears, and concerns in God's hands. He always cares for you.

Elza C. dos Santos

Facing My Jericho

By faith the walls of Jericho fell down.
Heb. 11:30.

THE ISRAELITES FACED the battle of Jericho with fear and trembling. The situation seemed impossible. The walls were insurmountable. The enemy within was invincible. They were so afraid. We too face Jerichos in life—problems that are insurmountable, an enemy within that is invincible, a situation that seems impossible—and we, too, are afraid. I faced my own Jericho in December 2006. I had been diagnosed with cancer. The enemy within was invincible. The situation seemed impossible. I was so afraid.

It started as a toothache. But the dentist said my teeth were fine, and he recommended a neurologist. An MRI revealed a small growth on my left trigeminal nerve, back near the brain. A biopsy proved it to be non-Hodgkins lymphoma. After a surgery of nearly five hours, the growth was gone. Then came a series of chemotherapy treatments.

The Israelites were afraid to face Jericho, but God said to march. So they marched by faith for seven days. And "by faith the walls of Jericho fell down." My march around the walls of my Jericho took not seven days, but seven months. I marched by faith, and by faith the walls of cancer came tumbling down. I praise God for seeing me through. But it was not just my faith—it was the faith of thousands around the world who prayed for me. It was the faith of my coworkers and my children and my husband. For those seven months Ron never left my side. If he had to travel on important business, he flew out in the morning and was home again that night so he could be with me at night when the battle was the hardest.

So many times I wanted to give up the march. It was a terrible journey. I wanted to stop. I wished to die. But I did not. By faith—the faith of a host of friends—I kept marching. By faith—the faith of my children, who called often to encourage me, who came when they could to be with me—I kept marching. By faith—the faith of my husband—I kept marching. When I was thin and weak and bald, with sunken eyes and wrinkled skin, he told me that I was beautiful and that I was going to make, it for he was praying for me.

I praise God for the faith of friends and family who believed the walls of my Jericho would eventually fall. And they did!

Dorothy Eaton Watts

The Helping Word

A word fitly spoken is like apples of gold in pictures of silver.
Prov. 25:11.

I RUSHED INTO THE BREAK ROOM, aiming for the snack dispenser—and right into an embarrassing situation. There was Karen, sitting on Tom's lap. I knew (and knew Karen knew) that Tom was married.

Tom, a very sensitive, intelligent, and helpful lead man on my shift, had helped me learn my job and had encouraged me during my first trial-and-error (mostly error) efforts. I liked and, until that moment, had respected him. Not sure what to do, I completed my purchase and left as quickly as I could.

Later that evening Tom came to sit with me in the lunch room. He wanted to apologize and tried to explain. He went into great detail about the breakup with his wife, and how Karen had reached out to him. However, it sounded to me as if Karen had inserted herself into his life in such a way as to facilitate the breakup. He went on and on, not only about the problems but about the joys of his married life. As the break period drew to an end and he ran down, he finally asked me for my opinion in such a way that I could tell he wanted my approval of his budding relationship with Karen. *Dear Lord, give me the right words to say!* I prayed as I picked up my food tray to leave. Finally I said, "It sounds to me as though you are still in love with your wife."

Not long after that, Tom transferred to a different department, and Karen left the company. A year passed before I saw Tom again. One day at lunch he led a coworker to my table and introduced us, telling his friend, "This is the lady I was telling you about. Her words saved my marriage."

The words of an old hymn sang in my heart, "God help me speak the helping word . . . and drop it in some lonely vale to set the echoes ringing." God had given me the exact words Tom needed to hear to clear away the confusion Karen had brought into his life, and set him back on the right path to happiness and faithfulness with his wife. God's promise to Moses, "I will be with thy mouth" (Ex. 4:15), is for each of us. We never know when we'll need to speak the words that can make a lasting difference.

Lord, may I always speak the helping words You give me to say. Amen.

Darlenejoan McKibbin Rhine

Under Construction

For we are labourers together with God: ye are God's husbandry, ye are God's building.
1 Cor. 3:9.

WHILE LEAFING THROUGH a novelty clothing catalog, I saw a couple of T-shirts I really liked. One design showed some owls perched on the branches of a tree, all of them in an upright position except for one little owl who was hanging upside down. The caption read: "Sooo? Nobody's perfect!"

The second T-shirt depicted a building site, complete with tools and scaffolding and an "Under Construction" sign. The caption stated: "Be patient with me, please; I'm under construction, and God isn't finished with me yet." I didn't buy the two shirts, but their messages made an impression on me that remains to this day.

For the past two years we've been remodeling our house. We've reroofed, installed vinyl siding, added a large comfy family room and an adjacent enclosed side porch. We've remodeled the kitchen and built a screened-in patio porch beneath the family room. We're also adding an unattached double carport.

After that we'll probably patch some places on the concrete floor in the unfinished part of our basement, paint some of the walls, and put drywall or paneling on others. I believe that any house or apartment, if it is kept in good repair, is a perpetual work in progress.

The same goes for our walk with God. We are "under construction," with God as the master designer and builder. We are already created in His image, but He wants to help us reflect that image more fully—help us "be all that [we] can be," to quote the U.S. Army advertisements. God knows that it takes time and patience to accomplish that. That's why one of my favorite songs is "He's Still Working On Me"!

I love to watch construction projects progress from the ground up. It's a thrill to see ourselves and others growing spiritually, too.

May our prayer be that we'll not be harsh and judgmental with others who, like us, are still "under construction," but will extend to them the same love, patience, and understanding that we would like to have them give us.

Bonnie Moyers

Gentle Dew

My teaching, let it fall like a gentle rain, my words arrive like morning dew,
like a sprinkling rain on new grass, like spring showers on the garden.
Deut. 32:2, Message.

AS I STROLLED DOWN the path toward the school building, all nature glistened in the sunlight after a gentle, misty rain. This was rainy season in South Africa, and many wildflowers nodded in the soft breeze.

Rainy season in this part of the world can vary from day to day. Only a few days before we'd had a terrific downpour. Rain had run in many rivulets down this same steep path, bending or breaking off the flowers and greenery by the heavy force of the wind and the rain. I had held tightly to my umbrella to keep it from blowing away. I hadn't enjoyed that walk, and I felt sorry for the flowers being swept back and forth in the heavy downpour.

But the gentle dew today was beautiful. The flowers looked so bright and cheery. They held their heads high, absorbing the warm sunshine. What a contrast to just a few days before!

I thought of the children we encounter day by day at home or school or church. Our words have such a great effect on their emotions. Children certainly need training as much as the grass and flowers need moisture, but how that discipline is rendered makes such a difference in their attitude. Too often we become upset, and our emotions are rendered in harsh, passionate words. The child is wounded and tries to escape the onslaught, just as the flowers bent under the rainy downpour. Some children may be affected for life. However, if in patience and love we can gently remind them of their need for good behavior, and we encourage them in a better way, the young ones are often able to smile and lift their heads and square their shoulders and try again.

Lord, how gentle You were to the erring children. Teach us Your words and methods as we interact with them day by day so that we may bring smiles and gladness into their hearts as they meet the stormy seasons in their lives.

"But Jesus called the children to him and said, 'Let the little children come to me, and do not hinder them, for the kingdom of God belongs to such as these'" (Luke 18:16, NIV). May the Lord bless as we bring them the gentle dew.

Frances Osborne Morford

The Ambrosine Rose

He will take great delight in you, he will quiet you with his love, he will rejoice over you with singing.
Zeph. 3:17, NIV.

SOME YEARS AGO a friend at church, an elegant, gray-haired lady, gave us a healthy rose plant. We planted it carefully, and it thrived. After a while a steady stream of flowers burst into bloom, sharing their glory with passersby. Each rose began as a creamy pink, but its color deepened as it matured. Neighbors often complimented us on their fragrant beauty.

I intended to send a note of thanks to my friend, but I never got around to putting my thoughts into action until one day, in a picture-taking frenzy, I shot several photographs of the lovely pale-pink rosebuds. When I had the film developed, I slipped a picture of the roses into a thank-you note to my friend.

She thanked me so profusely when she called two days later that I had to ask about the reason for her fervor. Reluctantly she shared her bittersweet experience. She told me that she'd given another friend a rosebush about the same time she gave us one. When she met the woman a few months later, she was told that the plant had 17 blossoms, "but she never even offered to give me a single bud," my friend wistfully reported. Then her tone brightened as she told about going through her mail that very same day and finding the card I had sent. The photograph of the pale-pink roses fell out even before she could read my note. She stared at the picture on which my scrawl indicated that I had named the rose Ambrosine in her honor. She said she joyfully turned to her Father, and prayed this poem: "Rose of Sharon, thank You for reminding me/ That I must rely on You, and only You./ Let the fragrance of Your love spread to others around me./ Thank You for valleys, Lord./ For it is there that I grow."

My friend's story gave me such a tantalizing glimpse of our Creator God's creativity that I had to bow my own head in praise-filled prayer when I heard it. While the thought of one unshared rose had brought my friend great pain, the sight of another had instilled in her pure pleasure. And my God had juxtaposed the two—just for her!

Thank You, Creator God, for beautiful flowers. Help us also to remember Your earthly angels who share their wonder with us.

Glenda-mae Greene

The Main Race

Do you not know that in a race all the runners run, but only one gets the prize? Run in such a way as to get the prize. Everyone who competes in the games goes into strict training. They do it to get a crown that will not last; but we do it to get a crown that will last forever. 1 Cor. 9:24, 25, NIV.

IN JANUARY 2006, when I established my goals for the new year, I determined to participate in the traditional São Silvestre Marathon that has taken place in São Paulo, Brazil, on December 31 for more than 50 years.

I began my training by participating in smaller competitions of from four to six miles (six to 10 kilometers). My first long competition was difficult. I kept asking myself what I was doing there. I felt tired, and sweat ran down my body; I wanted to sit down on the sidewalk and call for someone to come and pick me up. My mind told me I would not succeed. But when I heard the crowd encouraging me at the finish line, everything changed. My steps became firmer, and a great big smile replaced my expression of fatigue.

During my lonely morning runs (since no one else wanted to come with me at 6:00 a.m.) I began to consider another race in which we all participate. Maybe some of us have already grown tired. Maybe we've injured our feet and have shed some tears for the loved ones we miss. Perhaps we cannot hear the angels cheering for us, nor can we hear our kind Coach saying that He is by our side, that He will encourage our success.

I have no way of knowing whether or not you are already tired of the run, but I want to share something with you. Do not give up! Christ, our coach, has already won this race, and now He has His arms open wide, ready to pick us up if necessary, ready to offer us His hand. He loves you and will never disappoint you.

Although I've trained a lot, I've neither won a race nor reached a high place on the podium. But this doesn't make me discouraged. I know that my reward is being kept for me, and not only for me but for all those who want to run with Christ. We can get up, dry our tears, and see Jesus waiting for us with a wonderful smile and our crown in His hands as He tells us, "I am happy that you did not give up. I have been waiting for you."

Lizandra Neves de Azevedo

The Perfect Picture

I saw the Holy City, the new Jerusalem, coming down out of heaven from God,
prepared as a bride beautifully dressed for her husband.
Rev. 21:2, NIV.

I HAD BEEN WORKING on a watercolor piece for more than an hour. I sighed happily. I was in the best of my creative moods and had made a beautiful picture: a bright sunny day in warm hues of golden yellow; clear blue sky with patches of white clouds; pink, red, and purple flowers in a lush green garden; tall healthy trees against the background of blue-gray rolling mountains; a little white house beside a silver lake . . . The colors radiated peace and warmth.

As I stood up to take a look from a distance, my foot caught the leg of the table, and I tripped. Something fell. When I regained my balance, I stared down at the picture in utter disbelief. The cup of water that I'd been using had spilled across the paper, soaking the landscape into shapeless patches. There was nothing that could repair the damage.

In the beginning the Great Artist sat down to create a world. He made a perfect picture that radiated His love, reflected His image. Then something happened. Satan dropped the cup of sin onto the perfect creation. The entire artwork was marred. As sin flowed down through the ages, the Creator could hardly recognize His own art. He couldn't see anything that reflected His love. He had to send His Son to repair the damage.

The media is abuzz with blood-chilling news every day: flood here, drought there; storm here, earthquake there; disease here, destruction there. The world reeks of violence and crime, deception and destruction. Nations fight wars to find peace; extremists terrorize to please God; there is a mad rush to hold on to sanity. The perfect picture lies ruined.

What can an ordinary Christian like me do?

First, be calm. God wants us to trust Him and know that amid all this expected chaos, He is in complete control. Second, study the Bible and pray unceasingly. This is more relevant now than ever before. And third, look beyond. We have a blessed hope. Though the picture now is far from perfect, our Creator has a plan. There will be a new earth that will never be destroyed. Colors of love and joy will glimmer, and somewhere in the center of it all will be you and me—new creations—with our Father.

Vinita Gaikwad

We Have a Friend in Jesus

I will never leave you nor forsake you.
Heb. 13:5, NKJV.

WHEN MY GRANDDAUGHTER, Ashley, was about 10 years old, she was playing in the front yard with her dog, Lacey, a really friendly blond cocker. She was dressing Lacey up, and, as a finishing touch, put a ponytail holder on Lacey's front paw. When Ashley was called in for dinner, she undressed Lacey and ran inside.

A few days later, when I put Lacey outside, I noticed that she was limping. When I brought her in, she was really limping. I discovered that her paw was swollen three times the size it should be. In checking further, I discovered that ponytail holder that Ashley had put there. I finally was able to cut it off, but I was really worried about that paw, so we took her to the veterinarian. After the vet examined and treated her, we had to wait to see if she would lose that leg.

Ashley felt so bad when she found out what she had done. She immediately wrote out a prayer to Jesus for help: "Dear Jesus, I love You very much, and I want to pray for Lacey. Please don't let her lose her leg! Sometimes I listen to sin. I don't like that, so please, Lord, will You help me listen to You? Then sin won't tell me to hurt others or any animals! I love others and all animals, but I love You best. Jesus, can You forgive me for what I did in putting the hair twist around Lacey's paw? Today was a sad day. Jesus, I won't do it again; just please let Lacey's paw be OK!" She closed her prayer with "Love, Ashley Anne Nelson, Your little lamb."

Aren't we glad that Jesus is so understanding of all our mistakes and blunders that we make through life?

After we got Lacey home, Ashley prayed again: "Jesus, thank You for forgiving me today. Thank You for getting Lacey home! Please continue getting Lacey better. Love, Ashley."

We can be so thankful we have a great and merciful God. He has compassion all the time. He is always forgiving. God does always care, and He answers our prayers. He says yes, He says no, and sometimes He says wait. However, He always answers all our prayers.

Dear Lord, thank You for Your loving-kindness toward us and for making Lacey well.

Anne Elaine Nelson

The Master's Voice

My sheep listen to my voice; I know them, and they follow me.
John 10:27, NIV.

ONE OF THE HIGHLIGHTS for me on a recent trip to New Zealand was a visit to the International Antarctic Centre in Christchurch. I had the opportunity to take a close-up look at a community of little blue penguins. The smallest of the penguin species, little blue penguins (also known as fairy penguins) grow to only 16 inches (40 centimeters) in height and weigh a little more than two pounds (one kilogram). Although a little ungainly on dry land, they are expert swimmers and divers, and I found it a joy to watch them through the glass walls of their specially built swimming pool.

While their enclosure is very small compared to the open ocean, the penguins at the Antarctic Centre aren't captives; they've been rescued. Each has an injury or disability that prevents it from surviving in the wild. A paralyzed flipper, for example, means that a penguin can't swim and maneuver fast enough to catch food. One little fellow, christened Elvis by his rescuers, had apparently been struck by a boat when he was quite young and was now permanently blind. As he was feeding Elvis slices of his favorite Dutch herring, the attendant told us that one day a woman visitor had surprised him by calling, "Elvis, remember me?" The little penguin had turned in her direction and cried out in recognition. He knew that voice! It was the very woman, a volunteer from the wildlife rescue service, who had cared for him after his injury and had nursed him back to health. She, in turn, cried tears of joy that after all the time and effort and love she had expended, without any expectation of reward, one little penguin still knew her voice.

Of course, penguins weren't a feature of ancient Palestine, but there were sheep aplenty (as there are in New Zealand, too). The story of little Elvis reminded me of Jesus' words in John 10. He says that the shepherd "calls his own sheep by name . . . and his sheep follow him because they know his voice" (verses 3, 4, NIV). He goes on to affirm, "I am the good shepherd; I know my sheep and my sheep know me . . . and I lay down my life for the sheep" (verses 14, 15, NIV).

I want to listen for Jesus' voice today, knowing that He is the only one who can save me from the deadly perils of this world.

Jennifer M. Baldwin

The Sandals

Since no man knows the future, who can tell him what is to come?
Eccl. 8:7, NIV.

I HAD A VERY COMFORTABLE pair of sandals that I wore every day. Because they were so comfy, I decided to buy another pair just like them before my old pair was completely worn out. However, I wore the new sandals only twice before the buckle broke. I was going to take it in to be repaired when my husband reminded me to take along both sandals so the new buckle would match. I put the pair in a sack and trudged up the road.

As I walked along it seemed as if I heard a voice: "Before going to the shoe repair shop, go first to the shop where you bought the sandals."

I decided that was what I would do. I thought I would mention my predicament to the salesperson in charge, but she wasn't there. The shop seemed unusually busy with women trying on shoes, and more coming in. Then I saw an older woman get out of a van and come into the shop. Although I didn't know who she was, I began to tell her about my predicament.

She responded, "We don't sell rubbish at our shop."

I looked at her in surprise and asked, "Are you the owner of this shop?"

"Yes," she replied.

She immediately took me over to the rack and told me to try on two other pairs. Both were too big. However, the owner told me not to worry, she would sort it out.

One of the workers phoned their other shop, but they didn't have my size either. The owner then wrote me out a credit slip. She told me to return to the shop the next week for a brand new pair of sandals. She didn't even ask me to produce my receipt for proof that I had bought the sandals in her shop in the first place. I was accepted at face value. No questions asked. I was amazed. God is so good! I was blessed by going to the store at the right time and by meeting the kind owner of the shop.

When we listen to the still small voice of God (1 Kings 19:12), He always leads us in the right direction—even when we have no idea what is going to happen!

Priscilla Adonis

Honoring Parents

Honour thy father and thy mother: that thy days may
be long upon the land which the Lord thy God giveth thee.
Ex. 20:12.

WHILE GOING THROUGH my e-mail inbox, I ran across an e-mail from a dear friend. We don't talk often, but I'd forwarded an e-mail on how children might respond to the needs of aging parents. Some suggestions included showing patience when listening to repeated stories and patience in waiting for a complete sentence when it's hard for the parent to remember. My friend responded by telling me how timely and worth "due consideration" the e-mail was because he had recently begun caring for his elderly disabled mother. It had become burdensome, especially when 24-hour care was needed. He was desperate and considering alternative care.

Taking care of our elderly parents is sometimes difficult—and often trying. Much loving kindness, compassion, and patience is needed. And those of us who acquire such demonstrate the love of Christ in doing so. For it is only through Him that these virtues are witnessed. Many unknown sacrifices were made by our parents on our behalf. Memory seems to fail us regarding the selfless acts they made when we were small and during those difficult teenage years. We forget the harsh words we may have spoken while being disciplined. Forgiving is not an option—they continued to love and were determined to direct us on the straight and narrow path.

How privileged we are when God allows us to lovingly care for our aging parents! To honor and care for them is what He commissioned in the commandments. To do less would be dishonoring God. My mother is 93 years old. She is a joy, and she never misses an opportunity to share Jesus' love with those she meets. When she's not gardening, most of her time is spent reading Scripture and in spiritual development. My sister and I lovingly assist in her care and welfare—when she allows us to do so—and she never fails to thank us for each caring deed. Perhaps listening to the same story becomes monotonous, yet I know how precious time is.

George Washington Carver once said, "How far you go in life depends on your being tender with the young, compassionate with the aged, sympathetic with the striving, and tolerant of the weak and strong, because some day in your life you will have been all of these." Honor your father and mother, for your reward will far exceed anything else you may ever do.

Sylvia Giles Bennett

Prayer of Faith

I have heard thy prayer, I have seen thy tears: behold, I will heal thee.
2 Kings 20:5.

MY 10-MONTH-OLD GRANDSON was the delight of our family. Kenric Adam followed me wherever I went. It seemed that he bonded to me with real and lasting affection. His eyes were full of life, and his smile always reflected joy and love. The very sight of him warmed my heart!

One night the room was quiet except for the ticking of the clock. A few minutes before midnight my daughter-in-law woke up suddenly and was shocked to see that our Kenric was having convulsions. She summoned all to come quickly. His tiny body trembled with high fever, and we sensed that immediate care was imperative.

We all rushed to the nearest hospital and waited the whole night. It was the first major crisis our family had had to face. Sleep wouldn't come. Fear gripped us. I breathed a silent prayer for a miracle.

The pediatrician was unable to diagnose the cause for the fever and convulsions. Four days passed. Every evening the fever became intense. Each day was like a nightmare. It was agonizing to see my son's pain-filled eyes and my daughter-in-law's tear-stained face.

Friday evening the temperature rose to 108° F. Sensing danger, all of us began to cry. I held the baby in my arms, bathing his burning body with ice water. The doctor tried different remedies—all in vain! He lost hope, and we shifted Kenric to another hospital. I thought to myself, *I am going to lose my grandson.* As he lay in intensive care, I placed the child in God's hands, saying, "I no longer ask for healing, Lord. I pray only that Your will be done in him." Although we knew that his life was in serious jeopardy, I believed that God always does the best for His children who trust in Him. No problem is too big or too small for Him to handle. I knew that God was leading, guiding, and supporting us.

Finally the doctors diagnosed cerebral malaria. They were then able to give the right medications, and Kenric responded well. The fever subsided, and he improved. God manifested His power. The doctors were amazed at his rapid recovery. And today Kenric Adam is a healthy, active, intelligent 3-year-old. He loves Jesus very much and recites lots of memory verses.

Thank God who does wonders in our lives—may His will be done in your life today!

Jean Sundaram

No Mistake About It

And we know that all things work together for good.
Rom. 8:28.

MY HUSBAND WAS ENDEAVORING to call my cousin's husband one evening on our cell phone when he realized he had punched in the wrong phone number. A woman, whose voice he did not recognize, answered; but instead of saying anything, my husband hung up. When he did get through to my cousin's husband, he kept getting an incoming call signal, which he ignored.

As soon as he hung up, though, the phone rang. It was a woman to whom I'd given Bible studies on the Internet. She had seen our phone number on her caller ID from my husband's mistaken call, and she returned the call. She was so happy it was our number, because she'd been having a lot of problems. She'd been baptized earlier in the year and was very happy in her church family. Then she moved to a new town and hadn't been able to go to church there because she was helping with her grandchildren. She really wanted to go to church but was a little shy about going by herself. Before we hung up, I was able to pray with her and assure her that all would be well.

I knew some folks who lived near her, and if it was all right with her, so I told her that I would give them her phone number, and maybe she could attend church with them. She was delighted to hear that, and as soon as I contacted my friends in the area, they contacted her. Not only that, but I found out that a young man, a schoolmate of our daughter's, attended the same church and was the personal ministries director. He also contacted her, and they had a wonderful visit.

She has now found friendship in a new church family and is once again worshipping God each week.

As I hung up the phone I was ashamed that I hadn't called her sooner. Many times I'd been impressed to make a call to her, but the days went by, and I got busy, and time passed. Although my husband was sure he had goofed when he mistakenly pressed the button to call Patti instead of Pat, I believe it was all in God's plan and in His timing that the call was made. I had not listened to God's promptings when He wanted me to call her, so He worked it out for me to talk to her anyway. I praise Him for that!

Anna May Radke Waters

Rotten to the Core

But the Lord said to Samuel, "Do not look on his appearance or on the height of his stature, because I have rejected him; for the Lord does not see as mortals see; they look on the outward appearance, but the Lord looks on the heart." 1 Sam. 16:7, NRSV.

I HAD EATEN A LIGHT BREAKFAST at 8:00 that morning, and now, three hours later, I looked forward to a snack. Before leaving for work, I had packed the only Red Delicious apple left on the tray. Always opting for fruit at room temperature rather than a cold one from the fridge, I reasoned that this apple would not be cold by the time I was ready to eat it. Besides, its dark-red color, shiny peel, and firm texture led me to anticipate the sweetness that awaited my taste buds. As I began to slice the apple, I realized my shiny red apple was spoiled on the inside. It revealed a dark-brown flesh emanating from the core. Unable to believe my eyes, I kept cutting the apple into smaller pieces. All revealed the same results. Immediately I thought of how easily I had been deceived by outward appearances.

Samuel was commissioned by God to choose a king to replace Saul (1 Sam. 16:1-13). David was not among the sons his father, Jesse, chose to present to Samuel for interview and consideration for the position of king. Only after God rejected the others was David called upon to appear before Samuel. Even loving and devoted parents tend to judge their children by their actions and outward appearances. God, in His mercy, created us so wonderfully that we are unable to read the thoughts or intentions of others.

We Christians, unfortunately, often mislead each other. We seem so righteous on the outside, but our thoughts and private actions are less than what God expects of us. I've had my trust in others destroyed by a careless word or action that revealed unexpected characteristics which were not readily identifiable. Conversely, I've been privileged to develop beautiful friendships with sisters with whom I did not initially bond. Thus the old adage "Never judge a book by its cover."

Dear Jesus, please help me today to live my life as an open book—the outside and the inside matching— telling others of Your love.

Avis Mae Rodney

Whiter Than Snow

Purge me with hyssop, and I shall be clean: wash me, and I shall be whiter than snow.
Ps. 51:7.

TO BEGIN WITH, I'll have to confess that I'm not much of a cook! I call myself a "short-order cook." Part of the blame I put on the fact that I've had to work all my life, married or unmarried. For 25 years I transcribed for court reporters. Some of this time I worked at home while my children were small. But even then, my meals were very simple: a protein, a green vegetable, a yellow vegetable, salad, and whole-wheat bread.

Nowadays my husband and I are retired and spend the winter months "camping out" in a small trailer in central Florida. We have two knives, two forks, six spoons, two bowls, and simple pots and pans. So I fix a simple meal and sit down to wait for it to cook. One time I smelled something burning. (Yes, my eyes are bad and my ears are not too good, but my nose works fine!) When I jumped up to take the pot off the stove, I saw that the bottom was black inside. Oh, no! Not again! After rescuing what was on top, I filled the pot with cold water and let it soak during our meal. Then I tackled the job of getting rid of all that black. It wasn't easy! I used the scrubber, then put Ajax on the scrubber and scrubbed some more. The last time this happened the black was so bad that I thought I would surely have to buy a new pot. But lo, after much hard work, the bottom was again shiny and clean.

The same pattern seems to repeat in my spiritual life. Each morning when I have my devotions I pray, "Thy word have I hid in mine heart, that I might not sin against thee" (Ps. 119:11). But during the day I find myself repeating an old habit, or speaking a cross word. At night I fall on my knees and beg the Lord for His mercy to cover my sins and to clean me up. It isn't He who is neglectful—I'm the one who has made a mess—but He once again willingly comes to clean me up. I read His promises in His Word and find assurance that He understands our weaknesses and freely forgives our shortcomings. As it says in Jeremiah 33:8: "And I will cleanse them from all their iniquity, whereby they have sinned against me; and I will pardon all their iniquities, whereby they have sinned." What a wonderful Savior is Jesus my Lord!

Rubye Sue

Golden Rule Days

So in everything, do to others what you would have them do to you, for this sums up the Law and the Prophets. Matt. 7:12, NIV.

SCHOOL DAYS, SCHOOL DAYS, dear old golden rule days." Remember that catchy little tune that Will Cobb and Gus Edwards composed in 1907? Most of us probably learned it at some time during grade school. There is a mystical magic in the change of seasons and new beginnings. A box of 64-count Crayola crayons with crisp, sharp points has to be one of the best-loved purchases for back-to-school children everywhere. Today there are many variations of that once simple choice—washable, glitter, scented, jumbo size for the tiniest of fingers, pastels, and a host more.

Rarely does anything seem simple these days. But the simple truth in 1907 was—and still is—the golden rule. For instance, "God is love," and how to grasp, comprehend, and live it, has been retold in a million words, songs, and voices. But it is children who are most like God: fresh, innocent, loving all with simple, pure, unconditional love. On the other hand, they will *unlearn* God's simple love and truth by watching you and me in our selfish, hurry-up worlds.

In the quiet of your morning, when the alarm clock signals a fresh start, enjoy the magic of a new season. Become childlike. May your prayer simply be: *Dear Lord, help me today to see You through the eyes of a child.* Make boats of your Cheerios floating in the milk. Enjoy the bouncing step of new tennis shoes. Talk to the cat on your way out the door as if you have all day and nothing else to do.

Thank God for small blessings, such as having all your teeth (or functional replacements). Dawdle in the bathroom making designs with the toothpaste and blowing bubbles. Giggle a lot. Sing a song on your way to work, something like "Making Melodies in My Heart."

Have a lunch fit for a child of the King: peanut-butter-and-jelly sandwich, an apple, and M & M's (and let them melt in your hands). Wash your hands, splash the water on yourself, the mirror, and your heart.

Get ready, get set, go—back to school! The lesson today is the golden rule. So simple, and yet we make it so challenging and complicated.

Judy Good Silver

My Worst Fears—Gone!

God is not a man, that he should lie; . . . or hath he spoken, and shall he not make it good?
Num. 23:19.

MY HUSBAND, OUR SON, AND I were all lying awake in bed, enjoying each other's company. Waynie in particular was having fun playing with his father and me. Waynie suddenly fell back really hard on my pregnant tummy, his head hitting directly on the spot where the 6-week-old fetus was. Based on the impact, I was absolutely sure I was going to lose the baby. I lay still for a while, wondering what to do, praying in my heart that the baby was OK.

After a couple of minutes I got up and opened the women's devotional book for 1998 to have my personal worship. The book opened to the reading entitled, "Living the 20/80 Rule." The text for the day was "Everything is all right" (2 Kings 4:26, NIV). When I read those words, I was overwhelmed with the fact that God is real and that He cared for this unborn child and me. I pondered the words in total amazement: God just told me, "Everything is all right."

A few months later I gave birth to a healthy baby girl. Thank God, everything *was* all right! God always keeps His promises.

But as time went by and I contemplated those words, I was compelled to read more fully the text as given in 2 Kings 4. To my surprise, this was the story of a woman who had lost her child. But instead of stopping to mourn, she sought help immediately from Elisha, the man of God, who under the influence of the power of God raised the child from the dead. Amazing! *Nothing is impossible with God.*

Do you need God to work a miracle in your life? Maybe it's to restore a dead relationship, or to come alive in Him spiritually. Remember, He is always there, and He is always near. His thoughts toward us are good: to prosper us and to give us a future (Jer. 29:11). We need not fear, but can call on Him, and He will deliver (Ps. 50:15).

Just as He spoke to me and gave me the assurance I needed at the right moment, just as He provided Elisha with His word at the right time, so He will demonstrate His love and care over you at the right time. Remember that God is still on the throne, and that He is still in control of the universe.

Thamer Cassandra Smikle

New Every Morning

Because of the Lord's great love we are not consumed,
for his compassions never fail. They are new every morning.
Lam. 3:22, 23, NIV.

I AM ABOUT TO LAND IN AMSTERDAM, Holland, for a women's ministries congress. Looking out the window, I see a bit of sun just breaking through the heavy clouds surrounding the airport. I didn't sleep well, but I thank God for the privilege to see a new day from up here.

A new day . . . Always a challenge. But I am grateful for new days, new hours, new minutes—even for the new seconds! New beginnings.

The question is Does God come first in our lives and our day? Hopefully He does. When we make God of secondary importance, we do ourselves great harm. But when we invite Jesus to be at the center of our lives, we can claim spiritual treasures that will endure forever.

God's promise is to give us a new beginning every morning. When I think about that, my heart overflows with joy. What an awesome God we have! No matter how my yesterday was, I can wake up in the morning, look up, confident that the compassions of the Lord will never fail; they are new every morning. Once again God's Word has given me a fresh perspective on life when my circumstances seemed bleak. We are never guaranteed an easy life, safe travel, a problem-free week, perfect children, or a perfect day. However, we *are* guaranteed help from God and success His way when we commit every detail of our lives to Him.

My plane is landing; I really don't know what God has in store for me today. But I have decided to trust in Him and be thankful for the blessing ahead.

Maybe today you will confront circumstances that trouble you to the very core of your soul. It is during these difficult times that you must find the courage to really trust in our loving Father. No matter what you are facing today, hold on to this promise: "Because of the Lord's great love we are not consumed, for his compassions never fail. They are new every morning."

Let go of any fearful feelings, and turn those worries over to the only One who can truly help you. Trust the Lord with everything.

Dear Lord, today I thank You for Your compassion and for another new day. Help me to trust You with the details of my everyday life. In Jesus' name, amen.

Raquel Costa Arrais

One Day at a Time

Take therefore no thought for the morrow: for the morrow shall take thought for the things of itself. Sufficient unto the day is the evil thereof. Matt. 6:34.

HAVE YOU EVER FOUND YOURSELF suddenly taken out of this game we call life and put on the sidelines, watching life go by as you deal with your situation? I recently had such an experience.

In December 2007 I had knee replacement surgery, and even though I was looking forward to a lengthy time of rest, I hadn't considered the amount of time it would take to recuperate. The first four weeks were painful but welcomed; however, by the fifth and sixth weeks I was eager to get on with my life. I was eager to go back to the office, to begin my travel schedule, and just get on with living.

But such was not to be. God had other plans for me. The first, and most important, lesson I learned was to be patient. Believe me when I say that this is not one of my best characteristics. I love to do things *now*. But when you are recuperating from an illness, and everyone is telling you to be patient, take time to heal, and loads of other advice, how do you cope?

One way I have coped is to keep busy. I do as much office work at home as I can. I spend time in my craft room scrapbooking and card making. I read; I rest; I spend more time talking with my family. I'm pretty busy, but the underlying frustration is still there. After much thought I discovered the problem was me: in my anxiety to heal and get my life moving again I was missing out on living today.

Are you ever so caught up with future plans and problems that you miss out on living today—a day during which everything goes by in a blur of things to do, people to see, places to go, and the worries of tomorrow? When I realized what I was doing, I asked God to help me to focus on each day I had at home—to live that day with all my might, to be purposeful in all I did, and to leave the future to God. That didn't mean that I stopped planning for the future, but it did mean that I put aside all my anxiety and focused on each day, one day at a time.

Now I thank God for each day and for the opportunity to slow down and really live each day. I take each day one at a time. Why not stop for a few minutes and give God thanks for this day? Ask Him to help you make the most of it. Tomorrow is not promised to anyone.

Heather-Dawn Small

The Clothes Hamper Perspective

Then you will call, and the Lord will answer; you will cry for help, and he will say: Here am I. Isa. 58:9, NIV.

IT'S FUNNY HOW OUR EVERYDAY ACTIVITIES can frame our perspective on the more important issues of our lives. For example, take our approach to laundry. Most people have clothes hampers into which they toss soiled clothing until washday, and washday is very often determined by the fullness of the hamper. Rarely will you find someone doing their laundry as each soiled item presents itself; they wait until they have at least a full washload. Others have a more systematic method that involves sorting the dirty clothes the very instant they are taken off.

The same tactic is often employed in handling problems: resolution is sought only when the challenges have accumulated to a bursting point. This type of problem solver thinks it unnecessary, even inefficient, to confront small challenges. This may be a learned behavior, as adults often chide a child, "Call me only when it's really important, when it's an emergency."

Is it any wonder, then, that we approach God in the same way? We pray only when the problem is too large for us to handle, or we think we must first sort things out and present them to Him in an organized way. This is the plan of the devil, who understands clearly that at the breaking point we are often too overwhelmed to pray. He knows that the more we try to sort our difficulties on our own, the worse they get. We lose the pleasures of a stress-free life as we struggle to manage our discomforts, thinking of God as an emergency service. We flinch at the thought of being a bother to such a good God, and so refrain from sharing our small concerns.

However, God already knows everything that crosses our mind and is eager for us to share it with Him. He knows our joys and our pains, our excitements and our disappointments. He longingly waits for us to call. Ellen White says: "Keep your wants, your joys, your sorrows, your cares, and your fears before God. You cannot burden Him; you cannot weary Him. . . . Nothing is too great for Him to bear, for He holds up worlds. . . . Nothing that in any way concerns our peace is too small for Him to notice" (*Steps to Christ*, p. 100).

Accumulating may work for the dirty laundry, but not for your relationship with God. Make your life one of perpetual prayer, sharing with Jesus every issue as it arises.

Patrice Williams-Gordon

The Flood of 1993

Behold, how good and how pleasant it is for brethren to dwell together in unity!
Ps. 133:1.

THE YEAR 1993 will long be remembered as the Year of the Flood. But I prefer to remember it as the Year of Unity. The company where I worked suffered during the raging flood. When we were forced out of our rented building because of high water, the employees pulled together to keep the company going, and that was a miracle and an answer to prayer. The president of the company often acknowledged this miracle in prayer during our meetings.

It rained for days, and the parking lot filled up, inch by inch. The water seeped under the front door and covered the steps leading to the offices. We could no longer park in the lot and had to park at a shopping area and be shuttled to the dike of Line Creek behind the building. We had to walk a distance on the dike before being ferried across the water in the back of a pickup truck to the ramp leading to the dock door. We worked together in solemn unity to keep the orders processed.

The dike eventually collapsed, in spite of the sandbagging efforts of dedicated employees. When the water rose to the rafters, the men constructed floating barges to rescue heavy equipment and save office fixtures. Months before, I had submitted the winning safety slogan which had been displayed on a large banner in the plant, and now it was not salvageable. Only my stapler was saved from my desk. (I continued to use it until I retired.)

We relocated to a hotel conference room, using rented typewriters instead of our computers to keep the orders processed. An empty building was finally made available to us, although it was across the state line 45 minutes away. Unity surfaced again as car pools were offered to those in need. We sat in lawn chairs at long tables and worked in cramped quarters, but no one grumbled or complained.

The next year we moved into a beautiful new building where unity and gratitude continued to reign. When I was ready to retire, I had the opportunity to express my appreciation to the president for his prayers and the fact that he never failed to give God the glory for saving this company, in which people of different denominations worked together.

My prayer is that my church will show comparable unity among confessed Christians.

Retha McCarty

The Honest Postman

Whoever can be trusted with very little can also be trusted with much, and whoever is dishonest with very little will also be dishonest with much. So if you have not been trustworthy in handling worldly wealth, who will trust you with true riches? Luke 16:10, 11, NIV.

ABOUT 70 WOMEN were gathered in my backyard around the pool for our annual ladies-night-out fund-raising event for missions. The women of the church and their friends had donned their muumuus and island clothes and basked in the magic of a night under the stars. The entertainment featured a Polynesian group who delighted them with their authentic, traditional costumes and their performance that combined music with mind-boggling illusions.

At the close of the program I showed a PowerPoint of the mission projects we had done previously. Each year, as a result of the good crowd and generous donations, we raise about $1,500 to fund our projects. This year was no exception—the offering totaled more than $1,600. We praised God for opening the hearts of the women toward missions.

I placed the money on my desk in an envelope marked "LNO mission funds: $1,609 in checks and cash." When it came time to take the money to the church treasurer, I laid it with other things that needed to go with me on errands that day, and dismissed the matter from my mind. The money would soon be funding mission projects in various parts of the world: women's literacy projects in India, Bible felts for needy Sabbath schools in Brazil, a shelter for Maasai girls in Kenya.

Four days later there was a knock on my front door. It was my mail carrier, holding an envelope in his hands with "LNO funds: $1,609" printed on the front. My mind whirled. What was he doing with this envelope that was destined for the church treasurer? He explained that it had been put in the mailbox a few days earlier. He didn't know which house it came from, but he thought it might be mine!

I thanked our honest mail carrier profusely as I clutched our mission funds to my breast! God had protected our money through one honest man. Our Scripture verse tells us that he who can be trusted with a little can be trusted with much. Let us each examine our trustworthiness this day so that God can trust us with the bigger issues of life.

Nancy Van Pelt

Out-of-Season Flower

Pray without ceasing.
1 Thess. 5:17.

ANOTHER MONDAY MORNING had arrived, and I had to go back to "that place"—my job, my vocation. Stressful, hostile, an unhealthy environment. There were a few staff members whom I found it difficult to be around. I saw them as manipulative, overconfident, over-assertive, disrespectful, and unappreciative.

Lord, how am I supposed to thrive in this environment? I prayed. Did I display any of these behaviors? I had to remind myself that prayer changes things.

Week after week it happened. Was it bullying or exploitation? Or was it just their way of behaving, and I was being oversensitive and analytical? *The battle is not yours, it's the Lord's,* I reminded myself. I remembered a bit of sage advice: when you go to battle with your enemies, do not use the same weapon. *Then what, Lord? How?*

David, I thought. *Remember David.* David used what he knew best, a stone instead of the weapons like Goliath's. God seemed to be saying, *Heap coals on their heads* (Prov. 25:22). I had to truly pray about the situation rather than cry, although the torment multiplied. However, I knew that I had to trust the God I know. With continuous prayer from my prayer group, friends, my mom, myself—and God giving me sustenance on a daily basis—there was a big shift. I also bought a book by T. D. Jakes, *The Ten Commandments of Working in a Hostile Environment.* I can assure you it was difficult to read, for it underscored that God is not going to take you out of your circumstance, but He will take you through victoriously.

I felt as Moses did when he was given a command, and he made excuses (Ex. 3 and 4). I was making excuses. God, however, reminded me that I was the best woman for the job, and I'd better learn to do it well. I started to blossom in spite of my circumstances; I felt like a little flower—an out-of-season flower. After some nurturing and support and a lot of prayer, I was able to smile again. Tough times never last, but tough people do.

God can turn every—and any—situation around. My attitude toward life and my colleagues has changed—and so have they. Pray, and pray one more time. He'll answer.

Susan Riley

What's in Your Juice?

But the fruit of the Spirit is love, joy, peace, patience, kindness, goodness,
faithfulness, gentleness and self-control. Against such things there is no law.
Gal. 5:22, 23, NIV.

I HAVE A HABIT of very loudly and happily saying good morning to everyone. Most people think I've had too much caffeine because of my energy level, but I am so grateful to see another day that nothing can suppress my joy the first thing in the morning.

During the day, though, I meet people who move too slowly, waste my time, do things improperly, or show no tact in their dress, behavior, or actions. I usually don't criticize or try to make comments, but if someone could read my mind, what would they think I was really drinking?

Had I had a shot of bitterness for breakfast? Is there evidence that I swished and swallowed envy on my break? Would someone detect the smell of gossip on my breath at lunchtime? Did I indulge in a large glass of discord at dinner? After leaving work, do I stop off to become intoxicated by negativity juice?

For Christians the fruit of the Spirit is the only trait that anyone should ever accuse us of revealing. We should think before we speak or act. Reflex responses should never be said without a word of prayer or careful consideration because those careless words could destroy our representation of Christ and Christianity.

If we hope to represent God in our walk and talk, it cannot be at our convenience. We should happily drink the juice daily from the fruit of the Spirit. This pure juice consists of staying in a spirit of prayer, repeating choice promises and words from the Bible at appropriate times, and studying the Bible with vigor and hope.

Look at your own life. What kind of juice would people say you sip during the day? If you are honest with yourself then magnify that response by 10. Remember that you are the only Jesus some people will ever see. If you try to introduce them to Jesus, will they say, "No, thanks; if He is like you, I'd rather not meet Him"? Or will they ask you to lead them to Jesus—the Man who gives you such peace and hope? We will stand before Jesus and have to account for our actions, thoughts, and words. What will you drink today?

Sharon Michael

Where Have They Gone?

Now we know that if the earthly tent we live in is destroyed, we have a building from God, an eternal house in heaven, not built by human hands. Meanwhile we groan, longing to be clothed with our heavenly dwelling.
2 Cor. 5:1, 2, NIV.

I JUST OPENED THE MAIL to discover an anticipated letter! My fiftieth high school reunion would take place in June! I recently saw pictures of three persons I had known in my early teens. *Oh, I thought, they've aged!* Immediately I realized how foolish my observation sounded. I look in the mirror every morning, but thankfully one's aging comes over time. So in spite of the wrinkles, I'm preparing to attend my fiftieth reunion.

The campus buildings bear little resemblance to what they did in my day; however, return visits have always left me with new memories and a desire to be in the new earth with my friends, where we'll enjoy the indescribable pastimes the Lord has in store for us!

Today I also received an envelope containing life sketches of several of my former classmates. I've been asked to write a page on 15 of them for a memory book that's being made for the reunion. How interesting to read each one! They tell about college days, children, travel, grandchildren—and oh, yes, there have been some trials, too. I felt as if each life story could be compared to a patchwork quilt: Some beautiful lacey patches, perhaps from showers and weddings. A few flannel ones, when children arrived on the scene. A bit of silver, from wedding anniversaries. And yes, there were some rough, painful patches, too.

While a reminder of another year or decade passing, reunions are a blessing. Going away to a Christian boarding high school was one of the highlights of my life. I loved the place, the young people, the memories, everything—except the food. But I realize that I'm going to find some sadness waiting on campus. Some of my friends have lost their mates; others are fighting health problems. But we will enjoy the time together. I'm scanning my old annuals, refreshing my recall of names and familiar faces, hoping I'll recognize my friends!

Oh, yes; we'll all keep adding patches to our personal quilts as long as life lasts, and then we'll rest until Jesus calls our names. But throughout eternity we'll enjoy our youthful bodies and minds. We'll celebrate our new home, where we'll never grow old. Come with us there, where we'll all be young again!

Rose Otis

Twice a Child

Teach us to realize the brevity of life, so that we may grow in wisdom.
Ps. 90:12, NLT.

FOR YEARS I'D BEEN PLANNING for the day when I would walk away from the formal work world and into retirement. I planned to do whatever I wanted to do, whenever I wanted to do it. I had plans for my spiritual life—attending midweek meetings and becoming more active in church activities, and doing things that I just couldn't do while holding a full-time job along with homemaking.

Was I in for a surprise! About 10 years before I retired, my mother came to live with me, as her sight was failing because of glaucoma. Then other problems developed. She began accusing successive helpers of stealing anything that she couldn't find. She couldn't remember where she had put them. Then she had a particular hallucination that stuck with her for years. I thought it was just her imagination running wild. I didn't realize what was happening. Today she is totally blind, the accusations continue, there are episodes of confusion and hallucinations, and more memory loss, all increasing at a rapid rate during the past 18 months since my retirement. I am finally facing the fact that my mother has Alzheimer's disease.

I now have a different 24/7 job as I supervise her part-time caregiver to whom she is sometimes abusive. I help to bathe and dress her and prepare her meals. I have to process her medical complaints, decide which ones are real, and treat them accordingly. My house has been reorganized to make it safe for her. All these things she did for me as a child. I must plan in advance where I can take her: Are there stairs? Is parking nearby? My life has lost spontaneity.

This causes me a lot of pain, pain as I watch the mother I love regress physically and mentally. Pain when I too become the object of abuse by a confused mind. Pain when I think, *This could be me in a few years. Will I have someone to care for me?* Pain when I sometimes feel so alone in my situation. Pain because crying out to God may give an answer that is too final. Pain when "friends of Job" make me feel guilty because I feel pain.

Today let us say a prayer for parental caregivers. Pray that we may learn coping skills, and that we get the support that we deserve from family and need from empathizers.

Cecelia Grant

He Shall Direct Your Steps

*Trust in the Lord with all your heart, and lean not on your own understanding;
in all your ways acknowledge Him, and He shall direct your paths.
Prov. 3:5, 6, NKJV.*

TOTAL KNEE REPLACEMENT! I had continued to put off the inevitable surgery for nearly nine years. As I waited for some new procedure for knees, I continued to ask the Lord for guidance. When, and where, should I have the surgery? And which doctor should I go to for the surgery?

My daughter wanted me to have the surgery done in Michigan. The problem was that my daughter, son, and their spouses work. No one would be available to take me to physical therapy three times a week.

Then my sister Joyce, a retired nurse, suggested that I have the surgery near her home in South Carolina and stay with her. Her home is on one level, and she could take me to therapy. My other sister, Peg, and her husband, Gene, are also retired, and live next door to Joyce. As it happened, I did need them to fill in for Joyce when she had to be out of town. Another bonus was that they live in Sun City, a lovely community in which to recuperate.

I researched two doctors in the area and made an appointment with the one who was doing a gender implant. A month before my appointment my brother-in-law, Gene, shared with me an article about a third doctor who was doing a new procedure with computer assistance. He made a smaller incision and did not cut the patella tendon, as the other doctors had planned to do. This would mean less pain and faster healing. He also used different sizes of implants to fit one's bone structure. So my surgery was done by doctor number three.

My recovery has been remarkable, and I haven't experienced the excruciating pain that I was told to expect by others who had gone through the regular knee surgery. I'm walking without a cane, and doing stairs just fine. It's been just six and a half weeks, and I'll be driving 400 miles to my home in a few days.

The Lord can be trusted. He answered my prayers, gave me guidance, and supplied all my needs. He is very interested in each of us. And He does guide us. I thank Him daily.

Patricia Mulraney Kovalski

Always Grateful

Be strong and of a good courage, fear not, nor be afraid of them: for the Lord thy God, he it is that doth go with thee; he will not fail thee, nor forsake thee. Deut. 31:6.

I WAS HUNDREDS OF MILES from my station when I got a call from one of my colleagues in Jigawa State, in the northern part of Nigeria, where we were serving our nation. The message was that they were going to pay the three months' salary owed us. I had to go back immediately. I left early the next morning on the 13-hour journey by bus.

When I arrived in Kano State, where I was to take the last bus to get to my destination, the bus had already left, and I was stranded. I didn't know anybody in that place, and I didn't understand their language. Fortunately for me, the bus driver was from the south, where I come from, and he offered to help me. He located an eatery, owned by people from my side of the country, where I was able to get food. Then, with other similarly stranded passengers, I slept in the bus—or attempted to.

I couldn't sleep because of mosquitoes, and I couldn't cover myself because of heat. I knew my parents were praying for me, because I had called them and told them of my predicament. My mother told me the next morning that she couldn't sleep either and had been praying all through the night. I thank God because He answered her prayers!

Early the next morning the driver helped me catch my next bus before he left. Even though I didn't understand the language, which caused me confusion, I knew God was in control. About 50 minutes later the bus stopped, and some people began to get off. I didn't know that that was where I was to get off and take another bus, but, providentially, one of the other passengers knew and told me this was the place. I knew that was God at work because if I had not gotten off, I would have been taken to another town entirely, and I could have been lost.

In today's text God says He will never leave us nor forsake us. I thank Him, because He fulfilled that promise in my life. He answered my prayers and those of the ones praying for me. In whatever situation you find yourself this day, pray and believe that God has answered your prayers. God never fails! I'm grateful, aren't you?

Omolade Ajike Dada

A Valentine's Apology

If we confess our sins, he is faithful and just to forgive us our sins, and to cleanse us from all unrighteousness.
1 John 1:9.

VALENTINE'S DAY CAME SIX WEEKS after our wedding. I had expectations for how that first holiday would go. I walked to the store and found a card idea I could make. That way, I thought the money my husband spent on a card for me wouldn't be so hard on the budget.

My husband wanted to get me a big bouquet and an expensive gift, but he knew we couldn't afford that, so he dismissed that desire. After work on February 14 he had his friend drop him off close to our house; then he jumped the fence that lined the freeway. Eagerly—yet innocently—he came running up the steps to our apartment to see me as soon as he could. When I gave him his card and realized he had not gotten me one, I went ballistic.

In the following years when Valentine's Day came, my husband would give me special gifts. But each year he also mentioned his failure on that first Valentine's Day, and when he told others he always said, "And she's never forgiven me." That puzzled me, because I would forget about it until he brought it up again the next year. It seemed as if we had switched roles—he was remembering, and I was forgetting.

One year Valentine's Day fell on the day I usually go to my husband's office for the staff meeting. The employees said he had told them about our first Valentine's Day, and that he had said, "She's never forgiven me." Again I was surprised, because again I had forgotten about it. So I told the employees my version: I had been home all day while he worked, and when he didn't bring me a card I had made a fool of myself in my immature, cruel response.

Suddenly I looked at my husband sitting next to me and said, "I don't think you've forgiven me." Now it all made sense. It wasn't *he* that needed forgiving—it was I.

That evening I talked with him about it and said he had done nothing that needed forgiving. I was the one who was wrong, terribly wrong, and I had hurt him so much he couldn't forget it. I asked forgiveness and told him that the way I would know he had forgiven me is if he never mentioned it again.

This year he didn't mention it, and I enjoyed the teddy bear he loved getting me.

Lana Fletcher

Sit, Stand, Walk

Blessed is the man who does not walk in the counsel of the wicked
or stand in the way of sinners or sit in the seat of mockers.
Ps. 1:1, NIV.

BEING A MOTHER has been a tremendous blessing, and having a little one around reminds me of the growth process. Not long ago our small son, Alsten Timothy, was at the stage in which he was able to sit by himself. When he first sat by himself, my husband and I stood in awe, watching his teetering attempts to stay upright without slumping over. Most recently we were all excited that he has been learning to crawl and pull himself up to stand. He is now standing while holding on to the furniture, but it won't be long until he will be walking on his own. That is how growth progresses. As we mature we learn to sit, then to stand, and then to walk. It is a natural progression: sit, stand, and walk.

Psalm 1 is a great psalm that talks about two ways of approaching life—either as the righteous, or the wicked. The promise is that the one who is faithful and does not walk in the way of the wicked will be blessed. But the implied warning is that to go down the path that the wicked follow leads to the road to ruin.

The interesting thing about the natural growth of a child is that they first sit, then stand, and then walk. But when our spiritual growth is reversed, we walk, stand, then sit. We begin by walking in the counsel of the ungodly, and then we stand in the way of sinners. And finally, we sit in the seat of mockers. The momentum is going backward until we stop completely. We begin by being able to walk, and end up immobilized. We are ready to stand to criticize anyone who is doing something. Finally we sit around complaining and finding mistakes in others for what they are trying to do.

When we place ourselves in the hands of God, we begin to sit and listen to His inspired words. He will restore us with His Spirit and strengthen us to stand for Him in this wicked world. When we are able enough to stand for Him, we become mobilized and will keep walking with Jesus Christ. We will be blessed when we look directly to God for His counsel. The Bible says that we are not to be misled.

Why don't we sit, stand, and walk for Christ, and Christ alone, today?

Jeba Andrews

The Sense of God's Presence

I will give them a heart to know me, that I am the Lord. They will be my people,
and I will be their God, for they will return to me with all their heart.
Jer. 24:7, NIV.

A LONG TIME AGO I needed to stay for an extended time far away from my home. My husband was in our house, and I was in a distant city. We didn't have enough money for either of us to travel by air or bus to be with the other one—the tickets were so expensive. Thus, we called each other every day by phone. Those were difficult days.

One night my husband called to say he was passing through a terrible situation. I felt overwhelmed—I wanted to be by his side, but how? I really had no time to help him, and in addition to this, I didn't have money to travel.

I didn't eat all that day, and I prayed all night. In the morning I understood that God was telling me that I should go to be with my husband, so I bought an airline ticket and boarded the airplane.

Suddenly I was feeling very alone. I usually like to travel by myself, but this time I missed the presence of my God, and I was scared! The day before I had spent a long time in God's presence, and I couldn't travel without His presence in my heart. So I prayed incessantly to my Lord. I examined my mind, asking God to remind me of my sins that I hadn't confessed.

Then I looked out the airplane window and saw a rainbow—not a simple rainbow, but a horizontal arc that had beautiful colors, and it seemed to follow the airplane. I was incredulous. I looked outside intently. I thought I was seeing a reflection of the airplane, but it wasn't. The rainbow remained for a time, and later disappeared.

In that moment I felt the sense of God's presence, and His presence continued with me. I wasn't alone. I had Someone by my side; I could talk about my worries and give thanks for His gifts to me. I was secure.

That experience taught me to claim the sense of God's presence until I get it. God desires to stay by our side, but we must ask Him for His perfect presence in our lives. Let us ask for more of His presence. We will be rewarded.

Iani Dias Lauer-Leite

Come Unto Me

*Come to me, all you who are weary and burdened, and I will give
you rest. Take my yoke upon you and learn from me, for I am
gentle and humble in heart, and you will find rest for your souls.
Matt. 11:28, 29, NIV.*

ON OUR DINING ROOM WALL hangs a large print of J. Reed's painting of the hands of Christ titled *Come Unto Me*. Our daughter gave it to us many years ago, but its appeal never lessens. No matter from which angle it's viewed, the hands extend toward the viewer. The right hand is cupped in the invitation to "come." One can almost see the fingers curl as they beckon. The left hand reaches out, palm up, as if to encourage or help.

In the busyness of day-to-day living I often glimpse the hands and remember who invites me to His presence. Recently, however, I've seen the hands in a different light—as giving and receiving hands. I see an open, nail-scarred hand stretching out, offering forgiveness, gifts, met needs, grace, and endurance to each of us. I think of the words from the hymn, based on Lamentations 3:23, "Great Is Thy Faithfulness": "All I have needed, thy hand hath provided; great is thy faithfulness, Lord, unto me." "They are new every morning; great is your faithfulness."

The right hand is cupped to receive and cherish my gifts to Him: my heart, my prayers, my praise, my life. The more I visualize the hands of Christ inviting, helping, giving, and receiving, the more it lends a sacred joy to my sense of relationship, of belonging. Herein, I believe, is our greatest human need—that of knowing we belong to God, and that He wants us with all His heart. This is true rest. All things, no matter how physically or emotionally exhausting, can be endured when we know He is with us, and that we are with Him.

"The Lord is my light and my salvation—whom shall I fear? The Lord is the stronghold of my life—of whom shall I be afraid?" (Ps. 27:1, NIV). "One thing I ask of the Lord, this is what I seek: that I may dwell in the house of the Lord all the days of my life, to gaze upon the beauty of the Lord and to seek him in his temple" (verse 4, NIV). When we fully accept Christ's giving and receiving, then we too become givers and receivers. We then find rest for our souls. He, the gentle and the humble, is today inviting us to take His yoke upon us: "Come unto Me."

Lois Rittenhouse Pecce

My Souvenir Spoon Collection

Fear not, for I have redeemed you; I have called you by your name; you are Mine."
Isa. 43:1, NKJV.

And you will seek Me and find Me, when you search for Me with all your heart.
Jer. 29:13, NKJV.

WHEN I WAS FIRST CALLED to work in faraway places, I began to collect tiny souvenir spoons that commemorate the places I visited. I wanted to remember those places with something that carried their names.

I had quite a collection saved up after a few years. I found spoon frames that hang on the wall to hold them, and I began to place them in the order in which I had acquired them in my travels. Some are engraved with intricate designs in the spoon or on the handle, and they make quite a lovely picture on my wall with their various shapes, shines, and colors!

When I had filled one case with all the little spoons from foreign lands, I found another frame for all the tiny spoons from domestic states and places I had visited in my own country. I soon needed another case just to hold the little spoons I had bought at national parks and memorial tourist sights.

Now I had three cases of the pretty little spoons. They are such an inspiring remembrance of my travels, and I enjoy showing my friends each little spoon when they visit me, naming the places where I have traveled, one by one. What wonderful memories are brought to mind as I contemplate each little spoon.

Those experiences remind me of today's verses about our Savior. I want to search for Him even more than I searched for those spoons. And I'm glad that He has a collection of our names written in His book of life. Someday soon Jesus will come to gather His people from the earth for His kingdom in heaven. " 'They shall be mine,' says the Lord of hosts, 'on the day that I make them My jewels' " (Mal. 3:17, NKJV). He knows us by name, and He calls us today to join the collection of His redeemed to be gathered into His kingdom forevermore. Let's be there!

Dear Lord, I thank You today for Your promises that we can be with You! Come soon to take us home where You are.

Bessie Siemens Lobsien

To Be Like a Pencil

Whatever your hand finds to do, do it with your might.
Eccl. 9:10, RSV.

IN 1945 WHEN I STARTED TO SCHOOL, slate pencils were used on a slate board here in South Africa. The rectangular slate board had a wooden frame. The following year, lead pencils were used. No more scratching on slates!

As I progressed to the next standard, the students sat in wooden desks, and on top of each desk, on the right-hand side, was a circular hole in which an inkwell fitted. To write, we used a nib attached to a length of rounded wood that we dipped into black ink. This was always so messy, so blotting paper was very necessary to blot up the smudges. Later, we students were allowed to use our own fountain pens with radiant blue ink. That was much better and neater. Then came the invention of ballpoint pens whose ink could not be erased.

Times have changed and technology has advanced since then, but as I look back upon those years, I still like using a pencil with an eraser, because when I've made an error, I am able to neatly erase it.

There are a few lessons that we can learn from the lead pencil that apply to our spiritual lives. I am useless unless Someone uses me and holds me up. The Master Craftsman wants me to be the best I can be, bringing a message of hope and love to the world. But this only happens if I allow myself to be held in His hand. Because I make mistakes, my mistakes can be erased by Someone who holds me close. And I cannot function effectively unless I have the lead of the Holy Spirit within my frame. My size, my age, or my color doesn't matter on the outside. The most important will always be what's on the inside.

The sharpening process is so painful to endure, but it has to be done so I can be effective and write a clear message. We all face challenges in our lives, but those experiences can make us stronger persons in Christ Jesus. No matter what my circumstances may be, I must always leave my mark—a good influence—on those around me, no matter how difficult the situation.

Everyone is like a pencil, created by the Maker for a unique and special purpose. Let us proceed with a meaningful purpose to do great things for God.

Priscilla Adonis

Bony Legs

For man looketh on the outward appearance, but the Lord looketh on the heart.
1 Sam. 16:7.

I WAS TINY WHEN I WAS BORN, and I've remained small all my life. Even after I had my two children, most of the weight that I'd worked so hard to gain fell right off. I look young for my age, and people often mistake me for a very young person. As I write this, I'm convincing myself that it doesn't sound at all bad. The truth is, however, that I was born small in the wrong corner of the world. I was born on the small island of Haiti, and to be small in that culture is a sign of poverty, hunger, and want. Without overgeneralization, some of my friends from other islands have told me that plumpness is also revered in their countries.

I was called Bony Legs as a child, and as an adult my weight is often the subject of discussion. "You never gain any weight." "I thought by now you'd be less bony." Or, "What size do you wear now?" These are some of the remarks that I often hear from friends and some family members. None, however, equals the way that my mom has dealt with my size. When I was a child, Mom fed me herself so I could "put some meat on those bones." She also bought me clothes that were many sizes bigger than my actual size. I loved to wear them because they made me feel big.

When I became an adult, Mom continued to buy me size 8 clothes for a size 2 body. She bought them as gifts, but I became increasingly uncomfortable with those "gifts." Why was I feeling so bad? I wanted to be bigger. Or did I?

A look inward and a lingering glance over my life tells me that I didn't choose to be small, and neither did I want to change myself. What I am is so much more than a small, insignificant body. I am a child of the King! He has accepted me just the way I am. In fact, I'm positive that He delights in my small size for it shows His creativity in making each person as unique as the snowflakes that fall from the heavens. He has redeemed me, set me free from sins, and called me His own. As if salvation were not enough, God has given me a wonderful family, health, friends, and a sound mind. These, not my weight, give me reasons to shout for joy!

Lord, help me to simply love others as they are. Help me also to value the things that are eternal, and to accept the things that are temporal.

Rose Joseph Thomas

Rescued

For God so loved the world, that he gave his only begotten Son, that whosoever believeth in him should not perish, but have everlasting life. John 3:16.

A SMALL GROUP OF PEOPLE in our little town recently decided to start a "no-kill" animal shelter. We have a local humane society, but the laws that come with city and county funds mandate that they take in all strays. They have the sad task of putting to sleep more than 2,000 dogs and cats each year. Many people had surrendered their pet, hoping that a new home would be found for it, only to learn later that it had been put to sleep because it was elderly or no one wanted it. The no-kill shelter plans to rescue these pets, to help people keep their pets in their homes, or to find other homes for them.

We seem to be a throwaway society today. No one wants those cute little kittens and puppies once they are grown or become elderly. Often it's the same with elderly people. When they are no longer useful and cannot care for themselves, they are placed in a nursing home and get few visitors, sometimes to live without hope, and are left to die alone.

In our small community there are many elderly people who live nearby. I'm thankful that most people are ready and willing to help others. Just this past week an elderly widow, who lives just a few houses away from my home, came down to see us, obviously in great distress. She had water in her garage, and it was ruining all her stored boxes. My husband and another neighbor soon located the problem. Her hot water heater had sprung a leak. They carried out her boxes and then called the gas company, who brought a new heater and installed it for her. She was extremely glad to be rescued.

When Jesus came to earth the first time, He was always available and helpful to the young, the sick, and the elderly. He came to rescue us from a sick and wicked world. Many of the things He did for others we can also do for those around us. If He had lived for self, as many do today, we would be eternally lost. He did not consider anyone a throwaway person. He died for each and every one—for all who will believe.

Dear Lord, thank You for sending Your Son to rescue us. Help each of us today to live for others as Jesus did.

Loraine F. Sweetland

A Tear to Remember

He will wipe every tear from their eyes. There will be no more death or mourning or crying or pain, for the old order of things has passed away. Rev. 21:4, NIV.

YOUNG AND CONFUSED, I knelt by my father's bedside in a large teaching hospital on the West Coast. My strong father, who was seldom sick, had had a major heart attack, and he lay there, pale and semiconscious. He didn't recognize me. Because I'd been in school when the heart attack struck, I hadn't had time to tell him goodbye, or even been able to go with him to the hospital.

He talked as I held his hand, but not to me. His words mirrored what had happened long before, before my time. His little son was named Johnny, whose happy pictures wooed me from the old family album. He was a little boy with a big smile and shiny black shoes. Johnny had died when he was 4 years old. My father had seldom spoken of him. Now he was calling for Johnny.

My heart broke. All I could do was hold his hand. I couldn't give him Johnny. I couldn't even tell him I loved him. I sat there for a while, tears rolling down my own cheeks. Then I heard the door open. Turning, I saw a young nurse, not much older than me, in a crisp uniform. She had a light-olive complexion and enormous dark-brown eyes—the largest, most expressive eyes I had ever seen. She stopped just inside the door, almost as if she didn't want to intrude on this precious, private moment, obviously not used to the sorrow often found in a hospital room. We looked at each other for a long moment, neither saying anything. Then one large tear made its way out of her eye and slowly trickled down her cheek. That one tear told me she cared. She understood. She was with me in soul and heart.

Did she hug me? Did she quietly leave the room and continue to give me privacy? I don't remember what happened next, but 40 years later I still remember her, the nurse with the beautiful dark eyes and that one, lone tear slowly moving down her cheek.

The Bible often speaks of tears, and that someday God will wipe all of them away. In the meantime, we can minister through understanding and sympathy—and maybe a tear.

Praise God, my dad did recover from his heart attack and return home to Mother and me.

Edna Maye Gallington

He Heard Me

Before they call I will answer; while they are still speaking I will hear.
Isa. 65:24, NIV.

AT 6:00 A.M. THE CELL PHONE ALARM advised me that I would have a test at 8:00. On that day, as I did my devotional, I asked God to show me the way, because I was not very certain of the location where I was to take the test.

After breakfast I got ready and went to the street where the bus would stop. It was still early, but I began to worry about the delay of the bus. Then I prayed, somewhat apprehensively, *Lord, send this bus soon, please!* Before I finished praying, the bus arrived. I thought about asking the bus driver where I should get off, but I remained silent since this was the bus that had been indicated when I asked for information. And once again I prayed, *Lord, show me the way!*

I had an idea of where to get off the bus, but I didn't know which direction to take from there. I got off the bus and started walking, and when I checked the address on my enrollment card, I realized that God had led me to the right street. Now I just needed to find the college. With a very thankful heart, I prayed, *Lord, show me the street; show me where the school is!* When I finished praying, I looked up and saw the school sign. I had arrived 30 minutes early!

God hears us even before we speak, and He answers us before we finish speaking.

How wonderful it is always to be certain of the Lord's presence! In His companionship we are assured that we are on the "right path." With Him we have nothing to fear. With Him we can be certain of the victory.

On that test day I learned how good it is to walk with God and to depend on Him each moment. How good it is to feel His presence with us and to know that we can trust in Him in all of life's situations.

The Lord hears us and is near to us. May nothing hinder us this day from speaking to God, telling Him all our difficulties, and also thanking Him because He always hears us and knows what is best for us.

May your heart say, *Lord, thank You for helping me to seek You! Be with me today; go with me and guide my steps in Your pathways. Amen!*

Carmem Virgínia

Unlimited Love

How good and pleasant it is when [sisters] live together in unity!
Ps. 133:1, NIV.

HOSTILITY IS A VERY DIFFICULT BARRIER to overcome among siblings. Like Joseph in the Bible, I experienced a similar situation, although it may have been to a lesser degree. However, it was no less painful. Perhaps because I was the oldest and first girl in the family, my grandparents had a strong, loving bond with me that caused jealousy among the other grandchildren. Our family, however, did not talk about our problems. I didn't understand the hostility.

When I was 11 years old, my parents separated, and the situation between my siblings and me became unbearable. So at 15 I married just to leave home. Then my father moved to São Paulo, and there he accepted Jesus as his Savior. A short time later three of my siblings moved into my father's home, and they also accepted Christ. When I was 20 and separated from my first husband, I also moved to São Paulo. In my father's home everyone was now Christian—except me. Because I loved my father and respected him, I went to church; but I didn't feel attracted to Jesus. My relationship with my siblings had hurt me profoundly. However, God's love is great. I learned of Jesus, and some time later I accepted Him as my Savior.

Contrary to my expectations, the relationship with my brothers and sisters grew worse, especially with one sister who was very dedicated to church work. I often asked God why this was happening. However, I decided to obey His commandment, repaying bad with good. Three years later my sister had emergency surgery. I dropped everything to take care of her. On day 41 of her hospitalization, she surprisingly improved. She squeezed my hand, looked into my eyes, and said, "Maria, God has a beautiful crown for you. I never would be able to do what you have done for me. Forgive me for everything." The following afternoon, while I held her hand, she passed away. I eagerly await Jesus' return so that finally we can enjoy a loving relationship.

I praise God, who makes us capable of loving even those who treat us badly. Like Jesus, we can have grace to handle difficult things with patience, repaying bad with good. Perhaps we will have the opportunity to see someone recognize their errors and ask for forgiveness. But this morning I ask that the love of Jesus will surround us in such a way that we are capable of loving others, regardless of how they treat us.

Maria Chèvre

Jesus Cares About Women

But a woman that feareth the Lord, she shall be praised.
Prov. 31:30.

JESUS ESTEEMS WOMEN EXCEEDINGLY, and there are numerous supporting evidences in the Bible. When Christ arose from the grave, the very first person He appeared to was a woman, and He commissioned her to bring the good tidings of His resurrection to the disciples. What a mission! Such a wonderful privilege she had!

Jesus used brave Queen Esther to save His people at a time when there seemed to be no other way out. And what courage she had as she went to the king: "If I perish, I perish."

At the death of Lazarus, Jesus comforted Mary and Martha, mingling His tears with theirs. Then He gave them back their brother.

I think of the woman caught in adultery. When everyone else turned against her, shouting that she be stoned, Jesus did not condemn her—He forgave her and set her free.

When the widow of Nain mourned the loss of her only son—her only means of survival—Jesus had compassion on her, and in love restored her son to life.

Yes, Jesus cares deeply about women. He is very tender toward us. He understands us, He loves us unconditionally, and He knows our frame because He made us. At Creation, when our Creator saw how lonely man was, He made a helpmeet for him: Eve was made from a bone taken out of Adam's side. God carefully choose the bone from man's side—not from his head, for she was not to be his ruler; nor from his feet, because he was never to walk on or trample her. He took the bone from the section nearest the man's heart—the seat of his affection—and made woman. Man is to keep the woman near his heart. Woman is to travel by the side of man as his companion, his friend, and his equal. This is God's plan.

It is such a pity that this bliss has been marred by sin. Nevertheless, Jesus still cares about us. His love for us has not changed. He longs to restore us to our original state, and Jesus has already made provision for us to be restored. He wants to restore our characters, our lives, and our homes to that of the Edenic family. Every woman will reach her utmost potential. Don't you long for that day? I do! Let's prepare for this!

Jacqueline Hope HoShing-Clarke

Twenty Years Later

Behold, the eye of the Lord is on those who fear Him, on those who hope in His mercy, to deliver their soul from death, and to keep them alive in famine. Ps. 33:18, 19, NKJV.

WHAT BETTER PLACE to be on a beautiful summer day than by the pool! My daughters and I were doing just that, but as they frolicked in the water, I stayed in the shallow end, trying desperately not to let my inability to swim deter me from the refreshing bath. To my astonishment, my youngest daughter, Jennifer, was easily swimming the length of the pool. Surprised at her prowess, I asked her, "Jenny, since when do you know how to swim? As far as I can remember I never let you swim unattended, and you've never taken lessons."

When she said she had learned all by herself, I asked how that could be. "Yeah, you know, when I was 6, and we went to camp meeting in Saint Damien, the kids always played in the pool while the adults were in the big tent prayer meeting."

"Oh, I see. So I guess that's where you learned to swim?"

"Well, not exactly. Here's the story," she replied hurriedly before I could get in a word edgewise. "A few of us were in the pool and, of course, I couldn't swim for beans, and Angeline, who was 7 at the time, promised to keep an eye on me. She was just joking around when she threw me into the deep end, but I sank to the bottom and was fighting desperately to come back up to the surface. I finally made it, but I'm sure it was the hand of God that pulled me out and prevented me from drowning."

Faint with emotion, I managed to croak, "You never told me anything! Now nearly 20 years later I find out that you almost drowned were it not for the grace of God! But you still haven't told me how you learned to swim."

"I guess when I was under water something miraculous happened when Jesus pulled me out of that water, because I never took swimming lessons, but here I am, and I can swim!"

The God I serve has always had His eye on my little girl. This same child, at the age of 2½, stood up before the church congregation to recite the twenty-third psalm. The words now have taken on a whole new meaning: "Yea, though I walk through the valley of the shadow of death, I will fear no evil: for Thou art with me" (Ps. 23:4).

Jeannette Belot

The Days He Carried Me

When thou passest through the waters, I will be with thee; and through the rivers,
they shall not overflow thee: when thou walkest though the fire, thou shalt
not be burned; neither shall the flame kindle upon thee.
Isa. 43:2.

I HAD MARRIED, and shortly thereafter I became pregnant. It was near time for delivery, and my husband and I were ecstatic. We were going to have a baby girl! I prepared for my visit to the doctor, but on the way there was an accident. I wasn't badly hurt, but I was in a great state of shock. I was hurried to the labor room, where the doctor told us, to our surprise, that my blood pressure had risen so high that if my life were to be spared they had to sever the baby's placenta and let her die. I delivered a beautiful baby girl, but she had died. It was a most painful experience. I was walking through the waters, but God was with me and saw me through my many nights of pain, anguish, and tears.

Time passed. Two years later I was back in the same hospital to deliver my second child—another girl. A new doctor and a midwife-in-training came to check on me and told me they were ready to deliver the baby. I asked them to wait until my doctor and husband arrived. They did not. Instead, they induced labor, and when they couldn't manage to get the child's head out fast enough, they used a vacuum extraction cap to assist them. In the process they damaged my child's brain. In the days and nights that followed, I walked through the rivers; the banks threatened to overflow and drown me, but God did not allow this to happen.

Ten years later my daughter was hospitalized and died shortly afterward. The day before her funeral, I felt that I would die. I had never before felt that kind of pain so deep down inside me. I was passing through the fire of affliction. Then two of my brothers, who are medical doctors, encouraged me to cry. When I finally did so, I was much relieved and felt as if I could carry on. In my deep sleep God ministered to me. I felt His presence near me. It was then that God carried me and allowed me to be in a position to attend my daughter's funeral the following day. He gave me peace of mind.

God has since rewarded me. He allowed me to successfully deliver two sons, one of whom is currently a pastor, like his dad, and the other a pilot. Truly I can sing of the goodness of the Lord, for indeed He keeps all of His promises.

Shirnet Wellington

Praying Can Be So Simple!

Give yourselves wholly to prayer and entreaty; pray on every occasion in the power of the Spirit. To this end keep watch and persevere, always interceding for all God's people. Eph. 6:18, NEB.

I WAS SITTING IN THE GARDEN, chatting with my 6-year-old daughter about the kindergarten, the school, Grandpa's upcoming birthday, and our last holiday in Austria. Suddenly Janina's face took on a pensive expression. She jumped up and ran into the living room and looked at the clock. For a short moment she just stood still, stunned.

When she joined me in the garden again, she sat down beside me, folded her hands in prayer, and closed her eyes. In a soft voice she murmured to herself. There followed perfect silence. I wondered what this was all about. Finally Janina opened her eyes and said, "My friend Samira is writing an English test at school today. She showed me at what time this would happen, and how the hands of the clock would indicate the exact time. I promised her that I would be thinking of her, and I know that God can help."

Touched by this child's faith, and lost in thought, I took my little daughter into my arms. How simple and natural for a small child to pray! Oh, that we adults would do the same! He loves to be included in our daily routine. He longs to share our joys and sorrows. God answers prayer. Prayer makes a difference!

What a privilege to leave every new day to God's loving care and guidance! Just to know that nothing can happen to me in life before first passing God's eyes helps me to tackle each new day with trust.

One of the most stress-relieving experiences that God offers us is prayer. At the end of a day we can hand over the day to God, leaving everything behind that has been a burden, a sorrow, or a pain. Further, He wants you and me to do this again and again.

However, it is not only the difficult times in my life that make me talk with God but also the happy moments. Some life situations may require more of me than I am able to give. In such moments it helps me to remember that God knows me and understands me.

Thank You, Lord, for this day, and for the joy You give me, and that You know me and love me.

Sandra Widulle

Preparations for Travel

All Scripture is breathed out by God and profitable for teaching, for reproof, for correction, and for training in righteousness, that the [wo]man of God may be competent, equipped for every good work.
2 Tim. 3:16, 17, ESV.

OUR SON, ERWIN, is 1 year old and is very eager to walk. This means that every time I must be aware of how I draw his attention to what he needs to do before he goes out. "Eri, listen to Mommy as I explain this to you," I say, speaking to him in two languages. "First, you dress in the T-shirt and pants; then you put on your sandals and then your cap; and then we will take 'tricy' [his tricycle] and go see Pa. All right, Eri?"

"Yes" comes the short answer from the little man who has already vanished to fetch his little sandals. And while we prepare, I reiterate the stages. Once he has put on his sandals, he runs to the door and tries to open it. In his excitement he has already forgotten a step.

"The cap," I remind him. He bows his little head to put on the cap, and off he rushes to the tricycle, raising one foot to be ready to jump on it. However, for that he likes to depend on his father's help.

We also receive daily instruction in preparation for our trip to heaven. This helpful information comes from our loving Father, who, through His Word, wants to teach, rebuke, correct, direct, and train all His children in righteousness. But we sometimes forget one stage, or we try to do it our own way. Then comes the advice of Scripture, which directs us to the way from which we may have departed.

In our excitement we may rush off without all the information we need. Are we willing to listen so that the woman of God may be competent, equipped for every good work for heaven? Are we ready to do our little part, and let Him help us?

And after that? I decided to copy my son, who, overwhelmed with joy, did his best to finally say, "I lo!" (I love you!) I also want to tell the Savior that I love Him, because He has planted in me the hope of eternity—and because He has promised us a wonderful trip.

Andreea Strâmbu-Dima

Mountaintop Experience

I will lift up my eyes to the mountains; from where shall my help come?
Ps. 121:1, 2, NASB.

THE 60S-PLUS RETREAT advertised in our church paper appealed to us, so my husband, Keith, and I decided to travel the 620 miles (1,000 kilometers) to join 23 others at the Alpine Village at Jindabyne. This pretty town in eastern Australia is snuggled against the mountains overlooking Lake Jindabyne. It's close to the snowfields and to Mount Kosciuszko, the highest mountain in Australia. It can be very cold there, with heavy snowfalls; however, we went in February when the weather is warmer down under and mountain roads are dry and safe.

The days spent in fellowship with others were memorable ones. I reflect on the times of worship, prayer, song, and the special messages of inspiration and hope given by the guest speaker. There were chats across the meal table when we could share experiences and encourage each other in our walk with Jesus. We enjoyed the spacious landscape with its gum trees, kangaroos, and birdlife. The presence of God was among us, and a feeling of peace and serenity filled the whole place. What a wonderful blessing we received! I opted to go with a few who chose to climb Mount Kosciuszko. Years before, I had reached the top, but I wasn't so sure I could do it now. We took the chairlift to the first level, which left another 4-mile (6½-kilometer) climb to the summit. I soon dropped far behind with only my gracious husband to urge me on.

We trudged on, enjoying the wonders of the mountainside. At times we were shrouded in heavy clouds, and it became cold. Then the clouds would part, allowing us a bright vista across to distant peaks. We crossed streams of icy water and photographed unusual flowers. Kangaroos hopped, and eagles soared. Two thirds of a mile (one kilometer) from the top the track became too steep for my aching bones, so I decided the 3½-mile (5½-kilometer) descent would be all I could manage. Nevertheless, I was content with what we had accomplished.

It's hard to leave beautiful mountain environments such as Jindabyne. The speaker had reminded us that mountaintop experiences are given for renewal; we can access that renewal each day by seeking our heavenly Father. It is He who gives strength and renewal so we can come down from the mountain and serve Him on the "plains" of daily living.

Lyn Welk-Sandy

Do Not Fear!

And he answered, Fear not: for they that be with us are more than they that be with them.
2 Kings 6:16.

WHEN MY HUSBAND DEPLOYED to a war zone, I felt as though I was always afraid. I feared for his life. I feared the unknown. I knew that God was watching over him, but I still had the uneasy feeling that something would happen. Watching the news coverage of the war, which gave daily statistics of how many soldiers had been killed, made me more fearful. To make matters worse, I received calls from idividuals who "cheered me up" by preparing me for the worst. No matter how much my husband tried to reassure me that he was OK, I always thought of the worst. In my time of need God used music to give me courage. The hymns I listened to put me at ease, inspiring me to believe that there was nothing in this world that God and I could not handle together.

The prophet Elisha's life was in danger. The king of Syria had sent out a great army of chariots and horses to kill the prophet. Elisha's servant happened to see the army approaching and ran with fear to inform Elisha. The servant didn't know what they could do. Here they were, two men against an army. You see, human eyes, covered by fear, cannot see God's awesome power. With fear the servant could see only the human army, but with the prophet's prayer and faith the servant was able to see God's stronger and mightier army encamping around them. "And the Lord opened the eyes of the young man; and he saw: and, behold, the mountain was full of horses and chariots of fire round about Elisha" (2 Kings 6:17).

In our lives we constantly overwhelm *ourselves* with fear. We are afraid to step out in faith. We are afraid of what is to come, and the more we think about it the more afraid we become. We forget that God is the owner and ruler of the universe, and there is absolutely nothing He cannot do for us. We become fretful when we have battles, not knowing that with God everything is possible. God has an army surrounding you and me today. He sends His guardian angels to watch over us while on the road and in our private spaces. He puts His loving arms around us to shield us from harm and danger. As you go about your daily routine, listen closely; God is telling you, "Don't fear; I am right by your side."

Diantha Hall-Smith

New Clothes

I will also clothe her priests with salvation: and her saints shall shout aloud for joy.
Ps. 132:16.

IT WAS A LONG SABBATH; many programs occupied the day. After leaving home at 8:15 a.m., I had stopped to pick up some church members who needed a ride to church, dropped off breakfast for one, and checked on a surgical wound for another. So after all the activities of the day—Sabbath school, Communion, and a council meeting—I was very tired.

But after the council meeting three of us council members remained behind to reflect on the happenings of the day and about items from the meeting. It wasn't long before Amireh, the energetic 4-year-old daughter of one of the women, entered the room, which was also used for the church school and other activities.

Seeing the toys stacked there, she wanted to play with them. But after several nos from her mother, the little girl decided that she was going to practice "fire safety" instead. To humor her, I asked, "What would you do if your clothes caught on fire?" Without another thought, the child responded quickly, "Get new ones."

We all had a good laugh. Then we told her that the proper thing to do is to lie on the floor and roll, and to get down on hands and knees and crawl out of the room, and to exit a smoke-filled building. That amusing interruption helped us to forget how tired we were.

This brings to mind what happens in our Christian lives. When our clothing gets burned from the trials that bombard us on a daily basis, it's so good to know that, as a child of the King, we can get new clothing. All we have to do is to stay connected to Him by reading His words and meditating on Him daily. I am looking forward to that day when this "mortal shall have put on immortality" (1 Cor. 15:54).

I pray that I will humble myself and, as a child of God, that I will be willing to learn and to remain focused on Him. I pray, too, that our little ones will continue to grow in the ways of the Lord so that, like the saints, we will be granted clothing as promised in Revelation 19:8: "And to her it was granted to be arrayed in fine linen, clean and bright, for the fine linen is the righteous acts of the saints" (NKJV).

Gloria P. Hutchinson

Home Sweet Home

Let not your heart be troubled; you believe in God, believe also in Me. In My Father's
house are many mansions; if it were not so, I would have told you. I go to prepare
a place for you. And if I go and prepare a place for you, I will come again
and receive you to Myself; that where I am, there you may be also.
        John 14:1-3, NKJV.

WHEN I THINK OF HOME, sweet home, in my mind's eye I often think of my beautiful country, Barbados, and of spending time with my 91-year-old mother and other family members. I get a warm feeling of excitement all over my body as I peer through the window of the plane as it descends to the runway. The ground is brightly lit, like an ocean of bright stars twinkling in the night. The excitement is short-lived, though, as we disembark and walk hurriedly to the customs area. There are already long lines of tired, anxious people waiting to clear customs.

We wait patiently, with our passports and hearts in our hands, as we observe the serious look on the faces of the customs officers. We pray silently that we will get the right one, and that he won't rummage through our luggage. The past few times we traveled home, we were lucky to get a baggage handler who was familiar with one of the customs officers. And now he beckons us to follow him. The customs officer asks if we have anything to declare. We don't. He stamps our immigration papers after asking us a few questions. Finally, we are free to depart to a friendlier environment where we can again breathe freely.

Outside the waiting area we look eagerly to see if anyone is there to meet us. What a disappointment—no one is there! I phone my mother. She is shocked to hear my voice, saying they expected us the following day. To avoid another hour's wait, we take a taxi. Finally, we arrive home, tired, hungry, and exhausted; but that soon fades into nothingness because we are home at last. My mom greets us with open arms as we enter the house.

There is another home to which I am longing to go—my heavenly home. We won't have to wait in a long line to get our passports stamped or our luggage checked. In fact, there will be no need for luggage or passport. Everything will have already been checked through. No fear of the customs officer, and no mix-up with the arrival time. And best of all, my Savior will be there to greet us with His "Welcome home, children; I've been waiting for you!"

Yes, I am homesick for my heavenly home. Are you?

Shirley C. Iheanacho

Stay Connected

Seek the Lord while he may be found; call on him while he is near.
Isa. 55:6, NIV.

OUR BIBLE STUDY CLASS met in the church. As one of our teachers, a retired biology professor, began to teach the week's lesson, his voice was feeble, and several voices chorused, "We cannot hear!" Someone placed a mike with a stand in front of him. He began the lesson again. It was no better. The connection cord was missing. Several voices said, "The mike is not connected!" Our teacher stopped and waited for the mike to be connected to the power. Once it was connected, we heard all that he taught that day.

This incident made me think how important it is to stay connected to my heavenly Father, the source of all power. It is important to hear what He says so that I can accomplish what I desire, so I can be successful and fruitful. How do we stay connected? The connecting cord is Jesus Christ. He once said that if we stay connected to Him we will bear abundant fruit. We stay connected to Him through prayer and Bible study. Prayer is nothing but talking to God as we talk to our earthly father or a bosom friend who is always ready to listen to our praises, thanksgiving, complaints, petitions, joys, sorrows, accomplishments, and disappointments. His ears are always open to hear us. In turn, we hear His voice through the Scriptures.

There have been days that I wrestled with my heavenly Father and disconnected myself. I cried out, "Why? Why did You let this happen to me? Why me? Am I not doing Your work? Where are my guardian angels? Why didn't they prevent me from falling?" Endless whys.

My Father didn't push me away. Instead, He worked with me patiently until I opened my ears to hear Him speak. He gently reminded me that He is always there, even in times of adversity. The more I tuned my ears to hear Him, the more I heard Him say, "Daughter, I will never leave you comfortless. I will be with you all the time. All that I permit to come your way, including the adversities, are for your good because you love Me. I will not permit anything that you can't bear. I will show you a way out. Cheer up! Be courageous! I will strengthen you to carry on your responsibilities and uphold you with My right hand."

I have renewed my pledge to stay connected to my heavenly Father at all times. How about you?

Hepzibah Kore

Auggie and Me

Grudge not one against another.
James 5:9.

ONE SUMMER EVENING I stopped to visit my friend Jeannie, who lives in the midst of her family's tree farm nursery. At the time they owned a rust-colored chow dog named Auggie. With his massive fur coat he looked like he belonged on a shelf in the stuffed animal section of a toy store.

The lawn slopes upward rather abruptly on one side of Jeannie's driveway, making the top about four feet higher than the driveway. As I left that evening, Auggie bounced along the top of the slope beside my car, joyously barking his farewell. All at once he disappeared, and I heard a thump under my car. I stopped immediately and jumped out, but Auggie was nowhere to be seen. Then, to my horror, I saw Auggie lying wedged under my car midway between my front wheels.

I raced back to the house, shouting for Jeannie to come. About that time her husband, Hally, and their son came upon the scene. Auggie was stuck so tight that all our efforts failed to remove him. Only one solution remained. Martin got the forklift and gently lifted the front end of my car. Like a bullet from a gun, Auggie shot out and away. At a safe distance he shook himself, turned around, and gave me what looked like a disgusted glare, which I read as a sarcastic "Thanks a lot, lady!"

Later that evening Hally called to say that Auggie appeared to be fine. How relieved I was! The cushion of thick fur was in his favor. I discovered, however, his pride had definitely been damaged. I tried to apologize, but his attitude and actions toward me and my car thereafter were far from friendly. It was obvious—Auggie held a grudge! He apparently blamed me totally for his having lost his footing on the grassy slope.

Auggie's response reminds me of those times I've held a grudge. Often the ill will I harbor against others is unknown to them. We tend to blame others for bad things that happen to us. Forgiveness is the key to resolution, and, when put into practice, grudges evaporate. Hally and Jeannie are still my friends, but Auggie, well, he went to his grave, grudge still intact. I was never able to gain his favor. Auggie never learned that grudges just aren't worth carrying.

Marybeth Gessele

Protected by His Angels

The angel of the Lord encamps around those who fear him, and he delivers them.
Ps. 34:7, NIV.

MY FATHER'S CHURCH was located near a very dangerous neighborhood. Many times we'd been afraid to go to that church to hold worship services with the members. One Sunday evening, when it was time for one of the regularly scheduled services, I was not feeling well. Actually, I couldn't even get up out of bed. My mother decided to stay with me, and my father and brother headed off to church. It seemed that it would be an evening just like every other evening.

At the time my father and brother should have returned home a member from the church telephoned to see if they'd arrived home. She was concerned because she had heard the sound of many gunshots near the church. We became very apprehensive that they had been caught in the cross-fire of a shootout. We prayed that the Lord's angels would protect their car as they returned.

Praise the Lord, they arrived without having been touched! However, the car had been hit by many gunshots. Thieves wanted to steal our car, and they aimed for one of the tires so that the car would stop and my father would give them the car. There were so many bullet holes in the car that we were unable to count them all. One bullet hole indicated that they had actually aimed for my father's head. Where had that bullet gone? Without a doubt, angels protected them so that that bullet—and all the others—didn't go through the car. God had saved the lives of my father and my brother.

Once again, God's promise, "For he will command his angels concerning you to guard you in all your ways" (Ps. 91:11, NIV), had been fulfilled. He promised that He would protect us all the days of our lives. He never abandons us!

We greatly praised the Lord for having placed His protecting hand over our family. At times we don't see God's hand as clearly as in this experience, but we must know that God always guards those who love Him, and He saves them. We will learn many of these experiences of salvation only in heaven when we talk with our guardian angel.

Will you thank God today for His protection as you return home in peace and safety?

Greice Marques Fonseca

Yes, Jesus Loves Me

I pray that you will be able to understand how wide and how long and how high and how deep His love is. I pray that you will know the love of Christ. His love goes beyond anything we can understand. Eph. 3:18, 19, NLV.

CHALLENGING JOBS require a strong character. Working with students who have special needs is one of those jobs. When you step into the school, those children have to be the sole focus of your attention. But that was almost impossible for me to do one Thursday. On Wednesday night I had been informed about a very negative opinion of me in my church, and it was affecting, if not inhibiting, my ministry. Me? How could this be? I had tried everything in my power to be the loving Christian God wants me to be. The pain was almost unbearable. I had considered one of these accusers my confidant. Throughout the day it took most of the strength I had to fight back the tears. The malicious words played again and again in my head. I almost began to believe them. Despair was setting in.

Finally it was recess time. Fresh air and solitude was much needed. I was alone—but not really. You see, I was caring for a severely challenged autistic child. The only time he spoke was when he was spoken to, and I was in no mood to speak, sing, play, or any of the other things we normally did at recess. So we both just sat there in silence, silence that I thought was much needed. But God disagreed. My autistic child broke the silence with a song. Because of his severely limited speech skills, his message came out as "Baaaaa, ba, ba, ba, ba." Then silence again. It only took me a few seconds, though, to recognize the tune. I almost caught whiplash as I turned around and shouted in disbelief, "What!" Again he started: "Baaaaa, ba, ba, ba, ba. Baaaaa, ba, ba, ba, ba." Again silence. The tears could no longer be held back. I joined in: "Yes, Jesus loves me; the Bible tells me so."

I work in a public school system; we had never sung Christian songs together. He had never had a musical outburst before that, nor did I ever hear it again. At that moment, the moment that I needed it most, Jesus came near to let me know that He loves me.

Listen closely in your moments of despair. He may use an autistic child, a donkey, a crow, a soft wind, or a strong flood, but He will come near so that you may know the breadth, length, depth, and height of His love.

LaToya V. Zavala

I Believe in Miracles

Blessed be the Lord: for he hath shewed me his marvelous kindness.
Ps. 31:21.

SOME TIME AGO I received a phone call from the headquarters of the Alberta Conference, asking if I could find the names and photos of the conference presidents since 1906. Finding the names was not a hard task; finding photos was, especially of the earliest ones. With quite a bit of sleuthing I found all but one—A. J. Haysmer, 1918-1920. Being the persistent person I am, I hated to give up. I didn't like the idea of a blank frame in the Alberta Conference calendar or their 2006 centennial book.

I went to the Internet telephone directory, rather dubious that I would have any luck, and placed a search for Haysmer. I found 21 names. It didn't seem like an insurmountable task to phone or write to 21 people, but I decided to phone. Letters are easy to ignore. I noticed that 10 Haysmers were from Michigan, and six of those lived in the town of Cadillac. That seemed to be a good place to begin.

I dialed the first number and got a recording: "The number you have called cannot be connected as dialed. Please try again, or call your operator for assistance." I dialed again to make sure I hadn't mixed the numbers. Same message. I dialed the second number and got a busy signal. When I dialed the third number, a woman answered. I explained my search and wondered if she might be related to, or know of, A. J. Haysmer. No, her family wasn't related to him, but she had come across the name in her search of family genealogy over the past 20 years. She thought he was a Seventh-day Adventist (she was Pentecostal). She said none of the other Haysmers in Cadillac had an interest in this hobby, so providentially I had reached the right person.

She offered to retrace her steps and would get back to me. Within 20 minutes she e-mailed me a picture of A. J. Haysmer and his family. The next day she wrote again and told me his name was Albert James Haysmer, and that he had been a missionary to Jamaica before coming to Alberta.

Some may call this luck, but I believe in miracles. "Now unto him that is able to do exceedingly abundantly above all that we ask or think, . . . unto him be glory" (Eph. 3:20, 21).

Edith Fitch

Follow Jesus—One Step at a Time

*Be ye therefore followers of God, as dear children: and walk in love,
as Christ also hath loved us, and hath given himself for us.
Eph. 5:1, 2.*

EVERY DAY WHEN I GET UP I ask God to lead me as I walk through the day, and I'm always humbled by the way God shows me new and wonderful things that I need to learn and know. My husband travels a lot for his job, and he'd been gone for about two weeks. My day would be a little different this Sabbath morning. So I began my prayer with What do I do next, Lord? As I moved through my morning, following God, He showed me, step by step. But time seemed to be running out.

I started to go to the small church in Naples, Italy, first by car and then by train. I knew that time was passing quickly. Nevertheless, I got to church just as the church service started and realized that today was Communion. A very friendly young woman moved over so that I could sit down. She translated some of the sermon for me, and when we went to the room for the foot washing, we visited with each other and shared God's love. She was from Romania, she said, and was teaching small children English in one of the schools in Naples.

She seemed to think that our church sometimes put rules ahead of God's love. So as we visited, I asked God to help me share His love for her. Back in the sanctuary again, those who wanted to partake of the bread and grape juice stood up. She hadn't washed anyone's feet, so she stayed seated. As they passed the wine and bread to each one standing, as I was, I asked Jesus how to share. I felt impressed to share my small piece of bread and juice with her. I've never done that in all my life, but both of us had tears in our eyes, and I was blessed for following God's voice.

The lesson God shared with me is one of the small miracles that brings tears to my eyes and makes me keep asking Him to lead me, step by step, through all my days. I hope that all of you will follow in His footsteps. I sometimes can't see the next step that He wants me to take, but He is there when I walk right behind Him—not ahead of Him, or even by His side. I am always blessed; I hope that those with whom I share Jesus are also blessed.

Susen Mattison Molé

Living on Borrowed Time

My times are in your hands; deliver me from my enemies and from those who pursue me. Let your face shine on your servant; save me in your unfailing love. Ps. 31:15, 16, NIV.

NEVA JIMENEZ HAS BEEN A MISSIONARY to the Pacific Islands for more than 20 years. While she and her husband, Levi, worked in Papua New Guinea, Neva was diagnosed with breast cancer. She spent three months in Australia receiving treatments, therapy, and an operation. This wonderful Christian woman of courage and faith was told she had a specific length of time to live. She has kept her love for the Lord, still works for the children of God, and, above all, she is healthy and strong—a living testimony to what God can do for those who love Him.

My family has the pleasure of being the Jimenezes' neighbors. Their children are my children's great friends. The music and beautiful singing from their home each morning and evening blesses us. We all love this couple, and we know that God speaks to us through them.

I too was taken ill and had to stay home for complete rest. This made me feel useless and hopeless. Many times I pleaded with God and told Him my desire to continue as a missionary in Papua New Guinea. One particular Sabbath I was feeling down and lonely when my children came from church and announced, "Mom, Aunty Neva said that the Filipino community is coming to visit you this afternoon." When they came, we sang, shared testimonies of God's love and care—and sang some more. I was richly blessed, and the focus on my illness disappeared as I heard some of these wonderful people share their testimony of how God had intervened in their illnesses and cured them—how God had worked miracles in their lives.

At the end, Neva held me close and, with a broad smile, said, "Fulori, you know, my sister, I am living on borrowed time. God has another plan for me, and I know He cares." She related her experiences and how she has been able to go on, serving the Lord and enjoying God's blessings. She chose the song "One Day at a Time," a song that fit her testimony well, and she sang it with the rest of us. I was strengthened that day.

God gives us time and wants His love to shine from our faces. Let us be courageous and tell others that with God all is possible, and that His love never fails. We are all living on borrowed time. Let's make each day the best by sharing His love.

Fulori Bola

Worship First

But seek his kingdom, and these things will be given to you as well.
Luke 12:31, NIV.

MY PARENTS BECAME CHRISTIANS during their first years of marriage. Reading the Bible and other religious books and Bible study became a constant practice. As soon as devotional books were published in Brazil, they acquired them each year. Family worship was an everyday habit.

Before breakfast the entire family went to the kitchen table for morning worship. Everyone got up, even if we weren't ready to start our day, and we returned to bed afterward. We sang one or two hymns, read the devotional book, studied the Bible, and memorized a Bible verse each week. We took our time as one member of the family asked a question and another found the answer in the Bible. No household activity began before the morning worship. My mother, Ubaldina, would frequently say, "First, worship time, then obligations."

We lived on a farm, and the hired hands who lived on the farm also participated with us in the morning worships—and the majority of them accepted Jesus.

Many years have gone by, and the farm no longer belongs to our family; however, there is still a little church in that area. Almost 20 years after my father's death they still talk of Tavin's (my father's nickname) church.

During the more than 85 years that my mother lived, nothing changed her dedication to family worship, reading God's Word, and intercessory prayer, in spite of weakened eyes and cataract surgery. Many results were obtained from the zeal of my mother. Even though she had attended school for only eight months, she remembered the reading and writing she had learned while as a child. (Her six brothers and sisters completely forgot how to read and write.) Thanks to reading the Bible, she was able to read until the end of her life. Her prayers and example kept the family united, something that gave her much pride. Of her eight children, including daughters-in-law and sons-in-law, all have remained firm in Jesus and are waiting for His return.

I miss her prayers. I thank God for the heritage she left us, and I ask our heavenly Father to give me faith, trust, courage, communion, and total dependence so that in this manner I also can be a blessing to my family and my fellow human beings.

Nair Costa Lessa

Just Can't Wait

*As the hart panteth after the water brooks, so panteth my soul after thee, O God.
Ps. 42:1.*

FOR WEEKS SPRING TEASED the Northeast with brief respites from the cold, dreary days of an unusually long winter. Gradually, as daylight overtook more hours, the winter doldrums finally lifted for good. After weeks of furious rainstorms the earth dried and trees began to bloom. One warm evening after work I pulled out the gardening tools. The workday had been stressful, and I looked forward to stretching my muscles outdoors. A thick layer of leaves had served to protect the flower bed by the driveway from frost and freeze. A variety of weeds poked between the dense layer of oak and maple vegetation, but now it was time to prepare the soil for seedlings. I envisioned overflowing flower beds lining the side of the house.

The twilight sun cast long shadows across the lawn where the neighborhood squirrels played tag between the trees. Robins, cardinals, and a bluebird serenaded my efforts as I raked and bagged an ever-growing pile. Soon I developed a rhythm that nearly blocked out the serene surroundings. Suddenly something caught my attention at the far end of the driveway. A nervous little red-breasted robin raced forward and then retreated, but inched ever closer. I continued to work, but curiously watched the strange little avian dance. Why was this normally timid little creature willing to charge forward? And why had a larger robin joined her in this anxious pursuit?

The birds saw and understood what I had overlooked. With each scoop of leaves fresh, dark soil was exposed, along with the tiny space that had been home to a layer of bugs. Those little birds became so eager that they ignored their innate fear of humans. They joined me in the flower bed, feeding just a few feet away. They were hungry. They were eager. They didn't share my dream of a future flower bed but of a feeding bed.

As I retreated into the house, more birds joined the two bold adventurers. Within a few minutes the bugs had discovered new hiding places, and darkness sent the birds to their nests. In the moonlight I lifted my eyes heavenward and prayed that I would hunger to spend time with my Lord the way those little robins hungered for my flower bed.

What gems would you seek in your Father's flower bed?

Shirley Kimbrough Grear

Traveling Mercies

The angel of the Lord encampeth round about them that fear him, and delivereth them.
Ps. 34:7.

IT WAS THE END of the National Youth Service Corp (NYSC), and I was going back home from the north to the south of Nigeria, a 13-hour journey.

The first phase of the journey took me to Jos, one of the middle belt states in Nigeria. I slept over in a friend's house before continuing on the next morning. Usually the bus drivers stop in a town called Lokoja, in Kogi State, to rest, eat, and repair whatever needs to be done before continuing the journey. I was looking forward to the stop because I hadn't eaten that morning. I planned to buy plantain chips to eat on the way. Unfortunately, the driver didn't stop where the other buses I have boarded used to stop. He was familiar with the place, but I was not. We stopped there only a few minutes, and I couldn't buy my chips. So I was annoyed—and hungry!

After spending about 40 minutes, we continued on our journey. Not five minutes later, as we were going up a hill, we saw two gas tankers also going up very slowly. Our driver tried to overtake them, but in the process of overtaking them he realized that there had been an accident, a head-on collision involving a bus and a car, which we saw as we passed. What I saw hit me hard. This could have been us! If we hadn't stopped where we did, we could have been involved in it, because it had happened just minutes before we got there. Immediately tears began falling from my eyes—I realized it was God directing us.

We parked, and some of our passengers went to help. Fortunately, there were no fatalities, but almost all the passengers were injured. The accident was so bad that it was aired on the national television news at 4:00. My parents had already seen the news before I got home and were afraid because they knew I was going to pass that place about that same time. So they began praying for me.

I thank God that He answered our prayers. In all my journeys to and fro, He was always there with me. I thank Him for traveling mercies. He never leaves His own children alone—God had kept me safe in an unsafe situation.

Omolade Ajike Dada

Real Woman

Favour is deceitful, and beauty is vain: but a woman that feareth the Lord, she shall be praised. Prov. 31:30.

HOW DO YOU KNOW if you are a "real" woman? From my experience, I found out that real women will not feel excited when they receive fake flowers on their birthdays. Real women will think about a wedding, whether they will ever have one or not. Real women will look at the mirror once again before they leave their room, delaying getting to work or meeting friends.

Some people would define real women in a different way. They say that real women pass through many experiences, such as being pregnant, being a mother, being a pretty woman, being a strong woman, or being a rich person. Some women try hard to be real women by working hard to earn money, by dressing up to look pretty, or by searching hard for love. But when everything doesn't seem to work out, it is too hard for them to find a real goal.

How do you define a real woman? I don't know. But I know that every woman is very precious in God's eyes.

I like to think that God expresses His beauty through women. Remember that He made woman not from dust, not from wood, neither from grass. Woman was made from precious bone. Bone is something important. If any of you have had a fractured bone, then you know. The bone from which woman was made was removed from under the arm of man, close to the heart of man. If women were not important in God's eyes, why would He make woman in such a wonderful way?

King Lemuel's mother taught him some truths about real women which you can read about in the last chapter of Proverbs (chapter 31). This passage describes a woman involved in many different things—no one description fits her. It was meant to be read by all women and men. As Lemuel writes: "Many women do noble things, but you surpass them all. Charm is deceptive, and beauty is fleeting; but a woman who fears the Lord is to be praised. Give her the reward she has earned, and let her works bring her praise at the city gate" (verses 29-31, NIV).

Every woman can be a real woman. If she has a heart to love God, she will find her way. God doesn't see a real woman from the outside, because He knows the inside of her heart.

Ho Yi Chan

Worm Jacob

*"Though you search for your enemies, you will not find them. Those who wage war
against you will be as nothing at all. . . . Do not be afraid, O worm Jacob, O little Israel,
for I myself will help you," declares the Lord, your Redeemer, the Holy One of Israel.
Isa. 41:12-14, NIV.*

THE MORNING SUN was making the day unbearable, and the creature crawled with difficulty over the uneven stone sidewalk. Its movements indicated it was in a hurry, as if seeking shelter.

I watched the drama as I waited for the bus on my way to church. Where did the worm come from? Its body was visibly dirty, and the cement dust from the old sidewalk clung all along its length. It stopped once in a while, apparently struggling because of this dust, and this is what caught my attention. Ahead, an army of ants was busy at work, and I was concerned about what might happen. Uncertain of my feelings, I didn't know if I should cheer the worm's victory, or if I wanted to see it defeated by the threatening ants. Finally, I could see the worm detouring, as if it somehow knew that doom awaited it if it decided not to change routes.

I began to think of the various occasions in which many people end up on dangerous paths in life, crawling in the dust of sin, wasting time trying to remove the dirt from their hearts by themselves. Some people give up along the way, perhaps because they have concentrated their efforts much more on removing the dirt and much less on letting the Lord Jesus do this for them. Others don't even realize that they're dirty and continue on, satisfied with their mediocre situation. Whether or not they are content, they continue unaware of the power that is offered to them. If only they would believe; if only they would ask.

Problems will always exist while we live in this hostile world, and like those dangerous ants, they can devour our peace and joy in life. We must always seek refuge in the Rock. Being proud of our efforts or despising them, we should never forget that we are like "worm Jacob, little Israel." What would we be without Christ? The only safe formula, if we want to overcome, continues to be the same: total surrender to Him. This world is not our home. Like that defenseless worm in the midst of the dangers of life, we want to flee from the scorching sun of this world. At times danger lurks behind apparently innocent things, leading us to reflect on the importance of accepting the Lord's offer: "I myself will help you."

Judete Soares de Andrade

Useful After All

Many are the plans in a man's heart, but it is the Lord's purpose that prevails.
Prov. 19:21, NIV.

WHEN ONE HAS AN EMPTY STOMACH and nothing to do, just sitting somewhere for about eight hours can be an ordeal. That was what I went through at a medical center one day. I was disappointed when I got the message at 10:00 a.m. that the earliest I could get a ride home was 6:00 that evening. Though I was very frustrated, there was nothing I could do but sit in the lobby, look into space, and wait.

Then a woman and three children came into the lobby. She went first to the security desk, then to the information desk. After about 30 minutes she was involved in an argument during which she even wept, but to no avail. She wanted to visit her sick mother upstairs, but those in charge refused to let her children go with her; neither would she be allowed to leave them on their own. A big notice on the wall read: "No child should be left uncared for."

They were right; children are not allowed in most intensive-care units, and the medical center is so big that if you left a child uncared for, he/she could get lost or get into some trouble. The woman understood why her plea was refused; nevertheless, she sat with tears running down her face. After making a 40-mile (65-kilometer) journey, she wouldn't be able to see her sick mother. It was then that I awoke from my trance and went to tell her not to worry; I would care for her children while she visited her mom.

"Who are you," she asked, "an angel, or something?" She hugged and thanked me; then she told her children to stay with me while she visited Grandma Jess. They weren't happy to be left, but I put the baby girl on my lap and told the boys to sit near me and wait. Supervising the children wasn't easy, but their mother came back after an hour all smiles, and she thanked and hugged me again, and then we said our goodbyes.

Her joy made me forget my misery, and my heart warmed for her and her mom. I felt good that I was able to help her, and I realized that maybe God had me wait there for a purpose. Do you see how God does things? He who knows the end from the beginning knew that I would be useful; hence, He left me there to wait on that needy woman. Yes! Just to put a smile on someone's face and peace into a heavy heart. I pray that I may always be useful to Him.

Mabel Kwei

Lesson Learned

And God will wipe away every tear from their eyes; there shall be no more death, nor sorrow, nor crying. There shall be no more pain, for the former things have passed away. Rev. 21:4, NKJV.

IT WAS LUNCHTIME after a nice Sabbath church service, and we'd been invited to be part of a shared meal at my daughter Jennifer and son-in-law Harry's home. (A shared meal is a planned meal in which each invitee is assigned a particular item to prepare and bring.) Our new associate pastor, his wife, and their baby son had been invited to be special guests, so we were looking for good fellowship.

I felt sorry for my son-in-law because he had just started a new job in a school setting and had contracted a cold that some of the sick children shared with him. Harry enjoys entertaining, and now he was barely able to speak above a whisper. Since I remembered an herbal tea my mother used to make when I was a child, I asked him if he'd like me to make some for him. He agreed at once.

After our meal I got out the ingredients, one of which is a bitter herb, and proceeded to entertain everyone with a rundown of what I was brewing—and my hope that my daughter would remember the recipe.

By the time the medicine was ready, I could see that our associate pastor was really very curious and seemed eager to have a taste, even though he wasn't the one who was sick. Using a toothpick, I fished out a small piece of lemon peel that was part of the mixture and handed it to him. He quickly popped it into his mouth. A second later the bitter taste reached his senses, and he quickly gulped it down while trying to keep a straight face. As soon as he caught his breath, he made a profound statement: "I am cured from all my illnesses!"

We laughed, but later that day I thought about his reaction and comment. This world has much in it to make us happy, such as meals shared with friends and loved ones, and various celebrations. But there are also the bitter times of disappointments and heartache. If only we could look at these distressing times and determine, "I am cured of all my sinning." Then Jesus would come!

Mildred C. Williams

Where Is Your Faith?

Now faith is the substance of things hoped for, the evidence of things not seen.
Heb. 11:1.

Blessed are those who have not seen and yet have believed.
John 20:29, NKJV.

I HEAR AND READ A LOT about the word "faith." The Lord has shown me much so that I may understand faith in my Christian journey. He has answered many of my prayers in positive and remarkable ways. But why can't I fully trust Him at all times? Why do I still doubt Him, as did the disciples of old?

Our son and his wife have been blessed with two lovely girls. Before the second girl turned 2, our son and daughter-in-law were expecting again. As soon as the baby's gender could be determined by the doctor, they went in for an examination. They came home very elated, for the film showed they were going to have a baby boy. They showed the members of our family that this grandchild was for sure a boy. I kept very quiet, thinking that perhaps when the day of delivery came my son and his wife, and all of us, would be very disappointed. I had heard so many stories about pregnancies in which the gender of the baby was predicted, only to be proven wrong later. So down deep in my heart I was praying that this baby's gender announcement would not be another false prediction.

My husband and I flew to Dallas, Texas, to be with our son and his wife to await the arrival of our ninth grandchild. Teresa had prepared the baby's things, all for a baby boy. The couple had even chosen the baby's name: Gavin Chadwick. They were very sure that it was a boy. On the day the baby came, we all went to the birthing center. Gavin came with a loud cry to announce that he had safely joined his family. What a joy to see him!

I was embarrassed, though, because even until the last day I thought we might be disappointed. I was glad I hadn't told my family that I nursed my unbelief even after they had shown me the film of Gavin while still in his mother's womb. Oh, me of little faith!

Lord, I know that faith in the prediction of a medical person, although very helpful, is not nearly as important as faith in Jesus Christ. Please help me to have the kind of faith that will lead me to Your heavenly kingdom.

Ofelia A. Pangan

The Lord Is My Shepherd

For thus saith the Lord God; Behold, I, even I, will both search my sheep, and seek them out. Eze. 34:11.

MANY TIMES I'VE OBSERVED the picture of Jesus carrying a lamb on His shoulders, with His staff in His hand, as He leads His flock. The significance of this portrait never occurred to me until someone recently brought something to my attention.

The story is told that the reason Jesus is carrying the lamb on His shoulders is that the lamb frequently wandered away from the flock. The story tells us that when this happened in times past, it was necessary for the shepherd to break the lamb's leg so that it couldn't continue to wander off. And that is why the shepherd carried the lamb. Although painful, this procedure kept the lamb safe from danger, gave the shepherd peace of mind, and, most important, created a close bond between the lamb and shepherd.

God has proved that He loves us more than shepherds love their sheep. Jesus knows that once we separate ourselves from Him we become prime candidates for Satan's snares. He loves us so much that He doesn't want to see even one of us lost.

Sometimes I become so overwhelmed with life's experiences I find myself unintentionally wandering away from my Shepherd's care, going my own way, incapable of seeing and protecting myself against the dangers that lie ahead. Sometimes He allows the discomfort of trials and tribulations to disable me so that I will draw closer to Him through fasting, prayer, and trusting His Word. These situations are often painful. They require time for healing. He brings me back to the fold, watches over me, and carries me in His arms during the healing process.

In Ezekiel 34:12 God promises, "As a shepherd seeketh out his flock in the day that he is among his sheep that are scattered; so will I seek out my sheep, and will deliver them out of all places where they have been scattered in the cloudy and dark day."

When I retire for the evening, He is there. When I awaken in the morning, He is there. No matter where I may be, He has promised never to leave me. No matter what you are going through, He is with you, too.

Cora A. Walker

People Will Remember—Cheers!

Hold on to what is good.
1 Thess. 5:21, NLT.

PURE JOY BEST DESCRIBES what family and friends were feeling as we watched Sonny walk so confidently and proudly to center stage when his name was called. He looked so handsome in his graduation cap and gown! His peers of the Peace-Wapiti Academy graduating class of 2005 stood, applauded, and cheered while Sonny flashed his heart-warming and contagious smile their way. He was beaming when he took his seat among the other 82 honored graduates. He sat listening so patiently, but not understanding what was being said. "This class will be remembered for their loyalty to one another," we were told. Wow! Talk about graduating with distinction and enriched diplomas!

For the second time Sonny's name was announced. As he received his high school diploma (his special prize for a job well done), again his classmates gave him a standing ovation. They were joined by his teachers, family, friends, and many others in the audience who stood, applauded, and cheered for him. Tears impaired my vision, but I think Sonny gave a thumbs-up to his classmates. He may have also counted "One, two, three, go" before his descent down the stairs.

Sonny is mentally challenged, his speech is very limited, and he'll always require a 24/7 support worker. It must be his gentle spirit (an unpretentious attitude of gratitude), his endearing hugs, his famous high-fives, and his innocence that helps him win hearts while making forever friends. Jesus has a special way of taking good care of Son-Man, Sonny's school nickname for the past three years.

I sensed a genuine feeling of unconditional love and acceptance initiated by his classmates fill the auditorium by this wonderful display of public affection for Sonny. They focused the spotlight on Sonny in hopes of giving him a day to remember, and in doing so they created beautiful memories for themselves and everyone in attendance. This child made us proud, proud to be among those who see beyond disabilities. Inclusion makes everyone a winner.

Was God trying to teach us something through Sonny's graduation ceremony? Yes. What wisdom can you find that is greater than kindness?

Deborah Sanders

Holy Spirit Translates Our Prayers

Likewise the Spirit also helpeth our infirmities: for we know not what we should pray for as we ought: but the Spirit itself maketh intercession for us with groanings which cannot be uttered. Rom. 8:26.

MY SON TZVETY was almost 3, but he couldn't talk yet. He had coined a few monosyllabic words that had nothing to do with the real names for the most essential everyday things. I didn't worry, because I could see he was smart. However, the other mothers at the playground would secretly watch us as we silently played with toy cars. They'd listen to the inarticulate cries of joy as the ball hit the goal, and sometimes they'd say, "Oh, he isn't talking yet!"

One day Tzvety and I were digging a tunnel in the sandpit in the warm spring sun, and all around kids were playing. We were hurrying to make our little shovels meet in the tunnel. "Tuss!" cried Tzvety. His little buddies near us looked at him surprised. "Tuss!" he repeated insistently. What did he want? I went to our rucksack and brought him his juice bottle as a few mothers monitored what was going on. Tuss was his coinage for juice. I was proud I was the only one who could get that. I had always been with him. I was there when he coined some of his baby words. There was no way I could not get what he was saying!

I suddenly thought that it is the same in our relationship with God. I recalled today's text. Who can say how many times the Holy Spirit has "translated" my prayers into the language of heaven? How many times, just like little Tzvety, have I asked God for many things, but my own human way has been so immature and inadequate? But the Spirit has always rightly understood what my needs are, hidden behind my inappropriate words that usually convey something quite different from what I really mean. And He knows what I mean not only because He is omnipresent and omniscient, but because I am His own child and He is, and has always been, with me, hearing my every word since my new birth. In our humanity we know neither for what or how to pray. But we grow in faith and in knowledge and in friendship with Him; and that is why there is no other one that can understand us better. And so He can help us efficiently.

By the way, Tzvety started speaking a month after his third birthday, and really did it well!

Pettya Nackova

Not Like an Orphan

Father of the fatherless and protector of widows is God in his holy habitation.
God settles the solitary in a home.
Ps. 68:5, 6, ESV.

I HAVE NEVER UNDERSTOOD why God permitted me to become like an orphan at the age of 11—exactly the age at which a little girl needs her mother most.

Life around continued on, but for me it seemed to stand still. Everything had to be changed, or started all over. We moved to another town, changed schools, colleagues, and teachers. I had a father with a broken heart and double responsibility who, being a pastor, was more away than at home. I was boarded around, commuting between two houses, not knowing which one was really mine anymore. There were pitying looks and a lot of loneliness. Life continued as if nothing had happened, as if everything was unchanged, and yet life was different; I was poorer, emptier. One of the pillars of the house was missing.

But God, in His infinite love and mercy, prepared me another mother. He who looks from the height of heaven, who knows us before we are born, and who doesn't stop taking care of us, had already prepared an alternative plan. Far away from the land where we were living, there was a faithful woman who feared God and had a great heart. Although she never had a family and children, she accepted to her loving heart two wounded beings. She had learned something totally unusual: to divide everything by three, instead of two, even from the first day. She had learned to give instead of to receive; to care for, to pray for, and to cry for a child who wasn't her own. The mother's place wasn't empty anymore—the house had once again the two important pillars.

Then the family increased by another member; and thus instead of one, I received two gifts: I had a mother and a sister. God is wonderful! He knows to add where the evil one makes desolate. This mother's example taught me what God's love for humankind is. May He reward her, and those who have done the same, plentifully!

If today you feel alone, if the evil one has made your house, your family desolate, if your soul is ravaged by storm, look upward. There is a Father of the fatherless and Protector of widows and orphans.

Gertrude Dumitrescu

The Family Prayer Chain

Be anxious for nothing, but in everything by prayer and supplication,
with thanksgiving, let your requests be made known to God.
Phil. 4:6, NKJV.

WE HAVE BEEN PRAYING for our family members every Friday over the years. Each of us did it in our own way. Some of us prayed and fasted, others fasted for half days, and still others just prayed. In October 2006 we decided to start a family prayer chain on the last Friday of the month. Since I was the one who made the suggestion, it was left for me to organize this family event. The family included people in Maryland, Pennsylvania, and St. Thomas, Virgin Islands.

It included my siblings, my mother, my aunts, and cousins. We began at 6:00 on Friday morning and concluded at 7:00 that evening, approximately 13 hours later. The group was relatively small, and we handed off every hour to the next person. It was left to each family member to be as creative as they wanted. They could just pray with the next person, read a scripture, or whatever they wished. We prayed for every person in our family, those associated with the family in any way, those who needed financial blessings, those on college campuses, those who had left the church, and any prayer requests we received. I felt good at the end of the first session.

My brother asked if we were going to continue every week. I told him no, since it took a lot of planning to accommodate everyone and their requested time, and I was highly stressed with all the arrangements. However, in November we met at a family member's home for Thanksgiving dinner, and my younger sister suggested that we get the younger ones involved in the prayer chain. I was reluctant, but explained the program. To my amazement, everyone signed up and gave their e-mail addresses and cell phone numbers. One of my nieces, who is computer-savvy, volunteered to assist me. Although I'm a person who plans way in advance, she's the opposite, so I had to wait on her because she had the computer knowledge. Initially, I was stressed with last-minute preparation, but the plans always worked out. The prayer chain lasted over an entire day the first time. It has gotten much larger in the months following. The blessings we have seen are too numerous to mention. We've had many challenges, but we know that God is certainly blessing our family.

Irisdeane Henley Charles

His Grace

But they who wait for the Lord shall renew their strength; they shall mount up with wings like eagles; they shall run and not be weary; they shall walk and not faint. Isa. 40:31, ESV.

WHILE I LIVED IN BANGALORE my health deteriorated day by day. Very often while walking on the road I would faint and have to be rushed to the hospital. After various checkups, I was diagnosed as a diabetic patient with hypertension. On one such occasion my pulse was very low, and the night-duty doctor came every hour to check my pulse. Toward morning my pulse returned to normal, and I was discharged. I was put on medication and placed on a special diet. A year later we moved to Hosur.

By God's grace we were able to build a small, two-bedroom house with a little garden space. The climate was very pleasant and suitable to both my husband and me. We used to walk daily, early in the morning.

With God's help I was able to wash clothes, clean, cook, do all the household work, and help my husband in the garden. We never stepped out of our house without having our morning devotions. At noon we would relax, read, write, and have our Bible study. We always waited on the Lord for all our needs, and He was our constant friend. We visited homes on Sabbath afternoons, conducting prayer meetings and Bible studies. We had no means of transportation, so we walked back and forth to visit people. This became our routine.

God's grace kept me healthy and happy. His grace made the impossible things possible. We completely relied on the Lord, and we were blessed by His grace, which enabled us to achieve many things. Our home is His abode. His grace enabled me to complete two years of a master's in English at one stretch. I am happy to tell my friends that we have a God who gives me strength in my old age to continue to work. Sometimes I wonder how I can do all the work, in spite of my spondylitis, hypertension, and diabetes. Now I realize that it is His grace that helps me do all these things.

The path of life is not always smooth and easy for the aged, but by His grace we can reach our goal. I am now 65. I'm glad I worship a living God who never fails those who look for His help.

Winifred Devaraj

My God Is Faithful

God gives wisdom, knowledge, and happiness to those who please him, but he
makes sinners work, earning and saving, so that what they get can be given
to those who please him. It is all useless. It is like chasing the wind.
Eccl. 2:26, TEV.

ONE OF THE MOST SUBTLE DANGERS in life is complacency, which numbs us to the importance of depending on God.

I was employed at the biggest pharmaceutical company in the world and enjoyed my job. Working in a lovely environment as a receptionist, I was paid to talk! Then there was a merger—a dreaded word in the corporate world—and with that came restructuring. At first, only the names changed. But soon there were changes in management, and with each change some of the original staff was eliminated. I comforted myself with the thought that they would always need receptionists and felt that my job was secure. Then we heard a rumor that management had decided to eliminate all the receptionists and use a centralized call center. I was shocked!

Although I'd been praying about my situation, one Friday I was suddenly impressed to pray again. I stopped what I was doing and knelt by my bed. I thanked God for His blessings and asked Him what I should do about my work situation. I prayed that He would show me what to do—from His Word. I opened my Bible, with my heart racing, and flipped through the pages. Ecclesiastes 2 caught my eye: "Nothing that I worked for and earned meant a thing to me, because I knew that I would have to leave it to my successor, and he might be wise, or he might be foolish—who knows? Yet he will own everything I have worked for, everything my wisdom has earned me in this world. It is all useless" (verses 18 and 19, TEV).

With those words came the realization that God was inviting me to rely completely on Him. My heart was at peace as I thanked Him for His assurance and asked for His continued guidance. Now, in spite of being unemployed for almost a year, God has been faithful, and I know He is in control.

God wants more from us than a spirit of complacency. If your world is spinning upside down right now, consider it a personal invitation from the God who loves you to trust Him more completely.

June Jepthas

588 Steps

But he was wounded for our transgressions, he was bruised for our iniquities:
the chastisement of our peace was upon him; and with his stripes we are healed.
Isa. 53:5.

WHILE ON A CRUISE to the Greek islands, we arrived at the foot of a high cliff. At the top was the village of Fira, with shops and hundreds of boxlike white brick homes of the islanders. My choices for access to these were cable car, mules, or climbing 588 steps! In spite of my fear of cable cars, this seemed to be the best option. I whispered a prayer, got into the cable car, and started the ascent. I prayed throughout the journey, keeping my mind fixed on the goal. Fearing the descent in the cable car even more, I went into denial about my return and wandered through the shops. I met members of our group who had climbed up the 588 steps, as they too feared cable cars. They planned to climb down, and I decided to join them.

My first challenge was the cobblestone surface of the steps, which was rough on the soles of one's feet. Then came the challenge of the approaching mules with their inexperienced riders heading straight for us. My biggest challenge, though, was the dried excrement from the mules, which made the stones slippery and, with the help of the wind, covered me totally. I used my knees as brakes, and about a third of the way down my brakes began to fail. Fortunately, the only weight that I carried was my money belt around my waist. I set my own pace, and finally, with pride, I reached step number one. I was exhausted and covered with sweat and manure. My knees and feet ached, and I was so thirsty that I finished a bottle of water in one gulp. Once back on the ship, I immediately cleansed myself with soap and water.

As I reflect on this event I remember a climb that my Savior made for me thousands of years ago. His climb was uphill to Golgotha. He was not on an adventure but a mission. He carried the added weight of a cross and the sins of the world. He slipped and fell several times and was whipped when He didn't move fast enough. When He needed water, He was given a sponge soaked in vinegar. He was covered with sweat, saliva, grime, and blood, which He was not allowed to wash away. After His last step He shed His blood and washed away all my sins, allowing me to have eternal life.

My 588 steps have just paled into insignificance.

Cecelia Grant

Pray Without Ceasing

I will therefore that men pray everywhere, lifting up holy hands, without wrath and doubting.
1 Tim. 2:8.

I HAVE A LONG LIST OF RELATIVES in my extended family: my parents, maternal, and paternal relatives. We were all very close when I was young. We went to the farm together and to the stream to draw water, with my older cousins as our chaperones.

I didn't actually grow up in my small town. My father was a pastor, and we were always being transferred from one station to another, but we always went home during the holidays. I always looked forward to these fun visits because my cousins treated me better than my siblings.

As I grew, my visits home became very infrequent, and, little by little, years passed without my seeing some of these numerous cousins on both sides of my family. As I grew in my spiritual life, I decided to be praying for these cousins even if I didn't see them often. I take different days to pray for different sides of my family.

A few years ago my thoughts drifted to these relatives as I took each name. I thought of how long it had been since I had seen some of them. Then doubts crept in. Why was I wasting my time praying for these people? *Suppose some of them had died without my knowing about their death?* I thought. I was troubled, and I didn't know whether even to continue to pray for the ones I hadn't seen for a long time, especially one cousin. I didn't reach any conclusion.

The last time I had this thought I was on a journey, and to while away the time, I prayed for my family and my extended family, as well. I attended a wedding ceremony in a town close to my hometown, and what a surprise awaited me! A group of women were dancing to the native drumming to celebrate the wedding. I went closer to see the group, and whom did I see? It was the same cousin I had wondered about. She was very much alive. We hugged and hugged. She could not believe it when I told her I had prayed for her as I traveled.

It is a good thing to lift one another up in prayer to our Father. Who knows who is praying for me? I believe God deliberately made it possible for me to see my cousin so that I wouldn't doubt the Spirit's promptings any longer.

Becky Dada

Story to Be Told

I will praise the Lord at all times; his praise is always on my lips. My whole being praises the Lord. Ps. 34:1, 2, NCV.

EACH OF US HAS A STORY TO TELL not only about an interesting life, but how the Lord has led us. Many people wait until they are retired to write their memoirs, but everyone can write how the Lord has been leading in their lives.

In reading Dan B. Allender's book, *To Be Told*, I was reminded of this. I've reached retirement and thought I would write about my life just so my children would know. However, while reading this book my story took another focus, as it is often said, "Lest we forget how the Lord has led in the past." Some of our memories are vivid about times God led, protected, and provided for us. Some we recognize later, thinking about a situation or crisis. Others we won't know about until we get to heaven.

I'm eternally thankful to God for being such a big part of my life. I always thought I was open to God's Spirit. Born in the mission field and raised in a Christian home, I mainly lived in large Christian communities. However, that didn't keep my mom healthy or my folks together. There was a three-year period during which my folks separated and divorced, my mother went into a mental institution, and my father remarried and gained custody of my sister and me.

Sometimes I think about how I could have ended up, and I shudder. At times during my life I made bad decisions, but the Lord often protected me from the fallout. Other times I had to suffer the consequences. "Though your sins be as scarlet, they shall be as white as snow" (Isa. 1:18), because "He will abundantly pardon" (Isa. 55:7).

Looking back, I see how God was always there for me. I felt loved even in times of separation and rejection. Did I have "issues" I needed to work through? Yes! However, with God's help I have lived a fulfilling, Christ-centered life. He has blessed me with family and numerous friends.

And I have learned that God is *always* good. Now I praise Him every chance I get through song or reading praises. We are told that God inhabits our praise and that He is never closer than when we praise Him. To be close to God is my desire. Is that yours today?

Louise Driver

The Touch of Jesus

He touched her hand and the fever left her, and she got up and began to wait on him. Matt. 8:15, NIV.

AMONG THE PATIENTS I VISITED as the hospital chaplain that morning, I discovered a Christian minister from my denomination. While he was traveling on vacation with his family, his car had skidded in a puddle of oil and collided with a truck. An adopted daughter had not survived; his wife was hospitalized in another hospital with fractured ribs, and he had fractures in his face and legs. I began visiting him daily, and we prayed and studied the Bible together.

After several weeks of treatment he contracted a staph infection, and his doctor informed him that he might need to stay longer in the hospital. Now when I visited him, it was necessary for me to wear a mask and gown. Depression took hold of him, and one day I discovered him crying. He had just talked to his little son on the telephone, and he wanted to be with his family. But his fever wouldn't break. After listening to his concerns, I shared that my husband is also a minister, and at times it is necessary for my husband to listen to others. I opened the Bible to Matthew 8:14 and 15 and read the story about the healing of Peter's mother-in-law, who had also suffered from fever until Jesus touched her. At that exact moment the fever went away, and she began serving the Lord.

The power of touch is tremendous; it decreases anxiety, generates hope, and makes healing easier. I touched the pastor's hand, and we prayed for Jesus to touch and heal him, according to His will. The next morning I knocked at his door and entered his room expectantly. To my relief, I found the minister smiling and fever-free. He told me that while we were praying he felt a shiver go through his entire body, and he believed that Jesus had healed him. After only two more days of hospitalization, the minister was discharged and was able to return home.

Many people in this world are sick, discouraged, and suffer from spiritual fever. They are in great need of Jesus' healing touch to cure their traumas, unresolved internal wounds, or even sins. Remember, prayer causes Jesus' hand to move, touching your life and strengthening you physically, psychologically, and spiritually. Then you will be able to stand up and begin serving Him.

Ana Maria Calcidoni Käfler

The Lost Suitcase

Look at the birds in the sky! They don't plant or harvest. They don't even store grain in barns. Yet your Father in heaven takes care of them. Aren't you worth more than birds? Matt. 6:26, CEV.

RAYLENE! One of the suitcases was left at the airport!" My husband sounded very excited—and upset. I knew this was not an April fool's joke. We had just arrived home from a harrowing two-week trip to the United States, and I had hoped that our arrival at our house, safe and sound, would have been the end of a very stressful day. But here we were, and one of our six pieces of luggage had been left at the airport more than 30 minutes away—without traffic. After a hasty decision to head right back to the airport, our family gathered around in a circle and prayed that God would keep our suitcase safe and help us to retrieve it.

What would make the recovery of the suitcase doubly difficult was that on arrival in Jamaica the handle, with all the flight information and our personal information, had broken off. So there was nothing on the suitcase—or in it, for that matter—to identify its owners.

That initial trip to the airport didn't produce the suitcase, but many prayers were lifted up for its safe return nevertheless. Public service announcements were faxed to two radio stations, asking for the suitcase's return, and the story of our loss was shared with friends and other family members. All promised to continue to pray on our behalf for the safe return of our lost piece of luggage. There seemed to be nothing else we could do.

The Sabbath after our arrival and the loss of the suitcase, we were impressed to drive back to the airport to look again for the suitcase. We hadn't received any calls or any word, but after a lovely service at church and a filling lunch, we jumped in our car and headed to Kingston.

Our first stop was the police post at the airport. No lost luggage. Disappointed but still somewhat hopeful, I was about to head to the lost-and-found area when a voice said, "Check with the airline's delayed-baggage counter." As I stepped up to the counter, there it was!

Praise to God, who cares about us so much that leading a suitcase back home is nothing for Him to do! He cares even about the little things. We left the airport that evening with our faith renewed and knowing we can always trust Him.

Raylene Ross

Gone

He is not here; for He is risen, as He said. Come, see the place where the Lord lay.
Matt. 28:6, NKJV.

IT SEEMED A FRIDAY like any other, and even though it was her day off, Nadine came in to work for a meeting and planned to leave right after. We chatted for a while, and then she headed downstairs. About an hour later there was a knock on my door, and someone informed me that my colleague had collapsed in the meeting. When I arrived on the third floor, I found Nadine with emergency medical services staff. Before long she was in an ambulance, heading for the hospital.

After lunch we learned that Nadine had had an aneurism and that the prognosis was poor. She wasn't expected to make it through the night. Everyone was stunned by the sudden change of events. We were conducting business as usual, and then tragedy struck. Nadine died in the hospital the following Sunday night, having suffered multiple aneurisms and a massive stroke.

Nadine's office, a place that was usually full of laughter, papers strewn about, pictures and other personal effects, and a woman in the prime of her life, was empty. Nadine was gone—nothing but a memory to her family, friends, and colleagues.

Early one Sunday morning Mary Magdalene and the other Mary arrived at the tomb where Jesus' body had been laid. They found the stone rolled away and the tomb empty. He was gone. An angel, who sat on the stone, told them that he knew they were looking for Jesus who was crucified. He told them that Jesus was not there, for He had risen, and invited them to see the place where He had lain. The women were admonished to go quickly and tell the disciples that He had risen indeed. The angel also told them that Jesus was heading to Galilee, and that they would see Him there. They rushed from the tomb with both fear and great joy to tell the disciples. Jesus met the women on the way and told them to rejoice. They were so excited that they fell at His feet and worshipped Him.

He is gone. . . . I thank God that nothing could keep Him in the grave. "O death, where is thy sting? O grave, where is thy victory?" (1 Cor. 15:55). Jesus has gone to prepare a place for you and me. He promised to come again to receive us unto Himself that where He is we may be also. Hold fast till He comes!

Sharon Long (Brown)

Jesus, Make Me a Magnet

Then drew near unto him all the publicans and sinners for to hear him.
Luke 15:1.

THE ATMOSPHERE AROUND JESUS was electric. There were those who were drawn closer to Him, absorbing His current of love, and it flowed through them. Others turned away. Then they had the same effect on others—some were attracted, and some were repulsed.

Jesus knew if He went after the rich young ruler, who turned away, it would only repel him further, as a magnet does. He was setting an example of accepting each person's choice. When people are left alone, they will more likely feel free to change their magnetic field to positive and be drawn later.

Jesus talked about the publicans and sinners' sense of need that drew them to Him, but the Pharisees' and Sadducees' choices repelled them.

The church leaders dragged the sinful woman into Jesus' presence, but His love drew her to His heart. Whereas their anger caused them to bring her to Jesus, His love toward her repulsed them, and one by one they left His presence.

Jesus watched His disciples bounce back and forth as they chose His atmosphere and then Satan's. In the same chapter Jesus tells Peter that men had not revealed to him that Jesus was the Christ. God had. In the following verses Jesus says that when Peter refused to accept that Jesus would be killed, he was speaking not God's thoughts but Satan's.

Yet Jesus believed in Peter and gently kept pulling him with cords of love that do not force or give up. When Peter denied Him, Jesus' unresentful look of love finally broke Peter's pull toward self-sufficiency. On the cross, one thief was repulsed by Jesus' submissive attitude, but the other thief was drawn by it. On the same night Judas chose to break all magnetic connection with Jesus and go with Satan's pull.

Father, thank You for loving me too much to stop drawing me to You. Sometimes I feel as if I'm being torn apart—polarized—when I'm trying to hang on to both magnetic poles, wanting my own way and wanting to respond to Your drawing. I know You are allowing experiences in my life to bring me to a final choice.

Lana Fletcher

Rabboni Grace

Jesus saith unto her, Mary. She turned herself,
and saith unto him, Rabboni; which is to say, Master.
John 20:16.

IT WAS A LONG-AGO EASTER MORNING, and our pastor gave us a wonderful message about the resurrection of Christ. A part of the message was how Jesus Christ was present for Mary Magdalene, who was crying that she wasn't able to find her Lord. She was disappointed and frustrated that the Roman soldiers hadn't even spared the dead body of Christ.

Her disappointment was only momentary, for Christ was present there and called her by name. She ran to Him with excitement, calling Him "Rabboni," and with this identification her disappointment was wiped out. The pastor concluded by saying, "Rabboni is resurrected; He is there for us to run to in our time of disappointment and depression." As a young girl, I was completely captured by the message and the word "Rabboni." made a covenant with God, saying, "Lord, when I am married, if You give me a daughter I will name her Rabboni."

I did marry, and God gave me a son. I called him Hanukkah. And my second issue was also a son. I was a little disappointed, yet we were very happy with our children. But God didn't forget the covenant I made with Him, and seven years later I conceived again. I had almost forgotten the experience of being pregnant and delivering a baby. I felt I was too old, but when some of my colleagues asked me "Are you expecting a girl?" I responded, "Yes." "Well, what if you get a boy baby?" they persisted. "Well, I will thank God and bring him up," I replied.

When I was admitted into the hospital for delivery, I had to undergo surgery, and my husband stood outside the operating room. Praise the Lord, God gave me a beautiful daughter. He had not forgotten the covenant I had made with Him. When the doctor told me that I had given birth to a daughter, I cried even from the surgery table, "Rabboni has not forgotten me." My husband wouldn't believe we had a girl until he saw her. I named my daughter Rabboni Grace.

We may forget the little things we say to God, but Jesus, our Rabboni, never forgets even a word we speak to Him. You may sometimes wonder if God has forgotten what you asked Him years ago, but I promise you, if it is God's will, God will give you what you ask for at the right time that His name may be glorified.

Beulah Sudhakar

Take Care of My Baby

There are many fine women in the world, but you are the best of them all!
Prov. 31:29, TLB.

MY MOTHER HAD DIED! After a week of extreme stress and sadness, I returned to work, feeling sorry for myself and expressing these feelings to my friend, Yer. "Poor, pitiful me" was basically what I was saying. "My mom is dead, and my father has died, and now I am an orphan." Yer listened intently, and then she said, "Yes, it is awful to be without a mother. I just wish I could have known my mother."

I glanced quickly at my Asian friend. "Are you adopted?"

"No," she answered. "My mom died when I was 1 year old. So I never got to know her." I immediately felt as if I was blessed, because I'd had my mom for 45 years, and now Yer was telling me that she didn't even know her mom. I asked her how that happened.

"When I was 1 year old, I lived in Laos with my parents and older sisters. The Communists were in control of the country, and they went through and mined the area. My mother and 16-year-old sister were clearing brush in a nearby field, not knowing that a grenade had been hidden on one of the branches. My sister hit the brush hard with her machete, and the grenade exploded, throwing shrapnel in every direction. My sister was hit in her leg, and she immediately fell and began to bleed. My mom, who had been hit also, was concerned only about my sister, and she picked her up and headed for the house. She had carried her for about a half mile when my father met them. Mother, weak from loss of blood herself, had to sit down. My father tried to help both of them, but my mother couldn't go on. She died soon after, and her last words were 'Take care of my baby.' That is why I never got to know my mother."

I thought about her statement "I wish I could have known my mother." I couldn't get this sad story out of my head. Then it occurred to me: Yer may not know her mom personally, but she knew her by her character and her actions. Her mom was a loving, caring woman who gave up her life so she could save her daughter's life.

I told Yer my thoughts, and said, "Someday you will meet her when Jesus comes back to take us to heaven. Isn't this so like our Father in heaven? When He died for us, we were the last thoughts on His mind." Truly, Yer's mother had the love of Jesus in her heart.

Charlotte Robinson and Yer Moua

My Advocate

He who dwells in the secret place of the Most High shall abide under the shadow of the Almighty. Ps. 91:1, NKJV.

I WAS BORN AND RAISED in Zimbabwe, and in 1987 I decided to relocate to the capital city, Harare. This meant leaving my job and looking for a new one. For some reason I couldn't get a transfer, which would have made things easier for me.

The first thing I did after renting a small flat was to look for a job before I exhausted my savings. I knew this wasn't going to be easy, as unemployment was high and job openings for the type of work I did were scarce.

I had learned to trust God from childhood, so I wasn't discouraged. I attended five interviews the first month. But the most disappointing thing happened when I returned home one day from my last interview—I lost my folder to thieves. It contained all my identification, résumés, and work references. This was a major setback, as it would take months to replace some of them. However, this didn't discourage me. I kept applying for jobs, praying, and fasting.

One day, not long after losing my documents, I was looking through the job finder's column in the local paper and spotted an advertisement from a company looking for someone with my skills. I called the company and was invited for an interview on the following day.

When I arrived for the interview, I learned that two other women were also waiting to be interviewed for the same job—three people competing for one vacancy. These women knew how to dress for an interview, and they were holding large folders, presumably loaded with proof of their skills. I was modestly dressed, and I had only God as my advocate.

The two women were interviewed first. When my turn came, I confessed that I didn't have any documents, but I knew my job. After the interview I was asked to join the other women in the reception area. After about 20 minutes of anxious waiting, I was called in and told that the job was mine. I don't know how to describe how happy I was! Further, that evening someone handed me my lost folder with all its contents. Whatever your circumstances, put your trust in the Lord, whose Word does not fail.

Peggy Rusike

Don't Be Afraid

Are not five sparrows sold for two pennies? Yet not one of them is forgotten by God. Indeed, the very hairs of your head are all numbered. Don't be afraid; you are worth more than many sparrows. Luke 12:6, 7, NIV.

MY LIFE WAS FILLED with anguish. I simply couldn't understand why I was confronted with so many struggles. God seemed so far away, and so incapable of hearing my pleas for help. Mentally, I knew He was there all the time; but my heart was so broken that I needed some assurance of His love.

When I was young, my mother was close to death, but I found comfort and strength in lifting my eyes to the nearby mountains. They were symbols of the unchanging stability and help that God could give me. "I will lift up my eyes to the mountains; from where shall my help come?" (Ps. 121:1, NASB). Now, many years later, a mountain across the valley beckoned to me.

I needed strenuous physical exercise to relieve my emotional stress, so I drove to a trailhead and began the steep, challenging trek up the mountain. The first snow of the season made the trail a bit treacherous, but nothing would deter me now that I had set out on this quest. I skirted rocks and snowbanks and trudged on. I'll admit that I was tempted to turn back many times, but I pressed on. At last my energy was totally spent; I could go no higher. My reserves were gone. Exhausted, I dropped down on a fallen log and began pouring out my heart to God. Suddenly I noticed a Steller's jay dancing a jig on the path below me. Occasionally it'd stop, stare at me, and cock its crested head from side to side. It held my attention for an amazingly long time. Through my bird-watching hobby God had encouraged me a number of times before. Now through this joyous encounter on the trail, God again ministered to me in a special way.

This precious jay entertained me, lifted my spirits, and helped me realize that I didn't need to be afraid of the future. I had a God who understood me. He knew the number of hairs on my head, and He would use the trials to prepare me for deeper fellowship with Him on this earth and glorious fellowship with Him throughout eternity.

Donna Lee Sharp

Songs in the Night

By day the Lord directs his love, at night his song is with me—a prayer to the God of my life.
Ps. 42:8, NIV.

SEASONS IN LIFE pass by quickly. Sometimes in the rush I forget how close heaven is to earth, and then I feel so alone. As old age makes its inroads into my life, my naturally high spirits and expectancy diminish. I struggle with pain and depression and seldom hear God's voice in the same ways I have in the past.

Yet I'm learning to listen for His still small voice in new ways. Instead of terrific insights and rapturous delight at His presence, I find Him giving me songs in the night that enable me to find sweet sleep. Walking by faith alone is the path the aged must take. When despondency threatens sleep, God brings to my mind the words and melodies of old hymns.

Last night I awoke with a now-familiar sense of loss—loss of bodily health, mobility, daily expectancy, of being in the center of life. A song immediately entered my thoughts, one I hadn't heard or thought of in years: "Will Your Anchor Hold in the Storm of Life?"

Yes! was my immediate heart response. *Yes! No need to fear or worry; my anchor is fastened to the rock of Jesus.* Peace filled my soul, and I immediately slipped back into sleep.

In the past I didn't realize the importance of the old hymns to my daily walk with God. I see it now. "I'm a Child of the King," "I Have Decided to Follow Jesus," "What a Friend We Have in Jesus"—God has used these, and many lesser-known hymns, to give me sweet sleep at night. Often I haven't heard or thought of the hymn for years, but there it is, the melody and many of the words, ringing in my mind. Sweet sleep comes. Sometimes I awaken in the morning with a song. I now keep a hymnal near my prayer chair so that I can refresh my heart with all the words of the song God has given me.

Do not think that I am a natural musician or singer. God has not gifted me that way. But my husband, who is musically gifted, remarked the other day when he chanced to hear me singing, that I carry the tunes quite accurately. So this is God's special gift to me in my old age—the gift of a song in my heart.

Thank You, Jesus, for songs in the night.

Carrol Johnson Shewmake

Obedience and God's Love

And this is love: that we walk in obedience to his commands. As you have heard from the beginning, his command is that you walk in love.
2 John 1:6, NIV.

HARRY AND I SEPARATED in 1993, and I received my divorce. However, God spoke to me and placed a burden on my heart: I felt that I must go back and heal that marriage. For me it was a matter of being in complete obedience to His Word. I went back, and we were remarried. In 1996 we discovered that Harry had progressive cancer and had only six months to live. If I had not gone back, he would have spent his last days in a nursing home rather than at home, which was his desire. So God's provision for him was supplied. I believe God always has a purpose for everything He allows in our lives.

As the days and weeks progressed, I spent many hours in personal care of Harry. One day I felt I needed to get away, and I asked a friend to sit with Harry so that I could do some Christmas shopping.

An unusually beautiful day shone bright as I got into my car and headed for the mall. I turned on the CD player for some praise and worship music, slid open the sunroof, and began to pray. The music was so beautiful that as I prayed, tears began to fall as the Holy Spirit surrounded me, and the love of God filled the car in such extreme power that I had to cry out, "Jesus, I can't stand it!" I felt His awesome love that day in a way that I shall never forget. He showed me His love for my obedience in returning to my husband and completing my responsibility to Harry and to God's commands.

God placed His loving hand upon my heart and filled it with a love, peace, and contentment that I cannot explain. His love is eternal, never failing, filling our lives with living water so that we will never thirst. But it will also continue to flow through us as life itself. My life is His—no reservations—just total love and trust that will see me through until He comes for me. Are you enjoying this sense of love as well?

I pray that you will experience the fulfillment of His love as I have, in whatever form it comes. There is no explanation for it—He is just so very beautiful to me!

Margaret C. Duran

Under His Wings

He shall cover thee with his feathers, and under his wings
shalt thou trust: his truth shall be thy shield and buckler.
Ps. 91:4.

IT WAS A WONDERFUL WEEKEND at the church camp by a peaceful lake. When it was over, four of us started home in a Jeep Cherokee, driven by the son of an elderly church member, who sat in the back seat with me. The sun was setting, and dusk was fast approaching. We drove for several miles on a hilly, curve-filled rural road before turning onto the highway. A slight mist filled the air and settled on the road. Once on the highway, our driver sped ahead with all the intensity of Jehu, a Bible character known as the world's leading charioteer, who drove furiously.

As the road turned in a long curve, our vehicle veered from side to side. I thought the driver must be dodging something on the road, but the Jeep didn't slow down. We shot across the highway, flew across a ditch, crashed through a barbed, wire fence, and came to rest on top of a small cedar tree. There had been no time to kneel and pray. A simple "Jesus, help us!" was all that I could utter in the seconds we seemed destined for destruction. The Jeep teetered on the edge of the ditch perpendicular to the highway. We all sat quietly in stunned disbelief. The silence was finally broken when the driver questioned, "Is anybody hurt?"

"No, we are all OK" was our weak reply. We didn't speak of the inner turmoil we had endured. My head had thrashed from side to side, and I could feel a scratch above my eye as a result of my glasses banging against the side of the vehicle. The landowner happened to drive by and saw the Jeep's headlights on his land and called for help.

While waiting for the tow truck, we sat in the dark with the rain falling. I tried to comfort the elderly mother. I recalled that during church services she didn't open a hymnbook because she had memorized all the words to favorite hymns. I wondered if she was thinking of hymns now—"The Lord's Our Rock," "Just When I Need Him," "Safe in the Arms of Jesus," and "Under His Wings."

When we are in times of stress and distress, it is good to have scriptures and comforting songs to fill our minds and remind us that we are, in fact, always under His wings.

Retha McCarty

God Provides for Our Needs

For the Gentiles seek all these things; and your heavenly Father knows that you need them all.
Matt. 6:32, RSV.

MY HUSBAND AND I were doing our doctoral studies in the Philippines and had already been there for four years. Our three sons had also been attending their school. We were almost finished with our program and were ready to write our dissertations, which would take a year, or less, to complete. Since we desired that our children continue their education without losing a year, we sent them back home to India.

This was the first time the children had been separated from us, and we wished to get back to them at the earliest moment, so my husband and I worked hard, day in and day out. The only rest we had was on Sabbath. One Sabbath evening after an evangelistic program, we reached home to find that our cooking gas had run out. We had nothing cooked for breakfast the next morning, and the store that supplied gas wouldn't open until 10:00.

We usually jogged every morning at 5:30, so the next morning my husband suggested that we not go because when we got back there would be nothing to eat until after the store opened. I agreed, but I soon felt an urge to go out to jog anyway, and so we went. The school has a one-mile (1.5-kilometer) circular road around the campus, and we usually made three rounds. That day, as we were finishing the first round, we noticed something round lying beside the road. Since it was too dark to identify it, we went closer and found it was a big coconut. I asked my husband to carry it home. He said he would if it was still there when we finished. By the third round it was daylight, and we saw the coconut—and a second one. We picked up both of them. After having our morning devotions, my husband cut the coconuts. Each coconut contained more than half a liter of sweet water and a plateful of tender coconut flesh.

We hail from Kerala, a land of coconuts, and are familiar with all kinds. In excitement I whispered, "It is manna from heaven that God sent us to meet our need for breakfast!" We thanked the Lord for supplying our need, even when we didn't ask for it.

My friends, the hands of our heavenly Father are not shortened. He will supply all our needs in time if we walk close to Him daily.

Ramani Kurian

The Bridegroom Is Coming!

Watch therefore, for ye know neither the day nor the hour wherein the Son of man cometh. Matt. 25:13.

THE DAY HAD FINALLY ARRIVED, and emotions ran high. The couple was about to proclaim their love one for another, and time passed quickly. They would spend the rest of their lives together, and they couldn't wait. Nothing was going to get in the way of their saying "I do." Everything was going according to plan. The church had been decorated, the feast had been carefully selected, and gowns purchased and fitted. Ten young women, unable to contain their excitement, went to meet the groom with burning lights. Of the 10 bridesmaids, five remembered to pack extra oil—the other five felt they had no need for extra.

To their surprise, the groom wasn't there. The news came that the groom would be late. The women, exhausted, fell fast asleep, their lamps burning while they slept. At midnight the women were awakened by a voice shouting that the groom was on his way. The bridesmaids scrambled to get themselves ready. By now the lamps had all burned out and needed to be refilled. The bridesmaids with oil could not afford to give any away; they admonished the others to go buy their own. While the women were gone to get their oil, the groom arrived. He and the bridesmaids who had been prepared went in to the wedding and celebrated. When the others returned from shopping, they realized that the door had been shut. Knocking and screaming, the bridesmaids called for the groom to let them in. He replied that he didn't know them (Matt. 25:1-13). In a short time five women missed out on the anticipated celebration. The lack of oil showed that they had not been prepared. Years of dreaming, wishing, planning—and now it was all over.

The story remains the same: the Groom is coming. He has been patiently waiting. Ready or not, He is coming for His bride. He has put on hold His glorious appearing for so long, allowing His wife-to-be time to get affairs in order. If she truly loves Him, she has no time to procrastinate or entertain other prospects. Time is running out. Will she be ready to meet her Love? Will she have extra oil? I pray that we take heed, watch, and pray, because we don't know when our Groom is to return.

Diantha Hall-Smith

Jack

So I commend the enjoyment of life, because nothing is better for a man
under the sun than to . . . be glad. Then joy will accompany him in
his work all the days of the life God has given him under the sun.
Eccl. 8:15, NIV.

IN A FAMOUS BUILDING at the heart of Manhattan his wheelchair is beside his mattress. Behind him a glass wall shows a spectacular view of New York City, enveloped in a colorful sunset. Down on the streets thousands of yellow taxis fight for green lights, and people rush.

By my side, Jack doesn't see this amazing postcard beauty. Not because he doesn't want to, but because his beautiful blue eyes cannot see. Neither can he ask me what I'm seeing, because he cannot talk. But he joyfully laughs with all his heart when I describe heaven and everything he'll be able to do and experience there. I tell him how he will run and play with other kids, feed the animals, and talk to Jesus about whatever he wants while they travel together to distant planets, or just sit with their feet dangling in crystal waters, feeding colorful fish.

That night, while I was being paid to take care of Jack, Jack gave me a free lesson in happiness. He showed me that it is not what you have or what you can accomplish; neither is it what you can see that brings you full happiness. It is the fact that you are able to choose, to meet new people, to laugh, and to see wonderful things, even without sight.

Even if he is only 8 years old, Jack knows more about happiness than the majority of the population of the world. For him, there is no trying to appear as something he is not. There is no running like crazy after something he doesn't have or losing precious time with someone who tells him nice stories while playing with his hair. He has learned to accept everything and to enjoy a good laugh. Not because he doesn't have any reason to cry, but because he's decided to always find reasons to laugh.

I hope that, just like me, you learn with Jack the simple secret of being happy no matter what limitations and injustices life brings you. It doesn't matter what your wheelchair is, or if you've never seen all the colors others have seen.

Make life simple. Be happy with what you have. Allow yourself to be loved by God and by the people He puts in your way. And together, have many laughs!

Kênia Kopitar

God Chose the Best

For thou art my rock and my fortress; therefore for thy name's sake lead me, and guide me. Ps. 31:3.

ARE YOU ANGRY WITH ME?" It was a long-distance call from my mother, who was in her twilight years. My husband and I had visited friends in a retirement village and came away with our names on a unit—despite the fact that we had said we were never going to live in a retirement village. We had also discovered that three small rental units were vacant, and immediately I thought of my mother. She could occupy a unit and, if necessary, later she could go into the hostel and nursing home.

After we arrived home, I phoned mother and alerted her to the fact that we were going to enter a retirement village and spoke glowingly of the advantages. I suggested that she could join us, as there were three small units available. As she had never envisioned such a move, her first reaction was that she could never move away, as so many folks depended on her—all people much younger than she. I suggested that she think about it and make a decision quickly, as the units would be spoken for almost immediately.

About a week later she called and asked if I was angry with her for saying no. I assured her that I was not. She said that a voice seemed to be going round and round in her head saying to ring Joy. I told her one unit was left. Mother canceled her holiday, and I took her to the village for an interview and to sign papers. Then began the task of sorting her possessions and selling my small home, which she occupied. An acquaintance passing by asked what was going on, and immediately he contracted to buy the house. After a tearful goodbye to her friends of many years, she settled into the village.

At first we were a little disappointed that only the oldest unit was left, but it was in an ideal location for her. She soon made friends and joined in the activities of the village. She never regretted God's leading, and continually praised Him for bringing her to a place where she was so well cared for in her twilight years.

At the right time the problem of Mother's future was solved in ways that we didn't plan, and we thank God once again for being a light unto our feet.

Joy Dustow

Architect of Dreams

If ye then, being evil, know how to give good gifts unto your children: how much more shall your heavenly Father give the Holy Spirit to them that ask him? Luke 11:13.

IN MY EYES MY MOTHER was a phenomenal woman. She worked tirelessly to make sure that we were taken care of. There are many things that I admired about her: her strength, kindness, stick-to-itiveness, and her ability to laugh in the face of difficulty. In addition, my mother held on to every dream I had. As a child I can remember summer holidays when I spent a lot of time coloring houses that I drew. When I showed them to her, she would always say, "When you get older, I'll get you a house." In high school my mother told me that she purchased a piece of property for me to build my house. I thought nothing of it then because at my age, who really cared about property? Little did I know that my mother was holding on to my dreams of owning my very own home. I was 24 years old when I moved into my new home. With the help of my mother, my dream had come true. While I thought nothing of it, my mother had been working hard behind the scenes to ensure that the dream of owning my own house was realized. Today it stands as a symbol of her love and commitment to me.

We have a Father in heaven who is an architect of dreams and is a specialist in planning lives and mending broken dreams. I'd like to introduce Him to your situation today, no matter where you are in your life. God is able to make your dreams and aspirations come true better than you could ever imagine. He said in His Word that He has plans that will prosper you (Neh. 2:20). Even when we treat His plans for our lives as insignificant, He is constantly there hoping that we will catch just a glimpse of the blueprints for our lives here on earth and in the hereafter.

There are times when our dreams don't correspond with His plans, yet He faithfully waits and waits on us. His plan for us includes happiness, peace, health, success in our jobs and our relationships. It's a free gift that is only a prayer away. My mother was successful in helping me attain my dreams of owning my own home; yet her gift to me could never be compared to what God has prepared for you and me. He has built a mansion, not just a house, for each of us. Won't you accept this free gift today?

Architect of my life, thank You for holding on to my dreams. Help me to trust You more.

Carol Robinson

Divine Design

We have many members in one body, but all the members do not have the same function. Rom. 12:4, NKJV.

IT IS SPRING. From my window I can see all the flowers blossoming again. Flowers are everywhere. Different shapes, different sizes, different colors—it is difficult to choose a favorite. All are beautiful in their own way and style.

As we observe the plants, flowers, and people around us, we are reminded that God made each one of us unique for a purpose. No one else fits your shape or mine. God gave us individual talents and spiritual gifts so that we can work together as a body. "But now God has placed the members," Paul wrote, "each one of them, in the body, just as He desired" (1 Cor. 12:18, NASB). And as it is with the human body, so it is with the body of Christ, which is the corporate collection of all who believe.

But this uniqueness goes beyond giftedness; it reaches as well into the depth of each of our experiences in our life of faith. No one else has your life. No one else has your pain, your hardships, your joys, or your sorrows. Everything in life shapes us, and we are shaped by everything for a reason: so that we can touch others in a unique way, based on who we are and what we've been through. God is amazing! He doesn't waste anything in our lives.

That's why we are the crowning jewel of Creation, and we shine brightest not when we see our own likeness reflected in others but when each of us performs the unique functions that God designed for us to do. There is an old saying that is true: "What you are in God is God's gift to you; what you become is your gift to God."

I believe that all of us have been touched by God in many ways, so we have something to offer. Every piece of our lives and experiences can be used by Jesus to touch someone else. Think about your unique gifts and ask yourself how those gifts are benefiting others. There are no accidents with our lives. Whatever we have received and experienced has shaped who we are, and because of that we are qualified. There is truly no one else like you—for a reason.

Today, promise yourself and God to use your talents to touch someone for Christ.

Raquel Costa Arrais

Drought and Water

Whoever drinks of this water will thirst again.
John 4:13, NKJV.

IN 2007 AUSTRALIA WAS GRIPPED in the most severe drought since records began. A national day of prayer for rain had been held a few days before I flew to visit my brother and sister-in-law, who live in the state of New South Wales.

Once I was clear of the international airport in Sydney the heat hit me. The sun beat down from a relentless blue sky, so it was a relief to settle down in a very comfortable air-conditioned coach to travel the 375 miles (600 kilometers) west to where my brother and his family lived.

When the city suburbs finally gave way to countryside, the drought conditions became obvious. For mile after mile I looked at pastures that were nothing more than brown dirt. There wasn't much in the way of livestock, considering the distance I traveled. The thin sheep I did see were struggling to find something to eat. Cattle were so lean that their ribs nearly protruded out of their skin. Farmhouses stood in fields of brown; their water tanks on stands built against the houses were useless in this terrible drought. My heart ached for both the farmer and his animals. *Please, God, send some rain,* I prayed. *Water is so desperately needed.*

A few days later, as my brother and I were driving to the city of Wagga Wagga, we suddenly saw a farm that appeared so very green. We saw water irrigation pipes giving the ground much-needed moisture. The water was pumped up from a very controlled, very low river flowing at the back of the farm. I learned that although many farmers had water rights, this farmer was the only one for miles around who could afford to pay for his water supply.

Back in New Zealand, not far from where I live in a beautiful valley, are farming properties, each with several hundred milking cows. One farm has a wonderful watering system. Although there are no drought conditions there, the difference between the farm that irrigates constantly and those that do not is obvious. Water is a precious world commodity, no longer to be taken for granted!

Jesus offers us water. He says, "Whoever desires, let him take the water of life freely" (Rev. 22:17, NKJV). It doesn't cost a single cent, because our Savior has already paid the cost. Let us drink of the Living Water.

Leonie Donald

The Helping Hill

I will lift up mine eyes unto the hills, from whence cometh my help.
Ps. 121:1.

BECAUSE OF UNCONTROLLABLE DIABETES, I was experiencing health problems. My second daughter was having her share of health problems also. Trying to be a good housewife and maintain a demanding job took a toll on my well-being, which resulted in my being hospitalized.

But in the hospital I worried about how I would cope with the stress. One day as I strolled up and down the hospital corridor, dismal thoughts accompanied me. Suddenly I came to an open door. Without much thought I entered the very tiny room that had one open window. As I looked straight ahead, out through the window, my gaze rested on a small hill and a little mountain in the distance.

The serenity of that peaceful scene immediately flooded my mind with the words "I will lift up mine eyes unto the hills, from whence cometh my help. My help cometh from the Lord, which made heaven and earth." Just as suddenly, those dark, dismal thoughts seemed to melt away, as light, happy ones swirled around in my thought process. How delightfully reassuring! *My* health comes from the Lord—but only if, and when, I lift up my eyes to the hills. He is the same big, great, powerful being who created the heaven and the earth.

Why am I so worried? Maybe I forgot to lift up mine eyes unto the hills. There is a big Daddy watching over me. He alone can give me strength, comfort, and relief. The longer I kept my eyes on the Lord of that hill, the more my thoughts circled from dark and dismal to lighter, happier, brighter things. I sensed God's presence overshadowing me, His arm around me. I felt happy.

I do not know how long I stayed in that tiny room, transfixed in glory, but when I left I was a different human being. Those new, healthy thoughts remained with me. Life didn't seem so unkind, so harsh, so unpleasant anymore. The next day I took a walk down that same hospital corridor to enter that tiny room. I was hungry for more. I never found that open door. I couldn't help wondering: *Did God provide that open door just for me?* It's a question I've never been able to answer.

Thank You, Lord, for being there for me when I needed You. Please keep me faithful.

Joyce O'Garro

God's Wonderful Healing

My comfort in my suffering is this: Your promise preserves my life.
Ps. 119:50, NIV.

And the prayer of faith shall save the sick, and the Lord shall raise him up;
and if he have committed sins, they shall be forgiven him.
                    James 5:15.

LIFE HAD BECOME UNBEARABLE FOR ME. My thoughts weighed me down as I contemplated my situation, and I worried about what would happen to my children if I were gone. I tried not to dwell on that thought too much, but I had to let my children know what was happening. So we gathered for evening worship and praised God for His care. Later I shared with them my physical condition and what was most likely to happen should my situation worsen. I praise God that my children took it calmly and encouraged me that God would never fail us. I am grateful for my children's faith.

That night I experienced the worst night of my life. I writhed with pain. The weight of the pain bore me down as if tons of rocks were upon me, and I couldn't move. In desperation I cried to God for help. I forced myself up and crawled to the living room, where I sat up all night, praying to God for healing—not necessarily physical healing but for forgiveness so my life could be healed of sin and made ready for His kingdom. I prayed as I had never prayed before and completely put my trust in His hands.

As morning dawned a glimpse of daybreak brought a new promise of life to my being. Turning to God's Word, the Scripture reading for that morning was today's texts.

Miraculously, the pain was gone. I felt a pang of hunger, and I knew at once that a new life had begun. God, my Father, had healed me in the night. I went into the kitchen for the first time in weeks to prepare some potato juice and salad. Life had a positive turn for me, and I praise God that He heals and forgives. Prayer warriors throughout the South Pacific had been praying too. God was indeed at work. I praise Him for His wonderful healing.

May this be our prayer: *Father God, sometimes we are overcome with pain and illness. We put our trust in You, O God. Please, Jesus, take the pain, because You have experienced pain through Calvary. I know You will bear it for me. You have done it for many, and You will do it again and again. We praise You today, for Your love endures forever. Amen.*

Fulori Bola

It Doesn't Look Good!

But the natural man receiveth not the things of the Spirit of God: for they are foolishness unto him: neither can he know them, because they are spiritually discerned.
1 Cor. 2:14.

MY HUSBAND, WILL, AND I were having a leisurely Sabbath lunch when suddenly my adult daughter, Jhovonnah, raced down the steps and toward the front door. Breathless and obviously upset, she called out, "Something is wrong with one of the girls. I don't know which one. The only thing Vernon [her estranged husband] said is 'Get here right away. It doesn't look good.' "

Jhovonnah was in her car and down the street before we could even react. Had one of the girls been kidnapped? Had there been an accident at their dad's house and one was severely injured, or worse? "It doesn't look good" rang out in my ears. I didn't have a phone number to call or an address to go to. *O Lord, please be with Kali and Ariyah. And with Jhovonnah on the highway.* I was wringing my hands and pacing with worry. Ten minutes later the phone rang.

"It's Ariyah," my daughter said. "She fell into the windowsill and her teeth are pushed back; the ambulance is on the way." Ariyah, my 3-year-old granddaughter, was the youngest of three sisters. We left immediately for the emergency room, where we found Ariyah moaning and crying, ice packs and towels on her face. We hated to see her discomfort, but were relieved that it wasn't worse. Hours later an oral surgeon determined that she had a ridge fracture. He forcefully pushed her gums forward and extracted one front tooth. She was in terrible pain, with bleeding and swelling, and was unable to eat for days. Then a second front tooth was removed. Despite continued warnings, she soon was jumping on the bed, enjoying the exhilarating feeling of bouncing and flying—which was the reason she was injured in the first place.

Aren't we adults just like Ariyah? We do things that could potentially inflict hurt or cause untold distress, worry friends and relatives, even threaten our very lives—while we have our fun and enjoy the exhilaration it brings. Yet before the wounds from our adventures are even healed or the memory of the trauma we've suffered has faded, we're back at it again. The enemy revels as we slowly lose our souls, but the Lord beckons us to give up the foolishness of this world.

O Lord, help us not to choose worldly things that injure us emotionally, physically, or spiritually. Guide us, thou Great Jehovah.

Iris L. Kitching

Faith in God

So Jesus answered and said to them, "Have faith in God. For assuredly, I say to you, whoever says to this mountain, 'Be removed and be cast into the sea,' and does not doubt in his heart, but believes that those things he says will be done, he will have whatever he says." Mark 11:22, 23, NKJV.

THESE ARE YOUR OPTIONS: chemotherapy or radiation—and neither are available here. Call your mom and have her make arrangements for you to have these done in the United States." Those were my surgeon's concluding words to me.

Immediately I called my mom and requested that my youngest sister, a medical doctor, call me so I could read to her the diagnosis I had gotten from the laboratory after a lumpectomy. She returned my call in the wee hours of the morning and advised me to ask God to give me peace of mind, and that I should make arrangements to travel immediately. I fell sound asleep after talking to God.

Leaving my family in Guyana, I journeyed to the United States. One week later our family surgeon called and confirmed my worst fears: "Yes, you have been diagnosed with breast cancer." My mountain was before me. How would I get over it?

Away from my husband and children, I bravely went through chemotherapy and radiation, with the usual side effects of hair loss, weakness, and low immunity. But I trusted God—I was so confident that He was with me. My family and church in the United States and Guyana prayed for me as I agonized daily, calling upon the Great Physician during every session of treatment, remembering every patient, the oncologists, nurses, and even the medication administered.

The support of family and friends and members of the support group I joined all aided in my recovery. By reading books on health and healing, doing research on the Internet, and talking to survivors on the subject of cancer, I have learned the proper diet, attitude, and general health rules to follow for the duration of the disease.

To adopt an attitude of gratitude and to give praise helps healing. God is still good. He is mighty to save and strong to deliver. Let us continue to place our faith in the Great Physician and trust His heart.

Ruby H. Enniss-Alleyne

Saved From Committing Murder

Out of the depths have I cried unto thee, O Lord. Lord, hear my voice:
let thine ears be attentive to the voice of my supplications.
Ps. 130:1, 2.

MY HUSBAND WAS A LOVING and caring person, and our home ran smoothly and happily. But we had no children, and I was worried that I couldn't bear a child of my own. So I prayed for a baby girl. God heard my prayer, and I was very happy—but disappointed to have a baby boy. However, I accepted His gift to me, and our home was filled with love, peace, and happiness. My baby was so dear to me! I was happy to see him smile, make noise, and move his hands and legs. I spent most of my time caring for and playing with him.

As the child began to grow, so did our home expenses. My salary was very meager, so I had to work extra hours to meet the needs of the family. My husband also seemed to be very busy. I didn't know what he was doing, but I knew that he wasn't paying much attention to me or our child. Many times I wanted to question him, because I felt neglected. Then I thought he might feel hurt, so I kept quiet and busy with my home responsibilities.

Finally I realized that he was drifting away from me and was having an affair with another woman. My heart broke. I tried to win him back, but he wouldn't respond. I cried and prayed to God, but no changes came in his life. In fact, he would abuse me, pick a quarrel, insult, and treat me ill. All my happiness turned to sorrow. I was filled with regret and anger, and experienced severe mental distress. I asked God for help, but nothing seemed to work in my favor.

Once I was so upset that I thought of killing the woman who had taken away my happiness and peace of mind. Day and night I thought and planned how to take her life. In desperation I cried to God. He touched my heart, and I realized that what I was planning to do was wrong, and I asked God to forgive me. Even though my husband didn't come back to me, God gave me courage and strength to live without my husband. I am thankful to God for holding my hand back from committing murder. If you are abused, mistreated, or face difficulties and problems, trust in the Lord! He will deliver! I am now married to a kind, gentle, loving man. My life is much happier than ever before. God heard me!

Esther Kujur

The Lord Is Wonderful

Jephtha uttered all his words before the Lord in Mizpeh.
Judges 11:11.

THE LORD GOD IS WONDERFUL TO ME! I am a nursing superintendent in a government hospital at Villupuram, Chennai, India. One day I had the most bitter experience of my 33 years of service. It was a holiday, and I was on duty. I went on my usual morning ward rounds. As I came out of the pediatric ward a young man came up to me and asked for the motor room key. I didn't know where it was, and I told him that I didn't have the keys. Immediately he and the two men who were with him began to abuse me with bad language. I tried to walk away to avoid the situation, but they followed me. I couldn't tolerate the abuse any longer and told them to stop it. They were frightening me, but I managed to be calm. Suddenly and shockingly, the man slapped me. As it is a criminal offense to manhandle anyone on duty, the issue now had become a serious one. I lodged a complaint, and the state government employees' association and the nurses' association supported me.

My family and I left everything to the Lord and were quiet amid the commotion. We surrendered everything to our God. I cried to the Lord as King Hezekiah had: *O Lord, why has this happened to me? Is this the reward for these 33 years of my sincere service?* Then I evaluated myself to discover what I lacked. I completely surrendered myself to Him in prayer and decided to spend most of my time in the Lord's work. He swept away my tears and answered my prayers. Peace filled my heart.

Later I learned that the man who had slapped me had a building contract for work on the hospital premises. He had asked me for the keys to use hospital water for his building work, which was illegal. His contract was immediately canceled. Previously there had been a lot of outside pressure and influence controlling the hospital, and all the workers were afraid to oppose it. The Lord used my incident to free the whole hospital from these bad forces. After that nobody entered our hospital to create any sort of trouble. Further, the hospital staff understood that I was a true Christian.

Our family thanked God for His wonderful guidance and deliverance during this time of trouble. I thank the Lord for the great things He has done for us. Are you doing that today too?

Victoria Selvaraj

An Abiding Optimism

I am greatly encouraged; in all our troubles my joy knows no bounds.
2 Cor. 7:4, NIV.

IN THE TOWN OF SOKCHO, located in the northeast region of South Korea, lives a very devout farmer who firmly believes that God takes care of him, no matter what, and that He knows what is best. The farmer faithfully tithed his earnings from the sale of his seeds in his little shop, and from whatever produce he harvested from his farm and one greenhouse. All the tithe was dropped into a little box and never counted before bringing it to the church each Sabbath.

When fear gripped the community as a horde of grasshoppers appeared on the horizon, this farmer was confident that God would take care of his crops, and he expressed this confidence to his neighbors. Contrary to the perfect ending of an "answered" prayer story, the grasshoppers tore through and destroyed the farmer's crops like everyone else's. Many of his friends began to mock his belief in a God who had no power to protect him. The faithful farmer replied, "The grasshoppers are God's creatures, and if He chooses to use my farm to feed them this time, let it be so." He refused to doubt; his abiding optimism was unshaken.

Later, when a typhoon hit the area, the farmers suffered the loss of not only their crops but their greenhouses as well. When they emerged from their homes after the storm, all were surprised that our faithful farmer's greenhouse was the only one untouched by the strong winds. This time God had chosen to protect and bless him. For this he gave thanks.

An abiding optimism is a result of faith, faith that has developed from a close relationship with God, trusting that He knows what is best. Through the good and the bad, we submit that God is still watching over all. When the grasshoppers destroyed the crop, our farmer didn't go hungry. In all things these people give thanks and look for God's hand and His plan rather than complaining. This type of optimism doesn't use faith as leverage to demand God's blessings. And even in the most trying circumstances, they can be assured that God is there.

An outstanding preacher and writer, E. E. Cleveland, calls this abiding optimism a character trait rather than a fickle emotion. "It has to be sought for and when received, cherished. It is imparted individually. It is handed down, not over or up. Heaven has plenty to spare." Those who know God have a joy and peace that money can never buy.

Sally Lam-Phoon

He Knows My Name

Come unto me, all ye that labour and are heavy laden, and I will give you rest.
Take my yoke upon you, and learn of me; for I am meek and lowly in heart:
and ye shall find rest unto your souls. For my yoke is easy, and my burden is light.
Matt. 11:28-30.

I FIND IT INTERESTING that when I walk on the street or through the neighborhood, individuals I don't know address me by name. One such incident resulted in an unusual reaction.

I was working at the front of my home and had just gone to the garbage bin to put away some refuse when a member of the family who had just moved in across the street addressed me by name. I had said hello to her before but was not yet properly acquainted with her. I felt shocked and surprised, but I didn't comment.

Sometime later I passed her and another female member of her family on the street, and they again greeted me by name. This time it was with a different expression and feeling, however, which brought a smile to my face and cheer to my heart. Later, as I thought about this incident, I compared it with our relationship with Jesus, and the words "He knows my name" came to my mind.

How often we are so caught up with our own thoughts, burdens, and cares that we neglect or are blinded to the simple things in life, such as greeting our neighbors. A few words—or even one word or a smile—can make the difference.

Jesus knows our name and is always aware of where we are and what our needs are. In today's text He says, "Come unto me, all ye that labour and are heavy laden, and I will give you rest. Take my yoke upon you and learn of me; for I am meek and lowly in heart: and ye shall find rest unto your souls. For my yoke is easy, and my burden is light."

Will you walk the path of Jesus today? Remember, if you reach a neighbor today, you are reaching Jesus; if you cheer a friend today, you are cheering Jesus; if you fill a need of hunger and thirst today, you are feeding and touching Jesus; and when we touch Him, we are blessed. The Holy Spirit can help us to be mindful of those around us and reach out to fill other's needs, which fills our needs as well. Won't you touch Jesus today?

Elizabeth Ida Cain

My Home Is in Heaven

In My Father's house are many mansions; if it were not so,
I would have told you. I go to prepare a place for you.
John 14:2, NKJV.

MY HUSBAND AND I were reminiscing and counting the many moves we've made during the past 43 years of our being together. We had recently moved to Hawaii, and this move marked the twenty-first house we'd occupied. I guess that should be no surprise—a minister's family is expected to move from time to time as needed. As the wife of a minister, though, I sometimes really dreaded moving, because packing and unpacking are two jobs that are not a joke. So when my husband finally retired last year, I was elated. That meant we could stay put in the house that God had provided for us. But then a call came from a small church in Hawaii, and my husband thought we should go. Of course I agreed and was happy that we could continue to serve, even though he had already retired. The best part about moving to Hawaii was that we didn't have to pack our furniture—the parsonage was furnished. The only thing we had to take was our clothes and books, although we took the least possible even of those things. There was even a car for us to use while serving here. What a privilege had been given to us!

I am looking forward to the time when the promise of our Lord in John 14:2 will be fulfilled. That means I won't have to move ever again. That means permanency in the heavenly mansion, although I know God's redeemed will go from one planet to another, exploring the vast universe. I am excited to think that we shall be like angels who will visit other planets and see what God has in store for us there. Although we will visit other places, we won't pack and unpack, as we do for our travel here on earth. Yes, Jesus' words in John 14:2 keep echoing in my ears—He is preparing a place for me! It will not be an ordinary three-bedroom house or a common place such as we have on this planet, for He Himself says, "Eye has not seen, nor ear heard, nor have entered into the heart of man the things which God has prepared for those who love Him" (1 Cor. 2:9, NKJV). So if my earthly home is not as elegant as I want or not as spacious as I wish, it is all right, because I know I have a better mansion up there. I can hardly wait to occupy the God-prepared abode. Have you accepted His promise as well?

Ofelia A. Pangan

The Last Breakfast

Jesus said to them, "Come and have breakfast."
John 21:12, NIV.

AT THE TIME I DIDN'T KNOW it was going to be our last breakfast together. My mom and dad, my sister, her roommate Cheryl, and Cheryl's brother—my best friend, Mark—and I went to Yosemite for a few days before Christmas. It was a long drive from our home in southern California, and I was a reluctant participant. My idea of time off from school was to be sprawled on the couch in front of the TV with a bag of Cheetos, not riding around in the mountains and becoming carsick.

The only thing that stands out in my mind about that trip was the last day and my futile attempts to build a snowman. I was still working on it when it was time to go, so Mark solved the problem by calmly ripping the head off an abandoned snowman and putting it on mine! We didn't stop for breakfast until about 10:00. Breakfast consisted of toasted cheese sandwiches and soda, and I don't know if it was the crispness of the weather or the pleasant company, but it remains one of the great breakfasts of my life.

Three months later Mark was dead, and my last photos of him were the ones I took at Yosemite. That was many years ago now. My father and sister are also gone. Cheryl married and moved back east. Only my mom and I remain in California.

Remembering that last breakfast together makes me think of Jesus and the Last Supper. Did the disciples realize that this was a special time, their last time together as a group? Would they have acted differently if they had? Would they have treasured their time together and savored every bite? Would anybody have had anything nice to say to Judas?

Most people know about the Last Supper, but they forget that Jesus and His followers had a last breakfast, too. After the Resurrection and before He ascended, He cooked a fish breakfast on the beach for His friends. Imagine eating a meal prepared by the Master's hands!

Both the Last Supper and the last breakfast give us hope—hope that when we eat in remembrance of our Savior we are really sharing a meal with Someone we love. And my own last breakfast with Mark and my family gave me a happy memory that has lasted longer than my mourning over his death.

Gina Lee

God Will Supply All Your Needs

I can do all things through Christ which strengtheneth me.
Phil. 4:13.

THEY WERE PLANNING a big retirement party for a good friend of mine. Russ had worked a long time and deserved to retire. He is one talented man who plays keyboard and accordion. He is always willing to help out at church with his talent. I wanted to get something special for Russ, so I decided to make him a tie blanket.

I shopped for just the right material and found a wonderful fleece that had a nice outdoor scene on it, with a white background. Now I needed the fabric for the other side; I wanted to get something that had music on it. Once before, I had gotten some fleece with black music notes on white. I began looking in all the stores that carried fleece. I couldn't find it at all. One store called three of their other stores to see if they had it, but to no avail.

I was disappointed. I went to a nearby city, but they didn't carry what I wanted. I went to Greenville, another town, and found fabric with music notes on it, but it was light brown with black notes. I bought two yards anyway so that I would have something.

It was getting closer to the date of the big party, and I was about to give up and make the blanket with the brown, even though I didn't like the two fabrics together.

I was over at a good friend's house who was going to her doctor's office for a checkup. She said, "I'll stop at Fields out on 44th Street when I'm finished to see if I can find your fabric." Later that day she called from Fields and said they had one fleece that was black and white with keyboards on it.

Helen got the fabric, and when she took the bolt to the counter, there were just two yards left on it. I knew before that it was true that God shall supply all our needs, but I had evidence once again. He had placed Helen at the very store that Fields had called. They said they didn't have any black-and-white music-note fleece, but never mentioned they had black-and-white keyboard fleece. God saved exactly the amount I needed.

Isn't the Lord wonderful? He cares about all the aspects of our lives because He loves us so much. What has God done for you lately? Are you praising Him for it? I know I am!

Anne Elaine Nelson

God Is Still Good

Before they call, I will answer; and while they are still speaking, I will hear.
Isa. 65:24, NKJV.

IN 2005 WE MOVED from our lovely home into a smaller townhouse, as I was finding the care of the house and garden too much for me. Within two months of moving I was diagnosed with cancer of the colon and had a hemicolectomy (removal of half of my colon), followed by six months of chemotherapy. I'm happy to report that after 18 months the follow-up colonoscopy showed that I was clear of cancer.

I was rejoicing in this and thanking God for His care and protection. Then the next blow fell. I had fallen twice before when out walking with family and friends, but when I fell again just walking across the parking lot of our local hospital after visiting a friend there, I felt there must be something wrong. So I went back again to our family physician. While I was talking to him he looked over at my notes that I had made and saw that my handwriting was extremely small and virtually illegible.

He said, "Ruth, I think you might have Parkinson's disease. I want you to see the neurologist." The neurologist confirmed that I probably had one of the Parkinsonian syndromes.

I was feeling sorry for myself one day after that announcement, so I prayed, *Dear God, please let one of my church friends phone me to encourage me.* I had no sooner stopped praying than the phone rang. Excitedly I answered it, but it was not one of my church friends but my next-door neighbor, a 90-year-old widow. She said, "I have something for you. Can I come over and bring it to you?"

A few moments later she was at my door with a beautiful bouquet of tulips. I love spring flowers, and these were especially lovely ones. I told her she was an answer to my prayer. She beamed and hugged me, and ever since then she has repeatedly brought me bunches of happiness. God must have had that all prepared for me before I even prayed, so I knew again the truth of the text "Before they call, I will answer."

Yes, God is still good, and He still looks after me and my family. I know I should trust Him more and leave the future in His hands.

Ruth Lennox

His Heart

You will keep him in perfect peace, whose mind is stayed on You, because he trusts in You. Isa. 26:3, NKJV.

WHEN MY DAUGHTER, DANIELLE, was home from college during her sophomore year, she brought home a puny, sickly, tabby kitten with the promise to take him back to school with her. A castaway from the litter at her summer job, she found him on the brink of being annihilated. With pleading eyes she begged me to allow her to keep him. I couldn't say no. He was such a timid kitten that I instinctively named him Timmy. Needless to say, when she returned to school she left Timmy with me. I suppose you could say that over the years he has infused himself into my heart, as we both have grown older together.

Whenever I sit in my favorite chair for reading or relaxation, I can expect that within minutes Timmy will be in my lap. He jumps up with such determination and skill that I'm always amazed at his agility. One day I took the time to watch as he lay sleeping on my lap. He purred sweetly as I stroked him. He looked so peaceful and content. The feeling was mutual, because I enjoyed him being in my lap. He didn't even raise his head to see whose hand was petting him. He knows and trusts the unseen hand. He trusts me to give him what he needs. He trusts me to feed him when he is hungry or give him water when he is thirsty. He trusts me to be there when he needs a lap to find comfort in. Yes, he trusts me, and I benefit from his trust.

As I sat quietly observing Timmy, a picture of my Lord and Savior vividly appeared in my artistic mind. I envisioned the many times I've gone to God as a child to her father and climbed into His lap. I thought how pleasing it must be to Him when we, as daughters of Zion, approach Him with such childlike trust. He must feel wonderful when we come to Him, trusting that He will take care of our every need, or that He is near to comfort our searching hearts. What peace and contentment He is so willing to impart to us when we just come to Him as children of the living God. We are His heart! His daughters! There isn't anything He wouldn't do to protect us or to provide for us. So why not trust Him? He loves us!

Do you see God as the all-powerful Father that He is? Do you take the time to climb into His lap and be content in His presence? Why not try it today!

Evelyn Greenwade Boltwood

Gift of Life

But God commendeth his love toward us, in that, while we were yet sinners, Christ died for us.
Rom. 5:8.

IT WAS AFTER 11:30 that Tuesday night when I got the call we had been waiting for. They were transporting my friend, Ilyn, to Toronto General Hospital, as there were double lungs available that might be a match for her. My friend had had trouble breathing without an oxygen mask for quite some time. She'd had to quit her job as a perioperative nurse in North Carolina and had come home to seek more medical attention. Now it appeared as if our prayers—the prayers of her family, friends, and churches—were going to be answered. It was a perfect match—the lungs would be hers. As we often say, God is good.

Ilyn was prepped for surgery at 7:00 Wednesday morning, and by 10:00 she went into surgery for the six- to eight-hour operation. Everything went fine, and the surgery was completed in only four hours. God was good once again.

Ilyn had so many volunteers in her operating room that morning that there was a veritable crowd—a crowd of witnesses for her life of faith, as Paul says in Hebrews 12. Many coworkers remembered her from her service with them more than five years before and wanted to be there for her. There was even one nurse who had retired a month before; she couldn't take waiting, and suited up to scrub for her. That even surprised the chief operating physician.

Her sister, Ivis, told me later that the number of doctors who kept visiting the waiting room made the other people who were waiting for loved ones in surgery wonder if she was some celebrity. Well, she *was* a celebrity in our sight!

This experience, though, made me think of a bittersweet reality. Someone whom we'll never know lost his or her life. Because of this my friend will live. However, all of this pales in the face of a historical and spiritual fact: Jesus Christ, our Lord and Savior, died so that we can live—and not just live but have a new body—in His heavenly home. He is the perfect match who can replace the sin in our lives and make us completely whole again.

My sisters, we do not know who is watching as we go about our daily lives. We have to live our lives so that others can know our donor, Jesus.

Loviere Pointer

Servant Leadership

For even the Son of Man came not to be ministered unto,
but to minister, and give his life a ransom for many.
Mark 10:45.

IN MY NEIGHBORHOOD I observed what reminded me of Christ's example of the servant leader that He exemplified while here on earth. He was the King of kings, yet He washed the dirty, grimy feet of His disciples.

Early one morning I saw the director of our neighborhood community center using a commercial outdoor sweeper, cleaning up the area in front of the center. This center provided child day care, as well as senior citizen activity programs, and other types of services, for the neighborhood.

An employee had been hired to do that job; however, that person was not there when the center opened. It was not in the director's job description to keep the area cleared of debris, but he wanted the exterior of the center to be clean and inviting. He didn't at all consider it beneath him to do any menial task, because his interest was for the respectability of the center, not the prestige or authority of his position as director.

Neither did Christ regard His supreme position as the Son of God too lofty to serve all and sacrifice Himself for the salvation of mankind. By His example Christ showed us that the absolute essence of a true leader lies in his attitude and willingness to serve faithfully in any capacity for the good of others. In fact, it says in Philippians 2:5-7: "Your attitude should be the same as that of Christ Jesus: who, being in very nature God, did not consider equality with God something to be grasped, but made himself nothing, taking the very nature of a servant, being made in human likeness" (NIV).

It was a living affirmation of servant leadership to see that director conscientiously cleaning up trash that was a blight to the front of the center, because he esteemed the appearance of the center of more importance than his ego. This gave me, a church elder, the living picture of what it means to be a servant leader—not just a sacrifice of time and energy, but ego as well. My prayer is that I too will not hesitate to serve whenever the circumstance necessitates. As Jesus Himself said: "The greatest among you will be your servant" (Matt. 23:11, NIV).

Dorothy D. Saunders

Keep a Song in My Heart

Speak to one another with psalms, hymns and spiritual songs. Sing and make music in your heart to the Lord, always giving thanks to God the Father for everything, in the name of our Lord Jesus Christ. Eph. 5:19, 20, NIV.

WHEN I WAS GROWING UP, I belonged to the Missionary Volunteer Society. Part of the pledge for this group has remained with me over the years: Keep a song in my heart.

Although I'm not a vocalist, I have the ability to carry a tune and have always responded to music. In the past few years I've learned that keeping a song in my heart is important to my well-being. I appreciate the modern praise music that glorifies God for His wonderful characteristics. It successfully leads me into praise and worship. However, recently God has renewed my interest in the old hymns of the church. There is meat in the words of the old songs that nourishes my soul. Like the psalms of David, they speak to my immediate need. They verbalize the thoughts I cannot find words for.

My husband and I are prayer leaders for our church and lead out in the midweek prayer service. Recently I shared with the group how God continues to speak to me through the words of my mother's favorite hymn, "I'm a Child of the King." God reminds me that my true identity is not an aging woman but a loved child of the King. I asked the group if any of them had a story about a song that had had an impact upon their relationship with God. Yes! Many had.

So we began a series centering on stories of hymns that have touched our hearts and lives in a special way. As we conclude each devotional time, the group sings the song of that evening. With minds filled with the message of the song, we go into our prayer groups.

Perhaps we would find deep renewal in our souls if, along with our search for revival in worship, we also sought out the old hymns to fill our hearts. Perhaps our young people might be attracted anew to the gospel message if they heard the gospel sung in words and melody.

Songs have power to play and replay again in our minds, lifting our hearts continually to the God of all wisdom and comfort who is surrounded by millions and millions of singing angels. Now is the time to learn these songs, in preparation for joining the massive choir in heaven. Let's keep a song in our hearts.

Carrol Johnson Shewmake

Clean

Who is a God like you, who pardons sin and forgives the transgression of the
remnant of his inheritance? You do not stay angry forever but delight to
show mercy. You will again have compassion on us; you will tread
our sins underfoot and hurl all our iniquities into the depths of the sea.
        Micah 7:18, 19, NIV.

MY SISTER AND HER FAMILY needed a break from the busy city life of New York. She lived in a concrete jungle where her kids had no place to play or run to their hearts' desire. So I left my country home in Pennsylvania to pick them up for a lovely weekend. She wanted the family to take the bus home, but I preferred for her instead to drive my new, safe car home. During her drive a tiny hole grew after a small stone hit the windshield. By the time she got home to New York City, that tiny hole had grown into a five-centimeter serpentine crack.

The procrastinator in me waited for another month until I called the insurance company and the windshield replacement company. The crack was too large to be repaired, so a $50 deductible would buy me a new windshield.

I took the car in that day, and it was ready by the time I left work. Gratefully I stepped into the car and smiled, realizing that the windshield was finally fixed. What amazed me was the intense clarity of the new windshield. I pride myself in keeping the car clean. All smears, smudges, and bird droppings are washed off weekly with an expensive windshield cleaner. Yet even my diligent efforts to keep my new car clean were worthless. My old windshield was still dirty, though I couldn't see it; it looked clean—it really did. But I couldn't see the difference until the windshield was replaced.

When confronted with his sin with Bathsheba, David wrote: "Wash away all my iniquity and cleanse me from my sin. . . . Cleanse me with hyssop, and I will be clean; wash me, and I will be whiter than snow" (Ps. 51:2, 7, NIV). It is Jesus, and only Jesus, who will do that cleaning for you and me, lowly, sinful creatures that we are. He will cheerfully replace our dirty, crimson-stained rags and clothe us in His righteous, spotless robe. His death on Calvary's cross allows us filthy creatures to stand clean on judgment day before His Father. If you haven't received Christ as your Savior yet, do it today.

Sharon Michael

Sharp Objects

Create in me a clean heart, O God; and renew a right spirit within me.
Ps. 51:10.

I WAS TRAVELING WITH MY MOTHER-IN-LAW from California to Washington, D.C. Check-in at the airport went smoothly. We checked our four bags, and then I requested a wheelchair for my mother-in-law. The attendant wheeled her as I followed behind. When we got to the security point, we put our carry-on bags and shoes on the scanner belt and went through the detector. One of the security guards asked about my mother-in-law's handbag. When he asked her what was inside, she said, "Just my personal things." Then he asked another question: "Do you have any sharp object in your handbag, ma'am?"

"Yes," my mother-in-law answered. "I have a small knife that I brought to open the bag of chips on board." The guard reminded her that no one was allowed to take any knife onboard.

He continued to search for the knife but couldn't find it. She finally took everything out of the bag—but still no knife. To speed up the searching, I asked Mom where she had put it. "It should be just there, because I dropped it in there just yesterday," she said. Another guard came and helped, and finally they found the knife inside an envelope. Apparently, when Mom dropped the knife into her purse, it fell into the open envelope. They confiscated the knife and cleared us to proceed to our gate.

In life we carry sharp objects. The apostle Paul reminds us that, as disciples of Christ, we need to get rid of sharp objects—objects such as materialism, envy, greed, gossip, hatred, and others that are dangerous in our Christian lives. Many times we keep these sharp objects to ourselves, trying to appear righteous when, in fact, we are keeping some sharp objects hidden. We think that we can hide them. We forget that "out of the abundance of the heart the mouth speaketh" (Matt. 12:34). As we pass the detector of trials and discouragement, those sharp objects are clearly seen in the way we respond to tough times in life.

The good news is that the Lord would like to take all those sharp objects from us. He wants to keep us safe from danger. All we have to do is surrender them to Him so that we can travel safely and happily with the other travelers. Surrendering those sharp objects will make us enjoy peace that passes understanding, and will make us loving and lovable Christians.

Jemima Dollosa Orillosa

Listening to God

Be still, and know that I am God; I will be exalted among
the nations, I will be exalted in the earth.
Ps. 46:10, NIV.

LISTENING TO GOD isn't always easy to do, but when you do, amazing things can happen. Often we can get caught up in pat phrases and clichéd prayers.

At a women's retreat we had a few hours of prayers and healing. We were learning to listen to God, allowing Him to tell us what to say. Now I've been learning more about praying. When you hear the Holy Spirit telling you things or giving you an image, it can blow your mind.

There are many ways to pray. It's nice to select a verse and meditate on it, and just listen. We can get too busy and too hurried to listen. Just think of the blessings God may give us if we listen to Him! But we have to follow through on what He asks.

There are three points to listening: *attitude* (our mind must be tuned in), *intention* (being strategic; doing what it takes to shut out distractions and allow our mind to focus on God's voice), and *action* (acting on what we hear from God).

Someone prayed for me that weekend, and she didn't even know what the desires of my heart were. She was told by God to pray for exactly what I wanted. I had never spoken to this woman before, and she didn't know what I needed prayer about until God talked to her. I have to believe she listened to the Holy Spirit.

This experience really taught me a lot. God has now given me a promise: the desires of my heart will come true. I claim Psalm 20:4 as my own promise from God: "May he give you the desire of your heart and make all your plans succeed" (NIV). I thank Him every day for that promise of granting my heart's desires. I also know that my plans will succeed. I thought I came upon that verse by accident; now I know that verse was God's leading me. Now I need to listen to the Holy Spirit and act on what He wants me to do.

We ask You, dear heavenly Father, to guide our thoughts and actions. Help us to listen to Your voice and Your will. I ask You to grant my heart's desire as You have promised.

Melanie Winkler

Making a Gift

Every good gift and every perfect gift is from above.
James 1:17.

MOTHER'S DAY WAS APPROACHING, and a little girl wanted to make her mother a gift. The girl decided the best gift to give her mom would be one created by hand. So she searched for a jar that bore the name and contents of another user. She carefully cleaned out the inside, and then began scraping the painted name off the outside. She continued working until she accidentally cut a slit in her wrist with the razor blade she'd been using.

She didn't want to tell her parents what had happened because that would spoil her surprise. So she climbed up into her bed and prayed, "Dear God, please sew my wrist back together. Amen." After taking a short nap, she looked down at her wrist and discovered the Lord had sewn it back together. Then she knelt down by her bed and thanked God for the miracle He had performed. Then she carefully continued cleaning the jar and filled it with pastel-colored salt. She covered the lid of the jar with fabric then fastened it to the jar with ribbon. Now her Mother's Day gift was complete.

Thousands of years ago Jesus decided to give His Father a gift. So He searched for vessels that bore the name and character of another owner. These containers carried such names as liar, prideful, covetous, greedy, gossiper, backbiter—and the list of sinful titles goes on. We wore the paint, the scars, the cuts, and the marks that represented the father of deception. We may even have been filled with alcohol, illegal drugs, nicotine, or other items that aren't healthy for us.

While Jesus was cleaning, scraping, and cutting away parts, and adding His character to His gift for His Father, some of these created beings didn't want to become gifts for Jesus' Dad. These creatures decided to cut Jesus with a thorny crown and nail Him to a rugged cross. Jesus didn't want to tell His Father how cruel we could be, so He prayed, "Father, forgive them, for they know not what they do." Later on, Jesus rose from the grave; and He is continuing to work on His gift for His Daddy. Do you want to be one of Jesus' presents for His Father?

Dear Jesus, please forgive me for carrying the name and character of another father. Please clean me up on the inside and the outside. I want to be a present for Your Father. Amen.

Quetah Sackie-Osborne

Mothers—a High Calling

Her children arise up, and call her blessed; her husband also, and he praiseth her.
Prov. 31:28.

A WELL-KNOWN MODERN PROVERB SAYS: "The hand that rocks the cradle rules the world." Though both parents are equally responsible for training their children, a greater responsibility often falls on mothers. I believe mothers are also the foundation upon which civilization is built. Mothers have a great impact on the moral and spiritual development of their children, influencing them either for good or evil. Mothers are the mirrors in which children see themselves; they are the keepers of their hearts. They are a powerful influence over their children. When mothers plant the seed of Bible truth in their hearts, it remains.

For children, mothers come next to God. Mothers nurture them. Affection and sacrifice are key roles for mothers. Children also need discipline, love, and self-esteem. The mind of a young child is like a sponge, waiting to soak in everything. Research determines that by the age of 3 a child's basic ideas of right and wrong are well set. During these three years mothers should spend more time with their children. But so often self, materialism, want—or necessity—or a whole host of other things take the preeminence or the priority in life, and children somehow get squeezed in between. Children learn by what they see and hear. So mother has the responsibility to teach her children honesty, integrity, faith, love, righteousness, and godliness by her life. This impact will be felt throughout entire families, communities, and nations; if parents did this there would be fewer problems with gangs, teenage pregnancy, violence, and drugs.

Lee Strobel tells about a mother's typical day. Her 3-year-old son was on her heels wherever she went, and she was having trouble doing her work. Several times she even tripped over him. She suggested activities to keep him occupied, but he said he wanted to be with her. In desperation she asked why he was following her. He said, "In Sabbath school the teacher told me to walk in Jesus' footsteps, but I can't see Him, so I am walking in yours."

Are we the model our children should follow? Someone has said, "We raise not the children we want, but the children that we—the parents—are." Children would rather do what they see than what they hear. We need to model aright so there will be no double standards to confuse young minds. May God bless our mothers to achieve their high calling!

Margaret Nathaniel

Mother's Love

As one whom his mother comforteth, so will I comfort you.
Isa. 66:13.

I OPEN THE LETTER FROM MY MOM with one hand and stuff down my breakfast with the other. It's the usual stuff moms write to their daughters: Don't sleep late. Don't forget to go to church. Don't forget the vitamins. Oil your hair regularly. Dress well . . . Blah, blah, blah!

Mom, why do you send a letter just to say the same things again and again when I call up once a week? "I love you very, very much" my mom had written at the end of the letter.

I throw the letter to one side and rush to my pediatrics ward. I walk over to the bed assigned to our team, and what I see makes the blood in my veins curdle. A child, about 5 months old, with multiple congenital anomalies lies there. I just couldn't call that "thing" a baby—babies are warm, cuddly, cute, with chubby cheeks and toothless grins. This child isn't anything like that. *O God*, I whisper in a silent prayer of anguish, *why did you let this thing be born—so he would lead a pitiful existence of degraded, lifelong dependence?*

I look up and see the woman who brought this piece of human wreckage into the world. She smiles at me. Just a smile. No false bravado, no defiance, no hatred, just blind acceptance. I looked down at the "thing" again. He waves his tiny arms and kicks the air energetically. Feeding time! Watching the mother and child together stirs something dormant and primitive within me. She puts the baby back on the bed, and I touch him tentatively. He curls his tiny fingers tightly around mine. How beautiful his touch feels! Suddenly I'm longing to hold him. I ask his mother if I may, and she nods. I pick him up gingerly and hold him close. He glares at me, as if warning me not to drop him, then smiles a little, cuddling up to me, and goes to sleep.

Standing there in the busy ward, my thoughts go to God's Word. I am just like this tiny babe—sick, filthy, full of weaknesses and flaws, marred by sin. But my Father in heaven loves me just the way I am. No defiance, no hatred, just blind acceptance. And love.

I bend down to give one last kiss before I leave. "Goodbye, Junior" I whisper, loving his soft baby skin and his warm baby smell. "I think I love you just the way you are." Back in my room, I pick up my mom's letter and hold it close to my heart. I begin to write, "Dearest Mommy, I love you very, very much."

Synthia Murali

Digging a Hole

Every branch in Me that does not bear fruit He takes away; and every
branch that bears fruit He prunes, that it may bear more fruit. . . .
The branch cannot bear fruit of itself, unless it abides in the vine.
John 15:2-4, NKJV.

LOOKING BACK ON LIFE, I see a picture of myself digging a hole. The hole completed, I gather all my worries, imperfections, wrongdoings, bad habits, along with all other evils, and toss them in the hole and cover them over with dirt. A symbolic gesture I was sure would work. Some people would call it turning over a new leaf. I complete filling the hole by planting a rose, an "apricot nectar," with the promise of a beautiful, golden flower. Like the rose, my life too was going to bear beautiful flowers.

Strange, I kept struggling with the same old problems. I thought I had buried them. As I tended to my rose I noticed it had problems too. Nearby plants were crowding it out. I trimmed these back. I made sure it had water and fertilizer. Buds began to form. Then I noticed beetles boring right into these buds, and the flowers were not as perfect as I would have hoped. But I rejoiced in the flowers it did have and savored the fragrant perfume. Sometime later black spots appeared on its leaves, and I applied some antifungal solution.

A dormant time followed. It was then I got out my pruning shears and cut the branches back. Now it looked very forlorn, and you could not imagine that there was still life within. But sure enough, in springtime shoots sprang forth from this plant, and a new life cycle began.

I see similarities in my life to that of the rose. Problems come my way and try to crowd me out, but there is One who tends my life, who sorts out my worries and generously supplies all the essentials of life. Other problems I encounter are much like the beetles that bore into my life to bring disruption and undermine my direction. Black spots have appeared from wrong decisions or actions, and pruning has been necessary. My life does bear flowers, though at times they are somewhat imperfect, and life's perfume permeates other people's lives, whether positively or negatively. But I rejoice in the good that my Creator puts into my life.

Now about my digging the hole: I've since understood that the only way to handle the problems of life is to lay them at the cross of Jesus. He will bury them for me.

Dawn Hargrave

God's Second Book

He has made everything beautiful in its time. He has also set eternity in the hearts of men; yet they cannot fathom what God has done from beginning to end.
Eccl. 3:11, NIV.

WITH EAGER ANTICIPATION my husband and I accompanied our daughter and son-in-law on our first outing in their new boat. As we skimmed over the smooth-as-glass water of Lake Michigan, I drank in the beauty around me. The sun on the water appeared as dazzling diamonds sparkling on its surface. The warmth of the sun and the breeze blowing warmly on my face and through my hair gave a sense of exhilaration. My mind seemed to clear, and the creative juices started flowing as I relaxed. No wonder nature is called God's second book!

Aren't you glad God is a lover of beauty? In spite of the blight of sin, nature's beauty still exists to tantalize our senses and calm our souls. God provided many opportunities in the natural world for pleasure and peace. We don't have to look far to see evidence of His love for the beautiful and for us: the towering trees, fluffy white clouds, the sun, moon and stars, as well as the many varieties of birds and butterflies that grace the air. Lush green grass, flourishing shrubs, and wild creatures all testify of that love. Even in cities there are parks where natural beauty can be enjoyed. Taking time to notice and appreciate them is something we don't always do.

There is nothing like a secluded place in nature for opportunity to commune with our Creator. How much my husband and I enjoy the birds that feast at the feeders in our wooded backyard, with squirrels feeding on the ground from the leftovers. Observing them, we are reminded of His watchcare for them, although they neither spin nor reap.

Planting and observing the miracle of tiny seeds or bulbs transformed into plants that yield their special blossom, fruit, or vegetable is an awesome experience. The gifts of nature were designed to draw us to the Giver of these gifts. Time spent in these settings may yield dividends for eternity.

Snorkeling or diving in some parts of the world gives opportunity to experience another dimension of God's creation. Fish of all shapes, sizes, and colors, along with varied and awesome shapes of coral that show off brilliant colors, are a sight to behold.

What a pleasant aid nature is to restoring the image of God in us!

Marian M. Hart

Lessons From the Flowers

But grow in grace, and in the knowledge of our Lord and
Saviour Jesus Christ. To him be glory both now and for ever. Amen.
2 Peter 3:18.

THERE IS A SPOT where I sit to have my personal devotions each morning, a special chair in one corner of my bedroom. I can look out of the high window to see the sky and the top of a tree. The blooms are mostly gone now, well into spring, but I noticed a beautiful little blossom bouquet one morning, clumped together on one obscure branch. It was a special gift just for me. Then I thought of all the flowers that grow in places where no one sees them. They bloom and die, doing what they were meant to do. They lift their little faces to the heavens in silent praise to God, blessing the bees and butterflies—and maybe an occasional animal guest. The world has been made richer simply by their presence, even if people never set eyes on them.

We can be a lot like those flowers—small, and seemingly insignificant, but not unimportant in the whole scheme of things. We may feel that what we're doing isn't of much value, but we can still add beauty to a bleak world for one person just by sharing a kind word or a smile. Until eternity, we may never know how significant our influence has been on others for good. Small things can have a large impact.

The little flowers that silently bloom without our knowledge are a tremendous testimony to God's love for the world. When I think of those faithful little flowers living to bring glory to their Creator, no matter where they grow, it gives an entirely different perspective to the phrase "bloom where you are." We are always in our Savior's care. Nothing is beyond His notice. He watches our spiritual growth with rapt attention, always attending to our needs. He knows exactly where we are at every moment. He's aware of every storm we pass through. Knowing how tenderly He loves us, we can fearlessly face each new day. And we can do this with complete trust, knowing He will bless our hearts with lasting joy and contentment, like the sunshine bestowing its life-giving warmth and nurturing rays on the hidden flower. And like the flowers, we can grow to richly bless others simply by living the life we were called to.

Think about the people around you. What would this world be like if no one did their work unless they were acknowledged and praised?

Joan Green

'Tis So Sweet to Trust in Jesus

I will lift up mine eyes unto the hills, from whence
cometh my help. My help cometh from the Lord.
Ps. 121:1, 2.

IT WAS MOTHER'S DAY 2003. My two daughters and I were some miles away from our home as they were participating in an athletic event. We left their father at home, not feeling well. My mobile phone rang. "Aunty Ruby, Uncle Ashton wants to go to the hospital. He feels worse!" cried the voice at the other end of the line. I immediately called the Davis Memorial Hospital to find out who was the doctor on call and to alert the chief nurse that Pastor Alleyne was on his way there.

My daughters withdrew from the remainder of the competition, and we headed for the hospital. By then my spouse had seen the doctor and was told to go home; however, he insisted that he must be admitted.

On my way to work the following day I stopped by to visit with him and noticed that his mouth twisted. He requested that I ask a few of his colleagues to visit and to pray with him. Before I could have the visit arranged, the telephone in my office rang. It was the doctor. "Ruby, your husband has had some kind of heart attack, and I think it is serious enough to let you know." I hurriedly rounded up the ministers, and off we went.

For the next three months my husband was hooked up to tubes and monitors as surgery and tests were conducted. During the first 25 days in the hospital, scores of friends and church members prayed and agonized with God on our behalf. He was then transferred to the Long Island Jewish Hospital in New York, spending several months there. Other family members and friends gave unflinching support.

All this was a mere two years since I had a medical condition that God so faithfully brought me through. Now my faith was again tested, but I took courage in the fact that "He can do it again." When we are down and feel that God has left us or that He has permitted us to walk through the valley of the shadow of death, just remember that we can grow through these experiences. I can testify that God is so wonderful. Do you have something for which to praise God too?

Ruby H. Enniss-Alleyne

Dealing With Prejudice

Then saith the woman of Samaria unto Him, How is it that thou, being a Jew, asketh drink of me, which am a woman of Samaria? For the Jews have no dealings with the Samaritans. John 4:9.

PREJUDICE CAN BE DESCRIBED as preconceived adverse opinion or judgment, formed without just grounds or before having sufficient knowledge. Prejudice can lead to an irrational attitude of hostility directed against an individual, a group, a race, or their supposed characteristics. How often we face real prejudice because of our gender, ethnicity, religion, and other related issues inside and outside of the church!

How does God deal with the issue of prejudice? We know that Moses was criticized by Miriam and Aaron because his wife was Ethiopian, and because they had become jealous of Moses' authority. God dealt with the prejudice and jealousy displayed toward His servant Himself and smote Miriam with leprosy. Moses had to pray for the reversal of her illness. (See Num. 12:1-15.)

Jesus didn't want women to be burdened under the prejudices of His time as second-class citizens. Neither did He want anyone to be so sanctimonious and steeped in customs that they could not conceive of the Sabbath as a day to do good. So on a Sabbath day He went into the synagogue to meet a woman who had "a spirit of infirmity for eighteen years, and was bowed together, and could in no wise lift up herself" (Luke 13:11). He healed her that day—much to the consternation and criticism of the Pharisees.

Think for a moment of the Samaritan woman whom Jesus met at the well. She was amazed at the nonprejudicial treatment she received from a Jew. She exclaimed, "How is it that thou, being a Jew, askest drink of me, which am a woman of Samaria?" (John 4:9). Jesus identified Himself to her as the Source of living water and continued to minister to her.

Jesus' mission to earth was to break down every barrier—including prejudice—and to let the oppressed go free. Would we not therefore like to be partners of Christ's mission by seeking to break down the walls of prejudice in our own lives and in the lives of those we meet? Our loving God, who hates prejudice, will help us to spread His unconditional love. So let's commit our ways to the Lord. The victory is already ours!

Shirnet Wellington

Far From Home

But Daniel was determined not to defile himself by eating the food and wine given to them by the king. He asked the chief of staff for permission not to eat these unacceptable foods. Dan. 1:8, NLT.

IF YOU WERE TO BE AWAY from people you know—friends, family, and pastor—what would you do, or not do? Daniel, a young Hebrew, had at least three good excuses he could have used while he was far from home and in captivity: 1. No one will know what I am doing—Mom and Dad aren't around. 2. I can do what King Nebuchadnezzar is asking me to do, because if I don't, he might kill me. 3. Everyone's doing it—why not me? He's the king, and I'm just a teenager in captivity. Those were excuses that could have been used, but Daniel didn't use them. Why? He had decided in his young heart to stay true to his God.

Daniel's God is also my God, and He did the very same thing for me. After I got my work permit, which allowed me to legally work in the United States, I applied for jobs. My first interview was for an assistant director position in Virginia Beach, Virginia.

I met with the regional director, a very nice woman, and the interview lasted more than 90 minutes. Then I was able to ask some questions. My first question was how much I would make per year, and the second was regarding work hours. I was told that I would not have to work on Friday but that I would have to come in for a few hours Saturday mornings.

I was speechless. She made it clear that there was no way I could avoid working on the Sabbath, even if I worked all day on Sunday. The interviewer told me that I would have to work that schedule for only three months, after which I would be promoted to branch director. And directors don't work on Fridays and Saturdays. "A little sacrifice," she said, and it would be OK.

Remember, God honors us when we decide to honor Him. I said no, because God always honors those who honor Him. Less than a month later I got a wonderful job.

I dare you today to be like Daniel. Say no, no matter how small or how big the temptation might be. "If you are faithful in little things, you will be faithful in large ones. But if you are dishonest in little things, you won't be honest with greater responsibilities" (Luke 16:10, NLT).

Natacha Moorooven

Take Time to Remember

*If thou shalt say in thine heart, These nations are more than I; how can
I dispossess them? Thou shalt not be afraid of them: but shalt well
remember what the Lord thy God did unto Pharaoh, and unto all Egypt.
Deut. 7:17, 18.*

IN 1985, WHEN I LOST my firstborn son, Joseph, Jr., I had no idea
that God had some wonderful things in store for me. It always
amazes me how God can take the worst experiences of our lives
and bring something good out of them. I want to share with
you one of those wonderful, amazing things that God gave me
during that experience.

The day after Joey died, as I sat to do my devotions, the
thought came to me that I should write down my thoughts and
prayers. I had never done this before. Journaling was an unknown experience for
me. But it turned out to be a wonderful way for me to express my feelings and
speak to God in an intimate and thoughtful manner. I haven't ceased journaling
since that time.

One of my favorite quotes from E. G. White is found in the book *Life Sketches*.
She writes: "We have nothing to fear for the future, except as we shall forget the way
the Lord has led us, and His teaching in our past history" (p. 196). But how do we
keep from forgetting? You know what I mean. It's easy to forget what God has done
in the past when some new trial comes our way. The Israelites forgot again and
again, and so do we. But with a journal I find I can't forget. I make it a habit that
every time a trial comes my way, I spend some time reading one of my old journals,
reminding myself what God has done in the past.

Doing this has a twofold blessing. First, I am reminded of what God has done
in my life. And second, it reminds me that if God did it before, He can do it again.
This gives me much courage and strength to face whatever comes my way.

What about you? Do you remember what God did for you two years ago, or
two months ago? I'm encouraging you to keep a spiritual journal that records your
walk with Jesus, and that you begin doing so now. If you do journal, take a moment,
from time to time, and read through some of your entries and give God the praise
each time He came through for you, each time He gave you the strength to make it
through another day of troubles and distress. Take time to remember.

Heather-Dawn Small

Prayer Makes a Difference

Confess your faults one to another, and pray one for another, that ye may be healed. The effectual fervent prayer of a righteous man availeth much. James 5:16.

IT HAPPENED ABOUT TWO YEARS AGO when my grandchild, Any, was 17 years old. On her way to school one Friday, a car suddenly stopped near her, and several strong men jumped out, grabbed Any, shoved her, into the car, and sped away. Shortly thereafter, she had a moment in which she could call her father. All she said was "Daddy, please, help me!" before the men took the cell phone away and tied her hands. The kidnappers took her to an uninhabited cottage outside of town, where they untied her but locked her up in one room. During the night she could hear voices in the next room discussing her destiny: should they ask for ransom for her, or should they take her across the border and out of the country? The last option would be especially dangerous for Any.

My son-in-law called the police. As soon as I knew that my grandchild had been kidnapped and was in danger, with prayer and tears I immediately called my sisters in the church to ask them to pray for us as they had done for others. We made a prayer chain and pleaded with our loving God to help us in that crucial moment.

Any wept the entire night. In the morning she noticed a blossoming flower in a pot. Because she loves flowers so very much, she went over to the flower to smell it. And it was then that she saw a key. Quick as lightning, she thought that it might possibly be a key to unlock the door. Trembling, she put the key into the lock—and the door opened! Wasting no time, she ran as fast and as far as she could away from the house. There was no one around to help her—no houses, no people, nothing. Unfortunately, one of the men saw her and ran after her, but just then Any saw a road and a bus that had stopped there, and ran toward it. Summoning her last strength, she reached the bus just as the driver was ready to drive away. "Please, help me!" she cried, weeping. "They are after me!" The driver helped her on to the bus, then sped away. As soon as possible, he brought her home.

When I was told that Any was home again, I hadn't words to thank my God for the wonders He had performed. Truly, He had answered our fervent prayers!

Ana Angelova

A Cure for Self-pity

But, Lord, you are my shield, my wonderful God who gives me courage.
I will pray to the Lord, and he will answer me from his holy mountain.
Ps. 3:3, 4, NCV.

A FEW WEEKS AFTER FINDING OUT that I might have Parkinson's disease, I had a morning in which I again wallowed in self-pity. The day before, I had had to go to the emergency room of our local hospital yet again, this time with abdominal pain and distention. The symptoms had settled down quite quickly once I was there in the hospital. The likely diagnosis was some partial bowel obstruction because of adhesions from my cancer surgery.

Altogether, I was feeling quite upset that morning and was finding it hard to talk to God. I felt impressed to go to the computer and look at my e-mail. There I found a letter from a previous patient. I had delivered her only child about 25 years before, and had treated her for many years for a chronic illness. She had found me again recently and sent me a "forward" with a prayer in it. This was so helpful at that particular time.

The e-mail said, in part, "Dear God, I thank You for this day. I thank You for my being able to see and hear this morning. Help me to start this day with a new attitude of gratitude. You have done so much for me, and You keep on blessing me. Forgive me this day for everything I have done, said, or thought that was not pleasing to You. Please broaden my mind so that I can accept all things. Let me not whine or whimper over things over which I have no control. Continue to use me to do Your will. Continue to bless me that I may be a blessing to others. Keep me strong that I may help the weak; keep me uplifted that I may have words of encouragement for others. Help me to remember that 'there is no problem, circumstance, or situation that is greater than God.' God, I love You, and I need You."

This prayer was just what I needed that morning. Yes, I could still hear and see, and I had much to be thankful for. I wanted to be a blessing to others, and I needed to remember that nothing is too difficult for God. I prayed that prayer that morning and have repeated it often since.

Yes, God does answer our prayers, and when we do not feel like praying, He even may use an e-mail to help us with the words.

Ruth Lennox

A Merry Heart

A merry heart doeth good like a medicine: but a broken spirit drieth the bones.
Prov. 17:22.

WE WERE DOWNSIZING from a 3,000-square-foot home to a 1,600-square-foot home, and I was overwhelmed with all there was to get rid of. Then in the midst of it all, I went into the laundry room one evening in my bare feet where there was just a little spot of water on the floor. As I hit that wet spot my right ankle turned over, and I caught myself sliding along on the outside of my ankle bone. Since I had an artificial right hip, I was trying hard to protect my hip, and my ankle twisted around even farther, and I sat down on it. I knew in an instant that it was broken, but how badly I had yet to find out.

It's now three weeks later, and I'm writing this from my wheelchair. Both sides of my ankle were shattered, and after 24 hours of waiting to get into surgery, it was plated and pinned and placed in a temporary cast. I'm told that I will not be able to place any weight on that foot for at least six weeks. I've learned that hopping around on one foot with a walker is not nearly as much fun as hopping was when I was a child.

As I thought about all there is to do yet, I made a choice. I was *not* going to feel sorry for myself. I know I'll walk again. There are many folks out there who never will. I decided that even though I'm a very take-charge person, I will let go and let others take charge. My husband and family are packing—not like I would, but doing their best—and I'm not worrying about it. I admit I'm a neat freak, but I'm able to laugh at some of the messes that have to be made as a part of moving. I'm enjoying my baby grandson when he comes with his mama to help, and somehow it is almost a relief to turn over all the responsibility to someone else.

I don't like what has happened, and I would not have chosen this to be, but I'm so thankful to the Lord for all I had already gotten done, for the wonderful meals our church family is bringing us, that I have such a kind and patient husband to care for me, and that my children are being such good help. I don't have a lot of pain, and I sleep well at night. I have also been able to keep my sense of humor, and I think that may help in the healing process as well.

Truly, the text that says "Be thankful in all circumstances" (1 Thess. 5:18, NLT) is good and helpful advice.

Anna May Radke Waters

Refiner's Fire

Everyone will be made cleaner and stronger with fire.
Mark 9:49, NLV.

AS MY HUSBAND, ROGER, AND I drove from Wyoming to Alaska, we passed through many acres of forest that had been scarred by forest fires started by lightning strikes. Trees were charred, and the soil blackened. We even passed land where trees and brush were still burning, smoke billowing into the sky. A forest ranger at one of the campgrounds where we stayed shared with us that forest fires have a purpose. They help make a forest stronger and healthier. The dead and diseased trees are cleared out of the way to allow room for new trees to grow, and the debris on the floor of the forest is burned away. There are pinecones that require the heat of a forest fire to open up and disperse seeds for new saplings. Some tree root systems, as well as shrub and grass roots, run deep into the soil to avoid the lethal conditions of a forest fire; therefore, they are able to send up shoots for new plants. The sun is able to reach the forest floor and allow fruit-bearing shrubs and seed-bearing plants to grow where previously there had not been enough sunlight for them to grow.

There are certain animals and birds that live in newly burned forest land. For example, the northern bobwhite and brown-headed nuthatch eat seeds that new plants produce. Other species of animals that live in recently burned forests are the pine barrens tree frog, fox squirrel, and gopher frog. These animals will live in burned forest land for about three to five years, and then move on to another recently burned forest area.

Just as forests have wildfires, so do our lives. As we go through trials and hardships, we wonder why God is allowing us to suffer from a lost job, the death of a family member, or the loss of friends or a spouse. If we have our roots deeply planted in Christ, He will carry us through these tough times. Our relationship with Christ and our faith can be strengthened through these trials. New situations will come of the hardships that we endure—circumstances in which we can sprout and grow into healthier, stronger Christians. We may be able to share our faith with those around us as friends and associates observe the situations we face. We will be able to offer words of encouragement to those who go through similar trials we have endured.

Dear Lord, help us each to endure the fiery trials that come our way and to trust You fully.

Linda Domeny

Good News

Let your light so shine before men, that they may see your
good works, and glorify your Father which is in heaven.
Matt. 5:16.

I WORKED IN AN OFFICE with mainly young people in their mid-30s who had just started or who were just about to start a family. When two of my female coworkers became pregnant about the same time, nobody actually knew until the pregnancies were really visible and could no longer be hidden. I found this a little bit odd; after all, they had both wanted to have a child, and there was nothing to be ashamed of. At least there was no reason for them to keep their happy expectations from their colleagues at work.

One morning a woman in my unit called in, telling me that she would be a little late to work as she had an appointment at the hospital. About two hours later, she entered my office with a big smile, declaring, "Good news—I am pregnant!" After receiving my congratulations and expressions of joy, she went around to every single office in our unit, telling each colleague her exciting news.

This incident made me think. There were two young women who were so hesitant to share their joyful expectations with their coworkers. But this woman could not keep it to herself. She was longing to share her good news immediately with everyone.

Shouldn't we be like that when it comes to the good news we find in God's Word?

In Acts 4 we're told about Peter and John who went to preach and teach the gospel wherever possible, winning many souls. The high priests didn't like this and "commanded them not to speak at all nor teach in the name of Jesus" (Acts 4:18). But these two men, imbued with the Holy Spirit, made it clear that they could not help speaking the things which they had seen and heard (verse 20). So although they didn't have permission even to tell the people about this good news, they couldn't keep their mouths shut!

Isn't it a pathetic display if we Christians, living mostly in countries in which we are allowed to proclaim the gospel, are hesitant to share this good news? Let's ask the Lord to help us by making us bold in sharing His marvelous deeds with the people around us—wherever He places us to serve Him!

Daniela Weichhold

Lost in the Woods

The angel of the Lord encampeth round about them.
Ps. 34:7.

UNCLE VERNON WENT INTO THE WOODS near his small log cabin. Having grown up in these Remer, Minnesota, woods, he knew his 40 acres so well that he didn't carry a compass. He knew where all the berries and lady slippers grew. Vernon was a retired pastor, and he called the woods his sanctuary.

On this day he noticed bark peeling off one of the birch trees, and he began to unwind it by going around and around the tree. In so doing, he lost track of his direction. Walking away, he found himself in an unfamiliar area. Incredulous as it seemed to Vernon, he was lost! He knew he needed to stay in one place, and, as always, he had a knife and matches along. When it began to grow dark and very cold, he built a fire for warmth and to keep animals away. Vernon had often slept outside under the stars, but this night was different.

Noreen, a neighbor, knew he'd gone into the woods, and drove by his cabin at dusk to check on him. She found no lantern light and no sign of Vernon. Alarmed, she called the police. Soon the state troopers formed a search party, but when it grew late, they called off the search until morning. They assumed he had died out in the woods. Noreen was very worried and prayed for his safety.

Uncle Vernon stayed by the fire all night and prayed. In early dawn he started walking in the direction of the sunrise. After some time he spotted an unfamiliar dirt road and followed it. Eventually it came out onto a road he knew by a big white house he recognized as the old Nimlo place. From there he was able to find the way home. How surprised he was to find a search party waiting, helicopters out looking, and the local newspaper there.

The troopers were surprised to see a bedraggled Vernon coming home. They had doubted he would last the night, and they wanted to know how he had found his way out to the highway. Although people looked for it, the road Vernon had followed was not to be found. The troopers said a road had never been where he said it was. The search party didn't know—but Vernon did—that the angels of God showed him the way out of the deep woods. And they didn't know about the prayers—both Vernon's and Noreen's.

Darlene Ytredal Burgeson

I Will Never Forget You

Then the righteous will answer him, "Lord, when did we see you hungry and feed you, or thirsty and give you something to drink? When did we see you a stranger and invite you in, or needing clothes and clothe you? When did we see you sick or in prison and go to visit you?" Matt. 25:37-39, NIV.

WE ARE WOMEN, the more sensitive gender, right? However, every now and then the native Bostonian that I am seems to emerge: business only, always on the go. *Go, go, go!* was all I could think as I watched the cashier casually converse with the customer in front of me. What's worse, I actually verbalized these thoughts. "I wish she would hurry up so we can get out of here," I whispered to my husband as we put our groceries on the belt. The rebuke came sharp and precise: "She's crying," my husband whispered back. How could I be so callous?

Just when I thought it was bad, it got worse. Together my husband and I decided to pay for her bill. *Duty done*, I thought as I proceeded to take our groceries out of the cart, while my husband swiped his card. Then I turned around just in time to catch his astonished look. His eyes were asking me, *What are you doing?* But the eyes were not enough for my Bostonian mind-set. So he had to blurt it out: "Hug her!" Of course! After recovering from the loving rebuke, I understood why the cashier took time to go beyond the limits of her job—beyond business as usual. She took the time to see a human heart and to care for it.

While my husband finished up her transaction, I gently rubbed the customer's shoulder to let her know that we sympathized with her. At the gesture she fell onto my shoulder and wept. We took her outside, prayed for her, and encouraged her. Before we walked away, she held my hand and said, "I will never forget you." I could have told her, "You reminded me that Jesus takes the time to notice me, to answer my prayers, to comfort me, and to listen to me. He is never too busy for me." But all I said was "I will never forget you, either."

Yes, somehow we become too busy to stop, look, and listen for an opportunity to give back to Him. Sometimes we—yes, even we Christians—get so caught up in daily life that we miss what's happening around us. We're so busy doing, doing, doing that we miss the very thing we are supposed to be doing.

LaToya V. Zavala

Contaminated

Be clean.
Luke 5:13, NIV.

IT WAS A COOL, BLEAK MORNING, and I was exhausted. I had just taken an early-morning flight from Edmonton to Calgary en route to Florida to visit my grandmother; I was ready to rest on some appealing airport chairs before embarking on my connecting flight. It was mandatory, however, that I clear customs before going to a preholding area to wait for my flight.

I walked to my assigned gate and bedded down to sleep. At 11:00 a.m. I suddenly had a distinct urge to get up, even though my flight wasn't scheduled to leave for another hour. Feeling hungry, I went to look for something to eat, but the holding area for U.S. passengers was closed off. *This is a bizarre phenomenon,* I thought. *Why is the door locked?*

The ticket agent told me that it was a holding station for U.S. passengers only. "But go on, sweetie, to customs," she directed me. Assertively I informed her that I had already been through customs. Suddenly everything took on a different perspective. With a loud exclamation her tone changed. She asked how I had gotten into that particular terminal in the first place. Meekly I informed her that the door had been open, and I had gone in. Perturbed, she called another supervisor. His response was brusque. "You are contaminated," he told me. "You have breached security. You must go through customs again."

Dashing madly through the airport, my heart racing, I could hear only the ugly word "contaminated" resounding through my head. Being rejected, not desired, and not belonging anywhere, reminded me of Luke's story of the leper. Unclean, contaminated, and rejected by society, this man was sentenced to a life of humiliation and physical and emotional pain until Jesus freed him with the words that meant the same as "Go, and sin no more. You are healed."

Fortunately, as in the story of the leper, my story had a happy ending. After a few calls and another 20-minute delay at customs, I was free to go. Smiling, I boarded the plane, knowing that I was no longer contaminated. I was a passenger who had every right to be there.

God has told us that, by His grace, He has removed all our sins. We too have full rights to His kingdom. Diseased, sin-filled, hardened though we are, God welcomes us all to His forever destination. There is only one condition: we must accept His cleansing power.

Christine A. Greene

Three Steps to Help!

The woman came and knelt before him. "Lord, help me!" she said.
Matt. 15:25, NIV.

MELISSA HOPPED EXCITEDLY from one foot to the other as bowl, pebbles, Greco-Roman ruins, fake seaweed, and a tiny goldfish were selected. Placing a small net on top of the package, the shopkeeper handed it to her and advised, "Ask for help when you change the water." Melissa nodded, but at the end of the first week she decided to just put her little fingers over the opening to the bowl and pour out the dirty water herself.

Unfortunately, Fishetta slipped right through those fingers and was last seen heading down the drain for parts unknown. After Melissa cried, moped, and saved her allowance, Fishinna arrived on the scene.

This time Melissa was sure she could clean the fishbowl without help—she had some experience. But Fishinna wiggled through those fingers, took a flying fish leap out of the sink, and landed on the floor with a *plop*. Gills working madly, the tiny goldfish flopped around as Melissa made valiant attempts to retrieve it. Her mother, hearing the commotion, grabbed the small net and came to the rescue. Alas, it was too late. Fishinna turned up its tiny fins and sank slowly to the bottom of the bowl. Time passed.

A week after Fishelda made her appearance in the household Melissa announced, "I need help changing the water."

"You finally figured that out," her father commented dryly.

"Yep," Melissa answered, and then added, a note of anxiety in her voice, "You will help me, right, Mom?"

"If you're willing to accept help," her mother replied. "Knowing you need it is one thing. Asking for it and accepting it . . ." Melissa's big blue eyes spoke volumes as she nodded her head vigorously.

"We're proud of you for doing all three," her father said. This time her smile was filled with both joy and relief.

Do you know you need help? Have you asked for it? Are you willing to accept it? Do it now!

Arlene Taylor

Three Prayers

Answer me when I call to you, O my righteous God. Give me relief
from my distress; be merciful to me and hear my prayer.
Ps. 4:1, NIV.

WHEN I WAS ONLY 20, I found myself without a home, without a husband, and without any financial resources, but I was the mother of a 1-year-old son. My greatest concern was to maintain the custody of my child, so my mother babysat him so that I could work.

Religion was not part of my life; however, when my son was 7 years old, I offered my first prayer for him. Looking toward heaven, talking to a God I did not know, I prayed, "My God, do not let me die while my child is small; he isn't able to take care of himself. Please, I trust You, Lord."

When my son was 12, he became very ill from tetanus; the doctors said it was fatal. During the 45 days he was hospitalized, I visited him every day. Once, when I opened the door to his room, the doctors and nurses were giving him oxygen and massaging his chest—his lungs were collapsing. I returned home, desperate and without hope of ever seeing my son alive again. So the second prayer was "Father, if You cure my son I shall give him to You. From this day forward he is no longer mine; he is Yours." To my relief, God cured my son.

The third prayer occurred years later, when my son was 23 years old, and we lived in New York. He was planning to marry a young woman. I was concerned about the situation because he liked her but did not love her. The date was set, and preparations for the wedding took place. I even made her wedding dress and his suit. Seven days before the wedding I returned to Brazil. I was still bothered about the proposed marriage and prayed, "My God, You know that my son does not love this girl, but if it is for the happiness of both of them, may the wedding take place. If not, let it be canceled." A month later I received a call telling me that the wedding hadn't taken place. The following year my son returned to Brazil. In 1973 we discovered the church we had been looking for and were baptized. He met a young woman of the same faith, and they've been married for 25 years and have four wonderful children.

Praise You, Lord, for hearing our prayers and responding in the manner that You know is best for our lives.

Maria de Lourdes Ferreira

Following the Directions

I will instruct you and teach you in the way you should go; I will counsel you and watch over you. Ps. 32:8, NIV.

I HAVE A JOB that requires me to travel to many locations, some in small towns and villages across western Missouri and eastern Kansas. Some of the addresses I have to find in these places are rather obscure, so I use a Web site available on the Internet called MapQuest.com. I can plug in almost any address and ask for directions from where I am, and the computer will come back with very explicit directions to help me get where I need to go. If I follow those directions, I usually end up in the right place.

However, sometimes I look at the directions and the map and think, *I'll bet I could get there easier, or faster, if I took this little shortcut or this other, easier-looking route.* This kind of thinking tends to get me into trouble. Sometimes I end up in the right place, but other times I find myself so lost I have to retrace my route until I recognize something from the directions and can pick up the trail again.

Of course, this Web site isn't infallible. Sometimes it doesn't take into account road construction that may be taking place, or exits that may be closed. One day I had to backtrack several miles out of my way because an exit I needed wasn't open, and the detour provided took me in the opposite direction from where I needed to go.

God's instructions for life, found in His Book, the Holy Bible, are pretty explicit instructions for us. But sometimes we get to thinking that we can take shortcuts, that there must be easier and better ways to get where we want to go. But there are no shortcuts to take, no easier routes. God's Word says, "This is the way, walk ye in it, when ye turn to the right hand, and when ye turn to the left" (Isa. 30:21). Furthermore, God's Book gives only good instructions and never goes out of date. The road may be rough and full of obstacles and difficulties, but following it carefully is the only way to get to our ultimate goal—heaven. Satan tries to make it seem too difficult by luring us into taking detours and backtracking, but keeping our eyes on God and reading His Word every day is the best and most direct route. I hope you have found, as I have, that He will never lead us astray.

Fauna Rankin Dean

Mustard Seed Faith

I tell you the truth, if you had faith even as small as a mustard seed, you could say to this mountain, "Move from here to there," and it would move. Nothing would be impossible. Matt. 17:20, NLT.

AFTER PROLONGING THE PROCESS and battling with myself long enough, I had to phone my landlord and inform him that I'd be leaving at the end of the month. My sister said, "Faith, woman!" with a chuckle in her voice. It appeared that what I was doing was not logical or sensible. However, the rent was too high, and transportation was inaccessible from my apartment. It had become too much of a strain. I started packing my clothes and kitchen utensils and storing them in the garage. My sister refused to pack her stuff and asked, "Where are you going?"

I was told that generally one couldn't find any place in Cambridge with a low rent. I laughed. My friend had given me an application to apply where she resides. My application went in, but it was taking so long to hear back that I inquired, but they said nothing was available.

I received a phone call some weeks later to come for an interview for an apartment. I was anxious, excited, fearful, and prayed all the way there. I received a key to my new flat (the one I was told I wouldn't be able to find in that area). Is my God good? When I told my sister, she finally started to pack. "I will answer them before they even call to me. While they are still talking about their needs, I will go ahead and answer their prayers!" (Isa. 65:24, NLT).

I moved to a much more affordable and easily accessible accommodation. I had had just a little bit of faith. I remember a song that we listened to on Sabbath mornings while my mom braided our hair for church: "A mustard seed, said Jesus, is the least of all the seeds, Yet a mighty plant will grow if a mustard seed you sow. Plant a mustard seed of faith in the garden of your heart, Plant a mustard seed of faith and it will grow, It will grow and grow and grow and grow, Till surely you will know, The Christ who the seed of faith did sow."

While reflecting on your daily life, think of the times you've exercised faith, of that seed that you've planted. Do you see it? Is it growing? With Jesus it surely will! Continue to trust and believe in Him.

Susan Riley

The Upholsterer

He restoreth my soul.
Ps. 23:3.

I HAVE A SPECIAL AFFECTION for the craft of upholstery. For many years we shared our home with my father's upholstery shop, and often I was his assistant. I remember seeing my father bring home old, beat-up sofas and love seats, those that others would consider beyond repair. Some would have missing limbs, broken springs, or a damaged frame. Lovingly, Dad would approach the job. First he stripped the piece of furniture, removing the old covers, the matting, and the rusty springs. These he discarded, then began the job of restoration. After several days of painstaking labor, Dad would look at his work and smile, because a fully restored sofa was ready to leave his workshop to beautify another home. Fully restored.

That is the job of a restorer—to take the old, the damaged, the one no one wants, the ugly and unattractive—and create from its ruins a thing of beauty. What potential for change we read in the words, He (God) restores my soul.

We come—or, actually, the Holy Spirit brings us—to our heavenly Upholsterer, worn out by sinful practices, damaged by years of neglecting our prayer life, battered by the stresses of life, or torn by ruined relationships and shattered dreams. We, who were once beautiful in our Edenic state, are brought in our shame to our Dad, the heavenly Restorer. He sees us as only an upholsterer can. He looks beyond the frayed edges, behind the lives wasted with substance abuse, beyond the ravages of sin. He sees how we can be restored.

First, there is the stripping. We've grown accustomed to our vices and the pollution of sin. He must take them all away and wash us with the blood of purification. Then, in our naked condition, we must face Him, face the One who made us perfect and now is willing to restore what sin has destroyed.

Finally, the real work commences. Slowly He begins the job. He works patiently with us through daily prayer and Bible study. We gain new springs, new matting, and a brand-new cover—a lovely robe of righteousness. He restores our souls to their former Edenic glory.

Just look at us now as our new lives humbly testify to His restorative power!

Annette Walwyn Michael

Protected

Shew thy marvelous loving-kindness, O thou that savest by thy right hand
them which put their trust in thee from those that rise up against them.
Ps. 17:7.

EVERY YEAR WE HAVE new birds in our backyard. It's fun to see the different varieties, and especially the babies. If they are seedeaters, they gradually learn to come to our covered-bridge bird feeder where they can eat to their heart's content. Other birds eat worms and insects, and since they feed farther away, I need my binoculars to see them better.

A few years ago, when one of the new bluebird babies left its nest, I happened to be going to the dog yard to clean at the very same time. The daddy bluebird was watching, and he was afraid I might harm or step on his newly flown baby. He came swooping down near both the dogs and myself to warn us and to be sure no harm would come to the little one. I carefully stepped back until he was sure the small bird was out of harm's way before I continued on my mission. Once the baby was again sheltered, the daddy bird left us alone. What a wonderful protecting parent he was!

How many times, I wonder, has God protected me and warned others not to harm me when I was unaware of it? I think of the many close calls while driving on the interstate highways from Maryland to Vermont, and from Tennessee to Vermont, and back again. Both are long drives, and I know the Lord has held His hand over my family and me many times when we would otherwise have had an accident.

I also think of the two times I nearly died while giving birth to a baby, but somehow God spared my life and let me live. One of our little babies, a boy, was stillborn. I look forward to seeing him in heaven when Jesus comes to take us home. I think of the little girl who was allowed to live, but for only 28 years before God permitted her to pass away. I am so glad we have a God who has promised to come back and take us home to live with Him.

Each day, I choose to think of all the blessings He gives us, and those great blessings yet to come—to live with Him in heaven where there will be "no more death, neither sorrow, nor crying" (Rev. 21:4).

And He is coming back—He promised!

Loraine F. Sweetland

No Tears in Heaven

And God shall wipe away all tears from their eyes; and there shall be no more death, neither sorrow, nor crying, neither shall there be any more pain: for the former things are passed away. Rev. 21:4.

ARE YOU SITTING DOWN?" No one likes to hear that question, as it immediately indicates that something is seriously wrong. One Sunday evening I got that call. One of my sisters, who was living in the United States, called with the devastating news that another sister's husband and two of her children had been in a serious car accident. The husband and my nephew had died at the scene, and my 13-year-old niece, Carla, had been airlifted to the hospital in serious condition and was undergoing surgery right then.

The problem we had was how to break the news to our mom. When she heard, she cried very hard and was not easily comforted. Meanwhile, my sister, Maureen, was having a difficult time handling what had happened. We tried our best to comfort her over the phone as we prepared to go to be with her.

At the funeral the tears flowed freely and it seemed that they would never stop. As I contemplated the deaths, I wondered where God had been when all of this happened. I had prayed for them that morning, so why hadn't He protected them and kept them safe? I was angry.

On Sunday, after the funeral, the doctor called and said Carla was not doing well, as there was a swelling on the brain that wasn't going away. As we all visited her, my nephews wept as we watched their sister being hooked up to machines and not able to speak to them. A friend of the family took them aside and told them that God listens to the prayers of children, and that they should pray for her and God would hear. They left feeling a little better.

Sure enough, on Monday morning, as two other sisters were leaving for Jamaica, they too decided to visit my niece. My mom, who went in first, came out and said that Carla was up and talking. I was so excited I just jumped and shouted, praising God for taking care of Carla. It was then that my anger toward God ceased—I saw how awesome is the God we serve.

What a glorious day it will be when we get to heaven and see our loved ones again! All will be joy and happiness forever.

Viveen McLeary

College Days

*And the child grew, and she brought him unto Pharaoh's daughter, and he became her son.
Ex. 2:10.*

*And when she had weaned him, she took him up with her . . . and brought him unto the
house of the Lord in Shiloh: and the child was young.*
1 Sam. 1:24.

MY DAUGHTER HAD TURNED 18 and graduated from high school. College loomed on the horizon, and I had thought about her leaving home for weeks—months, actually—and every time I thought about it I have to admit tears were somehow in the equation. To send my soon-to-be 19-year-old away from home was just unthinkable in my eyes. And heart. Jessica, however, seemed excited about it. We had decided to let her go to a college about 700 miles (1,135 kilometers) away from home. Soon the time came to take her to college. Instead of having a family vacation that year, our vacation was taking her to school. I'd think of it and quietly cry, not letting her know I was crying. Our trip was fun, just the five of us, and Jessica seemed thrilled at the idea of being independent, on her own, and living in a dorm. Then came Sunday, the day we were to leave. There would be four of us leaving, still the little pack that Dad had always said we were. It was then that Jessica realized that she would be alone, all alone, and she too cried at our exit.

"How can we leave her?" I cried to my husband.

"She is in God's hands," he answered, himself a little teary-eyed.

It was then that I thought of the mothers in the Bible, the mothers who had given up their children. I thought of Jochebed, who was given a small amount of time with her son, Moses, and had to see him off to the palace near the age of 12. I'm sure she cried and prayed as I did. *Twelve . . .* I thought. *At least I had Jessica seven years longer than that.* And what about Hannah? Hannah was barren and cried to God to give her a child. He had heard her cries and given her Samuel, a wonderful little boy, whom she gave to Eli, the priest, to raise at a very young age. I guess I was blessed, as I had my daughter up to adulthood. I still wasn't ready to let her go, but with God's blessing, I turned her over to Him. He who calmed the seas could calm my sad heart and give me peace. I still miss her every day, but every day I pray that God, her new protector, will guide her in every way.

Charlotte Robinson

The Sacrifice

For God so loved the world, that he gave his only begotten Son, that whosoever believeth in him should not perish, but have everlasting life. John 3:16.

I WAS IN LOVE, and I was going to be married. I felt that God had brought us together, and I didn't need to think about anything else. Or did I? I knew the words of the wedding vows, but I had not thought too deeply about what they really meant. I hadn't stopped to think about what I might sacrifice for this man, or if I would give my life for him. Does anyone think about these things before their wedding?

In November 1993, when I married James, I had no idea that I would ever be faced with making a decision that would decide whether he would live or die. He was a seemingly healthy Christian man. To my knowledge he had only a problem with the vision in his right eye, and he no longer had his appendix. I had no reason to believe that approximately 10 years later he'd be in kidney failure, and none of his siblings would be healthy enough, or willing, to give him one of their kidneys. Some have told James that God gave him the right partner, because they don't know if they could have made the decision that I did. I loved the Lord and trusted Him to know what was best for me, so how could I make any other decision? I pledged to love my husband, no matter what. Shouldn't I love him enough to give him a kidney, if I were able? Jesus gave His all to save me, so why would I have a problem making this small sacrifice to save my husband?

Without hesitation, I made the decision to give James one of my kidneys. Since then people have asked me if I was afraid, and I can honestly say that I was not the least bit fearful. I believed with all my heart that God knew this day would come, and just as He put Esther in the right place at the right time to save her people, He had also put me with this man for just such a time as this.

How deep is your love, and what are you willing to sacrifice in the name of love? God loved us so much that He sacrificed the life of His only Son to give us a chance at eternal life.

Dear God, You made the ultimate sacrifice because You loved. Help me learn to love as deeply and completely as You do.

Theodora V. Sanders

Not a Murmur

Though it linger, wait for it; it will certainly come and will not delay.
Hab. 2:3, NIV.

I'VE BEEN PRAYING AND WAITING for God to bless me with good health, a job, and health for my daughter. But there have been many problems, even though the Lord has been keeping me through the help of my church members.

Our daughter, Marian, had been very ill and had had surgery twice, but was still battling the illness in spite of prayers and all that the doctors could do. My husband kept encouraging me to hang in there and wait on the Lord with hope and trust.

How long were we to pray and wait? Were we so sinful that our prayers were not recognized by God? No, He does not deal that way. A small voice told me that He loves us all as His Word tells us.

The Bible tells me about the people of old, and that encourages me. I thought about the man with the infirmity near the Pool of Bethesda, who was there for 38 years! What about the woman who bled for 12 years? Then old Sarah—can a woman bear a child at the age of 99? I also remember that Father Noah had to work, preach, and wait for 120 years. Poor Rachel had to wait for seven years to be married to the man she loved, and had to hang on in her marriage for a long time before having Joseph and Benjamin. And how about the people of Israel? They were in bondage in Egypt for about 400 years.

Does it mean that they didn't pray? They surely did! But why did they all have to struggle for so long? That I cannot tell. But one thing I know is that God loved them all, and He loves my daughter and me, as well. So at His own appointed time He will heal Marian and me, and bless me with a teaching job. All we need to do is hang in there meekly and murmur not—knowing that God is in control.

Thus, I say, you hang in there too with hope and not a murmur. We haven't even waited half as long as the people of old. Remember, they struggled, hoped, and waited. And they were blessed.

Father, I sincerely thank You for blessing me with life after five years of battling cancer. Please keep an eye on our Marian, and if it is Your will, heal her completely to Your glory.

Mabel Kwei

Granting Permission

If ye then, being evil, know how to give good gifts unto your children: how much
more shall your heavenly Father give the Holy Spirit to them that ask him?
Luke 11:13.

I FEARED MY OLD PC COMPUTER wouldn't survive the trip across the nation. It was then that my caring California son purchased a new iMac computer with a 20-inch screen for me. I was delighted! Knowing I wasn't familiar with a Macintosh, he thoughtfully sent it to my Maryland son to have him install all the software I would need—and so much more. Then they equipped it so they could, by remote, help me transition to a Mac. When they had it all set up, they sent it to me in my new home in Tennessee.

I wasn't sure how it would all work until one day I called my son and asked him to help me through a problem. He went to his computer, and suddenly a window appeared on my screen, asking me if I wanted to give him permission to access my computer. I clicked on "Yes," and soon my curser began to move magically across the monitor, seemingly at will. It opened windows, clicked on programs, adjusted defaults, and resolved all my problems. I was amazed at this new long distance technology, and I was especially grateful for the loving care of my two sons.

All this reminded me of the heaven-designed computer minds God has given us, equipping us with varied talents—just because He loves us. But in our humanness, we often fail to make wise choices. Perplexities confirm that we need help, and on our knees we seek divine guidance. We say yes to the Holy Spirit and give Him permission to direct our lives as He knows best. Sometimes He solves our problem in a seemingly miraculous way. More often, He impresses us with His will and allows us to make the final decision. To be sure, it's a learning process. Granting permission is our part. We will find our lives are more productive and enriched for the experience.

And so I have dedicated this iMac to my wonderful Savior Friend, and I have resolved to carry out His will to bless others in its use. More important, I have dedicated my remaining span of life to Him as well, to be used as His instrument for the great purpose He has designed. And yes, every day I must remember to give Him full control!

Lorraine Hudgins-Hirsch

The Promise Box

And if you are Christ's, then you are . . . heirs according to the promise.
Gal. 3:29, NKJV.

IT HAS ALWAYS BEEN THERE—the Bible Promise Box—on my parents' dressing table. My mother thinks they bought it at a church camp meeting back in the late 1940s. When we were children we would use the tiny tongs on a silken cord attached at the side to pull out a promise and read it to the rest of the family. The little round box, covered in a pale, pink satinlike fabric, was the most beautiful thing I had ever seen.

I grew up, married, and moved out of the family home. Over the years my parents had a few shifts, but wherever they lived, there on their dressing table in exactly the same spot would be the Promise Box. With the passing of time the tiny tongs were lost, and the pink on the box faded, but God's promises remained the same: "I am the Lord, I change not" (Mal. 3:6). My father has now passed away and my mother is in a rest home—and the precious Promise Box is still on her dressing table.

At the end of 2005, after a lot of prayer and discussion, my husband and I put our own house on the market to move to the country. We had keen buyers in a very short time who were prepared to pay an excellent price for our house, but then we were asked if the finance settlement date could be extended for another week. We naturally said yes; however, when that week was up and the settlement was due at our attorney's office, we were asked for yet another week. This happened two more times, and I was beginning to think our house sale would fall through. It just wasn't going to happen!

Tuesdays and Thursdays were the weekdays for visiting my mother, and the following Thursday I drove to Bethesda from work. After greeting Mom, who was having her evening meal, I went down the passageway to get her a cardigan. In her bedroom I hesitated, looking at the Bible Promise Box. "My house, Lord?" I whispered as I pulled out a promise. Tears overflowed as I read Matthew 19:26: "With God all things are possible."

Reaching home a few hours later, my husband told me our house sale had become unconditional that very afternoon. Our attorney had the money, and all was well. Nothing is impossible with God!

Leonie Donald

Loud Hands

For ye shall go out with joy, and be led forth with peace: the mountains and the hills shall break forth before you into singing, and all the trees of the field shall clap their hands. Isa. 55:12.

IT IS NOT UNUSUAL for me to go to an event and have people look my way when I clap. I couldn't understand it, and it took me many years to figure out why they were looking at me. The answer? As strange as it may be, I have a quirky talent to clap loudly. The strange thing is that I'm not a big person, and I have small hands. What is even stranger to me is that I don't have a loud voice.

As I've recognized this unusual talent, I have also noted the impact it has on others. If I'm at an event that is honoring someone, I can stand up and start clapping and everyone will rise to their feet and do the same thing. I must be careful of my actions. There are those times when I find something clapworthy and begin to clap. I soon discover that no one else feels the way I do, and my resounding clap becomes disruptive.

I remember when we were trying to potty-train our daughters. They loved it when my husband and I would clap after they made a successful deposit. One time I walked past the bathroom and heard one of our daughters clapping. As I peeked in the room I saw her sitting on the toilet, clapping and saying to herself, "Good job!"

Although most of my clapping experiences have been positive, there are times it hasn't been so. There are times I will clap and my husband will say, as he covers his ears, "Why do you clap so loud?" My youngest daughter, Rachel, has said, "Mom, something is wrong with your hands; they are hurting my ears." I have to wonder, of course, how many other people are feeling the same way.

As with any talent, there can be an upside, and a downside. My hands are an example of our service to the Lord. In serving God I hope to use my hands to lead, encourage, and motivate. I don't want my clapping to be offensive, disturbing, or distracting.

Lord, thank You for all my talents—even the funny ones. Please help me to use my talents for Your glory and to recognize when I am working against You. May I raise my hands to heaven in Your honor, and clap as I am filled with joy.

Mary M. J. Wagoner-Angelin

The Right Words

Pleasant words are as an honeycomb, sweet to the soul, and health to the bones.
Prov. 16:24.

TODAY WAS THE LAST DAY of Youth Week of Prayer, and as such it was going to be a full day. Part of the day was allocated to the Pathfinders and Adventurers for an induction service, a formal ceremony during which new members are officially added to the club roster. We knew that our youngest, Cassandra, age 5, would be a flag bearer, carrying the Eager Beaver flag during the flag ceremony. During the church service we had a little surprise. Although our oldest, Lillian, age 10, was scheduled to tell the children's story, we didn't know it. When it was time for the children's story, Lillian got up, walked to the front of the sanctuary, and read the children's story as if she had been the storyteller all her life! When she was finished "telling" the story, she asked if anyone would like to pray, and Cassandra raised her hand. She prayed a simple but beautiful prayer that touched many hearts.

We take every opportunity to praise our children. We want them to know that we see not only the negative behaviors but the positive ones as well. Therefore, on the way home from church, as is our custom, we praised our children for not only doing a good job but also for using their talents for God. First, I praised Cassandra and told her that it always touches my heart to hear her pray. Then I told Lillian how pleased I was with her choice of stories and the great job she did. Not wanting to be left out, Cassandra piped up, "Yes, Lillian, you did a better job than I thought you would!"

In my heart I know Cassandra was giving her sister a compliment. Although it was amusing, coming from a 5-year-old, and our 10-year-old didn't read into the words what an adult might have, Cassandra's comment made me think: How often do I give backhanded compliments? How many times have I made a statement, thinking it was positive, only to learn that it caused pain? How often do I discourage instead of encourage—no matter how unintentional? How often do I complain? Do I see the negative when what the person needed was for me to find something positive and uplifting? I must answer yes more often than I would care to admit.

Lord, don't let this be the case. Help me to find words that are sweet to the soul.

Tamara Marquez de Smith

Two Prayers

Before they call, I will answer; and while they are yet speaking, I will hear.
Isa. 65:24.

I WAS BORN INTO THE HOME of a Christian minister. At a very early age I was taught about Jesus and God. I learned to love Jesus and believed that He could help me. I treasured the moments spent together in my daddy's study. He prepared his sermons audibly for my benefit. He showed me pictures of Jesus on the cross with a crown of thorns on His head. I could see the blood dripping. My young heart was touched.

One day when I was between 6 and 7 years old, I got a needle and thread to try to sew. Now, my mother had always told us, "Do not sit on the bed to sew." Not remembering, or not paying attention to her words, I sat on the bed to sew. When I was finished, I rested the needle on the bed. When I was ready to rethread the needle, it was gone—I couldn't find it anywhere.

Fear gripped me. I had disobeyed. I would be scolded. Someone could sit on the bed and get stuck. As my trauma escalated, I remembered Jesus. *He can help*, I thought. Kneeling, I prayed earnestly. "Dear Jesus, please forgive me for disobeying Mother. Please help me find the needle. Amen." A short, to-the-point, heartfelt prayer. Opening my eyes, I saw the tiniest piece of steel lying on the sheets. I closed my eyes again and whispered, "Thank You, Jesus." My personal faith in Jesus was sealed to this day. I knew then that Jesus is *real.*

Years flew by. I grew up and matured, always trusting and praying. My faith in Jesus grew also. As an adult a very serious yet mysterious pain developed in my right arm from the shoulder down the middle of my arm, forearm, and hand, down to the tip of my middle finger. The intensity of the pain drove sleep away and weakened my entire system. The constant loss of sleep left me almost useless for each day's activities.

I decided to try Dr. Jesus. As I prayed I thanked Him for the pain and asked Him to give me the strength to bear it and to learn whatever lesson He was trying to teach me. I prayed the same prayer for three nights. The fourth night the pain was gone. That was 17 years ago. I've never felt it again.

Dear God, help each of us to always trust You with our problems.

Joyce O'Garro

When God Gives, Your Cup Overflows

You prepare a table before me in the presence of my enemies.
You anoint my head with oil; my cup overflows.
Ps. 23:5, NIV.

ONE OF THE GREATEST CHALLENGES I ever faced was when my boss gave me a job description that included recruiting 500 people for a church Bible study program that had only 15 people currently enrolled. I had just graduated from the university in Cameroon, and gone back to serve in my home country, Mauritius, an island in the South Indian Ocean. I felt lucky to have the opportunity to serve as an intern pastor and director for the correspondence Bible study course. This was quite a challenge for a young woman of 23, especially since I was the youngest in the ministry and the only female.

I wasn't shocked to have to get 500 students until I heard the current number of students. My first response was "Pastor, how can this be possible? Nobody has done it before, so how can I? I am just a young woman." But then I pulled myself together and agreed with the president on the daunting figure of 500. I supposed he was realistic to think of such a high number. He had been in ministry for a long time, and I guess he thought nothing was impossible.

When I arrived home that evening, my first prayer request was "Lord, the pastor wants 500 new students, but between you and me, I want 1,000. You are God, and I am Your servant. Show me that You can do that for Your glory. Amen!"

From the time I started to work in January until June, I was blessed to work with wonderful church members. We organized a special week when each church member was asked to enroll 25 people. Of course some didn't accept the challenge, but by the end of that very week we had registered 450 people. And it was only June! We had six more months to reach the goal.

In October we did another promotion, working hard and praying even harder. By the last week we had enrolled 1,040 people. Amen!

Yet, when I think about my request to God, I get very sad. I should have asked for more. I asked for 1,000 and He gave me 40 more. When God gives, our cups overflow. Praise God for the blessing! I want to challenge you to test our God. See how good and powerful He can be when we simply trust and obey.

Natacha Moorooven

Grace

For by grace you have been saved through faith, and that not of yourselves; it is the gift of God. Eph. 2:8, NKJV.

WHEN I WAS A LITTLE GIRL, living in the small country town of Latty, Ohio, I would occasionally wander over to the Baptist church that was just a stone's throw away from our house. Well, maybe not a stone's throw away, but certainly very close. The church was small, but the folks would gather faithfully every Sunday to worship. The majority of the members were related by birth or marriage, which made the church extremely close in its fellowship, and included my extended family. There wasn't anything grand about the services, but the songs always pulled at my heart because of the serene and reverent presentation. Although I was raised Catholic and was used to songs in Latin, those old-time gospel songs became an integral part of my soul.

The town of Latty held the best and worst of times for me. It was there that I experienced forthright hatred against me as an African-American from my fourth-grade female teacher. Then I encountered the kindest fifth-grade teacher, Roy Jenkins, who contradicted that prejudice. It was in Latty that maternal family reunions were attended with fun and laughter. But it was also in Latty that my immediate family experienced poverty, escalating alcoholism, and spousal abuse. In retrospect, I can say it was those gospel songs I heard from that country church that perpetuated my hope. But it took me years to realize that it was all about God's grace enveloping me, grace that He gives as a gift to each of us.

Today a song came to my mind from that old church of my past, and it brought tears to my eyes. My tears were not of sadness from long-ago memories but rather tears of awe for a loving God. The chorus simply says: "Grace, grace, God's grace, grace that can pardon and cleanse within. Grace, grace, God's grace, grace that is greater than all our sin." My heart swelled as I thought of how good is my God. I thought of all the tumultuous times in my life; all the times I've doubted, stumbled, and feared; all the times I've been disobedient and failed. Yet His grace covered me like a gift, wrapped tenderly by His own divine hands! What unfathomable love! What an awesome God! Won't you join me today and praise Him for His infinite grace?

Evelyn Greenwade Boltwood

Lost

For this my son was dead, and is alive again; he was lost,
and is found. And they began to be merry.
Luke 15:24.

MY DOG, MINNIE, was very cute and active, following me wherever I went. Because she was so tiny, we never chained her. She'd go out with us, but never knew how to come back home, so we always kept her inside the gate.

One day someone came to visit us, and the gate was left open and Minnie wandered out. Someone caught her and tied her up inside their house. We searched everywhere for Minnie but couldn't find her. And every day we prayed for her. One day someone spotted Minnie with a woman and told me, so I went to look for her. When I saw her, I called, "Minnie!" Immediately she ran toward me, and I picked her up. "Where did you find her?" I asked the woman.

"I saw her walking aimlessly, and thought she was lost." We were so happy that God answered our prayers.

Once my 4-year-old son became lost. He had made a long train journey to Hyderabad with me, and upon reaching the station we hired a cycle rickshaw to get home, which he enjoyed very much. Later, we enrolled him in a school to which someone had to take him every day, and then bring him home again. One day when the person who was supposed to bring him home was a bit late, my son watched other children go home by cycle rickshaw. Suddenly he joined the group and sat down in a rickshaw. After the rickshaw man had dropped the others off, my son was left alone, enjoying the ride. The rickshaw man asked, "Where is your house?"

"Very far," my son replied. Now the man was worried, and since my son was wearing the school uniform, he decided to take him back to the school. Meanwhile, when the person came home without my son, we all became worried, and all of us went different directions to look for him. When I reached the school, there he was—but he wouldn't get out of the rickshaw, and the driver related the story. We were relieved and happy that my son was found.

When we become lost in this world, God must feel as we did. This world is full of temptations that draw us away from our home and God. It's easy to get lost. But when we repent and turn back from all the worldly attractions and retrace our steps, God rejoices.

Winifred Devaraj

The Last Birthday Gift

For your Father knows the things you have need of before you ask Him.
Matt. 6:8, NKJV.

MY FATHER CELEBRATED his seventy-fifth birthday the day after Christmas. Usually, when people reach that age, a party is held to celebrate the gift of life. In my part of the world, it is very rare for individuals to reach their 70s, and that's why this needed to be a grand celebration.

I wanted to give my father something special, to throw him a party, but I was broke, as I had been out of a job for nine months, and my budget wouldn't allow that. With the few pesos left in my pocket, I had only enough to give him a simple birthday present. Though I know my father would appreciate whatever gift I could give, I still wished to give him more. He deserved something special for being a very good and loving father.

Every Christmas Day our clan holds a reunion to have fun, play games, and eat together. Everybody is given a chance to join the parlor games and win some prizes. Representatives from each family participate, and no one leaves the party without some goodies and money to take home. When I was called to be a participant to represent our family in the last game, I saw an opportunity to add some pesos to my purse since the grand prize was cash. That would be a wonderful gift for my father's birthday—better than what I had for him!

During the game several questions were asked of the contestants. I successfully passed the elimination round. There was so much excitement! Of all the contestants, I was perhaps the most anxious; I needed the money more than my opponents did. As the game continued, I kept praying, "Please, Lord, help me win." When the last question was asked, my opponent missed it, and I knew I had won. I thanked God for hearing my prayer.

Joyfully, I handed my prize money to my father as an advance birthday gift. He was very grateful for the gift. I didn't know that that was the last birthday gift I could give him. He died four months later.

This experience showed me how God works in the most wondrous ways as He provides for our needs. He knew my heart. He knew how I sincerely wished to make my father happy on his birthday. And He knew that that would be my father's last birthday. God is in control of the events of our lives. Even before I asked Him, He had already given me what I needed.

Minerva M. Alinaya

Removing the Decay

I will sprinkle clean water on you, and you will be clean;
I will cleanse you from all your impurities and from all your idols.
Eze. 36:25, NIV.

MY COUNTRY, BRAZIL, is very hot in some locations, including the city where I live in the interior of the state of São Paulo. It's known as "Morada do Sol," Dwelling Place of the Sun.

Opening the windows and inviting the sun to come in is something I really enjoy. So I am pleased that my house receives a lot of sunlight. Working enthusiastically in the kitchen one morning, I began to smell an unpleasant odor. There was no trash in the kitchen, so I went to the refrigerator. *Perhaps something has spoiled,* I thought. But I found nothing and the bad smell continued. The sun seemed to make it worse.

Finally I found the problem. Though it was not yet 10:00, I realized that the hot sun was shining brightly through the window and onto a basket where I keep the potatoes and onions. When I lifted the basket, I discovered the cause of the odor. There in the bottom, where no eye could see it, a rotten potato was hidden. Looking at the top of the basket, all the potatoes seemed perfect!

If the sun had not invaded my kitchen and shone brightly on the basket, perhaps I would not have been able to deal with the damage, and that unpleasant odor would have persisted. Maybe I would still be looking for it in the wrong places!

Many times we live like those potatoes. Apparently, everything is fine; but in the depths of our hearts and our minds we are rotting with impure thoughts, hidden sins, resentment, jealousy, desires for revenge, and other things that only the Son of Justice can reach.

When we offer praise to God, only He knows the true aroma that comes from our heart! Only He can remove that rotten potato that is ruining our life and leading us astray. He knows everything, He sees everything. He knows even our secret thoughts. Let us allow God to remove whatever may be spoiled in us. Let's choose to emit a wonderful fragrance that pleases those around us.

O Lord, wash my heart and my mind. Remove everything that is impure and rotten.

Marinês Aparecida da Silva Oliveira

Irresistible to Me

For where two or three come together in my name, there am I with them.
Matt. 18:20, NIV.

IN A RECENT CONVERSATION with friends, my husband said that he knew a person who could not survive without a prayer group. He said this while smiling and looking at me. I reached the conclusion that it is true—I really do like prayer groups. However, I enjoy experimental groups, where we test new techniques of praying.

Prayer groups became of interest to me when I read the book, *What Happens When Women Pray,* by Evelyn Christenson. The author narrated her experience in creating prayer groups with women. I marveled, for the ideas in the book opened and promised thousands of possibilities. However, it wasn't until a few years later that I finally began to put the ideas contained in the book into practice.

My sister and I started a prayer group with two friends from our church. We experimented with some ideas we'd gotten from the book, and each meeting became a pleasure. Then we moved the location of the group, but we didn't give up on the prayer groups. We participated in various groups—some were excellent, others were mediocre. We learned a lot from each group that we founded. In the groups of women we learned to trust in our prayer partners; we learned that we could put them into action for urgent prayer. We felt loved and supported.

Not everything is perfect. There are sometimes conflicts and misunderstandings that need to be resolved. As participants, we are very different from each other. But when I am kneeling to pray with my friend from the group, I realize the union that only Christ brings.

Our current group keeps up lively and efficient dynamics. If there is an urgent necessity, we call the one in our group who is in charge of passing on the request to the other members. We are always eager to meet together and tell the group how God has responded. I've also observed that we've become more attentive to the spiritual necessities of the people close to us.

I would like to encourage you to participate in a prayer group—or even create your own group. As I've led prayer groups, I've realized that I was the one who gained the most, because the sense of working with God to decrease human suffering is incomparable.

Iani Dias Lauer-Leite

We Never Know!

How precious to me are your thoughts, O God! How vast is the sum of them!
Were I to count them, they would outnumber the grains of sand.
Ps. 139:17, 18, NIV.

ANNA AND I WEREN'T ESPECIALLY CLOSE. She was older, from another culture, and very set and reclusive in her ways. I knew her mostly in her later years—the bitter years of losing her job and alienating her friends. Once, terribly distressed, she asked my husband if he could pull strings to help her get her job back or get her retirement checks. The institution she worked for had lost her work records, and that was holding up her pension. Ed said he held no strings but suggested someone she should talk to. I sent her a small check with a note, hoping it could help a little. Anna never acknowledged the check, and never cashed it. It seemed she tried to avoid us the few times we saw her at church. I felt dreadful. I just knew I'd offended her. The uncashed check on my bank statements was monthly proof.

As I carried the outstanding sum into a new year, I hatched a plan. Anna was an excellent seamstress. I would hire her to make pajamas for our granddaughter. "Make them yourself," said Anna. "I have a pattern. We'll shop together for material."

We actually had fun. She knew as well as I that I couldn't afford her skilled services, but she seemed happy that we were doing this small adventure together. "I thought that you and Ed were mad at me," she said.

"Whatever for?" The idea shocked me.

"Because I asked him to help me find a job."

I assured her the request never caused either of us distress or anger. Then I ventured: "I thought you were mad at me for insulting you by sending a check, and that's why you never cashed it."

A smile wavered on her lips. "I never cashed it because I framed it with your note and hung it on my wall! No one ever did anything that nice for me before. I wanted to remember it every day." We hugged each other and laughed so hard our faces were wet with tears. We never know what's in someone else's mind or what God can make of our lives, words, or deeds. But we can know that what we do for love of Him will bless someone, somehow.

Lois Rittenhouse Pecce

Do You Have a Valid Visa?

*Blessed are they that do his commandments, that they may have right
to the tree of life, and may enter in through the gates into the city.
Rev. 22:14.*

I SAT IN THE UNITED STATES CONSULATE in Panama City while I waited
for a United States visa. As I watched the anxious and tense faces
of hundreds of people forming the long lines in that office, my
attention was attracted particularly to those who had received a
visa. To receive a visa to travel from Panama to the United
States there are certain requisites the applicant must fulfill. As
I sat in that office, I reflected on the spiritual applications.

We are all travelers on the highway of life, and one day,
through faith, we hope to fly to heaven with our Jesus. Not on a jet
airplane or Copa Airlines or on Eastern Airlines, but, according to the Word of
God, we'll meet the Lord in the air (1 Thess. 4:17). You might ask, "And what about
those who have died?" Verse 16 tells us, "For the Lord himself shall descend from
heaven with a shout, with the voice of the archangel, and with the trump of God:
and the dead in Christ shall rise first."

In the same manner in which most countries have certain basics in order to
enter into their countries, there are certain requirements to enter the celestial city
of God. Our devotional text indicates one of the requirements—we could call it
your heavenly visa. However, there's an outstanding difference between God's kingdom and that of earthly countries; there is no monetary price that can secure for us
a visa for the heavenly country. The Bible says we were not "redeemed with cor-
ruptible things, as silver and gold, . . . but with the precious blood of Christ (1 Peter
1:18, 19).

Yes, my dear friend, you do not need any application form or job letter, bank
statement or affidavit—only faith in the sacrifice of Jesus on the cross of Calvary,
maintaining a living relationship with Jesus, and keeping God's commandments,
because what He has done for us opens heaven's door.

*Dear heavenly Father, thank You for Your matchless love for us, Your sons and
daughters, and for the sacrifice of Your dear Son that made entrance into Your kingdom possible. Thank You for Your promise to take us with You one day. Amen.*

Olga Corbin de Lindo

The Last Shall Be First

So the last shall be first, and the first last: for many be called, but few chosen.
Matt. 20:16.

WHEN I ARRIVED AT CHICAGO'S O'Hare Airport on my way home from the United States to Belgium, I was praying I'd be able to get on the plane without any problems. I was still traumatized by a not-so-pleasant delay I'd experienced at another airport in this country. To my dismay, my anticipated fear became a reality when it was announced that the airplane had technical problems, and we'd have to wait for another plane. As I was pondering my delayed arrival in Brussels, a second announcement informed us that another airplane had been found. They needed to begin boarding without any delay as there were many passengers with connecting flights in Brussels, and there was only a short time margin left for the plane to take off. The only difficulty was that this plane still had to be catered, and the catering trolleys had to be moved from the very end of the plane down to the front—which made it impossible for the people booked on first and business class to enter the plane first. So they decided to let the economy passengers board the plane first, pass straight to the back of the plane on the right aisle, and let the catering trolleys move forward on the other aisle. Only after that could the passengers booked on first and business class enter the plane.

I found this quite amusing. Those people who had paid considerably more for their tickets had lost their privilege to board the plane first. This incident reminded me of the important words in today's text. This was the conclusion of the parable about the landowner who had hired laborers for his vineyard. He gave the same money to everyone, no matter if they had worked only one hour or the whole day.

When I was younger, I had a problem understanding this parable. I found it so unjust that everybody got the same reward for different work. Are we sometimes like "first-class" Christians who take God's kingdom for granted? Do we think that we deserve it because we have been laboring and living for the Lord for such a long time already? What about those "second-class" Christians who are converted later and don't have so much time to serve the Lord and win souls for the Master?

Let's be thankful today for the Lord's grace, and that His justice never fails!

Daniela Weichhold

Impromptu Visits

I hope to come to you and talk with you face to face, so that our joy may be complete.
2 John 12, NRSV.

IT WAS OUR LAST FAMILY VACATION with our teenagers. We concluded that with adulthood looming, chances were slim that the four of us would vacation together for quite some time. Our route took us through northern Ontario, through Manitoba, and into Alberta, where we planned to spend a few days visiting friends. After Alberta, we crossed into the United States, and that's where my geography failed me. I relinquished all rights to a vote and gave my husband, Leon, full range to map out our course. To my surprise, we ended up in Wisconsin. We were on our way to visit "Grandma" Byrka. We had become acquainted when my husband was a university student. As our family grew, so did our friendship.

Leon knew that my penchant for formality wouldn't allow me to consent to this impromptu visit, so he said nothing until we were almost at the retirement home. When I saw that Grandma had lost her feisty spirit and sense of independence, I felt ashamed of my earlier protests, feeble though they were. She was so happy to see us and was absolutely amazed at how much the children had grown. I have thanked Leon repeatedly, especially since Grandma passed away a short time later, at age 97.

We had a similar experience in the summer of 2003, when, on a return trip from Quebec, our car suddenly detoured to visit another aged and ailing friend. Vie used to be a robust woman. She and her husband, Charlie, had a country property that was beautifully maintained with flower beds, a vegetable garden, and manicured lawns. Now that Charlie had passed away and Vie was alone and in ill health, her home and property were no longer the showpiece they once had been. It broke my heart to see her in such a state. We continued to visit with her by phone.

On October 31, after failing to reach anyone for a couple of weeks, Leon finally reached someone at Vie's home. He was told she had died October 15. It is uncanny that my husband spoke with her on the phone the morning of October 15 before leaving on a trip out of the country.

Help me, dear Lord, to take time to visit with some lonely, aching soul today.

Avis Mae Rodney

Thou Shalt Not Bear Any Grudge

Thou shalt not avenge, nor bear any grudge against the children
of thy people, but thou shalt love thy neighbour as thyself: I am the Lord.
Lev. 19:18.

"I'M GOING HOME FOR MY VACATION," Marge said to her office neighbor. Marge sat three desks over in the row ahead of me. This woman had taken a dislike to me before she'd met me just after I came to work at the Los Angeles *Times* in 1974. She never spoke to me without a cutting edge to her words.

Trying to be friendly to her in spite of her attitude, I asked, "Where's home?"

She answered without looking around to see who had spoken: "Minnesota."

"I have family in Minnesota."

"Oh? Where?" Marge asked, glancing over her shoulder, trying to identify who spoke.

"A little town no one ever heard about—Swanville."

Marge actually fell out of her chair in surprise. As she picked herself up she said, "That's my hometown! Who are your people?"

When I answered "My grandfather is Herman Ganz," her face registered her shock as she said, "Herman Ganz is my father's best friend! My brother went to school with his son, Buddy, and I was in the same class as Ralph!"

"Buddy and Ralph are my uncles," I told her.

The change in Marge after that day was marked. She no longer spoke sharply to me, frowned at me, or shunned me. Every time we had occasion to work together, she pleasantly asked about news from my family.

I had done nothing wrong to turn Marge against me, nor did I allow her nasty attitude toward me to affect the way I treated her. Now, whatever had turned her against me was forgotten. She always treated me as though I was a dearly loved member of her family.

Harboring ill will toward others, for reason or for no reason, is not Christlike. He forgave those who drove nails into His hands and feet. We are all children of Adam and Eve. We are family. We benefit first when we treat each other—no matter the ethnic, political, or religious differences—as though they are dearly beloved family members.

Darlenejoan McKibbin Rhine

My Parents

Oh, that men would praise the Lord for his goodness.
Ps. 107:8.

ALVARO AND MAXIMA were in their early 20s when they met; both were new Christians, learning to live a better way of life and hoping to help others by serving the Lord. Eager to learn, they were diligent students. When Alvaro completed training, the missionaries there in the Philippines deemed him ready to go and preach the gospel. Maxima improved her musical skills so she could play the pump organ and double as a Bible instructor. They were teamed to conduct evangelistic efforts. As their love for the Lord and the work grew, so did their mutual admiration; and seeking God's leading, they decided to team for life.

On May 29, 1922, in a simple wedding ceremony they were pronounced husband and wife. That was how they became my parents (Pa and Ma, to their children). Ma worked with the evangelistic team until their first child was born, when she chose to stay home. Pa continued preaching, making his immediate family his first priority. A disciplinarian, he believed in "to spare the rod is to spoil the child." Ma was a visionary, kind and loving and widely read, like Pa. These parental influences are among many I thank the Lord for daily, and their prayerfulness was the strongest tie that bound the family together.

Early each morning, singing "Lord, in the Morning," Pa called the family together for worship. Always, he made mention of each child in his closing prayer. Before bedtime Pa sang a hymn to call the family together for evening worship. Each family member who was able offered a brief prayer. In Pa's absence, Ma led in the family's morning and evening worship.

After evening worship the younger children sprawled on the floor around Pa for a bedtime story of Daniel and his friends, Joseph, Moses, and Jesus' birth. Sometimes we waited for the rest of the story, only to find Pa asleep! Awakened, he continued from where he left off. As he told the story of Joseph being sold and looking back to the tents where his father lived, Joseph sobbed, promising to love the Lord as his own father loved him. We sobbed along with Joseph.

Thank You, Lord, for giving us our loving Pa and Ma. As a family, we look forward to worshipping Jesus in the earth made new. Today please bless all the mothers and fathers as they guide children to You.

Consuelo Roda Jackson

Why Weepest Thou?

Jesus said to her, "Woman, why are you weeping?"
John 20:15, RSV.

THE DATE HAD BEEN SET for my admittance to the hospital to receive a stem cell transplant to help in the fight against my cancer. I had to make one last visit to the ear specialist who was monitoring an infection in my ear. She took one look and said, "I definitely would not advise having the transplant at this time. Your ears are still too infected." It was not the news that I wanted to hear.

When I went back to the cancer hospital with that news and spoke with my doctor, I started to cry. I had so hoped that they'd be able to start the procedure. I wanted so badly to be well. I'd been through all the preparatory tests, but, no, it was not to be— at least not right then. My doctor was not a native English speaker, and sometimes I had a hard time understanding him. But he said very plainly, "Woman, why are you weeping?" I looked at him to see if he realized he had just spoken words directly from the Bible, words I recognized. Whether he did or not, he assured me that the procedure would happen—I just had to wait.

The next morning I was encouraged by this psalm: "Wait for the Lord; be strong and take heart and wait for the Lord" (Ps. 27:14, NIV). And I began to think about what the doctor had said to me—why was I crying? The angels first said those words to Mary when she came to the tomb, looking for the body of her Lord. She didn't realize that Jesus was right there beside her. Even when Jesus said those very same words to her, Mary still didn't recognize Jesus. Why was I also so slow to recognize Jesus right beside me?

I had claimed the promises. The pastor had anointed me. I knew people all over the world were praying for me. I had cards of encouragement from so many friends and even people I didn't know. It was time to be of good courage, knowing that my life was in the hands of my comforter and redeemer, Jesus. And yet when there was a delay (not a cancellation) in my treatment, I lost courage.

May each of us today know that Jesus is right beside us, ready to comfort and cheer, ready to listen to everything we have to say, ready to carry our burdens. When you are overwhelmed with something in your life, ask yourself, "Woman, why are you weeping?"

Carol Nicks

The Hesitant Smile

And if you greet only your brothers, what are you doing more than others? Do not even pagans do that? Matt. 5:47, NIV.

IN BUENOS AIRES, ARGENTINA, we often travel by train—it's the fastest way to get places. One evening I wanted to arrive as soon as possible at my daughter's house so I could see my little granddaughter. I was alone. One, two, three stations passed. People got off, and people got on. I began to pay attention to the other passengers. Some were very well dressed, while others were dressed more casually. My eyes delighted in looking at the different colors and clothing combinations, the shoes, the purses, the well-chosen accessories.

Suddenly my eyes stopped on a stroller holding a baby of about 15 months. His little legs kicked, his restless hands strained to grasp anything within reach. I raised my eyes to the baby's face, and in the instant in which I was going to smile and greet him from afar, I could see a strange lump on his forehead. Some abnormal growth had "ruined" his beauty.

I pretended to be distracted, but out of the corner of my eye I could watch him. The little one waited, as if wanting to see if I would "play" with him. In that moment the train arrived at the next station, and the mother and child were lost among the platform crowd.

The train continued its journey, but my mind was unsettled; a feeling of confusion came over me. Why had I reacted like this? Why hadn't I smiled at the little boy with the lump on his forehead? I concluded that, faced with something unusual, we try to be indifferent.

Have you found yourself smiling at a precious baby? But how many times have you smiled at the old woman in worn-out clothes, at the man who is missing an arm, at a baby with unattractive features, at the mother with a large scar across her cheek?

Don't stop smiling at those who are different. Don't be a coward and avoid their glance as if they don't exist. Many have confined themselves to indifferent isolation. Break this wall! Smile at the unattractive baby! Smile at the woman in threadbare clothes! Smile at the one who does not have an attractive appearance, and give them the gift of your acceptance. Don't hesitate. Perhaps your smile will be the only present they've received in a long time. Smiling is an act of kindness that you will never be ashamed of.

Susana Schulz

Learning to Trust in God

"Bring the whole tithe into the storehouse, that there may be food in my house.
Test me in this," says the Lord Almighty, "and see if I will not throw open the floodgates
of heaven and pour out so much blessing that you will not have room enough for it."
Mal. 3:10, NIV.

DURING THE SUMMER OF 2001 I decided to join the Oregon Youth Challenge, a ministry that involved selling books. I've had many wonderful experiences; however, the most impressive experience I had started the fifth week of sales, just three weeks before the end of the program. In addition to the fact that my sales began to fall drastically, I was unable to find ways to talk to others about Jesus. It didn't matter how hard I prayed, it seemed that God didn't hear my pleadings. Day after day, I asked God to show me what was wrong in my life; however, nothing seemed to happen until the Thursday morning of the seventh week.

When I studied the Bible for the lesson I was going to give that afternoon, I came across Genesis 3:3: "You must not eat fruit from the tree . . . and you must not touch it, or you will die" (NIV). The lesson was about tithe, and at that moment I realized my sin—I was touching the tree. During the previous two months, I hadn't returned my tithe. For reasons that I thought were fair, I had decided to return the tithe for the summer at the end of the program. But I was using money that wasn't mine; it belonged to the Lord. After recognizing my sin, I decided that the following Monday, when I received payment, I would put aside $100 to pay my entire tithe.

Monday came, and I cashed my check around 5:00 p.m. As soon as I had the money, I put aside my tithe. I returned to work, and less than 30 minutes later I met a girl who had just graduated from high school and was really interested in my message books. After talking for a while, she decided to buy *The Great Controversy, Peace Above the Storm, Angels Among Us*, and two copies of *He Taught Love*. I left her house speechless—I had worked all summer long, and I hadn't sold more than three books at any one door.

By the end of that day I had sold 10 books. The next day I sold another 14. In two days I sold more books than I had during any other complete week.

God has taught me to really trust in Him, and more than ever the words of today's Scripture text became real in my life. What do they say to you?

Alessandra Cholet Moreira

I Wish You Peace and Joy

"For I know the plans I have for you," declares the Lord, "plans to prosper you and not to harm you, plans to give you hope and a future."
Jer. 29:11, NIV.

FOR MUCH OF MY LIFE I felt very miserable and was a very miserable person to be around. Friends who've known me through those years now tell me, "You sure have changed!"

Sometimes we Christians believe that all a person needs is more Bible study and prayer to get over emotional pain and confusion. But religion only gave me another addiction. God answered my cry for help by forcing me into counseling, where I was exposed to the Twelve Steps of Recovery. The first step was to admit I am powerless over other people, places, and things. That was a revelation to me. I thought I believed God was in charge, but I acted as if I was in charge. I needed to believe a Power greater than myself could restore me. I needed to turn my will and my life over to the care of this God. Now that I wasn't so defensive, I was free to take an honest look at myself.

Once this thorough searching was written down, I admitted to God, to myself, and to my female counselor the exact scope and degree of these wrongs. I was ready to have God remove my defects of character. I realized selfishness was the root of every one of them. As God showed me areas of my selfishness and began to free me from them, it took care of the specific defects.

I asked God to make me aware of the people I had harmed, and I asked Him to make me willing to make amends. Recovery taught me that until that happened, I wasn't ready to make amends. Once I realized how good this freedom of conscience felt, I wanted to become aware when I fell back into my old ways and take care of them right away. Now my prayer and meditation could become effective in improving my conscious contact with God, in making clear what His will for me is, and in letting Him empower me to do His will.

I know that applying these steps to my life has brought about a spiritual awakening. I love carrying this message to others who still live miserable lives (though they may be oblivious to it), and I am determined to practice these principles in all my affairs. Working these steps in a group for support makes the process easier and the progress unbelievable.

I wish for you the life of joy and peace that I have found in those Jesus-led steps.

Lana Fletcher

Living by Faith

Therefore I tell you, do not worry about your life, what you will eat or drink. . . .
Is not life more important than food, and the body more important than clothes?
Matt. 6:25, NIV.

AFTER MANY FRUSTRATED ATTEMPTS to hold my marriage together, I decided to separate from my husband. From the day of separation forward, I began to experience all the promises of God in my life. My children and I were happy during this difficult time, in spite of our struggles. I remember well something that happened one Friday about eight months after the separation.

On Friday evenings I had the habit of reading a devotional book at sunset. On this special day I was feeling tired, sad, and afflicted. I didn't know what I would give my children for breakfast on Sabbath when I arrived home from the small group that we attended every Friday evening. I went to bed without reading the devotional book. Since I couldn't sleep and after many hours of tossing and turning in bed, I decided to get up and listen to the voice of the Holy Spirit. That voice seemed to be telling me to read my devotional book, especially the message for that day. As I read, it was so comforting to find Psalm 23:1 and 4, which says: "The Lord is my shepherd, I shall not be in want. . . . I will fear no evil, for you are with me; your rod and your staff, they comfort me" (NIV). To confirm God's guidance in my life, I also read Matthew 6:25: "Do not worry." If we observe the birds, they are not anxiously gathering up food for the next day. They trust that they will find everything they need the next day. They have no worry and anxiety.

I soon fell asleep, my heart at peace. On Sabbath we woke up to go to church without breakfast. But soon I heard the voice of my sister, who is my neighbor, requesting that I come to the fence to receive a loaf of whole wheat bread that she had prepared for me. The food problem was solved. After church my friend, Gislene, our small group leader, handed me an envelope that contained approximately $75 that the group had collected on that Friday night after our meeting. These funds were useful for purchasing groceries.

In spite of unfavorable circumstances and the anguish we sometimes experience, God is in control of our lives. We should place all our burdens and worries in the Lord's hands and rest in Him. I can truthfully say, *Thank You, Lord, for always providing for my needs.*

Rosângela Ferreira Nery

My Desired Gift

Then shall ye call upon me, and ye shall go and pray unto me, and I will hearken unto you. Jer. 29:12.

AS MANAGER OF A CHRISTIAN RADIO STATION, my husband is constantly on the lookout for electronic equipment. While visiting my mom and sister, I decided to get him something that he really would have loved to get for himself. There was a particular item he'd been reviewing but refrained from buying because he was waiting for the technology to be "debugged." I had delayed somewhat in ordering it while checking to see if he was satisfied that it was now working optimally. When I was certain it was what he wanted, I placed the order online. When confirmation came, I saw that delivery was scheduled for the day after my departure.

My heart fell. I told my mother my predicament, and she was also disappointed because she knew what it meant for both of us—my getting it for him, and his using it for the Lord's work. After we had discussed the situation, we decided to make it a matter of prayer. Every day I tracked the package's progress online. For a few days it seemed that the package was stationary. Then Hurricane Dean threatened to foil any further movement—Dean changed course!

On my final day I constantly thought of my husband's gift that had not yet arrived. I went to my mom's room and had a talk with God, reminding Him of my request for an on-time delivery so that I could get my husband his gift. Time seemed to rush by.

My 5-year-old niece, who always heard the doorbell, was informed that Auntie was expecting a very important UPS package, and she should look out for the delivery truck. She did so, and kept us posted with constant updates. By 6:00 p.m. she informed me, "Auntie, I haven't seen any truck, but we still have time." She had heard us discussing that the latest delivery time would be 7:00 p.m.

By 6:30 my faith was wavering, but at 6:38 p.m. my niece jumped and screamed, "There's someone at the door! There's someone at the door, and I think it's UPS."

It was—with minutes to spare.

Once again God had proved that He is in control. He knows our deepest desires, and He hears our earnest pleas.

Brenda Ottley

Listening to His Voice

And thine ears shall hear a word behind thee, saying, This is the way,
walk ye in it, when ye turn to the right hand, and when ye turn to the left.
Isa. 30:21.

WE WERE RETURNING HOME from the mission field following a series of providences that led to our move to Loveland, Colorado. One morning, while still living in Penang, Malaysia, I reviewed the events by which the Lord had provided a job, a house, and a car in Loveland, all within a week's time. Back in Penang, He had also orchestrated the timing of the expiration of the house lease, as well as the work permit and visas, to coincide with the time we needed to leave. Reflecting on these events, I prayed, *Wow, Lord! You are much better able to manage the details of my life than I am. Please take charge of my day.* I then went to the morning market to get some produce.

As I left the market, I noticed a skinny mama dog sniffing my bag intently, obviously hungry. I was impressed to buy some food for her. While I felt sad about her plight, I also had a lot to do. I thought of paying a gardener to buy her food but decided against it. I'm sorry to say that I decided to leave.

Although I had just purchased a new car battery the previous week, the car wouldn't start even after several attempts. I didn't know of anything I could do, so I sat down to reflect on the situation. *I have plenty of time to buy food for the dog now,* I mused. *I guess I'd better act on that prompting.* When I returned with food for the dog, I also found two small puppies with her who ate eagerly as well.

I was then impressed to try starting the car again and, amazingly, the engine roared to life immediately. How much easier it would have been for the Lord—and for me—if I had just obeyed the initial impression!

I am thankful that God loves us and is patient with us. I'm gradually learning that He is interested in every detail of our lives. He is trying to train us to listen to His voice and follow His promptings. When we give Him permission, He will rearrange our priorities, it's true; but although it may cause some temporary inconvenience, it will also bring unexpected blessings as the God of heaven makes His presence known—sometimes in amazing ways.

Teresa (Proctor) Hebard

Through the Valley

Yea, though I walk through the valley of the shadow of death, I will
fear no evil: for thou art with me; thy rod and thy staff they comfort me.
Ps. 23:4.

IT IS ALWAYS DIFFICULT to walk through the valley with the shadow of death looming overhead. We begin that walk with the physician's diagnosis: failing kidneys, cancer, and congestive heart failure. The names may vary, but the slow walk through that frightful valley seldom does. And as we walk, the mountains loom overhead: What will happen to my children? How will I pay these astronomical medical bills? How much longer can I bear this pain? Will I ever get out of this hospital bed? Each mountain appears taller and more menacing as we tremble in its shadow.

Often we approach the valley not for our own illness, but for a parent with Alzheimer's disease, a daughter with breast cancer, a sister with leukemia, or a husband with prostate cancer. We visit the hospital rooms where loved ones lie in pain, wishing we could take their place. The beeping lifesaving machines frighten us. The invasive tests scare us, and the treatments terrify even the brave.

But as we look up, as we lift our eyes to Jesus, we find comfort: "I will fear no evil: for thou art with me." And like the gentle morning sun, the realization dawns. In the midst of the searing pain, in spite of the mountain of bills, with concerns for the future, we are not afraid because we trust our Walking Partner.

We could not want a more experienced companion through that valley. He walked the streets of Galilee with Jairus, whose daughter was terminally ill. When the desperate father came to Jesus, He spoke only the word and the little girl lived again immediately. He touched the blind eyes, and they were cured. He met the 10 lepers and healed them all. In Bethany Lazarus had been dead for four days before Jesus arrived, and then He raised him to life again. With such evidence, why should I worry? Why should I fear my personal struggle through that dark valley?

You, my friend, may still be in the valley of the shadow of death. Even though the mountains tower overhead, let the world see you smile. You are not taking that walk alone. You've got company. Your Shepherd is right beside you.

Annette Walwyn Michael

Maranatha!

And behold, I am coming quickly.
Rev. 22:12, NKJV.

ON A VERY BUSY SABBATH MORNING I rushed to get everything ready. There was going to be a baptism that day at the Maranatha church. Among the candidates for baptism was a member of my family, so it was to be a double celebration.

I had eight guests to take to the church but only one car. It was clear that I'd have to make at least two trips. Furthermore, I had my 6-month-old son to get ready, and then I had to pick up two other family members in a totally different area of Bucharest. Already under a time pressure, we had packed our lunch, finalized our plans for the day, and made the final preparations to leave.

It took about 50 minutes to pick up the first group of guests and drop them off. I rushed off to pick up the second group. As I approached the church with the second group, I received a telephone call from someone in the first group. "Come quickly," the person said excitedly. "The baptism is about to begin and—and this is not the Maranatha church!"

Then I realized the mistake I had made. In the confusion of the morning, I had taken them to another church, located at a considerable distance from the Maranatha church. I couldn't afford to think too long because I now had to cross the city twice. All finally ended well, and we had a good fellowship together. I believe the angels of those who had decided to surrender to God rejoiced as well.

In my spiritual journey, am I losing sight of the target in my desperate rush to cope with the avalanche of daily activities? Even on that Sabbath, I again picture myself dragging after me bunches of flowers, guests, lunch, my little son—but to where? In the wrong direction! Well, not necessarily wrong, because we could have enjoyed a wonderful worship service in any of the 17 Adventist churches in Bucharest, but we would not have been at the event we had prepared for.

Another event, a celebration of the entire universe, is challenging us to get ready. Is it possible that in spite of our good intentions and our feverish preparations we could lose sight of our true objective—meeting our Savior? Maranatha! Lord, come!

Andreea Strâmbu-Dima

A Grateful Heart

Give thanks to the Lord, call on his name; make known among the nations what he has done. Sing to him, sing praise to him; tell of all his wonderful acts.
1 Chron. 16:8, 9, NIV.

SOME TIME AGO, while the dew still clung to the edge of every grass blade and the sun started to spread rays of sunshine, I began rushing through my daily routine at school, hoping to finish all the requirements and reports for the day. Then an elderly woman caught me by the arm, her eyes sparkling as she said, "Oh, you look pretty in that dress." She had once complimented me with "Here's 10 points for the lady in pink." Now she smiled at me, and I blushed. Deep inside I felt elated and thanked her for the kind words. My day then went really well.

The incident taught me a lesson to be kind and generous to all around me—to say some genuine little words to those we encounter in the daily walk of life.

Our life can be compared to an ordinary clothesline where varied problems and happenings hang in colorful linen apparel. Many people are represented on this line. They are like those around us. They have cheerless souls and are unsatisfied with the world. So many sad people are living a most vulnerable life. We cannot measure their hurts or their thoughts. But one thing is sure: they long for some kind words that may lighten their burden. Life can be wonderful and meaningful if we face it with courage, faith, hope, and cheerfulness, and strive to share positive thinking with those around us.

The dress I had worn that day was an old, rose-colored dress made of the cheapest fabric, but I liked it. Every time I wore it the memory of a friend who had complimented me flooded in. Her smiles, her encouragement, her kind words, and her act of supporting my programs in the church meant so much.

From that time on I strived very hard to find ways to make others happier—not just women, but couples and children, as well. They are worthy to experience the same encouragement I did.

Appreciation for good things around us should encourage us to sprinkle sunshine in the lives of others. We can be a blessing to others by gratefulness for every little thing in life. God's goodness and surprises are always there. Take a challenge! Share your heart and be grateful!

Leah A. Salloman

My Comforter

May your unfailing love be my comfort, according to your promise to your servant.
Ps. 119:76, NIV.

LAST NIGHT I ONCE AGAIN used the comforter that had been my mother-in-law's. She had come to live in the nursing home my husband and I operated, so to personalize her room we purchased a comforter for her bed, among other things. After her death we brought it home.

Some nights falling asleep is a challenging experience for me. When I find myself tossing and turning so much that I'm afraid I'll awaken my husband, I go into the guest bedroom. Not wanting to disturb the bedding, I sometimes get out the comforter, lie on top of the made-up bed, and throw the comforter over me. It is so soft and inviting; I snuggle under it and relax, close my eyes, and invariably go off to sleep in no time. No matter the season, it provides just the right level of comfort to keep me from getting too hot or too cold. My hope is that it will not wear out before I do!

There is another Comforter I cherish much more than this one. He is available to you, too. Like the one I sleep under, God—through the Holy Spirit—comforts us time and time again. He not only knows our every need and desire but is always available every hour of the day or night. His Word promises that He will answer when we call (Jer. 33:3). Whenever we ask Him, He is willing to take our burdens and worries (Matt. 11:28).

During our most difficult losses—the death of a close family member, friend, or special relationship—He sees us through. When we are ill, stressed out, or perplexed by a seemingly impossible situation and we don't know which way to turn, He gives us comfort, strength, and solutions to our problems. There is no situation He doesn't understand, no heartache He can't relieve. Nothing is too hard for the Lord (Jer. 32:17).

In His Word God has given us promise after promise to sustain us during every situation. Through the Holy Spirit we are often reminded of them just when we need them most.

The best comfort He gives us is His assurance that we may have eternal life and live with Him forever. Jesus' death on the cross makes salvation available to every one of us.

What a Comforter He is! Let's allow ourselves to be wrapped in His love and comfort!

Marian M. Hart

Mind the Gap

I would have lost heart, unless I had believed that I would see the goodness of the Lord in the land of the living. Wait on the Lord; be of good courage, and He shall strengthen your heart; wait, I say, on the Lord!
Ps. 27:13, 14, NKJV.

IF YOU'VE EVER TAKEN THE TUBE (aka subway) in England, there is a distinct announcement you can't avoid. At every stop a voice comes over the intercom, reminding you to "mind the gap." This repeated instruction is a source of amusement for tourists. For some reason there is a large space between the platform and the car. At some stations the gap is wider than at others. But regardless of the size of the gap, all travelers are warned to "mind the gap."

When Abram received His promise of a son from God, he must have jumped for joy. God told Abram, "I will make you a great nation . . . and in you all the families of the earth shall be blessed" (Gen. 12:2, 3, NKJV). When Abram reached Canaan, God reiterated His promise. Abram was so grateful to God that he built an altar. It would have been easy to praise God then. It would have been easy to declare the awesome power of God. I imagine Abram had a contented smile on his face as he looked into the future and imagined the life of his son.

This would have been a good point in the story to have a voice announce, "Abraham, mind the gap." He had no idea how many years it would be until that promise was fulfilled, but there was purpose in that gap: to build faith in Abraham. "Mind the gap, Abraham; you will have so many tests and trials before those dreams are fulfilled." "Mind the gap, Sarah; jealousy will eat you up." "Mind the gap, Abraham and Sarah, if you try to fulfill the promise on your own."

You may be in the gap. Perhaps you are waiting for employment, a child, a relationship, a doctor's report, a loved one to turn to God, emotional healing, or perhaps improved finances. Know that there is purpose in the wait. Use this time to develop your relationship with God. Let God rid your life of excess baggage and hurts that you may not even realize you have. Do not lose heart. Your heavenly Father will take care of you. Abraham had to wait for a son, but he became the friend of God because he allowed God to work in Him. The lesson learned during his gap landed him in Hebrews 11, the hall of faith. Your heavenly Father will come through for you—but mind the gap.

Laura Henry-Stump

Fireflies

Let your light so shine before men, that they may see your
good works, and glorify your Father which is in heaven.
Matt. 5:16.

WHAT FUN WE CHILDREN HAD on hot summer evenings, chasing tiny fireflies around the yard and catching and putting them in our glass jars. It was always a disappointment when we came into the house to see that these little lights were just small, ugly bugs. However, when we were in our beds and the room lights were out, we'd watch when first one and then another small light in the jar would blink on and off.

I hadn't thought of those days for years. Then I grew up and went to Africa with my own two children, and one night, as we sat outside on the steps in the deep blackness, I noticed a bright flicker in the bushes, then another, and another! The children spent many happy minutes trying to catch those flickering lights.

It was even more years later that I came in contact with fireflies again. We hadn't been in Uganda very long when I had my first bout with malaria. First, I noticed the aching in my bones. Then the chills began; my teeth chattered and my jaws ached. The fever took over. My head and neck ached, and I was totally miserable. In the middle of the night I began hallucinating. In my fever I couldn't figure out who I was or where I was. I was frightened. Just then, as I lay there hot, miserable, and scared, I saw a tiny bright light flicker across the ceiling. My eyes followed it across the room. Then I saw another, and another. My mind began to clear, and I realized that what I was seeing were God's little fireflies. Fear left, and a deep peace settled over me. Long into the night, before falling back to sleep, I followed those lights as they flickered back and forth across the room. I thanked God for His answer to my cry of fear.

What a wonderful God we have! He supplies His little creatures to share their tiny lights to guide us in the darkness. He cares about each of us and sends His light to let us know. Because He cares so much for us, we should be always ready and willing to share our light with someone who is crying out in fear and darkness to show them the way to the true light. Jesus said, "I am the light of the world. Whoever follows me will never walk in darkness, but will have the light of life" (John 8:12, NIV).

Frances Osborne Morford

Independence Day

To the Jews who had believed him, Jesus said, "If you hold to my teaching, you are really my disciples. Then you will know the truth, and the truth will set you free." John 8:31, 32, NIV.

MY HUSBAND AND I were having a Fourth of July picnic for family, friends, and neighbors. I had purchased each of our grandkids a piece of red, white, and blue clothing. Cody's T-shirt didn't come until almost time for the festivities to begin. As he slipped it on he grinned at me, and with all the wisdom of a 6-year-old he said, "It's because we won the war, isn't it, Grandma?"

"Yes, Cody, it's because we won the war," I answered as he ran out the door. I shook my head and thought, *He doesn't have a clue that it happened more than 200 years ago. He doesn't under-stand the blood, suffering, and death that it took to win the war. He only knows it was won.*

The party was a great success. More than 175 people ranging in age from 6 months to 90 years attended. There were family members we see all the time, and friends we hadn't seen in months. There were even several families we didn't know but had been invited because they were new in our neighborhood. We used our flatbed trailer with a 22-foot deck as the buffet table. It was covered from one end to the other with all kinds of wonderful food. As friends and family came together, we reminisced about the past and shared plans for the future. The fellowship put me on an emotional high through the day and into the night. I woke in the early morning hours and had to smile even then, remembering the enjoyment of the previous day. As my mind went into replay, I couldn't keep from making some comparisons.

There was another great war (Rev. 12:7-9) that was won more than 2,000 years ago (John 3:16). Do we really understand the blood, suffering, and death it took to win? Or are we, like Cody, clueless? Jesus says we will find truth if we search with all our hearts (Jer. 29:13), for He is truth. Yet even now many have not heard the news of victory, and skirmishes with evil continue.

Soon we'll be celebrating the end of that conflict, and there will be a grand party (1 Cor. 2:9). The invitations have gone out (Matt. 25:34), the party clothes have been purchased (Isa. 61:10), and all God's family will be there. PS: Bring a friend! (Matt. 22:9). What fun we'll have fellowshipping and planning our eternal future! Spread the news and RSVP today.

Diana Inman

Nothing Too Hard for the Lord!

Trust in the Lord with all thine heart; and lean not unto thine own
understanding. In all thy ways acknowledge him, and he shall direct thy paths.
Prov. 3:5, 6.

THE DAY FOLLOWING MY COUSIN Claude's funeral my sisters and I were scheduled to return to Jamaica. Our ride arrived about noon, leaving us with very little time to run some important errands and get to the Miami, Florida, airport.

We completed our errands and started for the airport, but everything seemed to indicate that we'd never make that flight. The traffic lights turned red each time we approached them (and there were legions of them), and the traffic flow slowed to a creep because of a five-vehicle accident. What should have been a half-hour journey became more than an hour. I even wondered why we had started out, knowing that we were late. I felt an enormous amount of stress weighing down on me. My siblings were very quiet; I sensed that they were praying silently. My cousin, who was driving, was silent too. I could feel the tension in the car. Then I began to verbalize my anxiety.

"I can't believe this is really happening to me! I am going to miss this flight, and I have to be at work in the morning. I think we should turn back. It is almost 5:00, and we aren't there yet . . . O Lord," I prayed out loud, "I can't manage this. I am so stressed. I can't bring myself to even ask You to help, because it makes no sense—we are too late. We'll never get through security. O God, it seems unreasonable to ask You to act, but if it is Your will, then cause the plane to be delayed. Lord, I give this entire situation over to You now; please take it from me, for I can't manage it."

We arrived at the airport at 5:30. I told my sisters that we should leave our luggage in the car and just go to the check-in counter to get rescheduled for the next day, even though we had no money to pay the penalty fee. At the counter, to our amazement, we learned that the flight had been delayed. We had a very smooth and safe flight, and I praised God all the way home.

God is in total control. He tenderly guides and watches over even His erring children. All the things that concern us become His concerns too, and nothing is too hard for the Lord. No situation is out of His reach or beyond His control. He works on our behalf, in spite of our faults.

Jacqueline Hope HoShing-Clarke

God's Second Book

*How beautiful upon the mountains are the feet of
him that bringeth good tidings, that publisheth peace.
Isa. 52:7.*

WE LOVE TO HIKE in the mountains, and the little biblical town of Berea, where we live, is ideally situated in the foothills of the Vermion Range at an altitude of 6,672 feet (2,033 meters). There is a variety of trails to choose from and heights to conquer. Then, just across the Aliakmon River, the Pierion Mountains (7,118 feet, or 2,170 meters) extend for miles in the opposite direction, offering many challenging peaks, including the highest mountain in Greece, Mount Olympus (9,480 feet, or 2,900 meters).

The beauty of nature, God's second book, more than rewards lovers of the great outdoors. In winter the stark nakedness of stately, deciduous trees and gentle sunlight, reflecting off deep snow, slowly gives way to the vivid and varied greens of spring—multicolored carpets of gorgeous wildflowers, and the harmonious melody of birdsongs. Gradually, they too are succeeded by the long, hazy days of summer, which in turn explode into the blaring colors of autumn with its misty fruitfulness.

Such beauty has a healing, calming influence on the hikers. They come from varied backgrounds and represent many different professions, but like most people today, many are struggling with seemingly insurmountable problems: marital friction, rebellious children, less than ideal health, and, of course, the everyday decisions, major and minor, we all have to deal with. Some walk alone, deep in thought, while others open their hearts to sympathetic ears, seeking for understanding, encouragement, or advice. They are not disappointed.

In such an environment it seems completely natural to talk of a loving God who is available and willing to interact with His troubled, human children. Hearts are drawn nearer to Him where the signs of His caring abound everywhere, from the humble wildflower blooming in obscurity, giving off a sweet perfume even as it is trodden underfoot, to the heavenly music of countless little birds, their lungs bursting with songs of praise to their Creator. Our finite gaze is lifted through vaulted heavens to rest in adoration, prostrate before the throne of the universe upon which reigns supreme our God, our Creator, our Savior.

Revel Papaioannou

Nobody's Cat

For every beast of the forest is mine, and the cattle upon a thousand hills.
I know all the fowls of the mountains: and the wild beasts of the field are mine.
Ps. 50:10, 11.

WE WOULD SEE THE CAT sitting on the wall beside the road as we took our evening walks. Every time we saw her we heard her meow just once, as if to say hi. We called her Puss. It seemed strange for a stray cat to be friendly and not afraid of people. We looked forward to seeing her and to being greeted by her. Then we saw her no more and found out Puss had gone to one of the homes in our colony and stayed. She was there for some time, even delivering a litter of kittens. When the kittens were big enough, Puss moved out.

After a time she found another home in this colony. The couple, delighted to have her, called her Kitty. We speak to her in English even though she probably is acquainted with the local Indian language. Kitty adapted to every situation and was well loved. She again delivered a litter of kittens and was a good mother. After weaning them, she brought rats or squirrels to her kittens, teaching them what to eat and what prey to catch. Then the mother cat moved again.

As I write this I now am the "owner" of Puss. Perhaps she recognizes us as the people whom she used to greet as we walked. The moment she came to our door she behaved like an old friend. She is very affectionate and behaves as if she owns the whole property. She has cleared all the mice and rats from our garden and the squirrels from our fruit trees. We don't allow her in the house, so it's very amusing to watch her sneak into the house to sprawl on the cool floor. She isn't bothered when we say, "Puss, go out." She won't look at me, as if to say, "This is my house too." However, she'll probably leave us, too, for another home.

One day I heard her muffled cry at the front door. I opened the door to see Puss drop a big rat at my feet. She mewed as if to say, "This is for you." I called my husband, and we both had a good laugh.

How many good things we can learn from a stray cat. We need to care for these creatures even if we don't own them. These creatures belong to God, and as we care for them we are rewarded with simple pleasure. One day in the new earth we shall enjoy these beautiful, innocent, and perfect animals.

Birdie Poddar

Our Wonderful Counselor

For unto us a child is born, unto us a son is given: and the government shall
be upon his shoulder: and his name shall be called Wonderful, Counselor,
The mighty God, The everlasting Father, The Prince of Peace.
Isa. 9:6.

JESUS IS CALLED OUR COUNSELOR. On many occasions He engaged in individual counseling with a view to helping the person involved. Counseling can be described as the process of disclosing personal hopes, desires, concerns, fears, and failures in an attempt to change behavior, alter external factors, and set future goals. This kind of intimate sharing and communicating is possible only in relationships founded on acceptance, understanding, and positive regard. Jesus accepts us all and understands perfectly the needs of the human heart. He came to save sinners of all races, and He is in the best position to help everyone.

A rich young ruler once engaged Jesus in a dynamic counseling session (Luke 18:18-27). Jesus was prepared to listen, to ask questions, to give feedback, to check perceptions, to summarize, and to help the client in the process of changing behavior and setting future goals. The young ruler came to Jesus voluntarily, and he came with a question: "What shall I do to inherit eternal life?" In his opening remarks he referred to Jesus as "good." Jesus then began to focus the discussion on the real matters at hand. He told him that only God is good. Jesus checked the ruler's perception of the Ten Commandments. The man self-disclosed and told Jesus that he had kept all the commandments from his youth up. As Jesus continued listening to him and checking his perceptions, He recognized that the young man's interpretation on the subject matter was not totally accurate, so He told him of the one thing he lacked. Jesus told him to sell all that he had, distribute it to the poor, and follow Him.

The young ruler made his decision. He was unprepared to make the sacrifice required. Thus ended this counseling session. Jesus then remarked on how hard it is for those who have riches to gain eternal life, but He didn't say it was impossible.

Today our wonderful Counselor and Savior is letting us all know that it is possible to be saved, but the decision rests with us. We should let nothing stand in our way for whatever we lose in this life we will gain more. The decision to follow Him is ours. Let's choose Him today!

Shirnet Wellington

Brain Files

I will praise You, for I am fearfully and wonderfully made;
marvelous are Your works, and that my soul knows very well.
Ps. 139:14, NKJV.

MY HUSBAND AND I had just settled down in bed when he asked, "Do you remember the name of that guy in Maryland who had the sanctuary model?"

I didn't. I knew his son's first name was Ned—he and his wife had been friends of ours, and I thought the father's name was the same, but I couldn't come up with the family name at all—a total blank. When I can't think of a name, I can usually think of the first letter of the name and eventually the name will come to me. So I started through the alphabet to see if I could recall the name. *Ned A* . . . Nothing. *Ned B* . . . Nothing. *Ned C* . . . Nothing. And on through the alphabet, *D* . . . *E* . . . *F* . . . Finally I got to T. *Ned T ,* and bingo! There it was! Filed under "T."

"Tenery,"* I blurted out to my husband.

"Yes. Ned Tenery. That's it," he agreed. "Thanks."

I lay there for a while marveling at how our minds work, how marvelously God created us. It had been at least 10 years since I'd seen any of the Tenerys, and I probably hadn't thought of them during that time. So how was it that my brain pulled the name out from the literally thousands and thousands of names stored there? And how many of them begin with T, as well? But without even conscious effort, the right name came up. I've read that we use only a small portion of our brains. Just think what we could do if we could access all that potential.

We're told that we'll be able to spend eternity learning more and more things, making use of our entire brains. Isaiah tells us, "They will neither harm nor destroy on all my holy mountain, for the earth will be full of the knowledge of the Lord as the waters cover the sea" (Isa. 11:9, NIV). Wow! No more dementia, no more Alzheimer's. Whatever subject we want to study will be open to our learning. We can study nature, psychology, mathematics, the universe. We will learn about God and what He has done for us through the ages—totally beyond what our sinful minds can comprehend. We will be able to fill our minds with all that knowledge and will always remember where it is filed. "Marvelous are Your works"!

Ardis Dick Stenbakken

*not his real name

Stranger in the Airport

Beloved, thou doest faithfully whatsoever thou doest to the brethren, and to strangers.
3 John 5.

THE AIRPORT CAN BE a frightening place if you're stranded in a foreign country without local currency. That was my situation. My husband and I usually travel together; we engage in some fun activities, including people-watching. This pastime doesn't work well when I am alone, especially if I feel stranded.

I was returning home from a friend's funeral, and while in transit in another country I had been bumped from my flight, which was overbooked because of a holiday. The airline wasn't certain what time I'd be placed on another flight because all flights seemed to be off schedule. I was stranded, and I needed to let my husband know where I was because he was expecting me home shortly. Earlier, while waiting for my flight, I had bought food and some souvenirs to finish using that country's local currency, so now I was out of cash. Situations such as these cause me to pray more than usual—I guess we all do.

I tried to make a credit card call to let my husband know of my predicament, but the phones weren't set up to access credit cards. While contemplating my next move, I observed a gentleman desperately trying to make an international call and becoming increasingly frustrated after numerous unsuccessful attempts. Being in a similar situation, I understood his frustration. I offered assistance when I recognized he was dialing the incorrect access code. He surrendered everything to me with a relieved expression. On my first attempt he was connected, and his gratitude was overwhelming. His conversation quickly over, he was ready to leave when he realized that I hadn't made my call. Immediately he offered to let me use his remaining call credit since he no longer needed it. Not expecting this goodwill, it was my turn to express gratitude. Finally I was in touch with my husband, who was worried because I wasn't on my scheduled flight.

As I returned to waiting, I began to reflect on what had occurred and realized that one act of kindness generated another. We really should help others, not just to receive a reward but to let everyone know by our actions that we are Christians. This is what God expects of His children. Our question should be "How can my actions reflect Christ today?"

Brenda Ottley

Maturity Is Pleasant

*You have made known to me the path of life; you will fill me with
joy in your presence, with eternal pleasures at your right hand.
Ps. 16:11, NIV.*

ONE BEAUTIFUL SUNNY MORNING I observed a woman of advanced age walking on the street, complaining about her age. What a sad scene! I thought, *Lord, aging like this is neither pleasant nor worthwhile.*

Seniors still need to catch a glimpse of the horizon and with hope see that the sun still rises. If you are already a senior citizen, know that you are a useful person to society even if you only offer optimistic messages. Life experiences are reflected in the creases on the face, originating through smiles, and not the wrinkles bitterness furnishes. Only those who are happy can convince someone that aging is pleasant. These individuals are able to demonstrate that while the years are added, wisdom is acquired as a blessing.

To me, that woman on the street wasn't old enough to have such a curvature to her body. Perhaps no one on her life's journey had shown her that life also has its good side. We must know how to turn things around when they go wrong. Instead of only complaining, one must understand that sad things are a part of life, and the heart must be an abode for happiness.

Some time later I met another woman, much older than the previous one, who in contrast transmitted a great deal of will to live. She shared with me a painful part of her life. She lived with a paralyzed grandson, who was her greatest motivation to climb up the steep slope! She also told me of her great love and trust in Jesus Christ. This filled me with enthusiasm, and I began to reflect that maturing in this manner is pleasant!

Dear friend, when you watch the sunset and still feel great hope, know that you are maturing only physically, but not in your spirit.

Christ states, "Let the little children come to me, and do not hinder them, for the kingdom of God belongs to such as these" (Luke 18:16, NIV). Let's become like little children—pure, happy, excited, and full of hope.

Dear Jesus, I want to be pleasant—always. May I learn to accept difficulties in life, and may I know how to send bright rays of hope to those who cross my path each day.

Maria Sinharinha de Oliveira Nogueira

She Can't Read the Bible or Go to Church

"For I know the plans I have for you," declares the Lord, "plans to prosper
you and not to harm you, plans to give you hope and a future."
Jer. 29:11, NIV.

COMING FROM THE INTERIOR of Brazil to study, the timid, observant, helpful 15-year-old was frightened when she arrived that Sunday morning. However, we noticed she liked children, and she began to adapt to her new surroundings.

One day her father, a very humble fisherman from the winding banks of the Amazon River, came to visit his daughter and get to know the family she was living with. As he verified our religious faith, he ordered, "My daughter can stay with you, but I do not want her to go to church with you, and I do not want you to teach her the Bible, understood?"

However, she heard the worship services and the religious music from a distance while she lived with us. After three years, my husband was transferred. Our affinity to that young woman was so great that we wanted to take her with us, and she wanted to go. Once her parents gave their permission, we were on our way to the metropolis of São Paulo. Our new home, near a Christian university and educational complex, afforded this young woman her first experience in a Christian school. She helped me with my two little girls, and since I wasn't home when they woke up, I asked her to tell the children a Bible story and sing hymns.

Two years later my husband was transferred again. The girl who had come to live with us was now a young woman who was totally involved in the Christian secondary school. She had wonderful friendships, and we felt that it would be unfair to make her leave that wholesome environment. Arrangements were made for her to stay as a boarding student on a work-study scholarship. God had great plans for her. Later we received a letter telling us, "I am going to be baptized!" Now she was of legal age; her father couldn't prohibit her decision, although he expressed his displeasure in a letter. After completing her studies, the girl who had been prohibited from reading the Bible married a Christian young man, and today they have a Christian home with two lovely children.

May God be praised for using our family as an instrument to carry out His plan of love in the life of that girl. He transformed her into a beautiful Christian woman. And He can transform us, too, if we will let Him.

Nair Costa Lessa

Just a Parking Space

And my God will meet all your needs according to his glorious riches in Christ Jesus.
Phil. 4:19, NIV.

I WAS TAKING ANA to her physical therapy appointment one Friday, and the traffic was heavy. Even though we started early, my watch told me that we barely had enough time to meet her appointment. But it didn't worry me, because I prayed that God would take us there on time. And He did!

I dropped Ana at the front entrance of the PT building then looked for a parking place. Parking in Baltimore around the Johns Hopkins area in the morning, when thousands of people come for physical therapy, radiation, or chemotherapy, is difficult. And that doesn't count all the employees, students, and others who work there! It was my first time in that place, and I really didn't know much about the parking garages. I asked a guard, who pointed to a parking garage about two blocks away.

Fine, I told myself, *I can just park there, and when Ana is done I can drive the car right to the front door and pick her up.* But my problem would be finding my way back to the building. There were so many one-way streets and I knew my weakness: directions!

As I slowly drove away from the building, I prayed, *Lord, would You mind giving me street parking not far from the physical therapy building? You know how bad I am with directions.* I smiled and continued, *Lord, would You spoil me today? Just with a parking place?*

What an amazing God we serve! Indeed, He is interested in all our needs and supplies them. Before I could even say amen, a car pulled out from a two-hour parking place close to the PT building. *Marvelous, Lord!* I smiled again and said, *Thank You, God. You're so awesome.*

Sometimes we go to God only when we have huge problems. We say to ourselves, *Should we bother God with the little cares in our lives?* Yet God isn't bothered with the little details such as a parking space. He is touched when we come to Him with the little things in our lives just as it makes us happy when our children come to us and tell us everything that happens in their lives. He loves us and wants us to trust Him not only in big stuff, but even in the little stuff in our lives. Yes, He even spoils us with a good parking space!

Jemima Dollosa Orillosa

God's Special Welcome

The Lord will keep you from all harm—he will watch over your life; the Lord
will watch over your coming and going both now and forevermore.
Ps. 121:7, 8, NIV.

MY HUSBAND AND I were invited to attend our granddaughter's wedding in Johannesburg, South Africa. Plans were made and the necessary arrangements completed. Flights were booked, accommodations were reserved. I was getting excited—I would meet family and friends again. I also eagerly anticipated seeing former neighbors who had once lived on either side of us. We'd had a good relationship when we lived next door to them 30 years before, and we hadn't seen them since.

The alarm system in our house had broken down the day before we were to leave. I knew the mechanic would never come out to our house in time to fix the alarm. And he didn't. We just had to commit the problem to our heavenly Father. We left our home Friday morning while it was still very dark. My husband "locked" the garage door, then I locked the gate. We did what we could to secure our home.

The wedding was beautiful, and we had a wonderful time visiting family, friends, and places. It was already dark when we got home the following Monday. As I unlocked the gate, the first thing I noticed was that the garage door was partly open, still with the lock on. What could have happened? We checked around, but everything seemed to be in order. We thought that the wind had been so strong that it had blown the garage door open.

We couldn't thank and praise the Lord and His holy angels enough for keeping our premises safe for the four days we were away, and also for keeping us safe from harm and danger on our trip.

The next morning, as I looked out my bedroom window, I saw a most beautiful sight. I called my husband to come and see. All 13 of our March lilies were in full bloom— prematurely. What a beautiful sight greeted us! God had prepared this special welcome for us. There had been no one to welcome us when we arrived home, but God was there, keeping things safe, and welcoming us. What a wonderful and awesome God we serve! He loves us and is faithful and true.

Priscilla Adonis

God Has a Plan for Us

I will instruct thee and teach thee in the way which thou shalt go: I will guide thee with mine eye. Ps. 32:8.

"YOU NEED TO TAKE THIS GIRL to the psychiatrist. She isn't normal. Children her age want to be a nurse one day, another day a teacher, the next a dentist or a lawyer; but not a missionary in foreign lands!" My grandmother didn't—wouldn't—accept the fact that we had left the church of our family, and with hard words she accused my mother of being responsible for a possible psychological imbalance in me. Attempting to "help" me, one day she gave me a keychain that displayed a little cannibal man with a bone in his hair. She made fun of my dreams and ideals.

In spite of her accusing words, her effort to change my plans, and her disapproval, I grew up with the desire to become a missionary. I read good books on the lives of missionaries that awakened in me the desire to imitate them. They were my heroes, and I resolved to pattern my life after theirs. With this objective in mind, I went to college to take theology. There, all the knowledge fascinated me, and I felt as though I was stepping on holy ground.

I never had the privilege of working in the mission field, but how many things I have learned where I have gone! Today I know that God always had a plan for my life, and I am pleased to see what a marvelous and audacious plan this is!

I've had the opportunity to work with children in an orphanage and to study the Bible with elementary and high school kids. I have given Bible studies in homes and directed Bible classes and public conferences. I have helped to create churches and establish recently formed churches. I have answered letters from radio and television program listeners. I have even worked in radio stations, led church departments, and worked in six different fields in Brazil. How many exciting things God has reserved for my life!

I am grateful to God that I listened to the desire of my heart; however, I am even more grateful that in His supreme knowledge He has placed me exactly where I would like to be. I don't know what His plans are for my life today, but whatever they are, I want to continue being thankful for His kindness in including me in His plans!

Sônia Maria Rigoli Santos

Engraved in Gold

This is the new covenant I will make with my people on that day, says the Lord:
I will put my laws in their hearts, and I will write them on their minds.
Heb. 10:16, NLT.

I HAVE MANY PRICELESS MEMORIES of extraordinary encounters with God. He engraved one of these in gold and sealed it within my heart and mind forever. I remember well the day in the early spring of 1969 when Ron and I toured the Idaho state mental institution near Boise with our school's church/state club. We were both seniors in high school, and we were also sweethearts and very much in love with each other. What an impact those scenes behind locked doors had upon our young minds. I remember lying in bed that night, talking with Jesus and praying. "Please, don't give me a child like one of those. I'd have to give the child away, for I couldn't handle the mental anguish or the disappointment." Heaven has proved me wrong, for God's glory.

In December 2010 Ron and I will celebrate our fortieth wedding anniversary. I didn't marry Mr. Perfect, nor did he marry Mrs. Right. We're still saints-in-training. We've been blessed with two wonderful children. Andrea and her husband are both warm, caring, and responsible adults. She is a music teacher, and Bill is a music librarian.

Our son Sonny will always require a one-on-one caregiver and the supervision one would give to a 3-year-old. Our man-child is kind and gentle in spirit and a fountain of joy to many. We are proud to be our children's parents. I have learned that psychomotor retardation and autism are a challenge, not a disgrace.

Heaven never lets me forget that we live in a war zone. Whenever life's ordeals become overwhelming, my mind revisits that mental institution. By the grace of God, there go I or someone I love. I hear Jesus whisper, "Don't give up! I am always with you." I believe Him, and we celebrate life together in the spirit of thanksgiving. My greatest joy is the prospect of heaven!

Thanks be to God who made us His captives and leads us along in Christ's triumphal procession (2 Cor. 2:14, 15, NLT). Now, wherever we go He uses us to tell others about the Lord and that He can always sustain. No matter what challenges we may meet. He has been with us. He will be with you too.

Deborah Sanders

Traffic Lights Versus the Father of Lights

When Jesus spoke again to the people, he said, "I am the light of the world.
Whoever follows me will never walk in darkness, but will have the light of life."
John 8:12, NIV.

WHY IS IT SO EASY for some of us to follow directions on the road, yet so trying on our human spirit to follow directions from God?

This question popped into my mind one day while I was driving. During my journey from work to home, I realized something quite obvious: people were stopping their car when the traffic lights were red, yielding when the lights were yellow, and going full speed ahead when the lights were green. Such a common observation led me to remember a Bible verse: "Every good and perfect gift is from above, coming down from the Father of the heavenly lights, who does not change like shifting shadows" (James 1:17, NIV).

Suddenly I realized that God doesn't change nor does He play favorites. He wants to safely guide each of us on our journey through this life. But He cannot do it as seamlessly as He'd like to if we're busy arguing with Him, ignoring Him, or faltering because of our sin-bent human condition and tendency to want to do things our own way.

Slowly, I began to pay more attention to how the other drivers behaved on the road. I watched as they waited for the green arrow signal to turn left. I became tense when I saw a car zoom by me and run through a light that was yellow but had turned bright red by the time they went through the intersection. I could almost sense the great anticipation of other drivers who figured when the traffic light was going to turn from red to green, seconds before the change. I smiled as I watched those drivers slowly release their brake pedals and inch ahead of the rest, mere moments before the green light, and then—*zoom!* They were gone.

We are all safer when we follow the traffic rules. *If only we followed our Father of lights with the same respect and obedience with which we follow traffic lights,* I thought. *Life would be a lot easier.*

Will you join me in following the rules, and will you pray with me?

Dear God, thank You for being the light of the world. Help us to follow Your direction and to accept Your will for our lives. In Jesus' name I pray, amen.

Alexis A. Goring

My New Stove

My Sabbaths ye shall keep: for it is a sign between me and you throughout your generations; that ye may know that I am the Lord that doth sanctify you. Ex. 31:13.

I USED THE SAME STOVE for 18 years. We had to screw and unscrew the fuse to get the right side of the stove to work. The oven door didn't close properly, so heat escaped when I baked. God was telling me it was time for an upgrade, as I kept getting mail about energy-saving tips.

My daughter and I went to a local department store to research the various models and prices. The next day my husband and I left a bit early for choir practice so we could check out stores on the way. I saw a flyer that had stoves on sale—with a $300 set of cookware as a bonus. A pretty good deal, as the price was the same as what I'd seen the day before, but without the bonus.

I purchased the new range, and two days later my husband picked it up. I waited with eager anticipation, as I'd not seen the bonus item yet. It felt like my birthday when I opened the box. I fell in love with the T-Fal cookware and other accessories.

I decided to break in my new stove and make lasagna for supper. I read the owner's manual and found out how to set the clock and use the timer, how to clean the oven, and a few other things. As I continued skimming through the book, I saw the words "Sabbath feature." I thought that I was seeing things. I began to laugh hysterically. Imagine—my new stove could be programmed for the Sabbath!

What about us? Are we programmed to toil and labor six days of the week and to rest on the Sabbath? Do we obey God's commands?

Some of us observe the first day of the week as God's holy day, others observe the seventh-day Sabbath, and there are those who don't even acknowledge that there is a God. In Exodus 20 the fourth commandment asks us to remember the Sabbath day to keep it holy. I don't know about you, but I am ecstatic when Friday comes because I know it is the end of my hectic work week. I look forward to the Sabbath rest, the worship, fellowship, and blessings that come with it. Come, rest in Him.

Sharon Long (Brown)

Glorify the Name of the Lord—Not Riches

But the rich, in that he is made low: because as the flower of the grass he shall pass away.
James 1:10.

I WAS BROUGHT UP in a rich family, enjoying all the comforts of life. My parents owned a big house, gold, jewels, property, bank accounts—the works. We knew about Christ, and our mother and grandma told us Bible stories and taught us the fear of God. But since we had all the comforts of life, we never bothered about anything. We had no strong hold on Christ.

A family of orthodox Hindus lived opposite our house. My mother and grandmother taught them about Jesus, and we took their two boys to Sunday school. They loved to attend and wanted to learn more about Jesus.

Then our family situation changed. We lost everything and were in desperate circumstances. We lost our house, jewels, property, and money. When our family moved to find work, our former neighbors also moved.

Our family situation went from bad to worse. Though we attended church we never had the opportunity to attend any big gathering or fellowship meeting or to share our testimony. Then we had an opportunity to attend an evangelical fellowship meeting. We learned to have strong faith in Jesus and to hold on to Him. But we still struggled for each meal every day. However, nothing is too hard for the Lord. Whenever we earnestly sought Him in prayer, we had a bag full of rice, wheat, oil, and all the necessary things. Like Elijah, God provided for us through His people, and we never went hungry.

One day we happened to meet one of our former neighbors, one of the Hindu young men. He said that he was not a Hindu anymore; he was a Christian pastor. He gave us Bible studies and answered all our questions. When he invited me to church, I accepted and went to Sabbath school with my parents. We stayed for a Daniel and Revelation seminar in the afternoon. It was very interesting, and we began to attend church regularly.

I surrendered my heart to the Lord, and I am now married to a Christian pastor. I am proud to say that the Lord picks up His jewels and makes them to stand as a witness for Him. I believe the mighty hand of our Lord does marvelous things when we submit our ways to Him.

Percy Florence Edwin Paul

I Shall Not Be Moved

And in my prosperity I said, I shall never be moved.
Ps. 30:6.

IF YOU DESIRE PROSPERITY, you have to be willing to do what it takes to achieve it. Yes, you can pray for prosperity, but the Lord is not going to just throw it in your lap. You have to do something. Perhaps go back to school to further your education to make more money on the job, or get a better job. Relocating to a different environment may be what you have to do. Making whatever changes are necessary is what is required.

Sad to say, but some people will sell their bodies to gain prosperity. Some people will sell drugs for wealth. But that's not a solution. What will it take for you? Will you sell your soul for financial prosperity? Is it worth all that? My Bible tells me: "For what shall it profit a man, if he shall gain the whole world, and lose his own soul?" (Mark 8:36). Philippians 1:19 says: "For I know that this shall turn to my salvation through your prayer, and the supply of the Spirit of Jesus Christ."

From what I have read, many of Jesus' followers were very prosperous, and He doesn't want us not to be. "Delight thyself also in the Lord: and he shall give thee the desires of thine heart" (Ps. 37:4).

In Matthew 6:31 we are told, "Therefore take no thought, saying, What shall we eat? or, What shall we drink? or, Wherewithal shall we be clothed?" So what should we make as our goal? The answer is found in Matthew 6:33: "But seek ye first the kingdom of God, and his righteousness; and all these things shall be added unto you." God will supply all your needs; just trust in His Word and believe. In wealth, or in little, we must pledge, "And in my prosperity I said, I shall never be moved."

Lord, there are times the struggle of life seems more than I can endure, the pain more that I can bear, and the cost of survival more than I can pay. In those times of weakness I choose to turn to You for strength, trusting that You will never fail or forsake me. In those weary times, help me never to forget the joy You have prepared for me in the end, as well as the promise of strength and power to overcome that I have now through You. I trust that our help is in the name of the Lord, who made heaven and earth and who has given us prosperity.

Hattie R. Logan

Behold Thy Mother

Then saith he to the disciple, Behold thy mother! And from
that hour that disciple took her unto his own home.
John 19:27.

MARY, CHOSEN OF GOD. The earthly mother of God's infant son had to understand the things of God, stand the ridicule of her town's people, and finally the death of her only Son.

We parents are very careful whom we choose as companions or caregivers for our children. God knew the dangers of this world into which He was sending His Son. He chose the most capable mother there was.

Imagine the fear, the burden, and the responsibility the visit from an angel must have placed in the heart of young Mary. When she shared it with Joseph, he thought she had been unfaithful. She faced social rejection and the loss of her beloved. She had accepted God's assignment but was losing her future.

As a young woman, Mary had to be strong and have an intimate relationship with God. He was sending His Son as an infant; the Creator of the whole world was coming here to be nursed by a human mother. Mary of Nazareth was chosen by God to diaper and bathe His Son. Mary was the one who rocked the Creator of this world to sleep, and the one who got up at night to satisfy the human needs of our infant God. Mary, chosen of God (Luke 1:30).

As the boy Jesus grew, life was especially tough for Him. The devil's attacks on Him were more intense than on any other human—ever. Mary had to be filled with patience and wisdom to deal with the children of Joseph as well as protect the Son of God. By homeschooling Jesus, Mary stood against the social structure of her time. She taught Him how to read and memorize the scriptures that He quoted throughout His ministry. She taught Him the things of God, not the traditions of man. Imagine the seriousness of being a human mother with the responsibility of teaching the Son of God about the God of heaven! Mary taught Jesus that He was the Son of God, and that He came to save the world from its sins. What she taught Him would determine the fate of the entire human race. What a blessed burden she carried!

Mary lived and died as does every human being. She isn't in heaven, answering our prayers or blessing us day by day, but she certainly was a saint. Mary, chosen by God.

Elizabeth Versteegh Odiyar

Having the Rug Pulled From Under You

So do not fear, for I am with you; do not be dismayed, for I am your God. I will strengthen you and help you; I will uphold you with my righteous right hand. Isa. 41:10, NIV.

I REMEMBER MY CHILDHOOD WITH JOY! Everything involved laughter and creativity in our childhood games. Rarely did we grasp the emotional or physical consequences these activities could inflict on other children. One prank, which I remember well, was pulling a chair or a rug from beneath someone at the exact moment they were about to sit down. The tumbles generally made the victim appear to be disjointed. Our little friend was usually caught off guard, or sometimes the victim would laugh with us to disguise their embarrassment in an attempt to discourage our enthusiasm.

What a risky game! Depending on the way the victim falls, serious injury can occur. Feelings of injustice and embarrassment can result, especially when these actions occur repeatedly, which is very common during this stage of childhood. As an adult, I have been surprised myself, and I have seen others caught off guard, when the rug was pulled out from underneath them. It is not by chance that we hear "I had the rug pulled from under my feet" when unexpected circumstances occur. When we don't get a job or when we are fired, when a child becomes seriously ill or is involved in a dangerous situation, when we are betrayed by others or people we love disappoint us and everything seems out of control, we ask, "Why me?"

Once again I had the rug pulled from beneath me, but this time I didn't fall. I realized that I was still on my feet. It was so amazing to be assured that I could remain on my feet! God's hand was beneath me, holding me up. Although I was above a profound abyss in my life, and, logically, I should have fallen, I wasn't frightened because He was there to support me and hold me in His faithful right hand.

Friend and sister in Jesus Christ, God invites us to be guided by His hand, even though we physically don't see it in our life. Prayer and faith need to be a part of our continuous walk. We must stop looking at our problems, thinking there is no solution. With God, step by step, we can slowly regain our balance and discover the marvelous assurance of continuing to be upheld by our Father's hands.

Ana Paula Costa Teixeira de Paiva

I Need a New Car

Delight thyself also in the Lord: and he shall give thee the desires of thine heart.
Ps. 37:4.

MY CAR WAS 16 YEARS OLD and creeping up on its last days. For many years I wondered if that would be the year God would bless me with a new car. December would roll around and my finances weren't to the place I could afford a car payment, and my vehicle was still running, so I figured that wasn't the year.

As my odometer crept over 266,000 miles and repair after repair became necessary, I knew that the year for that new car had finally come. However, knowledge of that fact didn't reveal a financial way to make the purchase happen.

My women's prayer group, my family, church family, and I prayed. I knew which car I wanted, and I even stepped out in faith and took a couple of test drives. I could actually picture it sitting in my garage.

The month that my car sat at the shop to be diagnosed with yet another problem, I was blessed with rides, and even the use of my family's vehicles. That arrangement couldn't go on forever: I needed a new car.

I inquired at work about when I might receive a raise. I've never been one to live beyond my means, and after being out of debt for more than eight years I knew the Lord didn't want me in debt again. So I trusted Him to provide when the answer never came from my job.

The day my father came over from Pennsylvania to go car shopping with me (I truly have an earthly father that emulates the love of our heavenly one), I still didn't see how I could afford a new car. After test driving my "dream" car again and knowing I couldn't afford it, the salesperson mentioned a promotion they were having on a model I hadn't even considered. It included a very affordable monthly payment. Praise the Lord! I didn't even think you could get a car payment that low anymore. Since the color I wanted was not in stock, the salesman allowed me to borrow his car overnight—my "dream" car, the one I pictured sitting in my garage. As I got home that night with the car tucked away in the garage, a big smile came to my face. There it was, sitting in my garage, just as I pictured it. What a wonderful God I serve—He gave me the desire of my heart, if only for one night. But He *had* answered my prayer!

Angèle Peterson

Dental Work—Prepaid

The people of Israel called the bread manna. It was white like coriander seed and tasted like wafers made with honey. Moses said, "This is what the Lord has commanded."
Ex. 16:31, 32, NIV.

RECENTLY MY HUSBAND AND I spent time away with our family, giving us the opportunity to enjoy the grandchildren. Prior to this trip I had started paying an extra electronic amount to our two travel credit cards just to make sure we'd have enough for the trip. When we planned this trip, we were aware that we needed some major dental work done but put it off until a later date—again. After all, we didn't want to go visiting with a sore mouth and pain pills and not be able to eat!

Our last visit to the dentist revealed that the dental work had to be done sooner, not later. I thought for sure there was time left to do it, but no, it needed doing yesterday. I checked with the credit cards and found that I'd been paying an extra amount for some time now, and the cost of the new dental work was not as pricey as I had expected. Did this mean we had extra funds left? It did. I said, "Thank You, Lord; You have always made a way for us in any predicament in which we find ourselves."

This reminds me of the children of Israel and the manna. The Lord knew their needs. They were not to stockpile manna ahead of time as it would spoil. God allowed the manna to come in double supply every sixth day so that they would have it for the Sabbath. And that supply did not spoil.

The Lord allowed those funds in our travel account to go unnoticed until the time we needed them. "But even the very hairs of your head are all numbered. Fear not therefore: ye are of more value than many sparrows" (Luke 12:7). *God, help us to always put our complete trust in You that You will provide for us on time, every time, at the appointed time. Amen.*

Have you ever worried and thought that God couldn't hear or take care of your needs? If, as Scripture tells us, God numbers the hairs on our heads and takes care of the sparrows and the lilies of the field, don't you think He can—and will—take care of our teeth if we ask Him? I can assure you that He does. I have experienced it.

Betty G. Perry

Magnetic Hill

The Lord hath appeared of old unto me, saying, Yea, I have loved thee with an everlasting love: therefore with lovingkindness have I drawn thee. Jer. 31:3.

I HEARD ABOUT A SPECIAL HILL with magnetic powers in Moncton, New Brunswick. It seemed unbelievable to me that a car could be drawn up a hill through the magnetic forces of the earth only. I had to try that out. So I drove to this hill with my rental car. I followed the instructions and drove down the hill to the spot marked with a white pole and put the car into neutral. When I took my foot away from the brake, the car began to move backward up the hill. Moving slowly at first, the car gained momentum as it was drawn by the magnetic powers of the earth. After a while the car slowed down and stopped—but even there, on the hill sloping down, the car stood still without rolling back, even though I didn't have my foot on the brake. That was incredible! I tried it out several times, and each time it worked just as well.

The magnetic powers of nature have always been there. Stories about a strange road on which the wagon would run up on the horses' heels when going uphill go back to the 1880s. In 1933 stories of cars rolling uphill without power piqued the curiosity of newspaper reporters from the Saint John *Telegraph Journal*. They traveled to Moncton and spent hours trying every hill they came to in hopes of unraveling the mystery. After five hours with no success they stopped to stretch their legs on the way home and, you guessed it, the car started to roll uphill. Slowly at first, and then with gathering momentum, the car climbed uphill without power. They spent a couple hours retrying the hill, using all the equipment they had brought to discover the secret. Was it just an optical illusion? They couldn't solve the mystery.

God has always loved us. He has drawn us toward Him because He loves us. God's love draws us like this magnetic power in the hill in Moncton. If we take our foot off the brake and put ourselves in neutral—give up our resistance and give our lives to God—the power of God's love will draw us toward him. It will hold us fast even on the downward slope of life.

It seems unbelievable, but it's true. Even if the powers of the magnetic hill might be an illusion, God's love is not. Will you submit yourself to the power of God's love today and let Him draw you into His everlasting arms where we can be sure that He will never let us fall?

Hannele Ottschofski

My Dream

I have heard the murmurings of the children of Israel: speak unto them,
saying, At even ye shall eat flesh, and in the morning ye shall be filled
with bread; and ye shall know that I am the Lord your God.
Ex. 16:12.

GOD BLESSED MY PARENTS with five children. I'm the fourth, and I was born on the Mvog-Betsi leprosarium campus where Dad had been working as a young nurse. I did almost everything with leprosy sufferers' children: church, school, games, and food. This experience impressed me. I identified with those children and with their poor and sick parents. I dreamed of helping and assisting these parents and many others, particularly those affected with painful illnesses such as leprosy.

A few years later we moved because of my father's work. But this also meant that we needed more money, which we didn't have. As a consequence, Mom had to work to help supply the additional financial resources necessary to keep us children going to school.

I became discouraged and seriously worried about life's toughness, but a powerful inner force kept me on track, motivating me and pushing me toward scholarly success while protecting me from adolescent troubles. I was a little like the children of Israel—murmuring and worrying.

I stayed very close to my father as he worked at the health center. This reminded me of our time at the leprosarium campus. Seeing Dad always busy, treating and taking care of people, gave me the motivation to become a doctor. Financial resources were few. Could my dream come true?

I always kept my faith in God. I knew He could do outstanding things for me if I were faithful to Him. I continued studying and working hard. My older brother, younger sister, and I all received our general certificate exams, advanced level. How could we all go on for higher education? Then one day a classmate handed me a letter from the superintendent. God had answered my prayers! I had received a scholarship from the sale of the women's devotional books. My dream had a real chance of coming true.

I will sing and praise the Lord my entire life. I'm currently in the second year of graduate nurse training, and I'm confident God will keep on assisting me, thanks to all those who have helped make this possible!

Julienne Lumière Ngo Massock

Adoption

He chose us . . . before the foundation of the world . . . having predestined us to the adoption as sons by Jesus Christ to Himself, according to the good pleasure of His will. Eph. 1:4, 5, NKJV.

MANY COUPLES WHO DO NOT HAVE CHILDREN of their own go through the process of adoption. In some countries adopting may be simple, but in others it can be complicated. Besides difficulties encountered at immigration, it can also cost an enormous amount of money. I knew a couple who had been told by the medical doctor, after they had gone through all types of examinations, that they wouldn't be able to have their own babies. They then decided that they would adopt a child. I knew a mother who had four children whose husband had died in an accident. She had no resources to take care of them all, or the fifth child she was expecting. She told me that she was willing to relinquish her baby to a Christian family. The adopting couple was very excited to know that there was a newborn baby whom they could adopt. They began to study the protocols for adopting the baby, but the long waiting list made it impossible for them to adopt that specific baby.

There was an interesting case at my work. An 18-month-old girl had been rejected for adoption by a young couple for cultural reasons. The first family, who wanted to have a baby girl, saw this baby and fell in love with her, in spite of the fact that the baby was a failure-to-thrive case. She had a tracheotomy, a gastro tube, and a diagnosis of vocal cord paralysis. This family took the risk of adopting her anyway. The grandfather, grandmother, parents, two brothers, nephews, and nieces all went to the court to witness the official adoption pronounced by the judge.

It was an awesome day for the new family! The child's name was changed to their own family name. A few weeks later they invited the community to a big party to celebrate the adoption with them. Many friends and relatives rejoiced with them.

We can all be adopted. The most powerful and rich King of the universe, the most loving and kind heavenly Father, wishes to embrace us with His loving arms, surround us with all the protection we could ask for, provide us with all we need, and shelter us with all the comforts in life. May we choose to be adopted into His family.

Esperanza Aquino Mopera

Make a Wise Choice

And if it seems evil unto you to serve the Lord, choose you this day whom ye will serve; whether the gods which your fathers served that were on the other side of the flood, or the gods of the Amorites, in whose land ye dwell: but as for me and my house, we will serve the Lord. Joshua 24:15.

OUR WHOLE LIFE IS FILLED with experiences in which we have to decide one way or the other—to make choices. Using the fruit of the Spirit, I choose love, joy, peace, patience, kindness, goodness, faithfulness, gentleness, and self-control.

It seemed when I was growing up that I was made to do things. Being a missionary kid, there were a lot of rules. How I dressed, ate, and what I said were important. I think that most of those things were good things to have in my life, but there was a much more important thing that I needed—a relationship with God. Worship was part of that. Going to church and Sabbath school and worship in the dorm I had to do. But most important was the time that I learned to spend with Jesus every day. Now, they may have made me go to worship, but I chose to spend time with my Friend and Savior. That is what made the difference.

Rules seemed to be things that made my life difficult and took away fun. But I began to see that every rule was giving me freedom to have a full and safe life. God's rules are that way. Human-made rules are sometimes silly and can make you unhappy.

When my girls were little, I would tell them to make their bed, and they did what I asked. That was the way with a lot of things. But as they got older, I noticed that when I asked, or told, them to do something, more and more often they had to decide what they were going to do, using their mind that God had given them to be wise and listen, then do what they knew was correct. I have also realized that I have to listen more and say as little as possible. Then when I'm alone, I pray and pray. I must trust in the Lord that they will listen to the best Friend that they will ever have.

God reminds me every day that we started on this journey together, and He and I will make it to heaven with my family. I want to live so that they too will make a wise choice and choose Jesus.

Susen Mattison Molé

Savannah's Sabbath Shoes

Before they call I will answer; and while they are still speaking I will hear.
Isa. 65:24, NIV.

HOW WONDERFUL TO SERVE a God who is interested in the small things in our lives as well as the big things. He sees the sparrow when it falls and knows how many hairs we have on our heads. How much He cares when we have a small crisis in our lives.

Our 4-year-old granddaughter often comes to our home to spend the weekend. One weekend when our daughter and Savannah arrived and we unpacked the car, I began checking off the things Savannah would need for Sabbath. As I went through the list, I realized her Sabbath shoes were missing. It was already sundown, and I was at a loss as to what to do. I didn't want to have to buy something on Sabbath.

"Oh, Savannah, what are you going to do for shoes for church?" I asked. She had no idea.

I lifted up my frustrations to the Lord, and it was then that He kindly reminded me of a pair of shoes that I had put away in my closet months before. When I had bought them they had been much too large for Savannah, so I'd put them up and had forgotten about them. Now, in this time of crisis, I took them down. When I put them on her feet, they fit, and Savannah was delighted with a new pair of shoes. They also matched her Sabbath dress perfectly! She didn't realize the dilemma in which I'd found myself or the miracle that was just bestowed upon me.

The next day at church Savannah showed off her new Sabbath shoes, and I was able to share the way in which the Lord had provided, even months before I had a need. He knew, and He had prepared to help me before I even asked. I was able to share today's text, as well as 1 Peter 5:7. Peter tells us to let our anxieties fall on Him because He cares for us. Don't you wonder, then, why we become so anxious and frustrated at times? God has so many gifts ready to give to His children. He plans ahead for our emergencies and answers our prayers in such wonderful ways!

Thank You, God, for showing Your love to me and helping me when I'm not able to help myself. Thank You for miracles, both big and small, that You do just for me. You make me, Your daughter, feel truly special.

Sharon Follett

Why Not Me? Sniff! Sniff!

Delight yourself in the Lord and he will give you the desires of your heart. . . . Be still before the Lord and wait patiently for him. Ps. 37:4-7, NIV.

AFTER LOSING TWO HUSBANDS TO CANCER, I moved from my native state of California to Virginia to be nearer my eldest son and his wife.

I settled in, bought a house, found the local Adventist church, and made some friends. I also volunteered one day a week at my son's nursing home and frequented several local restaurants at lunchtime (I don't like to cook for just me).

I found the local hospital and a number of doctors. Because of slowly declining health, I've been in the hospital quite a few times. I seem to keep a number of doctors busy. I'm very grateful for all that help and for the fact that my son has been available when I needed him.

But I missed California—my church, relatives, and friends. It got so that every time I saw a moving truck I'd say to myself, *Why can't that be me?*

I dwelt on Psalm 37:4: "Delight yourself in the Lord and he will give you the desires of your heart" (NIV). *What am I doing wrong, Daddy?* I would ask. There was no answer.

Finally, I read on down to verse 7: "Be still before the Lord and wait patiently for him." H'mmm. "Be still before the Lord." Those five words hit me in a different way than they would someone else. Oh, I still wanted to move back to California, but I knew I could not. (I do fly out once in a while for a good visit.)

"Be still before the Lord." I felt He wanted me to stop moaning, groaning, and whining! He was probably weary of my *Why not me?*

Now when I see a moving truck, whether big or small, I say, "Lord, bless them as they move." I also appreciate more the text in Philippians 4:12: "I know what it is to be in need, and I know what it is to have plenty. I have learned the secret of being content in any and every situation, whether well fed or hungry, whether living in plenty or in want" (NIV).

Thank You, Daddy, for helping me to change my attitude and learning to be "content in any and every situation."

Patsy Murdoch Meeker

The God of the Impossible!

O taste and see that the Lord is good: blessed is the man that trusteth in him.
Ps. 34:8.

I WANT TO SHARE A MIRACLE that God worked for me on October 25, 2007. My boss, Mike Ryan, asked me to bring him his travel folder for Brazil since he was flying out that evening at 9:30. But as I walked to my office to get the folder, I suddenly realized that I hadn't gotten the necessary visa for Brazil. I panicked! I immediately called our visa office to see what could be done. They informed me that it is very difficult to get a Brazilian visa on such short notice. They told me that the only slim chance there might be was to have Mike go to the Brazilian embassy and personally appeal to them. And even that wasn't guaranteed!

Mike went to the Brazilian embassy about 10:30 that morning. While waiting to be called to the counter, he saw three people wanting visas turned down—the embassy said it would take four days to get the visa. When he was finally called, he went to the counter, gave them his application, and informed the agent that he urgently needed a visa to leave that very night. The agent immediately shook his head and gave back his application, saying that it was impossible to get a visa so quickly. In the meantime I was constantly praying for God to intervene and had asked others in the office to pray regarding this urgent matter.

Suddenly Mike thought of something and told them that he had a five-year visa for Brazil in his old passport. He phoned and asked me to check the expiration date. To my dismay, I saw that it had expired on April 18, 2007! My heart sank in despair! When Mike told the embassy officer that it had recently expired, the man said they couldn't do anything for him.

God, however, impressed Mike not to give up. He told the man at the counter that he had numerous speaking appointments in Brazil that weekend, and that he had to leave that night. The man gave Mike a puzzled look, then took his application and went inside to check with someone else. He came out after five minutes and said to Mike, "Don't do this to us again, but we are giving you a visa this time!" When Mike phoned to tell me this good news, I praised and thanked God for this wonderful miracle. Our God is great—nothing is too hard for Him! We just need to trust in Him!

Stella Thomas

I Knew Thee

Before I formed thee in the belly I knew thee; and before thou camest forth out of the womb I sanctified thee, and I ordained thee a prophet unto the nations. Jer. 1:5.

JEREMIAH WAS ACCUSED of political treason. He was tried, persecuted, and imprisoned for the words he had spoken. What was God thinking before He formed Jeremiah in his mother's womb? What was God thinking before He formed *me* in my mother's womb? These questions haunted me for many years until I came to the beautiful realization that it was not about me. Never has been. It's all about bringing glory to His name.

I'm a survivor of childhood sexual, mental, physical, and social abuse from the tender age of 6. For many years I couldn't understand how God could allow this to happen to me. I'd been taught that Jesus loves me, but where was that love? Now I know that in all these misfortunes God truly had His powerful hand on my life. For 23 years I lived in a foggy state of mind, influenced by heroin, cocaine, alcohol, and whatever else I could find.

Revelation 7:13 says, "And one of the elders answered, saying unto me, What are these which are arrayed in white robes? and whence came they?" I like to imagine that some of these folks were those whom Christ delivered from the awful pain of the abuses that Satan attacks us with. When I think about the ways God has worked His will in my life to teach, guide, love, talk, listen, warn, feed, clothe, and visit His children, I can see little pieces of the spiritual puzzle coming together. It strengthens me every time God uses me to touch a life.

I often think of Paul's statement to the Corinthians that he would most gladly glory in his infirmities that the power of Christ might rest upon him (2 Cor. 4:17). Therefore he took pleasure in infirmities, in reproaches, in necessities, in persecutions—for Christ (2 Cor. 12:10).

No, I don't claim to have all of the answers; but one thing I do know is that whatever God was thinking before He formed me in my mother's womb, His thoughts toward me were thoughts of blessings and goodness. For His thoughts are not our thoughts, neither His ways our ways, but He did promise in Isaiah 61:7: "For your shame ye shall have double; and for confusion they shall rejoice in their portion: therefore in their land they shall possess the double: everlasting joy shall be unto them." And God alone shall receive the glory.

Cereatha J. Vaughn

Shhh! Listen!

The heavens declare the glory of God; and the firmament sheweth his handywork.
Day unto day uttereth speech, and night unto night sheweth knowledge.
Ps. 19:1, 2.

IT WAS FRIDAY EVENING AT SUNSET. From our cruise ship's west balcony we could see the unusually peaceful Atlantic Ocean, and beyond it the never-ending line of the horizon. Then we noticed it. Above the gently rolling sea, near the blush of the setting sun, a cloud formation looked like the outspread wings of a dove. Its feet appeared to be tucked under in flight, and its head was turned downward as if descending. It seemed to be a benediction on the Sabbath, a blessing on our worship of the Creator. My husband rushed to capture the moment on film, but I couldn't move, afraid that the dove would disappear. Even as we sang songs to welcome the Sabbath, my eyes were riveted on the red blush of the setting sun and the still-hovering, cloud-formed dove.

"The heavens declare the glory of God," a God who seemed to have put on a glorious aerial display for two of His children in the middle of the Atlantic. Although we were on a ship with thousands of other passengers, I wondered if anyone else witnessed what we had seen. "The heavens declare," as the psalmist notes, but if we hadn't looked and listened at that moment, we would have missed a spectacular revelation of God's glory.

I think about the heavenly wonders we miss every day as we rush out of the house with barely a prayer. We fight traffic, contend with the normal stresses at work, then return home to pay bills and prepare dinner, all the things that keep our eyes downward. We may see only the potholes in the streets, the car that needs washing, or stuffed laundry bins crying for attention.

Even the beauty around us can't compare. A hilltop mansion with gleaming hardwood floors has its charms, and the new custom kitchen with sparkling ceramic tiles has its allure. But compared to the glory revealed in God's quiet heavens, how insignificant they appear!

So I invite you to take a moment. Maybe go outside if you can. The heavens are speaking—often with thunder and lightning, sometimes with silvery moonlight, sometimes with twinkling stars. If you look up, if you pay attention, you may both hear and see God's glory. You will never be the same again.

Annette Walwyn Michael

My Grandsons' Powerful Prayers

Train up a child in the way he should go: and when he is old, he will not depart from it.
Prov. 22:6.

MY FAMILY AND I were sitting at our friend's wedding reception when my husband said that he was considering leaving Orlando the same time as our daughter, Ngozi, instead of the next morning. So all of us rushed upstairs to our hotel room and quickly packed. Chioma, our second daughter, and her son, 4-year-old Nikolas, would stay till the next day (his reward for being the Bible-bearer in the wedding). When we were all set to go, we gathered in a circle to pray. Nikolas asked his Mom if he could pray. She said yes, and he began: "Dear Jesus, thank You for my grandma and my grandpa. Please help them not to get a [speeding] ticket. Bless the people who go to Chicago [he lives in Chicago], bless the people who go to Atlanta, bless the people who didn't go anywhere, and bless the people who stayed home. Bless my toys and—"

In my eagerness to get on the road, I blurted out, "Nikolas, cut it short! We've got to get going!" And Nikolas' prayer ended abruptly. I've often thought of my words and the impression they made on his little mind.

Everything went well until it got dark and the holiday traffic increased. We had difficulty keeping up with Ngozi and her husband, Tim. There were accidents on the way and police activity slowing things down. We finally reached Roswell, Georgia, safely after a long and stressful seven-hour journey (thanks, I believe, to Nikolas' prayer).

After a good night's rest and breakfast, we again formed a circle for prayer. Timothy, Ngozi's 4-year-old, asked his mom if he could pray a "powerful" prayer. She said yes, and he closed his eyes: "Dear Jesus, thank You for Grandma and Grandpa. Please give them traveling mercies so they can get home all right. Thank You for my mom and my dad. Bless everybody. Amen." Then he looked up and asked, "Mom, was that a powerful prayer?"

"Yes, son, that was a powerful prayer," she said.

As we traveled home to Huntsville, Alabama, a flood of joy filled me as I thought of God's precious gift of our two wonderful grandsons. Are we modeling and teaching powerful prayers? May that be our aim on this and every day.

Shirley C. Iheanacho

Why God Allows Troubles

Though I walk in the midst of trouble, You will revive me; You will stretch out Your hand . . . and Your right hand will save me.
Ps. 138:7, NKJV.

WHY DOES GOD ALLOW His children to have troubles? Well, there are many reasons, but they can best be summed up in one word: benefits. He sees the benefits. Tests and trials strengthen and shape our character. They make us better people and better Christians. I have faced many trials and troubles. I had an external growth on my head operated on and was then healthy until I was severely affected by chikungunya (aka chicken guinea fever), a very dangerous disease. I suffered a lot with joint pains and was unable to walk and couldn't eat. When I attended the funerals of my four relatives who died from chikungunya, I was troubled and scared. After four months of no relief for my joint pains, I visited another doctor, who said that there is no specific medicine for this disease and advised me to take certain medicines and painkilling tablets.

Then I suffered many side effects, such as severe headache, ear pain, stomach pain, giddiness, and nausea. Because of the physical instability of my health, I was unable to attend to my regular office work, and I felt that this disease would bring an end to my life.

One night I was alone in my house. My mind was troubled, and I wasn't able to sleep. I got up from my bed and knelt down and prayed to God with tears to give me peace of mind. The next morning my daughter took me to a woman village doctor who gave me four tablets and one injection. Within two days I was able to walk and do my work. I had suffered for six months and spent a lot of money and time visiting hospitals. But the night that I prayed, God answered my prayers and miraculously led me to the village doctor. It is my Lord who helped me in times of trials and trouble. I have committed myself to serve Him.

When we realize His greatness and love, we learn to depend on Jesus. He is always there to help His children on the mountaintop—and the deep valleys, too. Unfortunately, when everything goes right, we don't feel a pressing need for God and His help and strength in our lives.

We should not run from troubles when they loom ahead. We should ask God to lift us above them on the wings of prayer.

Vinodhini John

Hurry Up and Slow Down!

Now therefore stand still, that I may reason with you before the Lord of all the righteous acts of the Lord, which he did to you and to your fathers. 1 Sam. 12:7.

IT WAS AN AVERAGE RUNAROUND DAY. I can't even remember all that we were doing, but I do remember the fast pace and overwhelming to-do list I had made. As I was issuing commands and rushing my kids into action, my daughter Barbara said, "Mom, hurry up and slow down!" Her comment stopped me in my tracks. She was right. I sat down for a moment to rest from the hurry and thought about how I wasn't only impacting my life, but I was teaching my children. It's been said that actions speak louder than words. How does that apply when action is amplified many times over?

Keeping up with kids, housework, a job, and all the other responsibilities of life can get me running in circles. The usual root causes are a schedule packed full of things to do, not planning ahead, not keeping track of time, and unreasonable expectations of myself and others. The kicker is that I allow hurry to take over.

In his book *My Utmost for His Highest* Oswald Chambers writes: "God is never in a hurry" (April 4). I look back at my life and think how God has taken His time with me. In every instance His timing was perfect. Even though I rush to and fro, He tries to tell me to "be still and know that I am God." And if I'm too busy to connect with that thought, He sends the message through my child, not to tell me what to do or to nag, but just simply because He cares about me and my family.

Since Barbara made her comment I have committed to God and my family to curb some of my activities and adjust my expectations. It's amazing how the Lord blesses us when we listen to Him. Our Father does know best. Now I have some time to breathe and to think. In the future I am sure He will have to reel me in again, but I'm so thankful He does not give up on us!

Lord, thank You for the individualized messages You send us. Please continue to work in my life and in others' who are addicted to hurry. Lord, I do want You to be in charge of my life. I do realize how busy I get and how that pulls me from You and my family. Keep on me, Lord!

Mary M. J. Wagoner-Angelin

The Giant

Listen, people of Israel! Today you are about to cross the Jordan River. . . . The people themselves are tall and strong. . . . But now you will see for yourselves that the Lord your God will go ahead of you. . . . He will defeat them as you advance . . . as he promised. Deut. 9:1-3, TEV.

I HAD JUST COMPLETED my final exams for nursing school and was looking forward to my holidays with my aunt and her family in the United States. I needed a visa and had requested a letter from my school a year before. Now I had finally received my papers.

It wasn't until I got home that I decided to check all my documents, preparing for my visit to the embassy the following day. I discovered that the letter from the school and my father's bank statement were outdated—in fact, a year old! Even so, I was determined to take them with me. My mom encouraged me to ask my dad to go with me, but I wanted to do this alone, with God. However, I felt impressed that I should listen to my mom (they often know best), so I did ask my dad, but he didn't respond.

When I awoke in the morning, I had my devotions and prepared myself to leave, packing my breakfast and making sure I was properly attired, and left early to avoid traffic. I arrived safely and early, yet there was a queue. However, I had an appointment.

Whenever names were called and seats became available, we'd move up closer. I prayed continuously until my name was called, checking my documents again and again. Then I heard "Susan Riley!" An adrenaline rush came upon me as I proceeded to the window and presented my documents to the officer. She scanned them well, then informed me that I was not eligible to travel. I responded with every argument I could think of as to why I should get my visa. I thought, *"No weapon formed against me shall prosper"* (see Isa. 54:17). She paused and then said, "We do not usually do this." As she was saying this, I thought, *Lady, you have nothing to do with this; this is my God.* I would receive my visa and passport in the mail, she said.

When we can't see the logic or way, for we are blocked by the giants, remember that God is bigger. He's able, so advance.

Susan Riley

Call Unto Me—I Will Answer

*Call unto me, and I will answer thee, and show thee
great and mighty things, which thou knowest not.
Jer. 33:3.*

I HAD AMPLE OPPORTUNITY to learn and also to teach Bible classes in schools. Teaching Bible changed my life completely. Our family was filled with rich spiritual experiences; we grew strong in faith, and the love of Christ filled our family. In spite of that, trials came to us. First, I underwent open-heart surgery. Everyone prayed earnestly for the healing touch. I had great faith and trust in Christ Jesus, who I prayed would help me to have a complete recovery. With prayer I went into the operating room. My God was with me, and I came out successfully. I thank Him every moment of my life for His saving grace.

Next, God saved my husband from a terrible accident and spared his life to continue in ministry. This is how the accident happened. My husband and Pastor Isaac had been conducting meetings and counseling young men and women all day, and drove back home the same evening. On their way they parked the car and bought some fruit from a roadside vendor. My husband found some nice ripe fruit and bent down to pick the best ones. Just then a tractor came crashing in. The driver had been unable to control the vehicle and hit my husband. He was knocked flat on the ground.

Pastor Isaac shouted, "He is under the wheel!" as people crowded around him. My husband says that within a fraction of a second an unseen hand pulled him out from under that tractor and placed him in a secure place. He says that it was God who sent His guardian angel to protect him from the fearful accident.

The bystanders saw him emerge without a scar or scratch and were amazed. They said, "God spared your life for some better purpose." The God who keeps Israel shall neither slumber nor sleep. It was a great miracle that God performed! I thank God for His guidance and help then, too.

I thank the Lord for the wonderful way that He has led me. I am sure my Father in heaven has a special purpose for my life, too. He has given me opportunities to serve Him in His vineyard, and I want to be faithful.

Kalaiselvi Jebamony

God Still Cares About the Ark

Then God remembered Noah, and every living thing,
and all the animals that were with him in the ark.
Gen. 8:1, NKJV.

AS A TEACHER I always strive to make each assignment fun and creative, as well as a learning experience, so I am constantly looking for new ideas. When we were studying about Noah's ark in Bible class, I found a neat art project that could carry the lesson over into art class. Excited, but not sure how it would turn out, I decided to try it first at home.

The first step was to draw a picture of Noah's ark. Only wax crayons could be used, because the second step required a sugar solution to be painted over the whole picture. The directions said that the wax crayons would resist the solution, not allowing it to soak into the picture, leaving the sugar solution to dry in large droplets, giving the picture the appearance of rain. After trying the project at home, I could hardly wait for my students to create their own pictures. I was sure they would enjoy the project.

The next day, after the students had created their drawings of Noah's ark, I opened the jar of the sugar solution to begin painting it over their pictures. It was then that I noticed that a few ants had found their way into my jar of solution. The realization then hit me that the *ants* were going to love this art project! Images of the art projects being carried away by ants filled my mind. Ants were a part of everyday life on our tropical island and could not be avoided. I really began to pray as I painted the sugar solution over the pictures.

I had no place to put the picture that ants couldn't find them, so I asked God to take care of the art projects and left them lying in the classroom. I knew that God had taken care of the ark when Noah was in it with all the animals, so I prayed that He would take care of these modern-day arks.

When I returned to my classroom after the weekend, I found the pictures right where I had left them, and not an ant in sight! God had truly watched over all the pictures just as He had watched over Noah in the real ark. It was a good reminder to me that God cares about even our tiniest cares and concerns and wants us to take every matter to Him, no matter how big or small.

Mai-Rhea Odiyar

A Merciful Father

*After the people saw the miraculous sign that Jesus did, they began
to say, "Surely this is the Prophet who is to come into the world."
John 6:14, NIV.*

WE WERE LIVING IN SOUTH KERALA, INDIA, where my husband was the
president of the church in that section, and I was the director for
women's and children's ministries.

Pandarathara church, in a village by the same name, is one
of many churches in Neyyattinkatra Taluk, and this church is
an old one, but it has a large group of people attending, including many children and youth. They have three classes for
the children, and many nonchurch children also attend the
Sabbath school.

This church has a very strong women's ministries program. Once a month they
have a fasting and prayer program. The other three Sabbath days the women go out
to do gospel work.

I would like to tell you about a miracle that happened here in this church. One
family with their two sons used to come to church every Sabbath. They were
Hindus, but they believed in God. Suddenly their 10-year-old boy became sick, so
sick that he lost his eyesight. His parents were, of course, upset. They took the child
to the hospital nearby, where they were advised to take their child to the ear, nose,
and throat section of the medical college. They took him there, and treatment was
started. The medical personnel all advised the parents that the boy needed an operation, but his parents weren't ready to do that. They were poor coolie workers and
didn't have enough money. In their crisis they thought of the women's ministries
prayer group in the church they'd been attending. They told everything to the pastor and his wife. The pastor and his wife asked them to bring the child for prayer,
and at the same time they told them to continue medical care as well.

The child was depressed. He stopped his studies, of course, because he couldn't
see anything. The women of the Pandarathara church prayed and prayed, with
tears, for this poor boy. At last God heard their prayer and answered affirmatively.
The boy's eyesight returned. His parents were baptized and joined the church. The
boy is now in high school, and this family is witnessing for our loving God in this
village. Miracles do still happen! God is a merciful Father.

Sosamma Varghese

Our Home

I will bless the Lord at all times; his praise shall continually be in my mouth.
Ps. 34:1.

WE OWNED A SMALL PIECE OF LAND, so after our retirement we pooled all our savings and began to build a small house with a little gardening space. We had many sleepless nights and offered many prayers because of finances, and sometimes for the want of good, faithful builders. At last, after two years of struggle, our dream house was ready, and we moved in. It was away from the city noise, dust, and pollution. We began living a simple village life with just a few basic needs. It was peaceful and calm, and we enjoyed it.

We began to collect flower and fruit seeds and plants. We spent hours in the garden, cleaning, weeding, watering, and enjoying the beauty of it. The thought always kept coming to mind of the Garden of Eden. When God created this earth, everything was beautiful. There was no flaw in it. God spoke, and it was done—no thorns, no weeds, and no thistles.

Someone gave us a few fruit seeds which would grow into big trees. My husband spaded up the soil, put manure on it, and put out the seed to germinate—and forgot completely about it. After almost a year a seed sprouted. One day as I was cleaning the garden I could see small leaves peeping out. I didn't know what plant it was and told my husband. He looked at it and said that it was a lychee fruit tree.

I wondered at the patience with which God works with each sinner to repent and to turn to Him. Forty long years God worked with Moses to teach him the patience to work with the children of Israel, and he became a great leader. This same God watches over us day and night, waiting for our spiritual growth. He guides and corrects us, but only if we trust in Him.

It was wonderful to work with the soil. There was one more flower that took almost seven or eight months to come to bud. We were eager to see it bloom, and when it did, it was a lily of beautiful maroon color. We admired the beauty: it had five petals, and bloomed for only a day. By evening it had closed its petals. The glory was just for a day! If God can take so much care of a little flower that is going to last just for a day, how much He must have loved us to make us, who are mortals, in His own image!

Winifred Devaraj

Sing Your Song

Talk with each other much about the Lord, quoting psalms and hymns
and singing sacred songs, making music in your hearts to the Lord. Always
give thanks for everything . . . in the name of our Lord Jesus Christ.
Eph. 5:19, 20, TLB.

I ENJOY ALMOST ANY TYPE OF MUSIC played on almost any kind of instrument. I realize that precious promises are found in the words of many of the old gospel songs and hymns that bring me joy, gladness, comfort, and calmness when distressed. They give me assurance that my sins are forgiven. When I think about who God is and whose I am, I remember that Jesus loves me.

I look at God's creation in the gorgeous flowers, the lofty trees, the stately mountains, the cloud formations, and when I hear the birds singing or the waves of the oceans. I know this is my Father's world and that He made all things bright and beautiful. It's no wonder that the songwriter penned "How Great Thou Art." When storms in my life rage, I hear God saying to me, "Peace! peace! wonderful peace." When my faith grows weak, I can sing "O for a faith that will not shrink, though pressed by many a foe."

No one understands like Jesus, because He is the best friend we could ever have. His love is greater far than tongue or pen could ever tell. So when you feel blue or doubt that your sins are forgiven, when you feel alone and sad over the loss of a loved one, just hum a few lines of your favorite hymns or gospel songs, and I guarantee that you will feel safe in the arms of Jesus. He will never leave you alone, and there'll be sunshine in your soul.

Because God has been so good to me I thank Him for the mountains He's brought me over, for the trials He's seen me through, for every blessing, and I give Him praise. Reflecting that someday all our trials will be over and all earthly cares be known no more, I keep my hope in the coming of our Lord. I rest, knowing that in that land of fadeless day I will never grow old. I will sit side by side with my friends at the welcome table. I will join with the angelic choir singing, "The Lord of hosts is the King of glory, and He will reign forever and ever." When we all get to heaven, what a day of rejoicing that will be as we behold Him face to face. I pray that we all will be there.

Marie H. Seard

A Fire in My Bones

He will baptize you with the Holy Spirit and fire.
Matt. 3:11, NKJV.

I OFTEN CHUCKLE at God's sense of humor whenever I tell the story of how He led me into Pathfinder youth ministries. My children's father had been exposed to Pathfinders (a church equivalent of Boy/Girl Scouts), but I had never heard of it until he registered our daughter in our church's club. Since it was his idea, I let him transport her to the club meetings while I stayed home and performed domestic duties.

Then a change occurred that required me to transport my daughter to the club meetings. Before long, the club director asked me to help one of the Pathfinders. When the club year ended, I thought I would return to my domesticated Sundays. But the Lord had something different in mind! I was asked to join the Pathfinder Club as a counselor. I gave every excuse possible, but God just laughed at my feeble attempts as I was assigned to five junior girls.

Here is where God's sense of humor revealed itself. Camping is an integral part of being a Pathfinder, and my idea of camping was the closest Holiday Inn. The Friendship camporee was being held that summer, and I was required to attend with my junior Pathfinder girls. A friend, an experienced Pathfinder leader, guaranteed that I would enjoy the camporee, but I wasn't convinced. And when I learned I had to sleep in a tent in a sleeping bag, I went screaming and kicking. Seven days of primitive camping? Me? I was unequivocally out of my comfort zone, and God was having a good laugh—and He protects babies and fools. He knew that I had an untapped propensity for nature. He planned to meet me anew at that camporee and put a fire in my bones to be used for His glory.

I grew to love Pathfinders and (can you believe it) camping! I even learned to pitch tents and build fires proficiently. But one of the most significant lessons I've learned from camping is a spiritual lesson. A campfire can metaphorically simulate the spiritual fire within us. Just as a Pathfinder must stir the campfire and put logs on it to keep it burning, we must do the same for our spiritual fire. If we don't keep the fire going, it will lose its flame and die. So remember to add logs of consecrated time to studying His Word. And don't forget to stir the flame with prayers of thanksgiving. Who knows where your spiritual fire will lead you!

Evelyn Greenwade Boltwood

The Day I Heard His Voice

You will . . . hurl all our iniquities into the depths of the sea.
Micah 7:19, NIV.

DURING A TIME OF IMMENSE TRIBULATION I fell into a deep depression, a time when I couldn't believe that the sun would ever shine for me again. My husband and I divorced, and I was sure that I wouldn't live a meaningful life again without him. Instead of feeling near to God, I felt as if I were drifting away from Him, further and further each day. I didn't believe that my sins were forgiven, and I was convinced that I was completely lost.

I prayed for help—for forgiveness, hoping that Jesus would listen and that He would give me the assurance of His love, assurance that He had forgiven me all my iniquities. But I didn't feel any better. It seemed as if my prayers didn't even reach the ceiling. I climbed into my bed night after night, crying my heart out because I couldn't believe the wonderful promises of the Lord.

While on holiday in the lovely town of Hartenbos in the Southern Cape, I strolled down the beach one morning without thinking of turning back. The cool water caressed my feet, and I felt very sorry for myself. I cried out to God, begging Him for a sign that would give me assurance that my sins were washed away just as the water was washing the sand from my feet.

At last I stood still, looking up into the sky where pure white clouds drifted by. *O Lord, why don't You listen to me? I've been carrying this bag of sins on my back for so many years! Now it is getting too heavy for me! Won't You please help me by throwing it into the sea?*

While still looking up into the clouds, something strange happened to me. I suddenly got the impression of two clouds drifting apart, and I could plainly hear a voice above the sound of the waves. "My child, so many times have I given you the assurance in the Bible of My love, My grace, My forgiveness. Haven't I promised you that I would forgive you all your sins on condition that you repent and confess your sins? I will in no wise cast out anyone who comes to Me. Why do you take Me for a liar?"

I stood there, petrified, feeling sure that God was talking to me. "Lord, I am a sinner!" I whispered, trembling. "Forgive me and take me in Your arms of love!" Oh, what wonderful love! Won't you make that your prayer as well?

Charlotte de Beer

Intervention

For where two or three come together in my name, there am I with them.
Matt. 18:20, NIV.

BEING A PART OF A PRAYER GROUP that has God as the central figure can have a positive effect on anyone. Thus, each member becomes stronger in Christ. This was my experience with my prayer group. Over the past 10 years our group has been meeting every first Sunday of the month. We take turns hosting the group in our homes, and this has brought peace, commitment, and unity. We have experienced many challenges over the years. If it weren't for the mercy of God and for our commitment to call on Him, we would long ago have separated and been doing our own individual thing.

When my 18-year-old daughter told me that she was pregnant, there was little that I could do. What does a mother, a parent, do at a time like this? Thank God, He had prepared a way for me. It was at that point that I made a call to my prayer partners, and in less than two hours we had gathered at one of our prayer homes, and there we decided to call on God. We fasted and prayed for guidance and wisdom.

I didn't tell my husband of the pregnancy just then because just prior to this event my husband had been hospitalized and had a heart catheterization. He was discharged with orders from his doctor to rest and to try to reduce his stress level. My concern was not to incur any additional stress that may land him back in the hospital.

It "happened" that on the same day I'd been given two days off from work, so for three days I fasted and prayed. God answered my prayer by sending my husband a dream about the problem before I could even tell him anything about our daughter's pregnancy.

On the third day of the fast, as my husband was leaving home, he mentioned a dream that he'd had. I dismissed it vaguely and told him that when he came home we would talk more about it. When he arrived home in the evening, I asked him about the dream. The dream was exactly what I would have told him, except God told him better. All I did was verify that it was the truth.

Dear God, thank You for sending the Holy Spirit to guide us, and I want to express gratitude and many thanks to my prayer group that has stood with me.

Selene Stewart

Praise—From Sadness to Peace

Praise the Lord. How good it is to sing praises to our God,
how pleasant and fitting to praise him!
Ps. 147:1, NIV.

FOR A WHOLE YEAR I studied hospital psychology at the university hospital in the city of João Pessoa in the Brazilian state of Paraíba. I had amazing experiences that were positive for my life despite the fact that we dealt with chronically ill to terminally ill patients. It was an environment in which we "breathed" the constant struggle for life and the imminence of death.

Among the patients I cared for was a woman with advanced stomach cancer; there was no possibility of surgery. She could only wait for her life to end. Consequently, her appearance was sad, and she had a yellowish aspect about her. Even when she was medicated she could barely speak because of intense pain throughout her body. Nevertheless, she demonstrated true praise to God from the depths of her heart and soul.

During our daily visits I found that her greatest dissatisfaction was that she couldn't sing. Her relatives had informed her that singing would cause her health condition to worsen. This information was not logical, and after I told her that she could sing, little by little her groans of pain were substituted with a song of praise to God. This brought joy to everyone.

Sadly, although she seemed to improve for a while, she passed away. However, a story I heard from another patient greatly encouraged me regarding the praises that had been offered by this suffering patient. She had demonstrated and lived the assurance of Christ's presence while walking "through the valley of the shadow of death" (Ps. 23:4, NIV). The patient told me, "She passed away whispering a song and with a gentle smile; it seemed as though she fell asleep."

As you read this, remember, above all, that you are God's creation. Perhaps you are experiencing a difficult phase of your life, or a turbulent and dark moment may appear. Always remember: it is only a phase, a fleeting moment, although it seems long. What is important is to decide to present a song of praise to God throughout your entire life. Then when pain presents itself, your life will be a song, resulting in the assurance that you are a child of a loving Father. After all, "a cheerful heart is good medicine, but a crushed spirit dries up the bones" (Prov. 17:22, NIV).

Ana Paula Costa Teixeira de Paiva

He's Got the Whole World in His Hands

Now all glory to God, who is able, through his mighty power at work within us, to accomplish infinitely more than we might ask or think. Eph. 3:20, NLT.

BEING A VERY VISUAL LEARNER, I appreciate object lessons and speeches with visual aids. One day I was shopping with Lance, my brother from Florida, and found what my mind labeled "a treasure." Ten years later it is still a great reminder to me that I can give it all to Jesus, for He is able. The treasure is a life-size ceramic hand that is palm up in a receiving position.

Sometimes in my life there are things I pray about, and there comes a surrender moment when I just know the situation is way too big for me. That's when I find a picture that represents what I'm dealing with, or I draw it on a small piece of paper and fold it up, and put it into the ceramic hand. In my mind I am telling the Lord that the problem is way too big for me, and that it is all in His hands.

The hand has held some peculiar requests, and the answers have been most surprising in some cases. There is one that I want to share. The object I put in the hand was a photo of my dad. Oh, how I longed to reconnect with my dad! After many years of heartache I fully surrendered this situation to God's loving hands.

The rest of the story is that before my dad died the Lord answered my prayers exceedingly, abundantly more than I could ever ask or hope or pray. It was such a huge gift God so sweetly gave to me to be able to reconnect—one many never receive. Dad's hand is one that I long to hold one day as we walk by the river of life, and together we can thank the Lord for the only human-made thing in heaven—His nail-pierced hands.

One of the best things about being a Christian is that we can trust that God is in control, that He doesn't make mistakes. We may not understand why things are happening in our life, but being able to surrender it to God is so wonderful. (Even though it sure isn't easy sometimes, it is well worth it!)

One day we will know the rest of the story, but for now I encourage you to put your life in God's hands this very day, for He has the whole world in His hands—including you and me, sister.

Gay Mentes

Lost and Found

And when he cometh home, he calleth together his friends and neighbours,
saying unto them, Rejoice with me; for I have found my sheep which was lost.
Luke 15:6.

I WAS IN THE NORTHERN PART OF NIGERIA, where I was in the National Youth Service. I went home during the afternoon break time in the secondary school I was teaching. After eating, I decided to rest a bit, but I went to sleep. The wind was blowing, so I got up and closed the windows, then went back to sleep. When my flat mates came back from school around 2:00, we discovered that my mobile phone was gone.

It dawned on me that it had been stolen when the window was open, because I had placed it on the window ledge. We used my friend's phone to call my phone, and it was answered by a Hausa man who told us the whole story.

The person who stole the phone was somebody we had helped. His 10 fingers were infected, so when he came looking for food we had given him an antibiotic instead. On the day the phone was stolen he had come to our house to ask us for money, but when he met nobody and when he saw my phone, he decided to take it and sell it. He thought it would get him more money than we would give him.

He took the phone to the next village. Fortunately for me, the person to whom he wanted to sell it was an honest man. The thief told the man an absurd story about the owner being in the hospital and needing money. The man took the phone and checked the addresses programmed into the phone. He realized that the names there were not the usual names of people found in the north of Nigeria; they were the names of people from the south. So he knew the man was lying. It was at this point that I called my own phone. The man decided he would give the phone back to me if I had enough evidence to show that it was mine. Thankfully, I was able to do that, so I got my phone back, and the thief was apprehended.

Throughout the time I was searching for my phone there was never a time I doubted that I would get it back. In all situations it is best to trust God. He is ready to help us at any time.

As in the Bible parable, I wanted to rejoice with my friends. But a phone is not nearly as important as people. Oh, how God longs to find each and every one of His lost sheep!

Omolade Ajike Dada

Is This Space Available?

Teach me your way, O Lord, that I may walk in your truth;
give me an undivided heart to revere your name.
Ps. 86:11, NRSV.

THE 9-YEAR-OLD accompanied her parents to an orchestra concert one evening. Knowing that she couldn't make a sound, she spent the time observing. She watched as some people took their seats. She heard a woman whisper to her mother, "Is this seat available?" Then she saw her mother's nod as the woman took a seat beside her. The concert began. The music was glorious, but what the child remembered most was that simple question: "Is this seat available?"

When her parents invited her grandmother and me to lunch the next week, the little girl sat on her grandmother's lap, regaling her with the highlights of the week. But when her grandmother had to go help in the kitchen, the young girl came to stand beside my chair. "Is your lap available?" she asked.

Her quiet question, gilded with innocence, pulled at my heartstrings. Cuddling her on my lap, I listened as she began our conversation. We talked about a thousand things in vibrant detail. But what I remember most is that question so ingenuously asked: "Is your lap available?" I learned that afternoon that there are special times wrapped inside an insignificant moment. There are lessons to be learned and riches to be shared. I knew that this was one of those times.

Each day our Best Friend asks a similar question: "Is your heart available?" How many times and in how many ways have you heard Him ask?

How we answer is crucial. When we answer gladly, the blessings will begin. Ellen G. White reminds us: "A heart of faith and love is dearer to God than the most costly gift" (*The Desire of Ages*, p. 615). When every act we perform is for God's glory, we shall never be able to measure the marvelous results.

Let us each watch for opportunities to tell our Jesus, "Yes, my heart is available to cuddle some lonely child, to comfort some wayward adolescent, or to teach some questioning adult."

Giver of all good things, help me to discern my mission, no matter how understated or how obvious it is. Use me, Lord. My undivided heart is available for Your service today.

Glenda-mae Greene

The Show Must Go On

While I live will I praise the Lord: I will sing praises unto my God while I have any being.
Ps. 146:2.

THE YOUTH CONGRESS was set for New Orleans, Louisiana. Our church drama group, ACTS (Adventist Christian Theatrical Society), was scheduled to perform. Everything was in place, but little did I know what horrors would befall me.

When the New York weather grew cold, I came down with the flu. My doctor gave me antibiotics, but something else began to happen that I didn't understand. As we loaded the bus, I was still feeling a little weak, and I slept most of the way to Louisiana, rarely getting up even for pit stops. When we checked into the hotel, I noticed several three-inch bruises all over my arms and legs. What should I do? Dress rehearsal was in two hours, and I had begun to have severe chest pains and shortness of breath. Two drama group members decided to take me to the hospital. When I told the triage nurse my symptoms, I became their top priority. I was rushed through to X-ray, ultrasound, blood tests—the works. I heard them page many specialists: cardiology, pulmonary, and renal doctors.

When the results came in I was told that my liver and kidneys were beginning to shut down. I needed to be admitted to monitor my condition. The doctors told me they weren't sure if I would survive. I told them that I needed to go and perform at the youth convention. I told them how important it was for me. "After all," I said firmly, "the show must go on."

The doctors were upset with my decision and made certain that I signed all the paperwork that would relieve them of any liability. I discharged myself "AMA" (against medical advice), but I could not let my drama group down.

Knowing that I had a tough decision to make, I prayed fervently. I told the Lord that if I were to die in New Orleans I wanted to go out doing something that would bring glory and honor to His name. And God was with me. In fact, He is always with each of us. Praise God!

Though I had to fly back to New York, I strongly believe that the Lord knew my heart and my determination to serve Him despite the threat of failing health or death. He allowed me to recuperate and survive, and so far there have been 22 more years to serve Him.

Arlene Clarke

Answered Prayers

I waited patiently for the Lord; and he inclined unto me, and heard my cry.
Ps. 40:1.

I COULD HEAR THE CLOCK ticking away at my bedside. As dawn approached, tears streamed down my face. I knew that it was time to have my early-morning talk with my heavenly Father; however, this morning I needed to communicate with someone whom I could see, feel, and touch. Someone who would just take me in their arms, wipe away my tears, and assure me that everything would be OK.

In my distress, I cried out to God. I told Him about the clothesline that had broken the night before with all my laundry on it. I told Him about the fish tank that needed cleaning so badly. I told Him about the many errands I had to run before the day ended. The list was endless. *O God, please hear my prayers,* I prayed. *Please send me some help today!*

I reached for my Bible and, blinking back the tears, I turned to Isaiah 43. Here I was again reminded that I was precious in the sight of God, and He loved me. Yes! God had a special love for me. Like a bolt of lightning moving through my body, I suddenly felt as though I was not alone. Someone had come into the bed beside me; the tears that were falling were now tears of joy, a joy that no tongue could explain. I suddenly felt secure; my strength was renewed. I knew that God would take care of all my problems.

As I was dressing for work, my phone rang. I could not contain my innermost joy when my landlord told me that he had come by earlier in the morning and had seen the clothesline down and fixed it. I now had a stronger line on which to hang out the laundry.

As I made my way home in the evening I gave God thanks for His wonderful blessings throughout the day. All my errands for the day had been accomplished. But God was not through with me yet. Can you imagine my amazement when I got home and found my fish tank all nicely cleaned? Yes, a friend came by to visit and, along with my niece, Latoya, decided to do the job.

Indeed, God is the God of impossibilities. Let us ask Him to give us the faith that will remove mountains and accomplish the impossible. "This faith will rise above the storms of discouragement and adversity, will triumph over time and continue to burn brightly while waiting for the accomplishment of its object. O for such a faith today" (Oswald J. Smith).

Donna Brown

I Be His Hands

He will wipe every tear from their eyes.
Rev. 21:4, NIV.

IT HAD BEEN MORE THAN a half century since I'd last stood here. Of the six gigantic cement dinosaurs only one remained: Dinny, towering over trees and creek. Its cyclopean tail (there were several large cracks), curving back almost to the monkey's enclosure, was now protected from little climbing feet by wire fencing. Dinny had been my favorite! We sat down on one of the massive feet, with plenty of room for both of us. As a little girl, no wonder I had been in complete awe of its size! "Your mom and dad brang you?" Melissa asked as she patted one of Dinny's enormous toes.

"Oh, yes!" I replied. "We would ride in our Model A"—and then I had to explain what that was. I gazed out across the water. It had seemed such a long distance across the old iron bridge to the zoo, sitting on its own little island in the middle of the Bow River. Same road, same river, same bridge, same zoo—although in some ways they seemed smaller. But not Dinny. Dinny was as impressive as ever. No parents now, though. Only memories. They flooded back as I reminisced aloud to Melissa.

"When I was your age," I began, "this was my favorite adventure in the whole wide world. Some of my earliest memories are of playing in this park." I told her stories about the other reproductions that had existed and promised to show her pictures when we returned home. Then it struck me. This leviathan replica couldn't have been all that exciting to my parents. There was precious little cash to spare for extras, yet they'd spent time, energy, and money to bring me here because I had loved it. Tears welled up, ran over, and splashed on my hand unheeded.

Suddenly I felt *pat, pat, brush, brush* as Melissa reached up to my face. "God isn't here right now," she said in her small voice. "I'll take your tears off. I be His hands." I squeezed her plump little body as more tears trickled down my cheeks. *I be His hands.* How lovely! Have I been His hands to others on this planet? I wondered.

We headed for the exit. The pilgrimage had brought back far more than I had expected. May I be His hands to others.

Arlene Taylor

Given Grace

And He said unto me, My grace is sufficient for thee:
for my strength is made perfect in weakness.
2 Cor. 12:9.

WE WERE HAVING THE ANNUAL Western Dinner Saturday night, so Ashley and I headed for the church. When we got there, however, we were the only ones who had arrived. It was 6:30, so we got busy carrying things in and started decorating the tables. I was hoping someone would come soon to take over because I still had to pick up Grandma Telfor and then go to the store for buns for the Grillers. Unfortunately, no one came until 7:15, and the dinner was supposed to be at 7:30. I took off to pick up Grandma Telfor and drove on to the store in Belding, where I dashed in and got the buns.

As I turned the corner on Ellis Road, I looked in my rearview mirror, and saw—you guessed it—a police car with its lights flashing. When the officer came up to my car I had all the things ready for him. "Do you know what the speed limit is?" he asked.

"No," I responded. "I suppose it is 35 [56 kilometers] through here?" It was 45 miles per hour [72 kilometers] on Ellis.

"I clocked you at 40 miles [65 kilometers] per hour over on the other street. The limit is 25 [40 kilometers] there."

I groaned, "Oh, no!" I explained about the Western Dinner, and how I was trying to get back to that. He took all my things and walked back to his car. *Anne,* I said to myself, *you always drive so as not to get a ticket, and now this is really making your day.* I used the time to pray—so did Grandma Telfor.

The police officer came back to the car and handed back all my things. He said he was letting me off with a warning. "God bless you!" I said fervently. I praised God all the way back to church! We didn't get to eat until 8:15; however, the program went well with guitars and singing. When I got up in front for my part, I told them all what had happened. Thank God for His mercy!

I am so glad that we have a Father God who takes care of us in each situation and who loves us every day, giving His grace and mercy to cover all our sins.

Anne Elaine Nelson

I've Got Your Back

You need not be afraid of sudden disaster or the destruction that comes upon the wicked, for the Lord is your security. Prov. 3:25, 26, NLT.

YOU'RE IN THE HOUSE ALONE at night when you hear a noise. It sounds as if it might be coming from the basement. You ask yourself, *Has someone broken in? Are they coming up the stairs? What type of weapon might they have? What should I do?*

Now, the typical person might have the police number programmed into their cell phone. However, if you're like me, you march to the basement to see if anyone really has broken in. Whatever danger is lurking in my basement, I don't want to be surprised by it. It's good to look fear in the face and confront it. But what would I do if I did find someone in the basement? Say, "Excuse me, but could you wait a moment while I run and call the police?"

A fine line exists between looking fear in the face and focusing on the fear. The Lord has helped me to confront numerous fears in my life and the truths that lie behind those fears. But in my attempts not to be surprised I have often focused too long and hard on the "enemy."

When Roy is out of town and I am staying alone, I hear many more noises than when he's home. So whenever a strange noise occurs, my eyes pop open and I look intently toward the door, wondering if someone is there. The last time Roy was away, I asked the Lord to help me to understand where this fear came from and how to get over it. For several nights after that prayer I performed my usual ritual of reading Scripture, and then I lay down facing the door and eventually fell asleep. However, one particular night I couldn't fall sleep. I kept changing positions. Sleep continued to elude me. I then realized that in all of these positions I could see the door. That left one position I hadn't tried: sleeping with my back toward the door.

I laughed aloud at this point and figured that God was laughing too! It was as if He were saying to me, "Bonita, you've exhausted all your options—except the one in which you trust Me." I then heard Him say to me in such a loving tone, "Bonita, trust Me. I've got your back."

I turned over with my back toward the door, praying for strength to resist the urge to turn over at every noise. I fell asleep almost immediately and slept more soundly than I ever have while being home alone. And I've slept with my back toward the door ever since.

Bonita Joyner Shields

Fruits of Patience

He who goes out weeping, carrying seed to sow, will
return with songs of joy, carrying sheaves with him.
Ps. 126:6, NIV.

IN SPITE OF BEING ERRING HUMAN BEINGS, many times we feel tempted to do the work that belongs only to God. When we study the Bible with someone who doesn't accept what is presented, sometimes we become disappointed and may even feel we are wasting our time. But it's important to remember that God's time is different. If we're doing our part, going to the world preaching the gospel, we can be certain that He is in charge of the results.

I met a young woman who was very interested in the Bible. We became great friends and frequently went to church together. We studied all of the Bible lessons and read many Christian books. We considered ourselves to be sisters of the faith. But there was one thing that kept her from accepting Jesus totally: her indignation with the problems she saw in church. It seemed she was using a microscope and always had a criticism. Many times we spoke about the importance of taking just Jesus as our greatest example. In spite of this, my dear friend became discouraged. Finally, she no longer went to church and moved to another neighborhood. Our friendship, however, continued strong—without criticism and with extra prayer on my part.

Six years later I received a card from her, expressing gratitude for unconditional acceptance. At the end of the message there was a little note that expressed her desire to attend church again. This card was a reason for more prayer. The Holy Spirit was still working on my friend's heart, and I continued praying and encouraging her to read the Bible.

After moving to another state, she wrote me asking what she should do to increase her faith. Besides praying, she was reading the Bible frequently; however, her faith seemed small. I explained that faith also comes from hearing the Word of God.

Thirteen years after those Bible lessons, I received a letter from my friend telling me of her love for Jesus. She also expressed gratitude for my patience, and that I had accepted her as she was.

Today I praise God, who gives us love and patience to love and accept our fellow human beings, allowing them the time necessary to mature in the faith.

Maria Chèvre

Buffy

And God shall wipe away all tears from their eyes; and there shall be no more death, neither sorrow, nor crying, neither shall there be any more pain: for the former things are passed away. Rev. 21:4.

I CLIPPED THE LEASH on Buffy's collar and walked to the car. When I opened the door, Buffy made her way inside. I would have given anything for this to be a horrible nightmare, but it wasn't. Sensing my pain, Buffy placed her head in my lap and licked me. I drove slowly because I wanted this time to last forever. I was thankful that our children were in Florida on vacation with my parents. I knew they would never understand. We'd been a family for seven years. Buffy had grown up with Lillian, now 8, and had watched Cassandra grow from a baby to a 3-year-old who enjoyed giving Buffy orders. I thanked Buffy for her watchcare over my family, for being a faithful friend, guardian, and companion. I thanked her for guarding the yard and keeping us safe from all types of dangers, from the perceived dangers of rabbits and chipmunks to the real dangers of strangers and stray dogs. I will always treasure those moments.

I had hoped we would never reach our destination, but all too soon we were at the vet's, and I knew what lay before us. When we walked into the office, a young boy asked if he could touch Buffy, and she wagged her tail. As the doctor gave Buffy the shot that would end her pain and her life, I held her as I cried, speaking to her so she could hear my voice. She trusted me to the end, looking at me and licking my hand as she closed her eyes.

Today, August 25, Buffy has been gone for two years. And as I write about her the tears run down my face. I still mourn her loss, but I realize that her death has made me think. We aren't living in the manner God had intended for this earth. He didn't intend for there to be illness in His creatures or in people whom He created in His image. God didn't want us to suffer and die. He created a perfect home for us; through sin it was destroyed. I thank God that He has promised to remove the pain, suffering, and tears. I look forward to heaven where we will live without the fear of pain or death. When the burdens of this world become overwhelming and I feel almost crushed by its weight, I claim God's promise found in Revelation 21:4 and look forward to it. Don't you?

Tamara Marquez de Smith

Needless Fear

What time I am afraid, I will trust in thee.
Ps. 56:3.

IT WAS JUST THE ROUTINE ANNUAL MAMMOGRAM. The pretty young nurse handed me a gown. As she operated the X-ray machine that scanned for lumps, she apologized for pressing so hard on my body. "But we have to get as clear a picture as possible," she reminded.

I was glad the annual ordeal was over and went about my errands with a light heart. When I got home, the answering machine light was twinkling. "Please call the X-ray department right away." *Perhaps the films didn't turn out right,* I assured myself as I dialed the hospital.

"Oh, yes, Mrs. Cove. We'd like to book you for an ultrasound. There was some suspicious-looking tissue on the mammogram film. Could you come in next Friday?"

When I hung up the phone, I began to sob uncontrollably. My mother had been a breast cancer victim. I pleaded with God for strength to deal with the idea that I too could face a slow and painful ordeal. I vowed to keep the horrible secret to myself until I'd had the ultrasound. Perhaps the mass wasn't too large. Perhaps they'd be able to remove it easily. All week I prayed continually for strength to face whatever was coming. I clung to God's promise in Psalm 23:4: even if I were facing death, God would comfort me and lead me through the shadows and valleys ahead.

Then came the fateful day. I was allowed to turn in such a way that I could see what the examiner saw as the ultrasound proceeded. There it was: an egg-shaped lump. The doctor rolled the instrument back and forth across the area, checking and rechecking the growth. Finally she looked at me and said she was certain that my lump was a cyst. Given time, it would simply shrink and disappear. Since it wasn't painful, there was no reason to remove it. She cautioned me to make sure that I continued having an annual mammogram as a precaution.

I left the hospital rejoicing and chastising myself at the same time. I had looked for the worst. I had spent a week torturing myself unnecessarily. At the same time, I was joyful in the knowledge that I hadn't faced that week alone. The Lord had been with me, helping me to deal with students and my family as if everything were normal. God doesn't promise to keep us from fears and problems, but He does promise to be with us as we face them, unfounded or otherwise.

Patricia Cove

The Choice

If you are willing and obedient, you will eat the best from the land.
Isa. 1:19, NIV.

WHEN I LOOK OUT THE WINDOWS from my upstairs veranda, in the distance I contemplate the magnificence of Ibituruna Peak. At 3,684 feet (1,123 meters), its characteristics make it one of the most famous places in Brazil to practice paragliding. What amazing and majestic beauty!

Looking down from my bedroom window, however, there is something totally different: a tall, unkempt man with dark eyes, who has an abandoned aspect about him. He lives right there on the street corner, and this is a fact known throughout the city. The local TV station once did a report on his living situation.

The news report gave me an opportunity to see this man after he cleaned up. His appearance was totally different. The TV station had even located his mother, who lived near the state capital. This news of an attempt to offer help pleased many residents from our city. However, after a few days, he made a shocking choice: he refused to go with his family and return home. His home of preference was the street corner.

A Christian couple offered him comfortable living quarters, which he also refused. "I don't want it! Later the demands will come: baths, haircuts, fingernails clipped. I like to live the way I am!"

On cold, rainy nights my daughter Ariane and I look out our windows and suffer because of this street dweller's choice. When she questions, seemingly suffering more than I do, I tell her, "Dear, it is very sad! But it is his choice." He had the opportunity to go to a home; however, the authorities have respected his choice. There are people who, like this man, refuse better things in life, even the best things that can be offered—the promises of God—because they do not want to be committed.

Many times human beings use their freedom of choice incorrectly, rejecting the best that can be offered to humanity: a land in which everything will be in complete balance and exuberant joy shall reign, where everything that we suffer here will no longer exist!

Lord, help me to choose the best, the things that will help to mold my character according to Your will—the only thing that we will take from this life to heaven for eternity.

Eny Ruella Silva

How Marvelous Is Your Leading

By thee have I been holden up from the womb: thou art he that took me out of my mother's bowels: my praise shall be continually of thee. Ps. 71:6.

I WAS BORN TO AND BROUGHT UP by Hindu parents. I didn't know anything about Christianity. Since my family was very poor, I was forced to discontinue my education by fifth grade. As years went by, I wove cloth and helped my mother to manage our family. I used to wonder whether I'd get another chance to continue my education.

After many years a pastor was sent by God to our home, and he invited us to attend church at Nagercoil. We attended regularly for a year. That pastor sent me to a Christian boarding school to continue my education. With the help of God I finished my higher secondary and college education in Christian institutions. God also helped me to establish a Christian home. I am married to a pastor, and God has blessed us with two sons.

We came across many trials and temptations, but God kept us faithful, and His promises led us to have a victorious life in Him. At times we've felt as if Satan was a roaring lion, seeking whom he may devour, but the God of heaven has been with us all the time.

When Elijah was taken to heaven his shawl floated down and fell on Elisha, who received the double portion of the blessing. He then did marvelous miracles with the help of God. Many times we feel that we are empty vessels. Are we really? No; not at all. Our thinking is wrong. God has special purposes for every human being. When we pour out our hearts to Him, without doubting, God can do wonders in our lives. If we submit ourselves completely to Him to control our mind and heart He will lead us in marvelous ways. He will hear our prayers and answer all our needs

Surely it is marvelous in the sight of the Lord, marvelous the way that He led us thus far. He picked me up from the miry clay, and His banner over me is love, His divine love that led us thus far.

But now God has placed a new mantle on our shoulders, and that is to bring many more souls to His holy temple. What is God asking you to do?

Jegatha Johnson Muthuraj

Care for the People

As it is written: "He has dispersed abroad, He has given to the poor; His righteousness endures forever." Now may He who supplies seed to the sower, and bread for food, supply and multiply the seed you have sown and increase the fruits of your righteousness, while you are enriched in everything for all liberality, which causes thanksgiving through us to God. For the administration of this service not only supplies the needs of the saints, but also is abounding through many thanksgivings to God, while, through the proof of this ministry, they glorify God for the obedience of your confession to the gospel of Christ, and for your liberal sharing with them and all men, and by their prayer for you, who long for you because of the exceeding grace of God in you. Thanks be to God for His indescribable gift! 2 Cor. 9:9-15, NKJV.

IN SINGAPORE we have many faithful Christians who take time to help the poor, the needy, and the orphans by donating money and resources in the form of clothes, toys, linens, shoes, and books to the people in Sri Lanka. People of all religions, including Buddhists, Taoists, Hindus, Muslims, and Christians of all denominations, help.

It all started when Ms. Goonasegaram, who lives in Singapore, visited Melbourne, Australia, and met Merilyn Beveridge, who was then the coordinator for orphanages in Asia and Africa. She asked Ms. Goonasegaram, whose parents came from Sri Lanka, to help the orphans and poor in Sri Lanka. Since then our church members in Singapore have been collecting, packing, and sending clothes and other needed items to Sri Lanka.

The Buddhist monks from a temple near where Ms. Goonasegaram lives came to know of the people's needs in Sri Lanka. They readily collected clothes and other useful things from the Buddhists who worshipped in their temple and sent the things to Ms. Goonasegaram's home to be sent as well.

This has been going on for about 30 years now. In spite of her age and poor health, every year Ms. Goonasegaram and other church members and old friends pack and ship four times a year. Their prayer is that many souls will be brought to Christ through this ministry. The Bible teaches us to care for all people, those who know Him as well as those who have not known Him yet. And praise God for all those who willingly help to make this happen.

Yan Siew Ghiang

We Too Must Have Fun

And he said unto them, Come ye yourselves apart into a desert place, and rest a while: for there were many coming and going, and they had no leisure so much as to eat. Mark 6:31.

WHEN I WAS A CHILD attending school, the majority of us had the innocent opportunity of not having to worry about our needs and to just have fun. When we reach adulthood, our minds often wander to those yesteryears of carefree fun, and often it is with great effort that we strive to achieve similar opportunities to "let down our hair" for a while. It's worth it, don't you think? After remembering those yesteryears of innocence, we usually feel rejuvenated, relaxed, and ready to return to our activities and busy schedules.

As I recall, it was with great effort that a group of us at work were able to organize and pull ourselves away to take a break from our regular schedule. We set out for the beach to have fun. The setting was calm and peaceful, with a little music that was pleasant to the ear. A barefoot walk on the beach provided the perfect atmosphere to reminisce.

Shortly after the walk on the beach, we gathered around a table spread with a feast fit for a royal family. Games and much laughter were plentiful and could only be outdone by our "call to order" after the meal, during which we shared comments and experiences, reflected on duties done during the work year, expressed our thanks, and gave best wishes for future days.

There was fellowship at the sea, friendly chatter and laughter, concern for each other, and feasting at the table spread for Jesus and His disciples. But at all times they were mindful of the great work that was ahead and the tasks that needed to be accomplished. We were determined that we too could—and must—have fun while we care, share, and fellowship together. The pounding waves, dashing against the seashore, filled the atmosphere with sound as we got ready to leave. All too soon it was time to face a new, untried, and unchallenged year. Slowly the vehicles left, one by one from our seaside venue. The hugs, sighs, and laughter drifted away until the last of us was gone.

Dear heavenly Father, thank You for opportunities to have fun and relaxation away from our busy schedules, and for the wisdom and strength to do and accomplish our tasks each day.

Elizabeth Ida Cain

Wet Pants

As a father pities his children, so the Lord pities those who fear Him.
For He knows our frame; He remembers that we are dust.
Ps. 103:13, 14, NKJV.

ONE EVENING I WAS PLAYING with some of my friend's children. We had decided to bake Christmas cookies and make gingerbread houses. As we pulled out the bag of white flour, I realized that my black pants were probably not the best attire for the occasion. So I went upstairs and changed into my sweatpants. Three-year-old Gabriella met me on the stairs, looked me over and exclaimed, "Auntie LaLa, you changed your pants." She looked at me again, then whispered in an all-knowing yet understanding tone, "Oh, you wet your pants."

In the mind of a 3-year-old, there could be only one conclusion: if you change your pants in the middle of the day you must have soiled the previous pair. My little friend could only relate my experience to what she had already experienced. At this point in her life she couldn't understand the value of putting away a perfectly good pair of pants in favor of an older one when nothing was wrong with them. I wanted to explain to her why I had changed my clothes, but then I remembered this was the same little girl who didn't understand when I told her she shouldn't go to bed in her new boots.

I wonder if that's how we sometimes appear to God. Sometimes we can see only one possibility—to our finite minds there can be only one logical explanation. We struggle with God's seeming refusal to explain why things are unfolding as they are. But perhaps God will not explain everything to us now because we simply don't have the capacity to comprehend. We know that God won't withhold any good thing from us (Ps. 84:11). So we must learn to trust in His love for us and believe that "all things work together for good" (Rom. 8:28).

We wouldn't fault my little friend for her lack of knowledge because we understand the difference between the knowledge of a child and of an adult. God understands that we're growing in Him. The challenge for us women is that we may have the head knowledge of God's promises while we struggle to get our heart to trust. It's easy to become discouraged with our immaturity. How comforting to know that we have a heavenly Father who takes care of what we cannot understand, for He knows that we are but dust.

Laura Henry-Stump

The Fragrant Garden

*You will be like a well-watered garden, like a spring whose waters never fail.
Isa. 58:11, NIV.*

MY SISTER, SEISINHA, has a very lovely flower garden that emits a wonderful fragrance. Much love and dedication are given to its care. She cultivates a wide variety of very beautiful flowers, and the roses especially provide us with a wonderful scent and a dazzling vision of beauty. When we pass her garden, astonishment fills us because of this exuberance of nature. Each one of the various species of roses demonstrates its beauty and enchanting power of captivation.

Each morning, with innumerable buds springing into bloom and the expectation of fragrances of love, hummingbirds transmit a message that profoundly reaches our soul. It seems they want to offer us a true understanding of our Creator's power. Who else could provide us with such tenderness, the various colors, and the sweet aroma that these flowers emit? No one but our powerful God. This is one of the greatest evidences to the universe of His power.

As these fragile roses exist to emit their fragrance, we should also offer ourselves to the Lord as the flowers in His garden. It's necessary that we learn how to join together love, charity, understanding, and unselfishness, and transform all of them into a large bouquet to deliver into His hands, saying, "Lord, take this bouquet and place it in Your garden. Help us to emit a fragrance by the service we give to be placed in Your heart." It's been said that if we learn the language of flowers and converse with them, we'll be able to feel that they also glorify and praise our God, who has infinite love for all creatures.

It is very gratifying to know that we are cared for by the most hardworking and most particular gardener, Jesus Christ, who in every instance cares for His small, delicate, and fragile roses: humankind. How wonderfully pleasant it is to contemplate the flowers as we imagine being part of those who one day will be in the Garden of Eden.

O Father, help us to be like the roses, receiving a very special fragrance from You and sharing it with the people around us. May our fragrance ascend to Your throne in the heavenly mansions.

Maria Sinharinha de Oliveira Nogueira

Losing My Mind

Let this mind be in you, which was also in Christ Jesus.
Phil. 2:5.

IT HAD BEEN A VERY CHALLENGING WEEK, with demands coming from every direction. Now it was Friday morning, and my hair was a mess. As I headed to Ms. Jerri's shop my mind was preoccupied with the cares of this world. Unfinished business from the day before, calls that needed to be returned, unanswered e-mails, bills to be paid, more errands to run, and preparation for the next day . . . A headache was fast coming on. I entered the shop amid a buzz of activity—women laughing and talking about anything from hairstyles and local news to politics. I relaxed as my body sank into the chocolate suede love seat. Before long Ms. Jerri called me back to the shampoo area. She wrapped a fresh, clean towel around my neck and gently forced my head back into the shampoo bowl. As the warm, soapy water massaged my scalp I closed my eyes and determined to enjoy this brief pampering session. I began to feel rested, relaxed, refreshed, and rejuvenated. For a moment it was all about me. My mind felt clearer and less burdened. It was as if the Lord Himself were cradling me in His strong yet gentle arms of protection. I wanted to stay there forever. Then just as I was about to enter into a deep sleep, Ms. Jerri said something that changed my day and my perspective.

"Girl, I'm losing my mind!" She almost whispered it, as if not wanting to interrupt my peacefulness. I quickly opened my eyes to see her expression. She was smiling as if to say, "You don't know what I mean, do you?" I was a bit confused, but she went on to explain. "When you're losing your mind to Jesus, that's the best way to lose your mind. His will becomes your will, and His thoughts become your thoughts." Ms. Jerri burst into laughter, hit me on my shoulder, and said, "I want to lose my mind!"

I joined in. "Me too!" Ladies, won't you join me in giving your all to the Master?

Thank You, Lord, for giving me hair that can be a mess. Thank You for bills that get paid, business to attend to, transportation, and e-mails from friends and family. Thank You for Ms. Jerri, who not only makes my hair look wonderful but reminds me of the importance of yielding my everything—especially my mind—to You. In the midst of everyday, ordinary things, I realize that I need to lose my mind in You.

Terrie (Ruff) Long

Apples of Gold

A word fitly spoken is like apples of gold in pictures of silver.
Prov. 25:11.

THE LAUGHING FACES smiled up at me from the picture in my high school fiftieth reunion memory book. I hadn't been able to go to the reunion, but the coordinators kindly sent me a memory book when I requested it.

Eagerly I looked at each picture, trying to match the laughing faces of the senior citizens looking at me from those pages with the laughing teenagers I remembered from my high school days. Then one man's face stopped me. I remembered that man as a tall, blond teenage boy in several of my classes, and an incident in which he taught me a wonderful lesson in kindness. These many years later I don't remember what grade we were in or what class it was for which I had to make the speech. I remember only how upset I was.

Speaking in public has always been difficult for me because I stutter. That day I had tried to begin my speech, and my tongue had locked. Rather than start with a string of repeated syllables, I stopped before I started again, took a deep breath, and opened my mouth to speak—only to have my tongue lock again.

Then Roger Butt, who sat in front of the lectern, said, "That's a pretty dress."

I looked down at him. He was looking at my dress, not my blushing face, and he repeated himself, his voice just loud enough for me to hear "Yes, that is a very pretty dress. It's the prettiest dress I've seen all day."

Distracted from my discomfort, I opened my mouth and made my speech without a single stuttered syllable or stammered word.

At least 50 years have passed since that autumn day when a teenage boy saw a flustered girl having difficulty starting a speech in class and spoke up quietly to calm and encourage her. Yet I've never forgotten his kindness, his perception, or his effort to distract me from my problem so that I could do what was required of me.

Lord, may I always be willing to support and encourage those around me. May I always seek Your wisdom in how I speak to those around me, and may I please be sensitive enough to know when to say the words You give me to say.

Darlenejoan McKibbin Rhine

A Table

You prepare a table before me in the presence of my enemies.
Ps. 23:5, NASB.

I'VE READ PSALM 23 many times, quoted it, studied it, and written in my journal about it, but today one word jumped out at me. A simple word of five letters. We learned to spell it in first grade, and every one of us has one in our home: a table.

Our table is the first piece of furniture we bought together as a couple. It's an oak claw-foot table, and it needs refinishing. Scarred from 30 years of use, it has resided in our four homes and has seen us grow from two to six—and now 10. At holidays four generations and 16 people gather around our table with a 4' x 8' sheet of plywood on top.

Our table represents family. I treasure the family dinners and special occasions when our family gathers around the table. We feel connected; we spend time in fellowship together; we are satisfied physically, emotionally, and spiritually; we feel listened to and refreshed, and, most of all, we feel loved.

To gather around the family table takes time. I spend time preparing the meal; the children spend time driving home. We take time after the meal to talk and then time together afterward doing something special. The next day I get to spend time washing dishes and cleaning up while remembering the good time we had . . . Precious memories.

God has prepared a table for us, and He hasn't just set out the dishes, food, and refreshment, and then walked away. God is waiting at that table for us because He wants not only to nourish us but to spend time with us.

How is your table time with God? Are you taking time to sit down and experience everything that God offers you? God wants to give you His time, His rest, His healing, a special spiritual feast He has planned just for you—everything your heart longs for can be found at God's table. Our excuses of "I'm too busy" or "I don't have time" or "I need to go" are enemies of our time with God, yet God's table is set in the midst of our enemies.

The enemies—struggles and problems of life—won't go away, but God's table is always right there in the midst of them all. At God's table you will find the answers, the rest, and the strength to face your enemies. Sit down and partake of God's goodness with Him.

Judy Musgrave Shewmake

Nah-ah

Also I heard the voice of the Lord, saying, Whom shall I send,
and who will go for us? Then said I, Here am I; send me.
Isa. 6:8.

IT WAS MY TURN to drive on a fall road trip around Lake Michigan. There was beautiful weather, beautiful scenery, and my husband was sleeping. It seemed like a good time to continue listening to the Bible on cassette. I pressed the button, and the book of Jonah began. Sometimes the Word is more easily grasped when listening rather than reading, and although I've known the story of Jonah for years, I was intrigued by what I was hearing. Here was a story about a man of God who didn't want to be God's man.

Have you noticed small children when they are learning to communicate? Nearly all of them go through a phase when the answer to every question is a simple but direct no or "nah-ah." Jonah's vocabulary seemed similarly limited. God told him there was a city that needed to be warned of impending doom and that he was to be the preacher. "Nah-ah," he said. As you know, some unpleasant circumstances (like being in a whale's belly for several days) changed his mind. But his attitude was still nah-ah.

Jonah finally went—one man on a mission—to the notoriously wicked city of Nineveh, which was three days' journey in size, a day's journey being 22 miles (35 kilometers), and had a population of 120,000 people. He began his preaching one day's journey into town. The people listened and repented. Even the king heard the news and proclaimed a time of fasting and supplication to God. "And God repented of the evil, that he had said that he would do unto them; and he did it not" (Jonah 3:10). Was Jonah happy for the success of his ministry? Nah-ah. Is there an evangelist anywhere who wouldn't love those numbers—120,000 converts from one campaign? As the book closes, God is still there, gently reprimanding. Jonah, however, is sitting in the hot sun, pouting, and contemplating suicide. I hope the final, unknown ending to this story was more upbeat.

Is God calling you and me to ministries that we can do but maybe don't want to? Are we quick to reply nah-ah until we've done it so many times that it seems the normal answer? Yes, God is calling. How much better to have the answer of Isaiah: "Here am I; send me" (Isa. 6:8).

Diana Inman

Wound-Care Specialist

I will answer them before they even call to me. While they are still talking about their needs, I will go ahead and answer their prayers! Isa. 65:24, NLT.

IT'S AMAZING HOW GOD presents Himself in ways we could never think of. When we need Him, He is there each step of the way, day by day.

About 12 years ago my husband had bouts of hospitalization because of diabetes, and he recovered well. Then about two years ago things began happening again. He had an amputation of a big toe, amputation of the left leg, and an ulcer on the right heel. Because the heel wasn't healing, the physicians wanted to amputate again. We prayed that this would not happen. We had heard of a world-renowned wound-care specialist in another hospital in the same system who'd had good results with such cases. His schedule was jammed, but my God intervened.

While we were praying, He worked things out. One of the resident physicians who cared for my husband also worked with this specialist. He told the specialist about my husband's case, and the specialist took my husband under his care. Before surgery the doctor told us, "I don't guarantee anything, but I have done a lot of these." I told him we would be praying. When he visited the next day to assess the results, he said "We won this one." Thank God!

The Lord put just the right people, who believed in prayer, in our path at the time when we needed them. When my husband was discharged from the doctor's care, I told him I thanked God for him and for his team. He admitted that it was indeed a team effort.

The process of rehabilitation is a lengthy one. Though we may ask why, and don't understand, we just trust God to do what is best. At this writing my husband is making good progress with his prosthesis and his brace on the other foot, and is otherwise doing well. We just thank God for sparing his life and drawing him closer to the Jesus who sacrificed so much for us. Each time we go to the doctor's office and see those who are much worse than he, we just praise God, from whom all blessings flow.

When Christ comes we will be resurrected, and my husband will come forth with a new body with two perfect legs. For what are you praising God today?

Marie H. Seard

Wild Hair Day

For it is God which worketh in you both to will and to do of his good pleasure.
Phil. 2:13.

I STARED AT MYSELF in the mirror one morning and saw what looked like a wild woman of the jungle. Brushing and combing only made my bushy hair look worse. I applied water, but now I simply looked like a wild woman of the jungle caught in a downpour. Tufts of hair stuck out in every direction. My hair was an absolute mess!

"Time for a haircut," I said to the face in the mirror. I thought briefly of getting the scissors and hacking it into shape myself. However, I've tried that before with results no less wild looking. So I reached for the phone and called my hairdresser for an appointment. Within an hour I was sitting in the chair at the beauty parlor. "Do whatever you need to do, but make me beautiful again," I pleaded.

She washed my hair and conditioned it. She combed and cut and blow-dried it. Forty-five minutes later she held up the mirror for me to see what she had accomplished.

"Marvelous! You did it again. Thank you!" I did look good again. Every hair was in place and sculpted to look its best. A transformation had taken place, but how much did I have to do with it? Nothing, except to decide to go to the expert to let her do what needed doing.

On the way home I thought, *What an illustration of the transformation of sanctification that can take place in my life!* The transformation is God's work, not mine. It is the Holy Spirit who changes me from a wild, willful person who wants her own way into someone who is obedient to God with His love and grace in her life. None of this is my work, no more than the change in my looks was my doing. My part was only to choose to call the hairdresser and then yield myself to let her do what had to be done.

So it is with my salvation. My part is to choose who will mold my life, to allow God the freedom to make the transformation as He sees is needed. The end product will be all His doing and none of mine. When I look into the mirror of God's law I see a wild, willful sinner. But when I let God have His way with me, I take another look in the mirror and am amazed at what He has accomplished. It is the work of the Holy Spirit that will eventually transform me into someone who really looks like a daughter of the King.

Dorothy Eaton Watts

God Is Our Healer

And call upon me in the day of trouble: I will deliver thee, and thou shalt glorify me.
Ps. 50:15.

WHY IS THERE SICKNESS in the world? Maybe we suffer because of our lifestyle and that there is sin in the world. Sometimes we have even inherited sicknesses, perhaps from our forebears. If that is so, we need to ask God to forgive our sins so we can be healed. Unless we go to Christ we can never receive this healing.

Women are susceptible to various illnesses and weaknesses. Sometime we get discouraged, too, and sometimes we lose hope. At times we're frustrated and worried about family situations, about our children or husband. At times there's no one to support us or to listen to our cry, and then we cry unto the Lord. He is always the present help to our need. I have personally experienced this.

One morning a number of years ago I got out of bed with a hurried prayer and rushed to do my morning duties. As I stepped out of the bathroom, I suddenly got a catch in my hip, and I was unable to move my leg or take a single step. I was paralyzed in place in pain. Everyone was still fast asleep, and I needed someone to support me and to help me out of the bathroom. I thought of shouting for help, but instead I began praising God. I just kept on saying, "Praise the Lord, for He is good. His mercy endureth forever. Praise the Lord, who is going to touch my hip and help me walk straight. Praise the Lord for touching the nerve in my leg." As I praised God, I began to feel less pain and was able to slowly move to my bedroom. I knelt down near my bed and prayed.

When my children woke up and discovered my situation, they called the doctor to come to our home and treat me. My friends rushed in and helped me to lie down flat on the floor. I suffered a lot till that evening. Though the doctor gave me two shots, I still felt the pain in my hip and legs. I kept on praying for recovery. I have heard people say that God heard their prayers and healed them immediately, but I never found that kind of answer to my prayers. But He who eventually made me whole is a loving and living Father. He is a much greater physician than any earthly doctor. He is the healer and the source of all my comfort.

No matter what challenges you face, call upon Him in your day of trouble. He delivers.

Victoria Jeeva Ponnappa

God's Grace of Acceptance

*Whatever your hand finds to do, do it with your might; for there is no work
or device or knowledge or wisdom in the grave where you are going.
Eccl. 9:10, NKJV.*

IT HAD BEEN A BUSY WEEK. Besides volunteering at the cancer society
shop, I had tried to finish a lap quilt for the terminally ill children's
camps foundation and fill the box I had started for them. In my
slow, elderly way, these and my regular home duties had been
my goals.

I remembered praying as I set my goals and read the verse
in John 15:5: "I am the vine, you are the branches. [She] who
abides in Me, and I in [her], bears much fruit; for without Me
you can do nothing" (NKJV). I prayed that I could really bear fruit
of my goals.

As the week progressed I was fulfilling each task with strength from above until
I realized I had neglected to read my Bible that morning. Distractions had gotten in
the way, so I stopped in the middle of the day and sank into a chair to rest and read.
It was nearly the end of the week, and I felt a bit discouraged as I took up the Bible
lesson for that day and read again in Ecclesiastes. This time my eyes fell on verse 7
of chapter 9: "Go, eat your bread with joy, and drink your wine with a merry heart;
for God has already accepted your works" (NKJV).

Peace filled my heart in great waves of comfort as I thanked God for that verse!
I had done what I could, and it was accepted! Even though I was exhausted and discouraged, God had sent me peace and assurance of His love and care and of His acceptance of my feeble efforts to bear fruit for Him.

Then I remembered another favorite verse I had almost forgotten: "He has
shown you, O [woman], what is good; and what does the Lord require of you but
to do justly, to love mercy, and to walk humbly with your God?" (Micah 6:8,
NKJV). *Maybe this old woman has done enough for now, even though "there is no
work or device or knowledge or wisdom in the grave where you are going,"* I said to
myself as I closed the book on that week. God in His grace had accepted my
earthly undertakings.

*Dear Lord, I want to thank You for Your wonderful grace and unfailing care in
these weary days of my feeble efforts. I know that it is only by Your strength that I
can do anything. And You have helped me do what I can! I praise Your name, my
loving God.*

Bessie Siemens Lobsien

Protected

The wolf and the lamb shall feed together, and the lion shall eat straw
like the bullock: and dust shall be the serpent's meat. They shall
not hurt nor destroy in all my holy mountain, saith the Lord.
Isa. 65:25.

THIS STORY TOOK PLACE when I was about 7 years old. My father was the pastor/teacher in a town that had once had a mission school and church. The school had closed, leaving only fallen walls to remind passersby that a building had once been there. When my father was assigned to that village he started a new school building project. There were about 20 students after some years, and the little church in which they met couldn't contain them any longer. So that was when my father started the building project. He and his members secured a new piece of land and began building. This, of course, necessitated his going to the school building every day to supervise the work.

On one of those days my father left for the site without eating breakfast. My mother was very concerned and began watching for his return. But when it was getting later and later, she sent me to go and call him to come back for his breakfast. It was not far to the school site, but I had to take a bush path to get there.

As I walked, I sang to make me forget I was alone. Along the way I met an animal that I thought was a dog. I passed by it and kept going. I got to the school and told my father to come home for his food. While he was putting the finishing touches to what he was doing, I waited for him.

As we headed home, we started hearing shouts. Within minutes we saw many people running about. My mother ran out from among them and came toward us. You could tell she was agitated until she saw me, and then she broke down, crying with relief.

The animal I met was actually a big gorilla. It could have hurt me, but the Lord protected me. The people had caught the gorilla. However, my mother thought it must have caught me, because I had taken the same path through which it had come.

A time will come when a little child shall be able to lead even the wildest of these animals. That time will come soon when our Savior comes back for me and you.

Becky Dada

The Passport

The Lord is good to those who wait for him, to the soul that seeks him.
It is good that one should wait quietly for the salvation of the Lord.
Lam. 3:25, 26, NRSV.

THE FALLOUT OF THE SEPTEMBER 11 TRAGEDY wasn't only physical, social, financial, and spiritual; it was also logistical in terms of our ability to move from one country to another. I'm a Canadian citizen, though I now live in Florida as a green card holder. A law was passed that by January 2007 everyone who planned to cross the United States' boundaries had to have a passport.

Clearly it was time to renew my outdated passport. I did all the things required of me—or so I thought, until the application was returned to me a month later. Attached was a notice indicating that I needed a signature from the photography studio. I wasn't surprised. I'd told the photographer that very thing, but leaning on his vast experience as a U.S. passport photographer, he'd said that it wasn't necessary. So I meekly mailed the corrected application again.

Nothing happened for another month. I called the passport office, and the answering machine message indicated that the process, which should have taken three weeks, was slowed down because of the unusually heavy load of requests. Yet another month went by, and still nothing happened. Now the answering machine messages at the passport office no longer suggested leaving a name and number.

I knew that God was sending me a lesson, and I prayed even more fervently to learn it. I was glad that I didn't need to travel anywhere soon, but I was still anxious. They had my original passport, a copy of my green card, and various other documents. I was truly grounded.

Then I got a phone call explaining the delay. I had written a credit card number that they couldn't process. I quickly corrected the number, but despite the correction I still had to wait.

Then one Friday the doorbell rang. It was a United Parcel Service man bearing a large envelope I needed to sign for. It contained my long-awaited, updated passport.

I thank God for that lesson in patience. I thank Him even more for His promise that there is absolutely no delay in getting my "passport" to His glorious kingdom. I need only follow His instructions for entry. And with God's help and the Spirit's guidance, I mean to do just that. Will you join me in responding to His invitation?

Carol J. Greene

For Me? For You!

I have been reminded of your sincere faith, which first lived in your grandmother
Lois and in your mother Eunice and, I am persuaded, now lives in you also.
2 Tim. 1:5, NIV.

AS I SMOOTHED THE WRINKLES from the white damask cover, my wandering thoughts settled on my grandmother. Memories of open arms and open heart flooded my vision. My fingers lingered on worn threads in the fabric. I saw Grandma remaking her guest bed for loved ones or yet-to-get-acquainted others. Grandma's welcoming hug wrapped us in assurance that all was well and that each person was cherished. Being special to Grandma meant knowing we were special to God, too.

Creeping from our beds and past the guest room, we slid into the fascinating bedroom of our grandparents. We girls tucked the eiderdown around us and settled in for another heritage lesson. Not that we knew it as such then. "Grandma," we'd plead, "please tell us about when you were . . ." And another special morning with Grandma began. The stories were always positive though difficulties weren't glossed over. You see, my grandparents trusted God and believed in telling others of His goodness in their lives. Our songs and laughter have evaporated, though the stories linger, arousing in me the knowledge that God cares and provides.

Heritage is something that is passed on: word pictures, attitudes, experiences, disappointments, and joys that molded the lives of my grandparents. Heritage—the challenging leaps I'm encouraged to take into each footprint ahead of me.

Timothy's grandmother must have been a lot like mine. "I long to see you [Timothy], so that I may be filled with joy" (2 Tim. 1:4, NIV). "I have been reminded of your sincere faith, which first lived in your grandmother Lois," wrote Paul. Wow! But there is more. ". . . and in your mother Eunice [real heritage] and, I am persuaded, now lives in you also" (verse 5, NIV). (An even richer heritage.) As Timothy read his second letter from Paul, I wonder if he saw his heritage as having value. Did the thought cross his mind to wrap up his heritage to preserve it?

Paul next wrote, "For this reason I remind you to fan into flame the gift of God, which is in you" (verse 6, NIV). Heritage is a gift to be used and passed along to those closest and others farther away. Each grandma and mom, aunt and sister, has a role in passing on the best of her life, allowing God to improve its richness. Heritage is something passed on with deliberate intention.

Glenise Hardy

What Do You Love the Most?

Set your affection on things above, not on things on the earth.
Col. 3:2.

PAUL GAVE TODAY'S TEXT as advice to the Colossians, as well as to us now. We have the ability to love, and this text tells us what we should love. It's not a blind love that is beyond our control. Neither is it a natural love for us humans, for we are asked to love that which is against our nature. We are to love things that are lovely and pure, things that are true and virtuous, simple and kind, and things that are ordained by God above.

We see things on display in shop windows daily as we walk down the streets in shopping areas. These exhibits attract and entice our eyes. Though we have no intention to shop, we still pause at the windows. Then we find ourselves inside the shop. Then we see if we have enough cash. If we carry a credit card it is easy to buy.

Quite often we have the urge to buy even what we don't need simply because the item is on sale or is fantastic and the price is within our budget. There are some who go into debt, and there are shops that encourage us to pay whenever we are able. With this arrangement we become slaves to shopkeepers, with a never-ending debt. Those who have the money and don't have to go into debt may simply buy for the sake of being able to afford to. We have no place for these things in our homes, so we dump them in the garage, and there they stay.

Paul advises us to focus our eyes on things above, not on all that is on display. It would be good if we put on our shopping list only those things that we need, and not buy what is not on the list. It's difficult, I know, so I pray that God will help me not to be greedy. Perhaps it would be a good idea to put on our list the name of a needy person and an item that person needs. In this way we don't have to dump things in our garage but rather into some poor person's hands. In this way we would be laying up our treasure in heaven (Luke 18:22). The real treasure then may be these precious people we have helped.

Let us remember that Jesus is coming soon and that all these material things will then go up in flames. Right now, while they have their value, let's use them for the poor and needy and for the spreading of the gospel. Putting our affection on things above is the only way to peace, joy, and eternal life.

Birdie Poddar

Someday in the Promised Land

And God will wipe away every tear from their eyes; there shall be no more death, nor sorrow, nor crying. There shall be no more pain, for the former things have passed away. Rev. 21:4, NKJV.

I NEVER THOUGHT that death could be so sudden until my father died of a heart attack. I never thought that in a matter of a few seconds I could lose my father. I had lost the man who had showered us with so much love and affection. No goodbyes were said. No words were spoken. When I saw his lifeless body, all I could do was cry, cry so hard, because I knew that I would never see his smiles again. I could never hug him anymore. I would never share my joys and my sorrows with him again. I still had dreams for him and my mother. But now that he was gone, all those dreams would never be realized.

It was so hard to accept that he was gone forever. When he died, I first thought of my mother. How could she cope with the loss of her beloved husband of almost 45 years? The two of them had been very close. Since their marriage there was never a time that the two of them were separated. They had kept their vows to be together through good times and bad times. They enjoyed each other's company so much. They could talk the whole day without getting tired of relating the same stories again and again. At times I was amused listening to them telling stories that I had heard when I was still a very young girl. And now my mother was left without the man she had spent her lifetime with.

Grief overtook our family. My mother was very much affected with depression. She became sick, and there were times that she didn't want to eat, that she couldn't sleep. Day by day she lost weight. I thought I would lose her, too. However, through God's providence and guidance, we were able to cope with our loss. He strengthened us and restored our broken spirits. He wiped the tears from our eyes.

Death is inevitable. It can happen in the most unexpected moment. When it strikes, it can devastate the family. The intensity of the pain is terrible. We who remain behind should not lose hope. We should be strong to face the reality of death. Above all, we should keep our faith in God and in our hope that someday we will be with our loved ones again.

Minerva M. Alinaya

Uncertainly Versus Certainly

It is better to trust in the Lord than to put confidence in [woman].
Ps. 118:8.

I COMPLAINED TO MY FRIEND BETSY, "As soon as the light turns red people step down from the curb and start walking across the street. They don't even look or seem to care how many vehicles are coming, at what speed they are traveling, or if they are going to stop." I'd also noticed that the timing of the traffic lights varies in different places. But it's also true that in any city or state in most of the world an amber light means prepare to stop. So I slow down when the light turns amber.

One day a man walked in front of my car just as I was stopping. I said, "Sir, you trust my brakes more than I do." He responded with a smile. He didn't know that I'd recently had the car serviced with new brakes. They were working fine, but who was to say that the automobile was going to stop for sure? "What if my brakes had failed just as he stepped in front of the vehicle?" I asked Betsy.

She said, "Do you want to know something? We trust the post office and the mail carrier to deliver our most important mail. We trust the train operator to get us where we have to go on the trains safely, the police officer for protection, and the dentist to extract our teeth. We trust surgeons for major operations, pilots to fly us from city to city, chefs to cook our food, optometrists to care for our eyes, pharmacists to give us the proper dosages and strengths of our medication that could result in a fatality—but we have a difficult time trusting God."

Society depends on these individuals daily to perform their duties, and we become disturbed if they don't do so at the highest levels. God is always on duty. He always performs at the highest level. He knows what we need before we ask. He knows all about our secrets. He is able to fix any situation that we might encounter. The above text is powerful: "It is better to trust in the Lord than to put confidence in man."

We have a tendency to share secrets with each other, but we don't even pray about situations until it seems as though nothing that we've said or done is working in our favor. When all else has failed, we take the matter to God as our last resort. How much better it would be to trust God in the first place, don't you think?

Cora A. Walker

An Epistle for Christ

You are our epistle written in our hearts, known and read by all men; clearly you are an epistle of Christ, ministered by us, written not with ink but by the Spirit of the living God, not on tablets of stone but on tablets of flesh, that is, of the heart. 2 Cor. 3:2, 3, NKJV.

SHORTLY AFTER OUR COLLEGE first-semester classes started, one of my students asked me if I could give him Bible studies. I was delighted, thrilled that a student would ask me instead of my asking him. Of course I said yes without hesitation. And he brought another young man with him when we started our first Bible study. I was grateful that in spite of their heavy program these two young men were willing to spend some of their precious time to learn about Jesus' love. So we embarked on our Bible studies every Monday, Tuesday, and Wednesday afternoons.

A few weeks passed by. Then the Week of Spiritual Emphasis came. At the close of that week I saw those two young men stand after an appeal made by the speaker. I didn't really think much about their standing until the following day when they stood up in church as candidates for baptism. I thought I was dreaming, but there they were, being immersed in the watery grave and rising up in the newness of Christian life. When I asked them why they hadn't told me before, they just smiled and said that they were ready to follow in the footsteps of our Master Teacher.

Two weeks prior to our final semester examinations, I gave a chapter test. As I checked the papers I noticed that one of the young men from my Bible study class got a perfect score on his test. Curious, I asked how he did it when most of the students in the class got average scores. Smiling, he said, "Teacher, I studied hard, and before I went to bed I asked Jesus to help me. And this morning, after you gave me the test paper, I asked God again to help me remember what I studied last night." What faith he had!

Then I thought of how I had been trying to witness for Jesus to the whole class. Sixty percent of my students are non-Christians. Indeed, I had been placed here as an epistle of Christ to be read by my students. What did they see in me?

O Almighty and Holy One, please help me to represent You always even in little and big acts of kindness.

Ofelia A. Pangan

To Know Jesus

And this gospel of the kingdom shall be preached in all the world for a witness unto all nations. Matt. 24:14

IT WAS A SHORT WALK to the museum from our hotel in Odessa, Ukraine. Maybe the jaunt would wake us up after the five-course, two-hour lunch. This visit was a part of our study tour in the Soviet Union. The building was set back from the street, surrounded by greenery of many varieties. The outside looked like a beautiful palace from the days of the czars. We stepped inside to an interior of gold and marble. Among this glory, the artwork was beautifully displayed. In a special tour for our group, Vladimir, one of the directors, showed us through the museum. He spoke knowledgeably, and we were impressed. Toward the end of the tour, however, we became a little tired. The lunch, heat, and hectic pace of our tour was taking its toll.

As we stopped in front of a picture of Mary and Baby Jesus, we were suddenly wide awake. We heard Vladimir telling in detail about the birth of Jesus and the significance of this to all Christians. Quietly we stepped over to the next picture, which was *Taking Christ Into Custody*. This magnificent painting was done by Caravaggio from Italy. We paused as Vladimir presented to us 27 Americans the complete story of the plan of salvation. All were captivated by his presentation and listened carefully. At the end of the tour he pointed out museum books for sale in the front doorway. We quickly went to the table. There was something about this experience that made us want to have the book to remember it by. I wanted to talk with Vladimir. When he was free, I introduced myself to him as a Christian. He replied, "I am a Jew."

"I don't understand this. I've never heard the gospel preached in a museum—and by a Jew." He looked intently at me and said with conviction, "I believe everyone should have an opportunity to hear of Jesus Christ." There was sadness in his voice as he spoke of the future for his country and for himself. When it was time to say goodbye, he pulled out of his breast pocket a tiny English New Testament and opened it and read to me, "Blessed are the pure in heart; for they shall see God." He kissed my hand and disappeared into the crowd.

Yes, everyone must have the opportunity to hear of Jesus Christ. Isn't that our gospel commission?

Dessa Weisz Hardin

Kaila's Song

There is therefore now no condemnation to them which are in Christ Jesus, who walk not after the flesh, but after the Spirit. Rom. 8:1.

IT IS 8:40 P.M., and the sun has already set as another Sabbath goes into eternity. My 2-year-old granddaughter, Kaila, and I were just returning home from a wonderful music day. We had had vespers and were given a charge for an untried week.

Kaila began singing a song. I could hardly make out the words—all I could decipher was "no con-nation." I began to pay more attention, and then I realized that Kaila was trying to sing the chorus to a song we had sung earlier in the evening: "For there is now no condemnation to them which are in Christ Jesus, who walk not after the flesh, but after the Spirit."

An hour prior to going to the Adventist Youth Society, Kaila had been fast asleep and, as a matter of fact, she had slept through the whole program. I was therefore quite surprised when she started singing. As we walked home, the cars on the street moved quickly and the neighbors were busy trying to get their last-minute shopping and laundry complete before returning to their homes. In the midst of all the traffic, noise, conversations, and various activities that were going on, everyone stopped and stood in amazement to listen to a little 2-year-old singing words that she could hardly pronounce to a lovely tune.

As I reflected on how the week had begun and how it ended, I realized that with each trial, whether it was at home or school, God had given me enough strength to withstand the pressure without becoming devastated. How wonderful that through the Spirit we can live a life without condemnation. It is so easy to get so caught up in the everyday challenges of this life that we sometimes forget that God says He will never leave us alone, even when we are going through fiery trials. "Beloved, think it not strange concerning the fiery trial which is to try you, as though some strange thing happened unto you" (1 Peter 4:12).

Dear God, thank You for reminding us of the promise that You will not leave us alone, and that You will not condemn us when we mess up.

Selene Stewart

I Am With You

Go ye therefore, and teach all nations . . . : and, lo,
I am with you alway, even unto the end of the world.
Matt. 28:19, 20.

AS A PROFESSIONAL GUIDANCE COUNSELOR, I was appointed as a counselor for the Pathfinders at a congress with a specific assignment to the Adventurers, the youngest group. Three days after the conference began, there was a mountaineering program in which I was scheduled to give a talk on nature on top of the mountain we were scheduled to climb. The serene beauty of the town below the mountain made us appreciate God.

The excitement made the Adventurers jump from one end of the area to the other. Though none were hurt, we adults were afraid of what could happen as a result of their pranks. So we decided to go down the mountain the same way that we had come up. A small and narrow, slippery portion slowed our movement. I had to go ahead to assist all the children to cross in safety. But alas, I myself fell. I had removed my shoes to have a firmer grip on the rock surface, but what I feared most had happened to me anyway.

After cleaning the wound with water and applying Sloan Liniment, the nurses with us tied my leg with the neckerchiefs available. A pastor's wife prayed. Later an X-ray showed a tibia fracture. I would have to be operated on. Fear raised my blood pressure, so for two weeks I was on hypertension medication. My leg was straightened with support and immobilized.

Thank God, the blood pressure became normal and the operation was successful. The hospital admission lasted for exactly two months, and then I was on crutches. The promise of the Lord that "with his stripes we are healed" (Isa. 53:5) came to pass. I never felt any pain. Every little Adventurer was praying for me, all their parents were praying for me, and church members all over the conference were praying. God heard them all. I praised the Lord. He said, "I will be with you always." Even on my sickbed, my God was with me.

People showered me with love. The medical personnel gave prompt medical care. When I was discharged, fellow patients cried; they said they wished I could go on sharing my faith and giving them lifestyle and healthful living tidbits. The Lord be glorified I was able to touch lives.

Lord Jesus, please use me always, whatever the circumstances, till You come. Amen.

Falade Dorcas Modupe

Lessons From a Capybara

Then Jesus said to his disciples: "Therefore I tell you, do not worry about
your life, what you will eat; or about your body, what you will wear.
Life is more than food, and the body more than clothes."
Luke 12:22, 23, NIV.

I LIVE IN SILVER SPRINGS, FLORIDA, and the principal tourist attraction is one mile from my home. I always buy an annual pass and visit when I feel like taking a relaxing walk, a boat ride, or just to read or do some writing on a comfortable rocking chair on the dock. The animals that reside there are an added attraction.

The other day I saw an amazing sight: a capybara and a domestic cat cuddling in the capybara's open-air pen. The capybara, the world's largest rodent, is from South America. They can weigh as much as 140 pounds. This capybara looked as though he were approaching a record weight.

I learned the kitty had showed up several months before. He won't allow anyone to touch him, but he moved in with Cappy. It is an incredible sight to see the cat rub against Cappy, nuzzle him, and settle down close by him for a nap. Cappy, in turn, lays placidly and returns what appears to be affectionate nuzzles.

Two beautiful black swans also live in the same enclosure with them. As I observed, enchanted by this scene, I reflected on the earth made new where the lion and lamb shall lie down together and all fear between people and creatures will be removed.

I thought of the differences embodied in this scene: various colors, species, shapes, sizes, and ages, and yet they all lived without conflict or animosity. None showed any need to express their seniority, importance, or superiority. A verse came to my mind from 1 John 4:12: "If we love one another, God dwelleth in us, and his love is perfected in us." That seems to apply to the animal world as well as to humans.

Daily, I am reminded that nature is God's second book, and how very much may be learned while enjoying and reveling in it. I thank Him for loving us enough to create all the wonderful things in nature for us to enjoy.

Isn't God wonderful?

Dorothy Wainwright Carey

Give Thanks in All Circumstances

Give thanks in all circumstances, for this is God's will for you in Christ Jesus.
1 Thess. 5:18, NIV.

TODAY'S TEXT SAYS to "give thanks in all circumstances." But how do we give thanks in such a frightful world? How can we give thanks in the midst of hunger, sadness, the death of a dear relative, or in tribulation?

The word *thanks* means an undeserved favor, an attitude that expresses gratefulness. This word was taught by the Great Master and transmitted to His disciples to help humankind. Part of being a grateful person is recognizing the generosity of others, showing affection and gratefulness in a visible way.

I don't know what you're going to thank God or your neighbor for, but I know that it's possible to give thanks in all circumstances. If the author of this text, even after being beaten and shackled in an uncomfortable position in a cold, dark prison in the city of Philippi, could be grateful, we can too. It's a question of attitude. There are people who see only the negative side of things and cannot find anything positive. Take a positive attitude toward your life. Even if things seem adverse they can still contribute to our good. You may be a person who has many problems, who has a troubled life, and everything seems to be going wrong. At this moment you may be questioning "But what am I going to be thankful for if I don't see any benefits?"

There are reasons for us to be grateful. Thank God for peace, protection, shelter, food, clothes, roses—and yes, even the thorns—for the forgiveness of our sins, for redemption, for His marvelous promises, and many other reasons. We can never forget the many benefits of God's love. Just the fact that you are able to read this text is a reason to be thankful.

Keep your heart thankful always, for this attitude produces happiness and health. It increases your self-esteem, opens the doors for forgiveness and God's infinite love. The author, Ellen G. White, wrote, "Nothing tends more to promote health of body and of soul than does a spirit of gratitude and praise" (*The Ministry of Healing*, p. 251).

What will your attitude be as you face life? Ask God to make you a grateful person! Certainly this will make you a happier person also.

Flávia Tiburtino de Andrade

Sisterhood

Wherefore receive ye one another, as Christ also received us to the glory of God.
Rom. 15:7.

THIS WAS MY THIRD Christian women's retreat, and about 200 women from all walks of life, cultures, religious affiliations, ages, and languages were in attendance in Red Deer, Alberta, Canada. There were laughter, tears, hugs, and kisses throughout the weekend. On one wall special messages of love, hope, and encouragement were left for others in the form of "warm fuzzies." We ate physical food and partook of the best spiritual "manna" that the Lord had to offer. We were spiritually filled, and my cup ran over. There were many reasons why God chose for us to be in that place at that time. He used ordinary women to share His love with their sisters in Christ. We were challenged to know His heart and be His hands.

During one of the sessions I looked at the faces of the women. Tears gently flowed down the cheeks of some. Others wore a smile in an attempt to cover up the hurt and pain they felt. Some showed the pain of mothers worried about their children's salvation. Others were filled with hope as they remembered loved ones they'd lost to death and longed to see again. A few of the younger ones looked as if they were wondering why their mothers dragged them along, but deep inside were thankful that they had. Others nodded as sleep overcame them.

Though our faces and our needs differed, we had one thing in common: the love of Jesus Christ and Him crucified. He was the reason we were there. We were spiritually parched, and we needed to quench our thirsty souls with the Living Water. Like the woman at the well we needed to drink from the fountain that will never run dry. We needed to bathe in His righteousness and wash in His blood.

As mothers, grandmothers, aunts, sisters, teachers, nurses, doctors, social workers, wives, lawyers, CEOs, clerks, or construction workers, and many other occupations, we are called. Our heavenly Father has a plan and purpose for our lives. As we go through our journey we are to be our sister's keeper and uplift one another. Let us endeavor to truly love one another and bear each other's burdens. That is what being a genuine sister is all about.

Is there a sister who needs a touch from you? Why not reach out and touch someone today?

Sharon Long (Brown)

A Precious Gift

For I know the plans I have for you, declares the Lord,
plans for welfare and not for evil, to give you a future and a hope.
Jer. 29:11, ESV.

AT THE BEGINNING OF THE YEAR I received a devotional book from my Christian friend. In this book the Lord sent me advice and help to believe in Him. I read the title, *Beautiful in God's Eyes*, then looked at my face in the mirror—the common face of a mature woman who had passed her first youth. I wondered, how many of those I have come in contact with during my lifetime have "looked" into my soul? How many have I labeled, based on some physical aspect of their appearance, not having the patience to get into their inner being, to see the seed of light and beauty sown by God in their soul? I realized that He created me with much love and gave me the Holy Spirit, and thus I became unique. He has blessed us, the Eves of this world, with good and beautiful gifts. He saw the beauty of the soul through our eyes, eyes wide open to the world.

And as in the depths of the earth carbon becomes a diamond by painful writhing, so do we, with white hair and faces wrinkled by life's vicissitudes, obtain a life-giving halo seen by those around us. I feel that the beauty from my soul lights my face, and the good God turns His face toward me with a forgiving smile.

I began to write fragments from the devotional book in a daily journal. Each page is a revelation to me, revealing events similar to those in my life. These wonderful women are talking to me, sharing their feelings and the way they found solutions to their problems. Some events in my life, which I hadn't been able to explain myself, were made clear. I realized that God saved me from death because He loves me and because He hasn't finished His work in me. He is still waiting to direct my steps on the straight way of salvation.

Reading every day, I don't feel the burden of my personal cares and problems. One writer put it: "Not all the days are good, but I am happy that I am in God's hands, and I have found the peace that surpasses any understanding." I've begun to study the Bible daily. God helps me to understand His Word and that He is permanently with me, and to feel a spiritual hunger and thirst. I believe that nothing will happen to me that I won't be able to solve together with Him.

Marilena Iorgulescu

Take Time With God

Thy word have I hid in mine heart, that I might not sin against thee.
Ps. 119:11.

HAVE YOU EVER EXPERIENCED a barren period in your devotional life? You know what I mean, those times when no matter what you read or how long you pray or meditate, it just falls flat. Maybe it was because of a problem you were dealing with or some area in your life where you keep faltering and failing. Whatever the cause, most of us have, at one time or another, met a blank wall in our devotional life. The question is What do you do?

A good friend who experienced the loss of her grown daughter helped me to deal with such times in my life. She shared that after her daughter's death she felt a need to focus on the words of God in the Bible. So beginning the day after her daughter died, she began to write out the New Testament. Every day during her devotional time she'd write out some verses, in sequence, from the Bible. I asked her if she also journaled her feelings as to what she read, and she said she did write her feelings and thoughts.

She had begun with Matthew and was now in the book of Philippians. Amazing! What better way to fix her mind on Jesus than to read and write His inspired words. She said that writing the words forced her mind to slow down and focus on each word, which didn't happen when she was just reading the Bible.

I knew God had sent her that day to visit me and share with me what she does, because I had found myself going through one of those difficult times in my devotional and spiritual life. No matter what I did or read, the words and thoughts just didn't seem to reach my heart. So I decided to spend my devotional time writing out one of the books of the Bible. I prayed about it and felt strongly impressed to write out the book of Colossians. What an inspiring book! Every verse has something that touches my heart, speaks to my life, or causes me to praise God.

If you find yourself going through a barren time in your spiritual life, don't worry. Try writing out the words of God in a journal. Take time to read, write, and meditate on the inspirational words of the Bible. By doing this, you too will be hiding God's Word in your heart, and, like a plant, your faith and love for God will grow and bloom.

Heather-Dawn Small

Too Busy for a Friendship?

Some friendships do not last, but some friends are more loyal than brothers.
Prov. 18:24, TEV.

HOW MANY FRIENDS DO YOU HAVE? I thank God for the blessing of having many friends. "Friendship is a two-way street," my husband says. And he is absolutely right! A friendship takes time, effort, and commitment from both sides in order to flourish.

How often do you share with your friends? I guess it depends on distance, the different interests that you share with each other, and such considerations. But one thing is for sure: if the friendship is to grow, it needs to be nurtured.

Some friendships require special care. They require more investment of time than others. In our high-tech world it's easier than ever to stay in touch with loved ones and friends. An e-mail or a short phone call will keep us up-to-date with each other even if we're miles away.

One day I called one of my friends. No answer. I called later with the same results. Many times during the following days and weeks I called, until I finally said to myself, *Well, I guess my friend is just too busy.*

Can you call yourself a good friend? Can your friends say you're a good friend? I often wonder how my friend Jesus rates my friendship and commitment to Him. Is He satisfied with the time I spend with Him? Is His friendship a priority in my life? Or is He calling again and again with no answer from me?

One thing is certain: He loves it when He calls upon me and I act in response to Him, just as much as I love it when He responds to my calls. He loves it when I make time with Him a priority and when I give Him a chance to nurture my soul. Jesus is a true friend. You and I can always count on Him. Can He say the same about you and me? Or are we just too busy for the friendship of a lifetime? After all, if I intend to spend eternity with Him I might as well get to know Him here and now, right? As it says in Proverbs: "A man that hath friends must shew himself friendly: and there is a friend that sticketh closer than a brother" (Prov. 18:24). That friend is, of course, our Savior, Jesus Christ.

Lord, help me not to be too busy for Your friendship. Help me spend enough time daily with You that our friendship blooms into eternity. Amen.

Rhodi Alers de López

Angel at My Door

For he shall give his angels charge over thee, to keep thee in all thy ways.
Ps. 91:11.

IN 2001 OUR FAMILY OF FIVE joined the Okanagan Adventist Academy mission trip to Costa Rica. Satan produced a number of difficulties preceding the trip, but finally all was in order and we left Canada.

Upon arrival in the village of Jicaral we encountered more obstacles. First, the houses that we were supposed to stay in were too far from the cooking facility. We ended up cleaning some rooms behind the kitchen (of the town pub) for the girls, and the boys made their quarters on the roof above the kitchen.

We went to bed exhausted our second night, looking forward to a good sleep. About 2:00 in the morning several of the girls were at our bedside saying, "There are ants in our beds biting us." Much excitement ensued as we moved half the girls to the hall in front of the toilets, allowing the army of ants to march through their room and suitcases.

Two toilets and one shower for a group of 30 was also a major challenge. One couple from our group stayed in the motel next door. They were very generous about sharing their shower with us and usually left the key in the kitchen to make the room available for our use even if they weren't there.

Thursday evening some people were still at the work site and others at the Vacation Bible School, so I decided to go have my shower early to beat the rush. I didn't want to lock the occupants out of their room if they were to come back while I was showering, so I left the door unlocked. I was feeling uncomfortable about the unlocked door, especially as I was able to hear loud voices out in the courtyard. I knew there was a room rented to some truckers, and it sounded as if they were drunk. I prayed for protection and asked for an angel to be posted by the door if they should consider coming in.

As I was leaving the room a few minutes later I looked around the courtyard and, sure enough, there was an "angel," sitting by the door. It was Mike, the building coordinator of our team, sitting there and resting after a hard day's work. Coincidence? No; I know God sent an angel named Mike! Could you be an angel for someone today?

Elizabeth Versteegh Odiyar

Fire Drill

Watch therefore: for ye know not what hour your Lord doth come. But know this,
that if the good man of the house had known in what watch the thief would come,
he would have watched, and would not have suffered his house to be broken up.
Therefore be ye also ready: for in such an hour as ye think not the Son of man cometh.
  Matt. 24:42-44.

THE THOUGHT OF A FIRE STARTING in one's home and getting out of control fills my heart with fear, as does a national disaster where the possibility of a fire looms on the horizon. Measures have been taken by many organizations to prepare people in their care should such a fire occur. Just as in these drills, we go about preparing for life. We go to school to acquire education, knowledge, and skill; we walk in the footsteps of our elders to pave the path for interpersonal relations; and then we find our way to maturity.

In the case of an impending fire, a fire drill and other necessary precautions lessen the likelihood of injury and help people know what to do. Our informed and practiced decisions and choices will aid us greatly in such emergencies.

I had a personal experience with fire drills. *Boom, boom, boom!* The warning could be heard along the corridors as the women hurried to vacate the dormitory. A warning had been given so everyone was on alert. It was time for a fire drill, and the firefighters were entering the premises. Alas, though they had been warned, some persons weren't prepared. Some ran to get items which they'd left behind; others scurried about in a frenzy. The women in my care had to learn how to react in times of crisis. Unfortunately, not all were interested, didn't care to be a part of what was happening, and saw it as a waste of their time. The dean's presence made a difference, and in no time everyone was out of the building and into the designated safe area. Goal achieved, but not without frills and flurry.

The fire drill is a physical, present-day experience and example, and as in the fire drill, we are warned every day of the coming of our Lord Jesus Christ and that we ought to be ready at all times. It is an individual preparation that deals with matters of the heart.

May our heavenly Father help us to know His voice and respond when He calls so that we will be ready for such an important event.

Elizabeth Ida Cain

The Promise

The Lord himself shall descend from heaven with a shout, with the voice of the archangel, and with the trump of God: and the dead in Christ shall rise first. 1 Thess. 4:16.

MY FRIEND JENNIFER died two days ago. I was introduced to her almost 20 years ago by a mutual friend. The fond memories that I have I hold dear to my heart. I want to thank God for bringing such a beautiful, dear person into my life. She had suffered many years with one illness or another, and she was on dialysis.

Every time she was hospitalized I talked to her about making everything right with God. After she was coded, I spoke to her the next day. She said that she knew and heard everything that the doctors did during the code. She was worried about her bills, and I helped her to turn it all over to the Master. I remembered from working in the intensive-care unit several years before that if a patient bounced back quickly after a code, it wasn't a good sign. That night I took my time to talk to Jennifer again regarding her soul's salvation. I pleaded with her to forget about her bills and turn her life over to God. She insisted that she owed Ingrid money for her braids, and I told her that I would pay it for her. I told her that God needed to be in control of her life; He had worked it out that she was at a different hospital—in the country, not like the ones in the city—where she could enjoy nature, get good care from the nurses, and get the peace and quiet that she so much deserved. She admitted that this was true and that the care was excellent. I then told her that after all the medical problems and difficulties that she had faced during her lifetime it would be sad if she didn't make it into the kingdom. She admitted that this was also true. We talked some more about the Bible and God. Then I prayed that everything would be made right and that God's will would be done. I then called another longtime friend of hers and encouraged her to call Jennifer and pray with her too. This she did.

We will all miss her. Whatever kindness you showed her, she was the type of person who was happy. I am convinced that she had settled it with her Master. The pain she had was bad, but Jennifer isn't suffering anymore. I am hoping to see her again when God comes for His children. "For God so loved the world, that he gave his only begotten Son, that whosoever believeth in him should not perish, but have everlasting life" (John 3:16).

Irisdeane Henley Charles

Fragrance of Christ

Then took Mary a pound of ointment of spikenard, very costly, and anointed the feet of Jesus, and wiped his feet with her hair: and the house was filled with the odour of the ointment. John 12:3.

EVERYBODY LIKES PERFUME—well, nearly everybody. I like to wear perfume very much. One day my perfume bottle was empty, so I decided to take some cologne from my husband's cupboard. I saw a beautiful, apple-shaped bottle and quickly removed the bottle top and sprinkled the cologne on my body. After a while I began to notice a strong odor that I didn't like at all. It seemed to be all over me. I didn't want to go close to anybody since I was wearing such a strong fragrance, and an unpleasant one at that.

That evening I went home with a severe headache. I asked my husband, "What is that bottle that you have in your cupboard?" He told me then that it wasn't cologne—it was a cupboard freshener.

Every Christian is a living bottle of perfume. When the love of Christ is poured inside us, it should diffuse the fragrance to the whole world. Sometimes we cork the bottle tight and keep the bottle closed so that no one knows that we're a genuine Christian. We may say that we have been a Christian for many years and may even attend church regularly and pay our tithes and offerings. But we have no relationship with God, no perfume to share.

We should never be bad-smelling perfume. A bottle such as that would be thrown in the trash no matter how much money had been spent for it. Many of us may look only at the outward appearance of the bottle, as I did. The bottle may carry a name brand, and unless we remove the cork we cannot say whether it is genuine. And if we don't remove the sin from our heart we cannot diffuse the love of Christ to the world.

When Mary took a pound of very costly spikenard and anointed the feet of Jesus and wiped His feet with her hair, the house was filled with the aroma of the ointment. So let us diffuse the love of Christ to the world.

May God help you to be a genuine, living bottle of perfume for Christ, filled with the fragrance of His love for others.

Hepsy Lincoln

The Big Test

Behold, to obey is better than sacrifice.
1 Sam. 15:22, NASB.

I WAS 12 YEARS OLD when one of my mother's cousins got married. In my culture, relatives are expected to help out with preparations at such special events. My mother couldn't go because she had small children at home. My older sister wanted to go very badly, but mother told me to go instead. The family lived quite a few miles away, so I would need to spend a night or two there. I wasn't too pleased to be away from home. When I arrived, there was already a crowd at the home. The family was wealthy and had a big house. I was shy and nervous as I didn't know all of the relatives. An older cousin took care of me, and I was glad to be in her company.

The next day was the wedding day. After breakfast the bride's father gathered the womenfolk of his family into his bedroom. He bolted the door and opened the big safe that was in his room and took out a lot of jewelry and spread it out on the bed. His daughters then handed necklaces and other jewelry to each of us to wear just for the day. When my turn came, she said, "This small necklace is for you." When I told her that I didn't wear these things, all were astonished. They tried hard to persuade me to wear it, but to no avail. Then they got serious and firmly said that I needed to wear it just for that day.

I became frightened. So they tried another tactic. They lovingly cajoled me and said that I could take it home and it would be mine forever. I rejected all their offers. All eyes were fixed on me, and I felt like a criminal. I wished I could run away. Then someone said, "Leave her alone," and I accepted a shawl they gave me to wear instead.

When my mother and sisters arrived for the afternoon ceremony, I ran and hugged my mother, crying. The ordeal of the morning had been too much for me. Mother felt my forehead and said that I was burning with fever. I told her that I wanted to go home, and my sister was overjoyed to stay in my place when my mother and I left. Once home, she gave me something to eat and put me to bed. I was fine in the morning.

I'm happy I did what I believed God wanted me to do, even though I didn't fully understand it all.

Birol Charlotte Christo

Childlike Faith

Then Jesus called a little child to Him . . . and said, "Assuredly, I say to you, unless you . . . become as little children, you will by no means enter the kingdom of heaven." Matt. 18:2, 3, NKJV.

IN THE SPRING OF 1982 my daughter was in the first form (grade), and my son was 1 year old. My life as the mother of two children was stressful. As soon as the holiday came, I packed my things and went with my children to my parents. I'd had a driver's license for two years, so I felt capable of driving 60 miles (100 kilometers). The holiday time spent in the countryside passed quickly. Being aware of the benefits of the fresh air and the pleasant spring sun, I went out in nature with my children, helped my mother in the garden, walked, and visited my friends and relatives.

But the two weeks came to an end. The morning I left, my parents and two younger brothers had already gone to work in the field. After I got the luggage in the car and put the children in the back seat, I got behind the steering wheel. I turned the key, but the car didn't start. I tried twice again, but no luck. I looked around to see if there was anybody passing who could help me, but there was nobody. I tried to start the car again and again, but without any result.

My anxiety increased even more as my children became agitated. Then my daughter asked me, "And what do we do now, Mother?"

"I don't know," I answered while I lifted the hood of the car. I don't know why I lifted the hood, because I don't have any mechanical knowledge; but as I looked at the engine I noticed a wire hanging loose near the battery. I saw that at the end of it was a sort of pincher. Then I noticed another wire with a pincher connected to a terminal, so I thought that the loose wire had to be connected to the free terminal. When I connected it again and turned the ignition key, the car started. And I was relieved! But I didn't get a chance to say anything before hearing my daughter say, "I knew it would start, because I prayed."

I learned an important lesson from a 7-year-old—bring everything before God, because with Him all things are possible. If you feel overcome by problems this morning, kneel down in prayer and put them in the hands of the One who can solve them.

Lidia Poll

That Very Day

A man's heart deviseth his way: but the Lord directeth his steps.
Prov. 16:9.

WE HAD MADE OUR WEEKLY TRIP to the grocery store. Eager to discover the state of my health, I rushed to the pharmacy window to have my blood pressure checked. Delighted with the reading on the machine, I hurried off in high spirits to begin collecting the items on my shopping list. Suddenly I heard my name over the public address system.

My first thought was that it was my husband, who had gone to park the car. I wondered if something had gone wrong since I had come into the store. Instead of responding immediately to the announcement, I walked toward the entrance, watching for my husband. We finally found each other, and, seeing he was all right, we continued going through the store together until an item caught my attention. After checking the price tag, I reached to get my bag from my grocery cart to see if I had enough money. There was no bag! I suddenly understood the reason for the announcement. I was not strolling anymore—I practically ran through the store!

At the pharmacy window a most beautiful woman did a most beautiful thing. She handed me my bag and said, "A gentleman handed this to me!" The bag was wide open, just as I had left it beside the blood pressure machine. As calmly and sincerely as I could, I thanked her, acknowledging the goodness of God. A quick check showed that not a single item was missing—credit cards, ID, checkbook, change purse, they were all there!

People say, "Where are the miracles? Why aren't they occurring anymore?" I say they are all around us, happening every moment. I consider every breath I take to be a miracle. Who can tell whether I will have the privilege of taking the next one?

When God performs a miracle for us, not only do we see with our eyes, but the physical perception enhances the spiritual. Then, as we contemplate the goodness of God, we are able to comprehend the true significance of the miracle. God is active in our lives, constantly performing inspiring, life-changing experiences. I believe God provided two miracles for me on that very day—the gentleman who turned in the bag and the woman who handed it to me. Every day God's erring but trusting children experience wondrous miracles, constantly repeated by a loving, gracious, and merciful Father.

Quilvie G. Mills

You Are Worth a Lot to God

Are not two sparrows sold for a penny? Yet not one of them will fall to the ground apart from the will of your Father. . . . So don't be afraid; you are worth more than many sparrows. Matt. 10:29-31, NIV.

THE YOUNG ROBIN, chirping plaintively, was following its mother around the yard. The mother kept on searching for breakfast and finally found a juicy worm. I smiled as I watched her present the worm to her baby. The baby accepted the gift, then promptly spit it out. Not deterred, mother picked up the offering and pecked it in several spots, as if to check that the worm was of the right sort, and offered it to the baby again. Again the baby spit the tasty morsel back at its mother. Mother picked up the worm for the third time and flipped it end for end before offering that worm once more. This time the baby promptly gulped it down, as a young child might swallow a strand of spaghetti.

I read many years ago that robins will not swallow worms backward. Earthworms have built-in ridges that help them to move forward through the earth. If a robin swallowed the worm backwards it would slice the bird's throat. Oh, to have the wisdom of a robin. Its built-in system kept it from eating the wrong way.

The only problem with that system is that it works by instinct and not through thinking processes. If I were to give up my thinking skills for a life based upon instinct I might have a simpler life. But would it be as interesting? I would be chained by instinct to react to each circumstance. Instead, I am free to formulate my own thoughts and course of action. My loving God lets me learn through trial and error. Hopefully, it doesn't take three attempts to get it right.

I take great comfort from the fact that I am worth a lot to God. Even as I stumble through each new experience, I know that He considered that I was worth dying for. Whenever I'm watching birds, I'm reminded to turn to my wonderful Lord for further instructions.

God's Book gives me daily advice on the best ways to run my life. When I prayerfully read His Book, I gain the wisdom to live a happy, productive life, free from disastrous results. Then when troubles come, as they surely will, I'll remember that God will be with me, and that I am worth many sparrows.

Patricia Cove

Imprisoned by Fear

Thou wilt keep him in perfect peace, whose mind is stayed on thee: because he trusteth in thee. Isa. 26:3.

IT WAS 7:00 IN THE MORNING, and the world was still asleep. Most businesses were still closed, to say nothing of banks and government offices, both of which I needed that fateful morning. I had to get downtown by public transit before 8:30, so I hurried out and on my way.

I found the door open to the building I needed, and as I entered I realized that the place was completely deserted, not even a security guard in the foyer. Now all I had to do was get up to the fifth floor to remit the envelope I had in hand. That should have been easy, but I'm mildly afraid of being in an elevator, and even more petrified of being in an elevator by myself. So I did the only sensible thing and went for the stairs. The door leading to the staircase was locked, so I went in search of another route. I entered a doorway that seemed to lead to somewhere, but as it closed behind me I realized it was a dead end, literally. I had now locked myself in an empty stairwell. I felt like a rat trapped in a very small maze, and I began to be very anxious.

Stronger than my panic was my knowledge that God is greater than any imprisonment. I began to sing a French hymn, *"Ne crains rien je t'aime, je suis avec toi"* ("Fear naught for I love you and am always with you"). The more panicked I became, the louder I sang, and when I no longer remembered the words to the song, I recited Psalm 23, interspersed with frantic calls for help and a simple prayer: "Dear Lord, do not leave me alone; please send someone to get me out of here!"

Thankfully, the stairwell was surrounded by glass walls, which quelled my mounting claustrophobia. In the middle of my singing and praying from within my glass prison cell, I caught the attention of a man who recognized my cries for help and was kind enough to rescue me. After thanking him profusely, I realized how that staircase had become a jail cell of my own making—I could have just taken the elevator, saving me from a world of pain.

If we don't claim the blood of Jesus Christ, how can we escape the self-made prison cell of sin? Let us go to Him without inhibition, confessing our sins and believing that our victory is assured.

Jeannette Belot

I Don't Fit

You, Lord, are my God! I will praise you for doing the wonderful things you had planned and promised since ancient times. Isa. 25:1, CEV.

SOMETHING GRABBED MY ATTENTION one midwinter morning as I was watching the news and finishing my oatmeal and strawberries. It was the Associated Press sports story recounting Toby Dawson's reunion with his Korean father. I don't usually watch sports news, so I had barely heard about Dawson, the freestyling Olympic bronze medalist skier. There were two things, however—haunting words and an unrehearsed action—that pulled at my heartstrings when the story rolled.

It appears that more than two decades ago, when Toby was barely 3, he had gotten lost in a South Korean market. Though his father had searched the surrounding orphanages and a host of other places, the little boy couldn't be found. Sadly, the father gave up hope. Somehow, an American couple, ski instructors in Colorado, managed to cut through bureaucratic red tape and adopt the young lad. Naturally, when they brought him home they taught him to ski.

But it was Dawson's anguished words that I'll always remember. "I didn't fit. I looked at my [adoptive] parents and I didn't look like them." Even when he went to Korea, he discovered that he didn't belong there, either. He was, in effect, "stuck between two different worlds."

As a counselor, I know the angst of the scores of people who, in their search for identity, feel like Dawson did—stuck between two worlds. They don't fit. Some, in their agonizing search, will choose the best from both worlds, while others find themselves still stuck between the worlds. Reporters recall that Toby told them that he felt most at home flying through the air on his skis.

The media noted that Dawson had memorized a Korean phrase to greet his father, "I've been waiting a long time, Father." We too have been waiting a long time, but not nearly as long as our Father has been waiting for us. From now on, I'll memorize at least one Bible text each week. Though I won't need to remember the words to greet my Father, they bring His presence closer to me until He comes. When we reunite with our heavenly Father, we will fit in with His family. And when we see our Brother's nail-scarred palms, we will reach out to touch them.

Glenda-mae Greene

Someday He'll Make It Plain

O death, where is thy sting? O grave, where is thy victory?
1 Cor. 15:55.

THE UNEXPECTED NEWS of Chidi's passing shocked everyone. We knew she'd been ill for several weeks, but we didn't expect her to die. She was such a loving and caring woman, with an effervescent personality and a heart of gold.

When my husband and I learned that she was in the hospital, we went to see her and took the devotional book *Colors of Grace* as a gift for her. It included a story of how God used her to perform a miracle for us a few years before. I read the devotional I had written entitled, "I Believe in Miracles," and shared with her that the station manager at a religious radio station had recently read it on the radio. Her face lit up as she held the book close to her heart and whispered, "Shirley, this is the best thing that has happened to me since I've been in the hospital." She was amazed how God had put people and circumstances in place at the right moment to answer our prayer. I told her I believed that the same God who performed a miracle for us could do the same for her.

Chidi had difficulty breathing as she talked about her plans to open an orphanage in her country and how blessed she was to be able to help needy people who came to her store. Several times she mentioned that when she got out of the hospital she was going to share her testimony of God's goodness at her church. Before leaving her room, we prayed for her healing.

Not too long after our visit, we learned that Chidi's condition had worsened. Then we received the sad and shocking news of her passing. All of us who knew Chidi were baffled as to how something so terrible could happen. We consoled ourselves that God is in control and that He knows best, and in the darkest moments of our lives, even when it doesn't seem like it, He's with us. One day He will make it plain.

Chidi didn't live to share her testimony at church as she had planned, but her kindnesses and beautiful memory will live on in my heart and in the lives of those she touched. I look forward expectantly to that glorious moment when in that day God "will remove the cloud of gloom, the shadow of death that hangs over the earth. He will swallow up death forever! The Sovereign Lord will wipe away all tears" (Isa. 25:7, 8, NLT). Death will no longer have victory.

Shirley C. Iheanacho

A Child's Prayer

And he said: "I tell you the truth, unless you change and become like little children, you will never enter the kingdom of heaven." Matt. 18:3, NIV.

AS MY HUSBAND, our two daughters, and I traveled on an unpaved road in the southeast region of Brazil, we knew the sunlight would be gone in a little while. Our family was returning home after visiting relatives and friends. We were happily singing our daughters' favorite songs when suddenly the car's electrical system went out. Nothing worked. We were stopped along a road with very little traffic, about 25 miles (40 kilometers) from home. There were no nearby houses, so my husband tried to fix the problem himself—without success.

Feeling incapable and totally dependent on divine assistance, we prayed. Oh, how we prayed! The night was coming, and so were the evening mosquitoes. Seeing no way to solve the problem, my husband suggested that when the first car came by, my daughters and I should ask for a ride to the city where we lived. Then I would go after help for him. "We will not go! We will not leave you alone. If necessary, we will spend the night in the car, but we will stay together," I said. Seeing my determination, when the first car stopped my husband sent a message to his brother requesting help. Would his brother receive the message? And we prayed some more.

Then our 4-year-old daughter, Regiane, said, "Daddy! Wait! I am going to pray now. And we are going to go." She took a few steps off the road and, standing among the weeds that were almost as tall as she was, she prayed silently. I don't know what she said in those few seconds, but when she returned she said to her father, "Turn on the car. Let's go!"

My husband, who had tried to start the car numerous times, did as he was told by his small daughter. To our surprise and joy, the car started normally. We continued our journey and arrived home safely. And that problem didn't ever require any work by a mechanic.

God hears our prayers!

Lord, thank You for guiding us and teaching us that we should be as pure and trusting as children in all situations.

Eny Ruella Silva

A Taste of Heaven

And God will wipe away every tear from their eyes; there shall be no more death, nor sorrow, nor crying. There shall be no more pain, for the former things have passed away. Rev. 21:4, NKJV.

HUSTLING THROUGH THE MALL, I quickly popped into another store. Although I don't like malls very much and I dislike shopping even more, one of the things on my list for the day was in that store. As I browsed, lost in my own thoughts, I was quickly pulled back to reality when I heard my name: "Mai?"

Looking up, I was first startled then overjoyed to recognize a friend from high school whom I hadn't seen in quite a while. We chatted, caught up on each other's lives, and then wished each other luck as we went our separate ways. It was only a brief encounter, but it made me so happy to see an old friend again.

It was like a little taste of heaven. Just imagine strolling down the streets of gold, stopping to dip your feet in the river. Later, as you meander past the tree of life, trying to decide which fruit you'd like to eat, your thoughts are interrupted by someone calling your name. As you turn to look, you quickly recognize a friend from the past. Maybe it's someone whom the sinful world took from you too soon, or someone who merely drifted away with time and distance. Someone you had lost track of for whatever reason. The sheer joy of seeing another friend who made it past all the trials and problems of this world and into the kingdom will make the moment so sweet. I can just imagine wrapping that person in a huge embrace. I will want to throw my head back with overflowing laughter and happiness. Won't that be amazing? But this time as you catch up and share the stories of how you made it through, it won't have to be a brief encounter. You won't have to wish each other luck and carry on as you go your separate ways—you'll have eternity to share together!

Sometimes life can be discouraging, but we have the hope of heaven. Having that hope makes this depressing world easier to handle. The goodbyes are still hard, but we have something to look forward to, and it also can encourage us to point everyone we meet to Jesus so that we will get to meet them in heaven again one day!

Mai-Rhea Odiyar

It Won't Be Long

And that repentance and remission of sins should be preached in his name
among all nations, beginning at Jerusalem. And ye are witnesses of these things.
Luke 24:47, 48.

I WAS ADMITTED TO THE UNIVERSITY teaching hospital on a Monday morning. I thought my fracture would confine me for only two or three weeks, at most, but alas, I was there for exactly two months and 10 days.

I asked my husband to bring Bible literature for me to share with fellow patients and for guests who came visiting. My first Sabbath in the hospital, members of my church came to sing, fellowship, and pray. Gifts were also brought for me to share with other patients, and it surprised them that a fellow patient would share things with others that she actually needed for herself.

There weren't less than five different groups visiting me every day during my stay, praying, and singing songs of victory. One patient asked a relative of mine to come to her bedside and pray for her as well. To God be the glory, she received relief! All her pains vanished, and she recuperated faster than the medical predictions had suggested.

The executive members of the Adventist women's ministries at the national level came one day to visit me, but they missed my ward. A worker in the hospital said to them, "I think I know the patient you have come to visit." They were surprised when she added, "It must be Mrs. Falade," and she led them to my ward. They wondered how she knew me. She said, "She is noted for her prayers" and that every Sabbath I got dressed for the church service. My younger sister, who helped care for me, was also engaged in Bible studies, singing, and praying to the Lord of the Sabbath.

A pastor came to pray in the ward one Sunday and was amazed that a patient could still feel happy and share Christian literature. Throughout my stay not one of us in the ward died; we all went home rejoicing, bubbling with good health.

While I went home to be on crutches for another four months, my local and district church members continued to shower me with love.

No matter our circumstances, we can be a witness for our Lord, making a difference for those around us.

Falade Dorcas Modupe

We're on the Wrong Train!

For this is God, our God forever and ever; He will be our guide even to death.
Ps. 48:14, NKJV.

MY HUSBAND AND I were on vacation in New York City, staying in Brooklyn with friends. This meant we had to catch the train to get into Manhattan for our activities there. One day we had just spent our time shopping in Manhattan. Tired but happy, we made our way to the train station to return to Brooklyn. As soon as we went down into the subway, we saw that a train was arriving at the station. We hesitated only for a brief moment as we concluded that we were on the right side of the platform. In New York City you must know if you are headed "uptown" or "downtown" and be on the correct side of the platform to catch the right train.

Quickly we hopped on. As soon as I sat down my eyes began to look for the subway map posted in each car. When I found our present train stop, I looked ahead to the names of other stops. None looked familiar. We had already passed one stop. I mouthed to my husband, "We are on the wrong train!"

"We'll get off at the next stop," he replied. So at the next stop we got off, went up the other side, and caught the correct train to Brooklyn. This time the map looked familiar. Once on the right train, we could relax and enjoy the ride.

Have you ever thought that you were going in the right direction only to realize that you weren't? Unfortunately, it happens a lot in our Christian journey. We don't remember to ask our Guide, Jesus, for directions. We may depend on others to confirm what we think we already know. Whatever your case may be, you need only to recognize when God speaks to you. I knew after reading the map that we weren't going in the right direction. Although I'm not from New York City, I didn't need anyone to tell me that. It would have been silly for us to continue on the wrong train.

Friends, when you read the Christian map, the Bible, and realize you are on the wrong train in your Christian journey, stop! Then get off! Ask Jesus for directions and continue on. You can then relax and enjoy the journey, knowing you will end up at your eternal destination.

Dana M. Bean

Is There Anything Too Hard for God?

He raises the poor from the dust and lifts the needy from the ash heap;
he seats them with princes and has them inherit a throne of honor. For
the foundations of the earth are the Lord's; upon them he has set the world.
1 Sam. 2:8, NIV.

BEING A STUDENT in pursuit of education but without financial assistance was a major challenge. A week before the beginning of the fall term I had no idea where the money to reister for college would come from. Failure to register would mean a violation of my foreign student status. The more I thought about it, the more anxious I became. I turned to prayer and fasting.

After pleading with God for three days, I got the idea to search for scholarship organizations. I boarded the train from Philadelphia to New York City. The African American Institute denied my scholarship request, but they offered me a meal instead. Well aware of my priority needs, I turned down the offer. I went to the United Nations next, but was again turned down. I didn't submit an application for the following year because I thought it wouldn't help. Finally, 15 minutes before the end of the business day, I entered the World Council of Churches director's office; they too denied me assistance. Desperately and persistently I explained my case. Suddenly the secretary reached for her checkbook and wrote a personal check for half the amount I needed and pressured the WCC director to match the amount. Surprisingly, he did! Suddenly I found myself with enough money to register for the first term.

A week later I unexpectedly received a communication from the UN informing me that I had been awarded a scholarship. Because I hadn't filed any application there, I wondered how in the world this could happen. The scholarship would cover any amount of tuition at any university in the United States or Canada! I was literally numb with the reality of such a miracle. I thought about Sarai, who laughed when God told her she would bear a child. Then it suddenly hit me: my one and only awesome God had proved that there is nothing too difficult for Him! God continued to provide for my needs miraculously throughout my educational and professional pursuits thereafter. In graduate school I qualified for full assistantship; in my doctoral program, working 24 hours a week qualified me for full-time tuition coverage. Whatever storms you might be facing, turn to God, because He is able.

Ruth H. Nyachuru-Muze

What Shall I Give Them?

Then our sons in their youth will be like well-nurtured plants,
and our daughters will be like pillars carved to adorn a palace.
Ps. 144:12, NIV.

IN BRAZIL, CHILDREN'S DAY is October 12. Months prior, advertising and the appearance of new toys and games leave the children excited. They are filled with requests and prepare wish lists! They understand very little about the subliminal advertising, and parents rarely perceive the consumerism hype that permeates society. Parents sacrifice to provide perishable things for children who use them briefly and go on to other perishable things. We all talk of the mixed-up values these days, but few people are concerned about passing on *eternal* values to children.

A truck's bumper sticker caught my brother's attention, and Nathanel shared the interesting phrase with me: "Two things parents should give to their children: roots and wings." I analyzed this "highway philosophy."

Roots contain the tree's source of nutrients and its support system in the soil. The deeper the roots, the stronger the tree will be; and it will not be easily affected by just any wind that comes along. Our example and lifestyle provide the same roots through which we transmit to our children virtues of honesty, loyalty, respect, compassion, faith, love, obedience, self-control, perseverance, dignity, friendship—the true fruit of the spirit and foundation of character. "He is like a tree planted by streams of water, which yields its fruit in season and whose leaf does not wither. Whatever he does prospers" (Ps. 1:3, NIV).

Why give wings to our children? No one wants to bring up dependent, fragile, insecure children, but parents desire to see their offspring exercising good earthly citizenship and preparing to live in the heavenly kingdom also. At an early age it is necessary to provide a child with the right amount of independence, responsibility, capacity for making good decisions, discernment, clear vision, and correct facts about life and the Word of God so that they are able to construct their own life history. With these wings they will be able to fly high, gaze into the distance, and reach the Christian ideal. "But those who hope in the Lord will renew their strength. They will soar on wings like eagles; they will run and not grow weary, they will walk and not be faint" (Isa. 40:31, NIV).

Nair Costa Lessa

God's Protective Care

They will call to me, and I will answer them. I will be with them in trouble.
Ps. 91:15, NCV.

WE HAD MOVED INTO A HOUSE that had numerous hidden problems, but being recently widowed and with two young children, it was the best that I could do. I soon discovered that one of the house's major problems was water leaks in the walls and ceilings because of faulty plumbing.

"Miss, if I were you, I'd have the whole system replaced," said one plumber.

So I spent several thousand dollars to have new pipes installed, all the while praying and hoping that this problem was now fixed. "Father," I prayed, "please let nothing else go wrong in this house." God answered that prayer, and for many years we lived problem-free. Then one evening as I returned from church, I noticed that the right post holding my front porch up was leaning, actually on the verge of falling off the landing. "If this post falls," I said aloud, "the entire front porch will collapse."

I pleaded with my heavenly Father before retiring for the night, asking that the angels hold the porch in place until I could get someone to fix it. When sleep failed to come, I decided to get up and check the post again. In just the course of a few hours, it had shifted closer to the edge and was now teetering at the point of falling and taking the porch with it. With fresh tears starting to trickle down my checks, I prayed again. "Father, please, please don't let this happen."

In the silence of my living room, I felt God speak. "Go to Psalm 91:9 and 10. The answer is written there." I turned as directed and read these verses: "The Lord is your protection; you have made God Most High your place of safety. Nothing bad will happen to you; no disaster will come to your home" (NCV).

The next morning my dad happened to stop by to check on us and noticed the leaning post. With a few tools he simply pushed it back into place and secured it. "I don't know why I felt impressed to drive in your direction," he said. "I was actually on my way to an opposite destination and just sensed that you needed some help."

Is not God true to His word? Since that day no disaster ever disturbed that home.

Thank You, Father, for being a wonderful provider and protector. Amen.

Yvonne Curry Smallwood

Count Sheep

Pray without ceasing.
1 Thess. 5:17.

ABBY, OUR YOUNGER DAUGHTER, had a habit of listening to some of Uncle Arthur's *Bedtime Stories* every night before she slept. As her dad was then a student and was busy with assignments, it became my responsibility to read to our 3-year-old, no matter how busy I was, or she would cry herself to sleep. May, her 7-year-old sister, tried to console her sometimes, saying, "Abby, Mommy is busy; just count sheep and the sleep will come."

"No! I can't. There aren't any sheep!" And Abby never counted sheep because she continued to claim that there were no sheep. She was just too young to imagine them in her mind's eye as her older sister did.

About three years ago I read a book written by Albert Waite, my science lecturer at Newbold College, and I found this statement: "Don't count sheep—talk to the Shepherd." He also said God's e-mail address is "prayer.com." This reminded me of Abby, now 20 years old, who couldn't see sheep when she was 3. She was right; there were no sheep, but there has always been a caring Shepherd, our Lord and Master Jesus. I am sure that even though Abby can now imagine and see sheep, she would rather talk to the Shepherd. He is ever present and ready to listen to us when we talk, even if we cannot see Him.

Praying is talking to the Shepherd. Paul says to "pray without ceasing," and with prayer.com we can easily send Him as many e-mails as we want and just wait for His will to be done. The good thing with prayer.com is that I don't need to be an expert in computing before I can send messages. All I need is to get on my knees and talk to the Shepherd, who, being omnipresent, will get the message without my even pressing "send." Remember, God said, "Before they call, I will answer; and while they are yet speaking, I will hear" (Isa. 65:24). The best thing is that the good Shepherd can keep secrets, so our secrets will be safe with Him. Let's feel free then to send Him all our painful and hurtful heartaches through prayer.com and stop counting sheep!

Father, please help me learn to talk to the Shepherd without ceasing; and thank You for Your ever-ready e-mail service for all who are willing to contact You.

Mabel Kwei

Thank You for the Popcorn

Giving thanks always for all things unto God and
the Father in the name of our Lord Jesus Christ.
Eph. 5:20.

DURING MY TEACHING CAREER of 14 years I taught many students from various ethnic backgrounds. One of my students, whom I still fondly remember, was from Puerto Rico. She was a quiet, pretty girl who wore braces on her teeth. She has since grown, married, had children, and those children are grown by now. We corresponded for years, but I've lost touch with her, which I deeply regret.

It was my practice to bring in the corn popper to school at least once a month, and after our lunch I made popcorn for all the children. Since popcorn is also one of my favorite foods, it was a fun time for all of us. Teachers need to have fun with the children they teach, as well as teaching and disciplining.

The first time I made popcorn the year I had the girl from Puerto Rico in my classroom, I didn't realize until after I'd made it that with braces she wouldn't be able to eat the popcorn. After all the popcorn was consumed by the rest of the students and myself, this quiet girl came up to my desk and said, "Thank you, Mrs. Sweetland, for making popcorn for us." She was the only one to thank me for it, and she wasn't able to partake of it!

How many times has someone prepared a treat for us, but we, not able to participate in it, are disappointed and are not very gracious or thankful for what has been done for us? Do we think to appreciate the thoughtful act?

The Lord prepares a sunny, beautiful day that we often take for granted. The next day may be rainy, breezy, and cool. Do we thank the Lord for that day—a day that may be just what the ground needs in order to prepare our gardens for seed? Or do we act gloomy and ungrateful for that day? I have to confess that I'm one of those people. I do thank Him for the sun, but not so often for the rain. Without the Son we wouldn't have the sunny days or the rainy days. Let's remember to thank our Lord for all our blessings, whether they are what we wish for that day or not— they are still blessings bestowed on us by a merciful God.

Loraine F. Sweetland

The Boxing Match

Even so, come, Lord Jesus.
Rev. 22:20.

THE WAITING AREA is full of passengers waiting for the flight to Manila. The flight was supposed to have left at 2:10 p.m., but the announcement over the sound system has told us that the flight has been delayed. Personally, I don't have any problem with this, because I don't have any appointment upon arrival in Manila. I was, however, expecting people to be complaining, but no one is. Instead, people are contented! Why? Well, there is a boxing match on the television, and people are glued to watching it.

The passengers are really enjoying the show; they seem to be one in their cheering. It is amazing to watch the men, especially; they act as if they're in their own family room. Children are left to amuse themselves with either food or video games. Even though I don't enjoy the show, I do enjoy watching the reactions of people.

After more than an hour's delay another announcement tells us that there will be further delay and we are asked to stand by. One man gives a thumbs-up sign, indicating that he's happy the flight has been delayed.

Some kids are getting bored, so more food is given and more toys are offered by parents who continue to enjoy the boxing match. One girl doesn't want food or toys anymore. The babysitter picks her up and tries to convince her to watch the boxing match, but she is not interested. She continues to be fussy, and finally the mother leaves to give attention to her girl.

The five-hour wait ends up with a cancellation of the flight because of mechanical problems. Now the people begin to complain; some even get angry, and harsh words are spoken.

As I contemplate the day's experience, I am drawn to the thought of our awaiting the coming of our Lord Jesus Christ. Many are busy watching the match of the world. We're so engrossed with work and other things that amuse us that instead of spending quality time with the family, we try to amuse them with worldly things. Are we becoming so comfortable with this world that we forget we're just transients?

My prayer today is that we refocus our attention on our final destination and do what we are commissioned to do—share the good news of salvation.

Jemima Dollosa Orillosa

My God Is Awesome!

Praise awaits you, O God, in Zion; to you our vows will be
fulfilled. O you who hear prayer, to you all men will come.
Ps. 65:1, 2, NIV.

I'D BEEN CRAMMING EVERYTHING INTO MY DAY, but the research paper that was due in two days was in dire need of editing. I badly needed help. My professor was renowned among the students for her ability to find a needle in a haystack, and I was sure there were dozens of needles in my "haystack." But what could I do?

I knew I could call on a friend, but it was close to midnight. I dared not impose on her then. The next day might not be any better, I knew, because I had to attend another church and then serve as counselor at the Pathfinder Club at my own church before noon.

With a prayer for God's instruction, I e-mailed the paper to my friend and hoped that she could work on it in the morning. But what if, as was her Sunday morning custom, she didn't even go to her computer?

Still praying for God's guidance, I asked Him to help me to leave it in His hands. I prayed all that morning as I performed my other duties. And when I could stand it no longer, I called her just before noon.

"Hi, Arlene," she answered, obviously reading my name on her caller ID. "I'm on page 10 of your paper. It's pretty good. I should be finished with it in the next half hour."

"Praise God!" I exclaimed, rejoicing in His goodness.

Then my friend explained how she had found my paper. "My cousin was visiting from California last evening," she told me, "but there were so many people at my house that he couldn't get a word in edgewise. So he text-messaged me on his Blackberry. As he was leaving he told me to read it." It was when she retrieved his message that she found my paper and began working on it immediately.

Now, nobody can convince me that my God doesn't work with tiny details! Yes, God does indeed answer prayers! I scored 100 percent on my paper, and I am still astonished at the amazing way in which God works miracles.

Arlene Walker-Adams

The Night the Angels Sang

But thou art holy, O thou that inhabitest the praises of Israel.
Ps. 22:3.

WE HAD ALL LOOKED FORWARD to the big event—had been planning it for months. Pastor Bullón was coming to Panama for a week of spiritual revival. People were traveling from different parts of Central America just to hear him speak. Hundreds of buses would be transporting groups from all over the country to the stadium where, night after night, he'd deliver a simple yet powerful message from God. And just as expected, the arena was packed every single evening with thousands of worshippers longing to hear more about Jesus.

Then one night the lights suddenly went out during the program. There was absolute darkness. I looked around nervously. I couldn't even see my own hands in front of me. It was as if everyone held their breath, imagining the tragedy that could result if the crowd panicked.

Not a sound was heard for a few seconds. And then the angels sang. It began as a sweet, soft whisper that grew into a majestic choir of thousands of voices as the entire stadium joined in the simple chorus, *"Dios bueno es . . . bueno para mí"* ("God is so good . . . He's so good to me"). We sang it again and again. The sopranos hit the notes in perfection; contraltos, tenors, and basses added flavor to the uncomplicated tune, and the Spirit of God filled the dark stadium.

Some say they got goose bumps, some cried quietly, and some prayed, but everybody joined the angels' choir in singing this fundamental truth: God is so good. We don't know how many minutes had gone by, but when the technical difficulties were finally taken care of the thousands gathered there were hungering and thirsting to hear more about this amazing God who sent His angels to start up an impromptu choir in Panama.

That memorable night, almost 15 years ago, remains as alive in our hearts as the night when Jesus Himself came down and sat among us. Imagine how awful it would have been if we had let despair and desperation overpower us! We would have missed out on a great blessing; we wouldn't have experienced what the Bible means when it declares that God dwells in the praise of His people.

Sister, it doesn't matter what you might be going through; determine to praise Him anyway, because the darkest hour comes just before daylight.

Dinorah Blackman

God Knows Our Needs

*O Lord, you have searched me and you know me. You know
when I sit and when I rise; you perceive my thoughts from afar.
Ps. 139:1, 2, NIV.*

OH, HOW GOD KNOWS ME—the time that I go to bed, and when I get up in the morning. He understands all my thoughts. And then there are my needs—He knows all of them.

I shall never forget the time a very valuable lesson was learned. I thought my problems were impossible to solve in spite of such a wonderful, understanding God who is always willing to attend our needs. My faith seemed to be so shaken that although I knew about God's power, I thought that no miracle could take place since I was a sinner who many times didn't dedicate enough time to God for prayer and Bible study. Although I wasn't trusting in a miracle from God, that morning I had prayed, "Lord, You know my necessity. Today we have to pay the rent, and there is no money. If we don't pay it today, certainly there will be a fine, and we'll still not have any money next week. Please work a miracle and show me once more, Lord, that You exist. Amen."

My husband went to the bank to check our bank account balance to see if there was any way we could obtain the funds necessary for the rent. As he was leaving the bank he met a Christian friend from college. His friend explained a difficult situation he faced and asked for advice. My husband talked with him for a while, and this troubled man began to feel better.

Before saying goodbye, his friend asked what my husband was doing in front of the bank. My husband explained that he had come to see the account balance, and that he didn't have money to pay the rent. His friend, moved by the Holy Spirit, invited my husband to go with him, and he gave him the amount of money necessary for the rent. "The advice you have given me is of much more value than this amount of money," he said. My husband arrived home with tears of thanksgiving in his eyes. God had solved our problems in spite of my weak faith, and in a way beyond our imagination.

Dear Lord, forgive my unbelief. Help me to always remember that in spite of living in a world of difficulties, You are in control of every situation, and You do know our needs.

Fernanda Paula Gomes Simão

Saved From Surgery

Pray for one another, that ye may be healed. The effectual
fervent prayer of a righteous man availeth much.
James 5:16.

IT WAS TUESDAY MORNING, and I was on my way to the hospital for surgery to have a pacemaker implanted in my chest cavity just below my left collarbone. This was my first surgery, and I seemed amazingly calm under the circumstances. I knew many prayers were ascending to God in my behalf. My sisters and my daughters were praying, as well as several friends. Members of my daughter's church were praying, as were members of my church. My other daughter asked her students at school to pray, also.

It took a while for me to give my consent for surgery after my young cardiologist first suggested—and then insisted—that the pacemaker would help regulate my heart. I read all the literature and watched the video about pacemakers. I asked the doctor if the atrial fibrillation would cease and if I could stop taking the prescription medication. He couldn't answer yes, so I questioned why he wanted me to have the surgery. He said, "Your heart cannot be regulated with pills."

When I arrived at the hospital, the woman at the admission desk took my information and fitted my wrist with a plastic bracelet before sending me on to the next department. There a nurse took my blood pressure and drew some blood. I was handed one of those unglamorous, tie-in-the-back gowns, and another nurse took an EKG reading and sent me for an X-ray of the heart area. Just as a nurse finished a second attempt at getting me hooked to the IV, my three friends entered the room to stay with me. Then the surgeon arrived and introduced himself and told me to get dressed and go home. After reviewing my case, he didn't want to take such a drastic measure as implanting a pacemaker; he wanted to try reducing my medication at this time.

Of course I was shocked and relieved by the doctor's announcement! I gave God the glory for being saved from surgery by the power of prayer. I praise God that prayers were answered far beyond my expectations, and I agreed that "we know not what we should pray for as we ought" (Rom. 8:26).

Retha McCarty

God's Plans

For who knows what is good for a man in life, during the few and meaningless days he passes through like a shadow? Who can tell him what will happen under the sun after he is gone? Eccl. 6:12, NIV.

SINCE CHILDHOOD I have praised the Lord. My dream always was to tell about Jesus through music and to make a music CD available to spread His gospel even further. My dream was placed in God's hands, and as I matured I began to understand God's plans for my life.

I was scheduled to sing in a special program in another city, but when I reached the bus stop I discovered that the bus had departed five minutes ahead of schedule. My transportation was gone! The next bus would leave four hours later. What should I do? Take a taxi?

Arriving at the cab stand, I discovered several people who were going to share a taxi to the same city as my destination. However, one more person was necessary for the trip. Perfect! Time passed quickly as I waited. I really didn't want to be late for the musical program. Suddenly the taxi driver arrived and looked right at me but said nothing. It seemed he was looking for someone else. He flitted here and there then disappeared. A few minutes later I went to the cab stand to inquire about my ride. I was told, "Your taxi has already left. The driver was searching for you, but he couldn't find you."

Tears filled my eyes. *Why, Lord? Explain to me why! I missed the bus, and now I have missed the taxi ride, and this musical program is to honor You!* Upset with God for allowing these events, I was going to be forced to cancel the entire program. My heart was shattered.

However, I didn't give up. An hour and 20 minutes later several more people arrived and decided to share another taxi to my destination, and I was included with the list of passengers. On the way we stopped at the scene of a car accident along the road. There was the taxi that I had missed. It had rolled over three times, and two passengers had died.

I bowed my head, ashamed of my anger with God. I hadn't been able to understand God's plans; now they were clear. I thanked Him for giving me another opportunity to live. We can't reach our objectives by ourselves, but with God we can all be victorious.

Adriana de Oliveira Lotério

Life Is Like a Picture Puzzle

God is our refuge and strength, a very present help in trouble.
Ps. 46:1.

WHAT DO PICTURE PUZZLES and life have in common? With both we may struggle to see the "big picture" if pieces don't fit or we discover some are missing. I found that out for myself while putting together a meadow scene puzzle of Gray's Basin, Wyoming, that I planned to frame and hang over the sofa in our new family room. Fifty pieces from completion, I realized five pieces had disappeared. Unable to find them, I used bits of the puzzle box top and a scenic calendar to create replacement pieces.

We may find that some pieces of our lives are missing because of accidents, illness, divorce, abuse, and loss of family, friends, health, or a job. It's easy to become depressed and to feel like giving up. So why didn't I give up on my puzzle? Because I really wanted that picture, and I didn't want to say that a 1,000-piece puzzle had bested me!

In life, the missing piece we most need to find is the one to fill the God-shaped void in our hearts. Once found, other parts of our lives will start falling into place.

How many hours did I spend on my picture? So many that I stopped counting. And the picture looks good. The time that God has spent working on the picture puzzle that is my life is measured not in hours, days, or weeks, but in months and years. And He has created some replacement pieces for me, including new friends, family members, or jobs.

Some problems may be so big and long-lasting that they may not be totally solved in this lifetime. Examples of this type of trouble may include severely strained interpersonal relationships or permanent health damage caused by former bad habits and lifestyle choices. Full healing for these might not happen until Christ comes back to earth and makes all things new.

Even if many of our troubles are self-created, God won't forsake us. He has promised, "Do not fear, for I am with you, do not be afraid, for I am your God; I will strengthen you, I will help you, I will uphold you with my victorious right hand" (Isa. 41:10, NRSV).

Enough issues will be worked through to give us hope for the future and make us feel that life is worth living. So why not invite God into your heart and life today (if you haven't already) and let Him help you start pulling the scattered pieces of your life together?

Bonnie Moyers

He Did It Again!

In my distress I cried to the Lord, and He heard me.
Ps. 120:1, NKJV.

MY TENURE AS DEAN was coming to a close, and these were the final commencement exercises over which I would be presiding after three challenging, hectic, and rewarding years in office. Anxiety and stress were mounting, even though I was prepared, my speech was well crafted (i.e., timely and neatly typed), but my sinuses were once again on the rampage. Breathing was a problem and, horror of horrors, symptoms of an asthma attack were all too evident. Besides that, a severe low-back pain had made its appearance that very morning. I was busy well into the afternoon discharging duties, all the while trying to keep my problems from interfering with the work of the day.

On the way home before returning to town for the exercises, I stopped at a clinic and got an injection of a combination analgesic/muscle relaxant. While there, I reviewed my speech and, after receiving the injection, proceeded to go home. Upon arrival, I realized that I had left the folder containing my speech at the clinic. Trying to remain calm, I called the clinic. I was assured that the folder was being held at the desk, and I could collect it on my way to graduation.

I took additional medication, including inhalation therapy, and set off for the graduation venue with an intermediate stop at the clinic to retrieve my speech. As I drove along, I prayed: *Lord, You know my condition, and it's too late to get a substitute. Further, the vice dean called in sick and will not be attending the ceremony. Without Your help, Father, tonight I will be unable to perform. Do intervene! Thank You.*

I arrived at the National Theatre, parked, and stepped out of the car without experiencing any pain. Miracle of miracles! My breathing was quiet and easy, my voice clear, and I was able to walk normally upright toward the entrance of the building where the master of ceremonies waited to usher me to my place on the podium. The program went smoothly; my speech was delivered and well received. Our administration's outstanding accomplishments and future plans were presented, and supporters acknowledged.

I returned home praising God for His merciful and effective help in my very real time of trouble. I had called to the Lord, and He had heard me. He always does!

Marion V. Clarke Martin

Sabbath

Remember the sabbath day, to keep it holy.
Ex. 20:8.

THESE WORDS ARE OF GREAT IMPORTANCE to all who believe that God created this world in six days and rested on the seventh day. I have repeated the fourth commandment many times in my life; in fact, we've been teaching the Ten Commandments to our children from their very childhood days. But in reality, for some it has no meaning. It has meaning only when we begin practicing Sabbathkeeping on a regular basis.

Our two boys have been observing me from their childhood, when I missed my master's degree exam because it came on a Saturday. I had to drop my master's program because two of my papers were to be presented on Saturdays. Our elder son, while appearing for his bachelor's exams, left his papers, which came on Sabbath. He was able to complete his degree in four years.

Last year our second son was admitted to one of the non-Christian nursing colleges for his nursing degree. He is allowed to have Sabbath off, and so he goes to church and then spends Sabbath afternoons with the pastor's family.

One day in April his principal called me and said, "Your son is not willing to write any exam coming on Saturday. How can he tell me he will not write his exam on a Saturday?" She seemed to be very upset with my son. I wanted to explain to her about Sabbathkeeping, but because of her mood, I tried to calm her down and asked my son to apologize to her for speaking to her in such a manner. At the same time it gave me immense happiness and peace to know that my son had made the right decision. He had shown courage when speaking firmly to the principal. This increased my faith in the Lord. We were praying that his exams would not fall on Saturday. When we sincerely seek the Lord and have faith to move mountains, He answers our prayers. Even though Satan works hard to bring all kinds of temptations to us, God has His own way of dealing with our problems.

It is essential for us parents to train our children in the way that pleases God so that they will not falter from God's will. To do so we must live truthfully ourselves.

Lord, help us each to be faithful in giving to You our hearts and the time You have asked us to spend with You.

Rebecca Singh

A Broken Piece of Magnet

Whatsoever thy hand findeth to do, do it with thy might.
Eccl. 9:10.

I WAS ASKED TO ORGANIZE, scan, and screen all the files from the year our mission headquarters was organized in 1980. It was quite a laborious process, and exposed me to the dust from the documents and also to the rusty staples that pricked my fingers each time I cleared up my desk. I was a bit annoyed, often asking myself why I had to do this dirty job. More discouraging thoughts came to mind, and my longing for my homeland intensified. But I still had two years of my mission service term remaining, so I had little choice.

One morning as I emptied the wastepaper I noticed a little black object sticking out from the bottom fold of the box. Seeing that it was just a broken piece of metal, I tossed it on top of my desk. Instantly the used staples and paper clips stuck to it. *So this is a piece of magnet—just what I need!* I thought as I ran it over the scattered staples and quickly cleared up my desk and saved my fingers from pricks.

One day while I was routinely clearing my desk of used staples, a thought struck me. This small, broken magnet, only half the size of a large coin, worked so efficiently. Besides making my job easier and quicker and saving me from pricks, I often found pleasure just watching its size double or triple, depending on the number of staples it magnetized. Then I felt the irresistible impression of the Holy Spirit telling me through this small magnet that He cared and understood what I was going through and that He loves me. He was also teaching me a lesson. The quotation in *The Desire of Ages* came to mind: "There is no limit to the usefulness of one who, by putting self aside, makes room for the working of the Holy Spirit upon his heart and lives a life wholly consecrated to God" (pp. 250, 251). I also thought of today's text.

The magnet, before it was broken and thrown away, was perhaps part of an important machine. But it didn't stop being a magnet. It couldn't do the original job it had been designed for, but it certainly could do a small but important task efficiently.

God gives me good health and endowments and He expects me to do willingly and with love whatever He wants me to do, and He supplies His abundant grace. One month before I left the mission field I completed the archive job with a sense of fulfillment and joy.

Dinah A. Maquilan

Call Upon Me

And call upon me in the day of trouble: I will deliver thee, and thou shalt glorify me.
Ps. 50:15.

ABOUT 3:00 A.M. I was abruptly awakened, not by an alarm or any noise, but by a strange, urgent feeling that something was really wrong. What could I do? I couldn't sleep; I could only pray. I immediately asked for God's protection for each family member. I pleaded with Him to bless and protect each and show that He was very near. I went through the names of our children, grandchildren, their spouses and in-laws, siblings, and extended families. Some were mentioned more than once, but God understood. Our youngest grandson, Timothy, had been seeing a doctor about severe abdominal pains. He seemed to get better with treatment but the pain would return, and there was no diagnosis. So Timothy was mentioned more than once. I relaxed and went back to sleep for a short time, leaving it all in God's hands.

Shortly after 8:00 we got a phone call from our daughter, Judy, saying that Tim was in the emergency room with extreme pain, upset stomach, and very high blood sugar. That was frightening but not surprising. I was so glad I had prayed for Tim during the night!

We found Tim in the intensive-care unit in a coma and very white. He was unaware of anything, and his breathing was assisted by a machine. It was heartbreaking to see him in such a serious condition. We joined his concerned parents and softly held his hand, lightly touched his face or his arm, and at the same time softly told him how very much we loved him. After a short prayer we quietly left the room to let him rest.

Two days later it was a special treat to see him awake and even smiling. We were all thrilled we could wish him a happy eighteenth birthday.

The diagnosis wasn't happy—his pancreas had lost all ability to produce insulin. He would still be very weak and need a lot of recuperation if he were to hope for a reasonably normal life. For the rest of his life he would have to test his blood sugar and administer injections of insulin before every meal and, of course, watch sugars, carbohydrates, and all calories, and balance his life with adequate exercise and work. We pray that he will have a long and productive life, kept safe in God's care. It is so comforting to know that we can call on the Lord in the night of trouble, as well as in the day.

Lillian Musgrave

Heart's Door

Seek ye the Lord while He may be found, call ye upon Him while He is near.
Isa. 55:6.

WHEN WE FIRST MOVED into our house our next-door neighbors were a mother and her teenage son. They had a rather fast lifestyle that included loud arguments, slamming doors, and lots of coming and going in the nighttime so that sometimes my husband and I had trouble sleeping. It even occurred to us that the young boy could be dangerous under certain circumstances.

One night we were again awakened by loud noises—tires squealing, raucous laughter, and then someone pounding on the back door just outside our bedroom window. This time Mom had had enough of her son's antics and had locked him out of the house. Over the next two hours we learned (by the two of them yelling back and forth through the door) that Mom had told him to stay home that evening and do certain chores around the house, but he had gone out with his friends, leaving his keys in the house. It was evident that he'd had too much to drink, and he was angry. "Mom, if you don't open this door, I'll break it down. You know I will!"

"And I'll call the police! Now grab a lawn chair and sleep it off."

He yelled, he screamed, he cursed, obviously never giving a thought to the two of us cowering in the house a few feet away. After a while he began to tire, and his attitude changed. Desperate to be let in, he became like a little boy again. "Please, Mom. Please let me in. I don't want to stay out here all night. OK, Mom?" He begged, he pleaded, he cried. Nothing was working. In one last effort he banged on the door, and his words nearly broke my heart. "Mom, you gotta let me in. I'm your son!"

They moved away soon after that, and we never heard from them again. But I've never forgotten that night or those words. I sometimes wonder if that's how it will be for some of us in the end-time. Instead of acknowledging God when He knocks on our heart's door and asks to be let in, will we wait until the last minute and then cry at the door, "Lord, You gotta save me; I'm your daughter!"

He promised He'd be back in a little while. Let it be that we will heed His loving call, obey the rules—finish our chores, so to speak—and be ready when He comes.

Carol Wiggins Gigante

Our Dog Benson

I am sure that God Who began the good work in you will
keep on working in you until the day Jesus Christ comes again.
Phil. 1:6, NLV.

A FEW DAYS AGO procrastination came to an end when Benson, our 7-year-old Dandie Dinmont terrier-poodle cross, got a homemade haircut, as usual. (I am, after all, a hairdresser.) It's always a major production, with him ever moving around and whining and sometimes even nipping my hand, the very hand that feeds him. My husband situates Benson in 10 different stances as I try to cut. First, lying down, then sitting a minute. Standing, and then belly up, all the while bribing him with treats and the assurance that soon he will feel so much cooler and be so glad we did this for him.

Most of the time it's stressful, because I'm afraid that with all the wiggling, I'll cut or poke him, so usually we do part of it and then quit for a while. But this time I was in it for the long haul until it was done. I began with that end in mind—a haircut from his head to the end of every little hairy toe.

After persevering way, way longer than usual, Benson pretty much became a submissive dog for the first time ever. I was able to let him lie down without being held, and I cut to my heart's content, with just an occasional complaint from him. By the end I actually had my husband take a picture, for this was unheard-of behavior for Benson.

We're a lot like Benson, you know. We kick and whine all the way when in reality God allows only those things to come to us that He knows will prepare us to be more like Him so we can spend eternity together. When will I ever learn to surrender and trust instead of fussing and complaining and asking why, and trying to bite the hand that feeds me? Truly He has begun a good work in me with the end in mind: heaven.

I'm so glad God is patient with me and doesn't give up, but continues to work with me and to ask me to be willing to trust Him yet another time. Things may not seem right or possible or reasonable in our lives, or to add up in our minds, but today is yet another opportunity to answer His question: "Will you trust Me?" I encourage you to believe that the Father knows best!

Gay Mentes

Who Is Your Leader?

The Lord is my shepherd; I shall not want. He maketh me to
lie down in green pastures: he leadeth me beside the still waters.
Ps. 23:1, 2.

I COME TO SCHOOL EARLY to look for books to fit the different classes I'll read to this morning. I have a third grade with Mrs. Hoy as the teacher. She has the perfect class—it should be, because she never stops disciplining them. Second will be a bilingual group. I find them still thinking in Chinese, and I must find an easy story that will have some meaning for them. Then there will be the bubbly first graders I had read to last year. It's great to watch them growing up in so many ways so quickly. And the last group will be the second grade, who will still have a lot of enthusiasm too.

I pick up a copy of "The Pied Piper of Hamelin." What a fun, mysterious story this is! The town of Hamelin has been overrun with rats, and they even bite the people's toes. The people can't get rid of them. So they go to the mayor to demand help from him to get rid of these pests. This will be a good time to review with the children their knowledge of who is in charge. I clarify who a mayor is and what he or she does, and I ask who their city mayor is. Several of the third graders finally come up with the correct answer. We discuss the office of governor, and there are more correct answers. When we come to who is the president, there is one child who strongly insists it's George Washington. When I have the group of bilingual children, they're lost and don't know what I'm talking about. I spend more time with them, and their faces light up.

We must know whom we're following, and why. Every few years we have the opportunity of choosing new leaders. I read in a public school, and therefore I'm not allowed to talk about God. Our list of leaders doesn't seem complete without this one more Leader of the whole world. But there is also a false leader who is contending for the leadership of this planet. We are free and have the right to study and find out the abilities and leadership of these two. We need to vote today. Whom will you choose?

Decide which leader you will give your allegiance to. God, the Creator, is providing a leadership that will last for eternity. He loves us, His children, with an everlasting love. Hold tight to His love and His commandments, and heaven will be your reward.

Dessa Weisz Hardin

Yes, Lord, I Come

Trust in the Lord with all your heart, and lean not on your own understanding; in all your ways acknowledge Him, and He shall direct your paths.
Prov. 3:5, 6, NKJV.

I'M SO AFRAID, LORD. *My desire to be successful, to be well liked by others, to be the best for You, as well as me. My need of approval of others . . . My need to make everything OK . . . I struggle with the concerns of my heart.* Releasing those concerns to God isn't easy for this frail Christian who wants to be successful in every way. But God says, "Release all to Me. I am the way. I will mend the brokenness of your heart, whatever it may be. You will be complete in Me. My success is not what the world calls success, but it is the best."

At times, in my struggle to surrender all to God, I try to be a Christian for Him. I search the Bible on how to be a better me. Christians such as I sometimes live our lives thinking that if we had perfect control of our lives we would have a better understanding of God and be accepted by Him. Then I search God's Word, and my heart sinks. He tells me I must surrender it all to Him. I must come to Him just as I am. He will give me rest. He will carry my load. My knuckles are white from trying to hold on, doing it my way.

Then God touches my heart to remind me why I'm really here. It's not the success or failure, but learning to love and trust Him with my whole heart and soul, that matters. I need to turn my reputation, my work, my family, my friends, and even my enemies, over to Him. Everything I am or hope to be must be surrendered to Him. In my need to be in control, the road to God isn't always easy. But He says, "My yoke is easy and burden light. Just trust Me."

He reminds me that I don't have to "be good" for Him—I need to surrender. I don't need to understand—I need to reach up and grasp His hand. To have faith and trust in Him. He knows a better way and will lead me in the way that is best. He tells me so in His Word. Sometimes as I go to my knees in tears with all the heavy baggage, I hear Him say, "Give it to Me now. Give it to Me, and I will make it better." Can I really trust God to see me through to a better end?

Ever so slowly I turn each concern over to Him. As I get up from my prayer each morning I don't let go of His hand. He leads me through the day. I have given Him control of my—everything.

Carolyn Voss

Life Abundant

The thief cometh not, but for to steal, and to kill, and to destroy: I am come that they might have life, and that they might have it more abundantly. John 10:10.

FROM THE PULPIT AND PEW is a newsletter I so enjoy preparing for our little church each month. I love writing the last page and am always eager to see what words the Lord will give me to share. It was the end of October, and I was preparing the November issue. Thanksgiving was just around the corner.

When we think of Thanksgiving, the things most likely to come to mind are pumpkins, Pilgrims, cranberry sauce, Indian corn, and the smell and taste of homemade pumpkin pie. Who would count a newsletter among their blessings?

"My" page was almost complete. Proofreading the contents, I found myself pondering how grateful I was for the bits and pieces that folks share for the newsletter. I tucked my previous page into the file and started anew to do some thanks-giving to the folks who commit their thoughts to paper each month. I was particularly grateful for an item that had blessed my life before it was printed.

On occasional Sabbaths we slip into "our" pew, brushing by each other with a quick "good morning," a shake of the hand, a smile attached to our faces, and yet our hearts are broken and fragmented. We've all been there. One Sabbath morning confrontations left my heart aching as I scooted my grandchildren into our pew. A friend sitting next to me asked if I had read the book review that she had prepared for the newsletter. Shuffling through my fistful of newsletter items so graciously given for the next issue, my eyes fell on the words of the first note opened: "I will never leave you nor forsake you" (Heb. 13:5, NKJV).

Peace, comfort, and the arms of Jesus seemed to wrap me as I read the text and her words that followed. Sometimes we quietly do the things we feel the Lord wants us to do. It might not be easy, and most of the time we will never know the rippling effect of a quiet, simple act. I am grateful for the "gift" of the newsletter that the Lord gave me to do and for the friends who share.

Thanksgiving is a time of thanks, harvest, bounty, and gratefulness. Jesus covers it all. He has come that we might have life and that "more abundantly."

Judy Good Silver

Who Called?

The Lord watches over you—the Lord is your shade at your right hand; . . .
The Lord will keep you from all harm—he will watch over your life.
Ps. 121:5, 7, NIV.

IT WAS DUSK ON A SUMMER DAY in the Southern Hemisphere. We lived in Monte Azul Paulista, a small town in the interior of the state of São Paulo, Brazil. Our children, still small, enjoyed participating in the worship service at church, and my husband, who had gone early to a Bible class, said he'd come back and pick us up for the evening service.

Because it was very hot inside the house, when we were all ready I decided to wait with the children on the veranda. After a time the children decided to go inside to watch television, but a soft breeze outside kept me on the porch.

Suddenly the telephone rang, and I went inside to answer it. When no one responded to my hello, I went back outside. When this happened several more times, I decided to stand beside the phone.

Then I heard a noise like fireworks and looked out the window. Armed men ran by on the avenue, shooting at each other. I quickly closed the doors and windows and drew the curtains and gathered my boys in my arms. The telephone rang again, and this time it was my neighbor warning me not to open the door because there were armed men in our yard.

I tried to call my husband to warn him not to come home at that moment, and soon the police arrived and the situation was resolved.

When I opened the door and we stepped out on the veranda, we could see blood where my sons had been sitting. We learned that the men were prisoners who had escaped from the town jail and were attempting to flee in a taxi. Thankfully, neither my sons nor I nor my neighbor suffered any injury.

But who had called on the telephone? Who was on the other end of the line? It was only the telephone calls that caused me to stay inside that night. I have no doubt that it was God who protected us from harm. He took care of my little boys and me.

Thank You, Lord, because You have many ways to reach us.

Elza C. dos Santos

Our Greatest Need

But seek ye first the kingdom of God, and his righteousness;
and all these things shall be added unto you.
Matt. 6:33.

WHAT IS YOUR GREATEST DESIRE? More brain power? Increased social skills? More money? What do you need most? Some time ago Hurricane Dean paid Jamaica an aggressive and aggravating visit. What did we need most then? Was it plywood or storm shutters? hurricane-proof roofs? lots of food? What did we really need most?

The day before the storm I sensed my need for the Lord in a special way. You see, the coming of Hurricane Dean carried with it dreadful memories for me of Hurricane Ivan. Knowing that I wasn't prepared, I went where I usually go when I am in trouble: my quiet place.

During my dialogue with the Lord I was inspired to read Psalm 91. It was in verse 4 that I found absolute peace: "He shall cover thee with his feathers, and under his wings shalt thou trust: his truth shall be thy shield and buckler." I asked the Lord to "batten down this house with Your feathers." Ever heard of feathers for storm shutters?

I'd like to propose that our greatest need is a closer relationship with the Lord. Find that quiet place. When we come near to God we begin to reflect His likeness, and we become changed. To those changes are added blessings that have no limit. "Seek ye first the kingdom of God, and his righteousness; and all these things shall be added unto you" (Matt. 6:33).

It was almost the end of the Bible story session, and the kindergarten teacher had nearly concluded the Bible story "The Walk to Emmaus." She recounted the experience of the two sad disciples walking to Emmaus and lamenting the death of Jesus. A stranger joined them, and they later discovered it had been Jesus. As the teacher concluded the story an excited little girl shouted, "Miss, Jesus walks with me every day!" The teacher was delighted to hear this and asked, "That is so wonderful! Now tell me, when Jesus walks with you, what do you do?"

"Oh, Miss, when Jesus walks with me I just move over and make more room for Him to walk close beside me!"

It is my prayer that we will all move over and make room for Jesus in our daily walk. That is our greatest need.

Jacqueline Hope HoShing-Clarke

Gossip

Thou shalt not go up and down as a talebearer among thy people.
Lev. 19:16.

THE PERSISTENT RING of the telephone caused me to glance at the clock on the wall. It was almost 9:00 p.m. *Who would be calling me at this late hour?* I wondered. When I answered the phone, a woman introduced herself as a paralegal from an attorney's office. She wanted to know if I'd be a witness in a parental custody case for one of the students in my class. The hearing would take place in another city, over a mountain pass, about 70 miles [113 kilometers] from my home. I was not thrilled.

I'd been to court before as a witness in another custody case. If I had a choice, I didn't want to repeat the experience. I knew that even simple court cases could sometimes take more than one day. In addition, I'd need to arrange for another teacher to take my class.

I told the caller that the boy in question came to school neat and clean, was making good progress in his studies, was a pleasant child, and got along well with the other students. I had noticed no physical or emotional signs of abuse, I added, and his mother sometimes volunteered to help in the classroom. "Why can't I just sign a statement explaining my findings instead of actually going to court?" I asked her.

"That wouldn't do," she said, "because the other party couldn't ask questions to defend his side of the case."

Her answer caught me off guard, and my mind took an unexpected detour, as though someone had dropped a big sign in front of me with large red letters announcing, "That's what's wrong with gossip!"

Gossip is so prevalent that it's easy to get caught up in it. But now I saw it from a different perspective. The wrappings of excuses were torn away to reveal the harmful scars such talk often leaves, made all the more unfair because the subjects under discussion aren't there to defend themselves.

The psalmist's prayer has now become my prayer: "Let the words of my mouth, and the meditation of my heart, be acceptable in thy sight, O Lord, my strength, and my redeemer" (Ps. 19:14). By God's grace, may it be so.

Marcia Mollenkopf

10 Percent, My Friend?

"Bring the whole tithe into the storehouse, that there may be food in my house. Test me in this,"
says the Lord Almighty, "and see if I will not throw open the floodgates of heaven and pour out
so much blessing that you will not have room enough for it. I will prevent pests from devouring
your crops, and the vines in your fields will not cast their fruit," says the Lord Almighty.
    Mal. 3:10, 11, NIV.

Each man should give what he has decided in his heart to give, not
reluctantly or under compulsion, for God loves a cheerful giver. And God
is able to make all grace abound to you, so that in all things at all
times, having all that you need, you will abound in every good work.
2 Cor. 9:7, 8, NIV.

WHEN I WAS A YOUNG GIRL, learning to be a cheerful giver was a problem for me. The very first time I received an allowance, I thought about the goodies that could be bought with it. I received 25 cents every week, to do whatever I wanted with, but my mother and teachers insisted that I give 10 percent tithe. By my calculations, tithe would be 2½ cents each week, and I figured that since I couldn't break a penny in half, I'd just keep it this week and add it in next week. This wouldn't be robbing God, I reasoned. Begrudgingly, though, I put in three cents every week.

As a college student I thought I couldn't afford to tithe, as my little budget included bus fare, eating, rent, and other living expenses. That didn't leave anything! (I didn't have to pay tuition or purchase books, as God had already arranged that.)

Later, as a young woman, I was hesitant about tithing since I had bills due and my budget was always in a bind. So I gave a small offering but no tithe. As I got deeper in the Word and strived to do what was right, I was impressed to try God for myself. He has proven to me time and time again how He will shower me with abundant blessings just for trusting and obeying. As a result, I enjoy being God's steward and gladly return my time, talent, and treasure to the Lord, my Supreme Provider. I cannot undo the past, but I acknowledge my loss of connection as I ask for divine guidance in my everyday walk.

God, please help all of us to be good stewards of Your resources. Amen.

Betty G. Perry

Thoughts About Death

Jesus said unto her, I am the resurrection, and the life:
he that believeth in me, though he were dead, yet shall he live.
John 11:25.

ON A HILL ABOVE THE LITTLE TOWN of Herrenhut is a cemetery with more than 6,000 gravestones, marking the place that faithful Moravians have been laid to rest since the days of Count Zinzendorf. They had devoted their lives to serving God, and the simple gray gravestones on which the name and dates of birth and death are engraved remind us of the devotion of these servants of God. On one side of the path I read only the names of women, on the other side names of men. It is no war cemetery, but all are heroes who rest here—heroes of faith.

My mother-in-law, buried in Bad Aibling, is a hero of faith, too. The simple white gravestones there resemble a war cemetery. And indeed, every one of the people who have been laid to rest there fought a heroic fight of faith.

When my mother was laid into her grave beside my father on a windy November day, we wept because we knew that we would not hear her cheerful voice again. It is a strange feeling when your mother is buried in the cold earth. But we also held on to the promise that one day she will arise again, together with our father, when the Lord will call them at His second coming. Then there will be no more tears, no more pain or suffering, because we will be with Jesus.

I've been at a number of funerals recently. But death has lost its sting: "O death, where is thy sting? O grave, where is thy victory? . . . But thanks be to God, which giveth us the victory through our Lord Jesus Christ" (1 Cor. 15:55, 57). Of course, it's still sad and painful to lose a beloved person, but the Bible doesn't leave us in uncertainty of what happens at death. You may want to read about it again in 1 Thessalonians 4:14-18. These truly are encouraging words!

Death just brings us a bit closer to the final victory. The fight is over. In Christ Jesus death is no longer a final separation but only a passing parting. We have the Lord's promise that whoever believes in Him will live, even though they may die now.

The challenge for us who are still alive is to live in such a way that we are sure to fight the battle of faith at Jesus' side. Jesus is the victor, and whoever is on His side cannot lose. He is stronger than hell, death, and the devil. Live each day with Him—there is nothing to be afraid of!

Hannele Ottschofski

The Flawed Quilt

As many as I love, I rebuke and chasten.
Rev. 3:19, NKJV.

QUILTING HAS BECOME one of my fun pastimes since I retired. After taking a quilting class at the local public library, I joined a guild and a quilting bee to plan and share various projects. As a newcomer to the world of quilting, I was excited about everything. At our guild meetings, held once a month, we're encouraged to share our finished projects for show and tell. It was at one of these meetings, shortly after I'd finished my first project, that I stood up proudly and displayed my quilted wall hanging. The women applauded, thanked me for sharing, and encouraged me to keep it up. When I sat down, a woman sitting near me began to inspect my quilt carefully. She commented that there were a couple of things that weren't done properly and suggested that ripping apart the flawed areas and redoing them was the best way to go. She even offered to help by allowing me to come to her house where we could work on it. I thanked her but told her firmly that I had no intentions of doing any ripping; however, I promised I would make another quilt that implemented all her recommendations.

She moved out of state before I could take advantage of her offer to help me. Nevertheless, I faithfully started another quilt, read books, purchased a quilting bible, and asked others to show me the right way to complete my quilt. My second project turned out much better. It was truly a joy to see the result of using the proper quilting techniques, and it gave me a true sense of happiness and satisfaction for a job well done.

It's never easy to undo something we've messed up, whether at work, with family, or in relationships or situations. Sometimes, when we're admonished to correct something, we are offended. But God's Word is our guide, and He always knows what's best for us. His offer to help is available all the time. He will not move away from us.

We'd be much happier if we'd allow God to direct our paths. Proverbs 3:5, 6 tells us to "Trust in the Lord with all thine heart; and lean not unto thine own understanding. In all thy ways acknowledge him, and he shall direct thy paths." Asking the Holy Spirit to aid us and to give us the desire to please Him in all areas of our lives will always prove to be a wonderful blessing and the results much more satisfying. We cannot produce anything good on our own.

Sharon M. Thomas

A New Home for Titus

*Are not two sparrows sold for a penny? Yet not one of them
will fall to the ground apart from the will of your Father.
Matt. 10:29, NIV.*

IT WAS LATE WHEN WE ARRIVED HOME Sabbath evening after traveling 372 miles (600 kilometers) to two different churches. I decided to check my e-mail messages before going to bed. One was from our son, who had experienced a divorce in the past year. His message was short and to the point: "Today is a very sad day for me. People have been complaining about Titus barking, so I have to take him in and give him up." Titus is a golden retriever dog that our son has had for 10 years. An earlier call from him indicated he had no choice but to find a home for Titus—but where? "I can't just take him out and shoot him!"

My son had recently moved to a new place where no pets were allowed. They did let Titus stay in the garage, but that was to be only temporary. Now what was he to do?

I went to bed that night feeling very sad. We all loved Titus. He was our "grand-dog," and the thought of losing him was troubling. The next morning I called a friend who lives on a farm. During the course of the conversation I told her about the plight of Titus. Without hesitation she said that she would have taken him, had she known. I told her I'd check.

I called my son to see what had happened to Titus. "No one was there when I took him in," he told me. I asked what he'd think if I told him I'd found a home for Titus on a farm. He seemed pleased, even though it would mean parting with him.

In less than 24 hours Titus was boarding a plane. We were there to pick him up, and when we let him out of his cage I realized what a beautiful dog he was. I also realized that not only does God care about us or the birds that fall, He loves all the animals, including Titus, who now has the freedom of living on a farm.

Freedom is God's desire for humankind, as well. We too are in a society that really doesn't want us. But we have a Father in heaven who is preparing a place for us, a place of eternal freedom. In the meantime, we have freedom of choice, freedom to decide to whom we will give our love and loyalty. We are of great value to our Father. Let's choose Him today.

Vera Wiebe

Protection in the Dark

He who dwells in the shelter of the Most High will rest in the shadow of the Almighty.
Ps. 91:1, NIV.

TWO MONTHS HAD PASSED since my husband had left for an evangelistic campaign in Argentina. The wives of other pastors who were involved, my 1-year-old daughter, Abigail, and I traveled to visit our dear husbands and father. This would certainly be an unforgettable weekend! We were overjoyed to see our husbands, to see the enthusiasm of young preachers, and to see the large number of people learning of Jesus. It was also a joy to reunite with old friends.

Exhausted by the activities of the day, we still had to move all the audio equipment because a bad storm had just begun. The lights suddenly went out, but fortunately a candle was found. Finally, we were able to go to bed in the children's meeting room. My husband and daughter were sleeping as I lay awake, remembering the day's activities. I finally fell asleep—but I forgot to blow out the candle!

I remember my husband's voice calling to me, but I just wanted to sleep. When I finally awoke, my husband was carrying me outside, and black smoke had engulfed the room up to his waist. Then he rushed back to get Abigail. While she was still in his arms, I noticed her hands and face were covered with something: Styrofoam had melted and dripped on her! The severity of the situation was beyond my understanding until the next morning when a pastor remarked, "What a miracle has occurred!" The only thing I could think about was my daughter's pain.

I now understand God's marvelous care. Our lives were in danger because of the gases from the burning Styrofoam, but this didn't keep the angels from waking my husband.

There are people around us who are confined in the dark smoke of sin, feeling that sleep has overtaken them, and they don't feel like waking up. "Right around you there are souls who are in danger of perishing. Will you not with the chords of love draw them to the Savior? Will you not cease your reproaches, and speak words that will inspire them with faith and courage?" (Ellen White, in *Review and Herald,* May 10, 1906, p. 8).

Certainly, when we reach heaven, we shall rejoice that in the midst of pain experienced on this earth, miracles will have taken place through the grace of our Lord.

Natalia Lorena Holm de Pérez

A Permanent Move

In my Father's house are many mansions. . . . I go to prepare a place for you.
John 14:2.

AS A MINISTER'S WIFE, I've had to move several times to different places. Some time ago we needed to move from one house to another within the same city. No matter the distance, moving is stressful. Much work was involved in preparing and packing everything, then setting things up and cleaning, unpacking and putting everything where it belongs. Finally everything was in place, and the house was organized and clean. What a marvelous sensation! It seemed like a small piece of heaven. That night we slept peacefully, ready to begin our routine once again.

Late in the morning on the following day we received a phone call from my husband's boss, informing him that we would be transferred to another city because of a need there. Unable to move, I collapsed on the floor, looking at the living room where everything was in place. We hadn't even settled into our new home, and we would begin the moving process again!

Although I was almost paralyzed with the news, my heart was comforted with the beautiful promise that Jesus is preparing a home for us. This move will be final. No packing will be necessary. Upon our arrival in heaven, things will already be in their place. Jesus will have prepared everything so that we can enter this new home and live there forever. No sadness, separation, tiredness, stress, or anything similar! Finally a life of peace and perfect harmony will be ours.

Preparation for this special move should begin now, because our Lord is waiting to welcome each of us with open arms.

Meanwhile, waiting for the day when I will move to that wonderful place that Jesus is preparing for me, I want to undo my pride, unpack my hidden talents, and clean each corner of my heart. I want to remove all the trash of evil, presumption, and intolerance. I want to throw away all the dirty clothing of my own justice. In my baggage for the new home I want to take only gratitude to Him and the hope of being able to embrace my Savior. In this manner I will be able to travel, free from all that attaches me to this world.

When I arrive Jesus will be waiting for me with the white robes of justice, and He will show me the home where I, through His grace, with the great multitude of the redeemed will live for all eternity!

Juliane P. de Oliveira Caetano

Crippled

The blind receive sight, the lame walk, those who have leprosy are cured,
the deaf hear, the dead are raised, and the good news is preached to the poor.
Matt. 11:5, NIV.

AS I WRITE THIS my right ankle is wrapped in a brace, and my left foot is in an air cast. No big accident or dramatic happening—I simply sprained my right ankle, and five weeks later twisted my left foot and broke a bone. It had to be pinned. Needless to say, it's made me think more about disabled people—and the crippled individuals in Scripture.

Remember Mephibosheth? "Jonathan son of Saul had a son who was lame in both feet. He was five years old when the news about Saul and Jonathan came from Jezreel. His nurse picked him up and fled, but as she hurried to leave, he fell and became crippled" (2 Sam. 4:4, NIV). Poor little Mephibosheth—no X-rays, and apparently no one to set the bones or offer any special help. So he spent his life as a cripple. Fortunately, King David provided for him out of his love for his father, Jonathan.

Interestingly, in the Old Testament no one who was lame or crippled in any way was allowed to serve as a priest and to offer sacrifices. God required only the best. And I can tell you that right now I can't be—and do—my best in so many areas. Very frustrating!

During biblical times the prophets had much to say about the lame, the blind, the widows, the children. The spiritual health of the nation was measured by how well these people in society were treated. And the promises of the better land always pictured the healing and support of these same people.

There were a number of instances of healing of cripples in the early church. One of the best known was the healing of the crippled beggar at the Gate Beautiful. That healing and their preaching landed Peter and John in jail. Later Paul healed a cripple in Lystra. It caused a problem there, too, and Paul was stoned and left for dead. These apostles weren't jailed and stoned because they helped the cripples but because of the gospel they were preaching.

Jesus too reached out to those who were lame, blind, sick, crippled. He was bringing the good news—physically and spiritually. And the good news is that someday there will be no more disabilities of any type. Oh, what a blessed day to look forward to!

Ardis Dick Stenbakken

Pete the Tramp

The tongue also is a fire, a world of evil among the parts of the body.
James 3:6, NIV.

WE GREW UP in the middle of Minneapolis and rode the old streetcar to and from church school every day. Mom and Dad were quite poor, but they sent all three of us to church school. I know our dad did people's lawns and gardens after work to pay the tuition. Our parents were very careful with their money, and we rarely had candy or treats. So when it was nice outside, we walked the nine blocks home and spent the carfare on candy or ice cream. (We never dared to tell our mom.)

On our way home at 29th and Hennepin, there was a bridge over railroad tracks. We'd heard there were tramps down there, so one time we peered over the edge and saw a man carrying a long stick over his shoulder with a large sack tied onto it. Then every time we walked home we watched for the man on the tracks, and we hollered over the edge of the bridge, "Are you Pete the tramp?" And then we ran away as fast as we could.

One day he shook his fist at us, but that didn't stop us. We thought yelling down to Pete and running away was a fun game. It became a habit to call down to Pete and ask if he was a tramp. Surely, it wasn't the same man we saw each time. (We didn't tell our mother about this either.)

We were coming straight from church school, where we had learned these verses: "Be ye kind one to another" and "Love one another as I have loved you." Still, at the bridge we were not very kind to Pete.

One day, though, remembering the memory verses, we decided to tell Mom about Pete. She was sad about what we'd done and sat us down to explain that those men had no families who loved them, so they lived under the bridge or else hopped on a train. Mainly, she said that they had very little to eat. Then we felt so terrible and wished we could apologize to Pete. We told Jesus and our mom that we were sorry.

How thankful we are today that we could go to a Christian school and have a godly mother who would set us straight about right and wrong. I've never forgotten Pete. He helps me remember to be more careful with words.

Darlene Ytredal Burgeson

Gracious Hosts

In my Father's house are many mansions: if it were not so, I would have told you. I go to prepare a place for you. And if I go and prepare a place for you, I will come again, and receive you unto myself; that where I am, there ye may be also. John 14:2, 3.

I MET LESLEY AUSTIN when I first became a member of the local MOPS (Mothers of Preschoolers) group. She was a sweet woman with a charming Scottish accent. What impressed me most was her talent as a host. Her goal was to make everyone comfortable and let them know how much Jesus loves them.

I was a little apprehensive about some of the activities that included food. I've been a vegan for many years and know that the way I eat isn't the normal fare at events. Also, I don't want anybody to go out of their way for me. After all, we're only talking about food here! Well, evidently Lesley didn't get that message. Once she discovered my veganism she made sure that there was something for me at every event, big or small. She'd even go so far as making sure there was something for me to eat at restaurants our group went to. After the food was served she'd say, "Is everyone doing OK?" then quickly add, "Mary, how is your food?"

And my good friend, Celeste Ruby Crosby, seems to have taken on the job of being my family's main food supplier when there's a church event. She brings several dishes to a potluck, pointing out the ones that she made special for the Angelin tribe. (The sad part is, she cooks the food we eat better than I do!)

It feels strange to have people take extra effort for me, especially since I enjoy serving others. I suppose I need to get used to it because my friends won't stop caring about me—and God won't either. He cares so much that He's promised to prepare a place for me, and I'm sure it will be beyond my wildest dreams. I can only imagine what heaven will be like and how the ultimate Host will greet me as if I were the only one there.

Lord, thank You so much for the bounty of friends You have given me in spite of myself. Help me to learn to allow others to serve me, and to learn to serve others selflessly. Help me to accept Your gift of grace without guilt or obligation. I can't wait to see the mansion You have prepared for me!

Mary M. J. Wagoner-Angelin

A Sea of Changes!

The Lord is a refuge for the oppressed, a stronghold in times of trouble.
Ps. 9:9, NIV.

AFTER NEARLY 15 YEARS my husband, Harold, and I made a remarkable return to Russia to a sea of changes and unbelievable sights. Harold had been invited to have the commencement address at Zaoksky Adventist University, and we were eager to see for ourselves some of the many changes that have taken place since the fall of Communism. The first taste of this transformation came when we made our way into the newest airport in the Moscow region—Domodedovo. Well lit, lined with shops full of expensive gifts, and a wide variety of inviting restaurants serving Russian food (even pizza!)—it was all so different from before.

Time changes people and places, and time can bring freedom, or snatch it away. But how marvelous to return to the former Soviet Union and find churches sprouting up like daffodils in spring, and young people receiving diplomas on graduation day and heading out to pastor in places their grandparents had suffered persecution. Russian music has always thrilled my heart, and if you go to Russia it will thrill your heart as well.

I felt as if our visit there was a taste of heaven to again be with dear friends from years gone by. I noticed that I wasn't the only one who had acquired a few more wrinkles and some gray hair. And I could look across large audiences and recognize smiles I hadn't seen in a couple of decades. Wow! Proof that we'll know each other in the new earth. There we'll have time to catch up on what's happened in each other's lives, and I can't wait.

Where had the children gone that we'd known? The lovely young woman directing the university choir had been the child who years ago had greeted us with the special Russian bread-and-salt welcome. Other graduates came to pose for pictures and give bear hugs. We toured the Source of Life Publishing House and came across many pastors who had received a set of the Bible commentaries as a gift from brothers and sisters across North America, Canada, and Australia. They told us how they'd learned English by studying the commentaries.

A taste of the new earth is what it was! We could preach without government permission and oversight. We could sing until our lungs were ready to burst. We could share Christian literature! I tell you—it seemed like a glimpse of heaven to me! *Come, Lord Jesus, come!*

Rose Otis

A Kind Deed Repaid

Evil pursueth sinners: but to the righteous good shall be repayed.
Prov. 13:21.

A MAN WANTED TO ENROLL his ward in a school where I worked some years before I retired from public service in my country. I was the officer in charge, and without much ado I quickly attended to him, placed the boy in class, and forgot all about the incident.

A few years later I had to travel a long distance to attend a women's ministries advisory meeting. I needed to take some days off from work, so I got permission and left.

We had a successful meeting, and I joyfully traveled back home. But the devil wasn't happy with success, so he tried to cause problems. Our vehicle broke down on our way back about three hours from home. The van couldn't be repaired in that place, and we had to tow it back to the nearest village and had to spend the night there. The following day, however, the van was repaired, and we got home safely.

Because of the repair delay I was late getting back to work. I went straight to my school, but when I got there the officer who had gladly waved goodbye when I left met me with a stern face. "What happened?" she demanded, and suddenly became officious. Inspectors had come while I was away and noted my irregular absence, and she couldn't cover or defend me.

The next day I went to the office to report why I had been absent when the inspectors came. I expected much difficulty but instead was met by a smiling officer. I told him my mission, and said I was to report my absence to the senior supervisors. He cheerfully told me to sign my name. As I did, I saw the names of the other members of our staff. When I finished, I still asked to see the senior supervisor. "Do you know who I am?" he asked. When I said no, he said he was the officer I had helped some years back, and that when he got to my school and found I was not around he asked about me. Other staff members testified that I wasn't a truant; so he decided not to submit the report until I was back and could sign the list. I didn't need to see any other officer.

I quickly thanked him. The Lord used this officer to cover for me. He repaid a kindness I hadn't thought much about. Kindness, even routine kindness, pays.

Becky Dada

Four S's

Whatsoever thy hand findeth to do, do it with thy might.
Eccl. 9:10.

LOOKING BACK OVER THE YEARS I see myself literally slogging through the days: cooking three meals for a family of seven, washing clothes, and the never-ending round of tidying and cleaning. For many years we didn't have a refrigerator or washing machine, which added to the workload. There were times we had a maid to help me out, especially when the children were very young, but as they grew up they helped out with whatever they could do; I tried to make work pleasant for them. Still, I rushed from morning till bedtime, with no time to fuss or feel grumpy, though there were times I felt as if I were serving a life sentence at hard labor. Being a tidy person, I had to put extra effort into my work. Where did I get so much energy? Many times my husband asked, "Don't you ever get tired?" I would reply, "No, there's no time for that." Night was the only time to rest. Once I hit the pillow, I'd drift into a soundless sleep till my husband woke me in the morning.

Years have flown by, and I find myself still working hard, though perhaps not quite as hard as I used to. I still wonder where all the energy comes from. I've come to realize that it was God who was with me all along, giving me the energy. I remember kneeling and thanking God for three S's: speed, strength, and stamina, God's special gifts to me—precious gifts indeed. Without them I'd have been so helpless. To make work and life complete, a fourth S was given to me at the same time: skill. God knew I needed skill to do my work efficiently. Without skill I wouldn't have been able to sew and knit for the family or make special birthday cakes for them. Truly, God has been wonderfully generous to me, and I give Him all the glory and honor and gratitude.

Since retiring I've had time to make use of my skill. I have so much fun making craft items, soft toys, and patchwork quilts. When looking at the things I made, someone asked me, "Where do you find the time to make all these things?" I answered that all of us have the same amount of time—24 hours every day—and time is a talent to be used profitably and not to be wasted. I'm glad that I'm not lazy and am not ashamed to work. Work is a blessing God has given to each of us.

Birol Charlotte Christo

What About the Small Stuff?

Are not five sparrows sold for two copper coins? And not one of them is forgotten before God. Luke 12:6, NKJV.

OUR GOD IS BIG, but, you may wonder, does He care about the small stuff? Let me tell you a story of how God took care of something for me.

Humidity is a fact of life on a tropical island. You get used to always feeling damp and having sweat constantly trickle down your back. Sometimes the air is so thick that your lungs feel as if they are filling up with water as you breathe. Your body eventually adapts, but other things may not.

My twin brothers had given me a watch for my sixteenth birthday. After about a year of living in Saipan, my watch began acting up. Sometimes it ticked; other times it just wouldn't. At first I thought the battery was failing, but after replacing the battery I realized that the humidity was taking its toll. For several weeks I was able to manage. When it stopped, I'd fiddle with it until it started ticking again. Then one day, without thinking, I stuck my hand into a deep jug of water to retrieve something, completely submerging the watch. Immediately I dried the watch off, but it had already stopped ticking. No amount of fiddling would get it ticking again and, seeing the condensation under the glass, I sadly realized that my special watch was finally dead.

I didn't know what I was going to do. To a teacher a watch is just as important as her red pen and whistle. All weekend I checked the watch to see if it was miraculously ticking again, but each time I was disappointed. Monday morning came, and knowing I'd need my watch, I decided to take it to school anyway. It seemed like such a small matter before God, but I sent up a quick prayer and mounted it on my wrist with the faith that God would help my watch start ticking again before school started. I checked during staff worship—it wasn't working. I checked while making my photocopies for the day—still wasn't working. I checked a few minutes before school was to begin—it was working! Joy coursed through my veins, and praise flooded my heart!

Not only does God care about the major problems in our lives—He truly cares about the small stuff, too. He had heard my prayer and answered just in time!

Mai-Rhea Odiyar

Open Windows

Prove me now herewith, saith the Lord of hosts, if I will not open you the windows of heaven, and pour you out a blessing, that there shall not be room enough to receive it. Mal. 3:10.

AS I WALKED THROUGH THE DOORS of the shopping center I saw a helium balloon floating in midair. Printed across its face were the words "When God closes doors, He opens windows." I kept walking, and before long there was another balloon carrying the same message. H'mmm . . . God opens windows. All my life I'd heard it this way: "When God closes doors, He opens doors" (not windows). When I caught sight of a third balloon carrying the now-familiar message, I seemed to be suddenly awakened from a daze.

Immediately I recalled a phrase from a text: ". . . if I will not open you the windows of heaven, and pour you out a blessing." God had showed me His message three times before it really got my attention. He was alerting me to the truth that He opens windows, not doors, when He closes other doors. An open door can accommodate a much larger amount than a window. Therefore, in opening windows I must expect less than if it came through open doors.

Acceptable idea, yes, but I thought further: *The text says that He will "pour you out a blessing." That means* one *blessing. "There shall not be room enough to receive it." Not room to receive that one blessing!* This blew my mind. God's blessing is small enough to be poured out of a window but so big that there isn't enough room for me to receive it. A little more elasticity in my thinking made me realize that the window is the window of heaven. So how big is the window of heaven? Bigger than I— or my needs.

Coming back to reality, I discovered that I was in the flower section of the store. I had no reason to be there and wasn't even conscious of my surroundings. I could conclude only that God had led me there to show me His message.

Shortly after that experience God opened, one by one, three windows of blessings as answers to my prayer of weeks before. If I hadn't seen those balloons I would not have recognized the blessings when they came.

Thank God for His guidance and messages!

Joyce O'Garro

Passing the Baton

I have fought the good fight, I have finished the race, I have kept the faith.
2 Tim. 4:7, NIV.

WHAT A GORGEOUS TIME for my walk! Strong gusts of wind have pushed away the clouds so that sunlight can bring a striking glow to the autumn leaves. I stumble along happily, blown to and fro by fitful bursts of wind playing among the rows of houses.

Suddenly I hear noises behind me. Thinking someone wishes to run by me on the narrow sidewalk, I step aside. As I turn to look, I'm surprised to see that my pursuer is a smattering of leaves that occasionally scrape the pavement as they spin in a swirl of wind. All the colors of autumn are represented in that flock of flying wonder—browns, reds, and yellows merrily dancing together. I laugh at their antics as they spin in my direction, and join in the fun by quickening my pace in an attempt to keep ahead of them. But I'm losing the race when suddenly the gust of wind stops—and the leaves fall to the pavement. A twinge of sadness replaces my playful mood. The leaves are motionless, their race over.

As I walked on alone, I found myself pondering a different race, one with greater consequences but no less delight. I thought of the many saints who had walked this earth before me. Being from every tribe and nation, they were gloriously colored by their inheritance from the Father. They ran their race for a season, dancing and swirling on the wind of the Spirit. Then all too soon they were gone. As they finished their race, though, they left something priceless behind. Like a relay runner passing a baton, they handed off the precious gospel of Christ to the next generation.

I smiled as I thought of brave Christians throughout the ages who persisted in their faith, despite trials and persecutions. Why? One day I could be handed the life-changing baton of the gospel.

Then it would be my turn, my day to dance on the wind of the Spirit. But before I fall lifeless to the pavement, I pray the Lord will strengthen me as I run diligently to pass that baton. Then I will say with Paul, "I have fought the good fight, I have finished the race, I have kept the faith" (2 Tim. 4:7).

There can be no greater success than to cross the finish line with a shout of victory.

Laura L. Bradford

Encumbrances

Wherefore seeing we also are compassed about with so great a cloud of witnesses,
let us lay aside every weight, and the sin which doth so easily beset us, and let us run
with patience the race that is set before us, looking unto Jesus the author and finisher
of our faith; who for the joy that was set before him endured the cross, despising
the shame, and is set down at the right hand of the throne of God.
Heb. 12:1, 2.

I WAS TRAVELING BACK to Lusaka, Zambia, from the United States. During my three-week stay in Maryland I had made purchases for my family and friends. And, of course, I had acquired a lot of resource materials from the two advisories I'd attended.

I had two suitcases: one was full of clothes, and the other was full of resource materials and gifts. The airline restriction was that each could weigh not more than 70 pounds (26 kilograms). I tried to make everything fit. Among my purchases were two leather jackets, one full length and very heavy. It became obvious that they wouldn't fit into my suitcases, so I decided to wear them during the check-in process. There was no place to weigh my suitcases, so it was difficult for me to tell whether or not I was overweight, and I wasn't prepared to leave anything behind. I wanted everything to go.

As the driver of the airport shuttle lifted one of the suitcases into the van he exclaimed, "This is overweight!" It was 4:00 in the morning, and there was nowhere to buy another suitcase. My only option was to pray to God either to make my suitcases light or help me find a way out.

At the check-in counter the porter told the clerk that I had overweight baggage and that I'd need to remove some stuff. I was panting and sweating profusely because of the two leather jackets. After she checked my ticket, the clerk guided me to the international check-in counter. My suitcase was six pounds (more than two kilos) overweight. I'd have to remove something or pay a lot of money.

The Bible tells us to remove every encumbrance that may hinder. There are many things that hinder us from having a fruitful relationship with Jesus, things that we aren't even ready to remove. *Lord, help me to put my life in order. Help me to tailor my life according to Your requirements so that on that day I may not be found with excess baggage.*

Caroline Chola

A Hole in My Heart

The Lord himself goes before you and will be with you; he will never leave you nor forsake you. Do not be afraid; do not be discouraged. Deut. 31:8, NIV.

I LOVE TEACHING! It brings me much pleasure to work with the youngsters and watch their minds expand when reading a passage or working on a social studies project. As I sat balancing our household budget one day, though, I realized that something had to give. Working at the charter school where I was employed furnished fewer dollars than working with a public school.

I got on the Web and saw an ad for a teaching job that I knew would suit me perfectly. And the pay was definitely better. I applied, was interviewed, and landed the job, but I was still unsure. I thought I should prepare my students ahead of time. "I'll be leaving this school on March 16," I told them. Some showed their sadness; others took it in stride.

But one little girl couldn't wait to pour out her sorrow at her mother's knee. "Miss Jones is leaving," she told her mom tearfully. "It feels like I have a hole in my heart."

I explained to the mother that though I loved the school, I couldn't stay because the compensation was not quite enough. The mother immediately contacted the school and complained to the administration. "Why aren't you paying our teachers?" she wanted to know.

Administration called me in for a meeting. They begged me to finish the year. They could not offer me more money, but they would write a letter of recommendation at the end of the year.

Confused and torn, I prayed that God would lead me in the right direction. I would be leaving a job in which I had worked hard with the children, not only in reading skills but in character-building skills. I felt appreciated and loved by the parents and faculty. But I would be going to a more mature bunch of students, and getting county benefits and a higher salary.

I decided to finish out the year at the charter school, and I needed to tell the other principal. I asked her if I could finish the year at the charter school and be reconsidered for the next year. Her reply was frosty. "If you can't commit to me now, I will not hire you in August." As I hung up the phone I knew that God was telling me to stay at the charter school.

Thank You, loving God, for helping me make decisions both big and small. When I make foolish decisions on a whim, I give You permission to intervene.

Raschelle McLean-Jones

Only God Understands

And God shall wipe away all tears from their eyes; and there shall be no more death, neither sorrow, nor crying, neither shall there be any more pain: for the former things are passed away. Rev. 21:4.

IN THE SMALL CHURCH where I worshipped for seven years I mothered more than 20 youngsters, teenagers, and young adults. Our relationship started with sign language classes and grew tremendously, evolving into deaf ministries, interchurch camping, and involvement in educational and social programs, among other activities. I certainly loved "my children."

There were three of us from the nursing profession in that church. We were always on duty for the community and happily served where we could. We were close friends as well, so a few times two of us went on vacation at the same time, but usually one of us was on duty at home. Then one fall, for the first time, the three of us all left together for a vacation in Florida. We were still only a phone call away. One morning at 6:00 one of my girls called, quite disturbed. She informed me that one of my boys had passed away suddenly after a very short illness. Of course we were shocked. He had died four days before his sixteenth birthday and five days before what would have been his first youth day sermon. Everyone had been looking forward to that, and now it was not to be. He had been courteous, loving, respectful, and dependable, well-loved by his peers and adults alike.

His passing was really difficult to take in. I thanked God for his life, though it was far too short. Pleasant memories linger still. He is missed, but I remember the expressions of the remaining children—"It could have been any one of us." That made us stop to think how uncertain life is, and the importance of living for God always.

No answers came for the questions we had. Was there anything nurses could have done to change the situation had we been there? Was that how it was supposed to be? The promised hope of life eternal in the New Jerusalem is ours to cherish. God knows each situation, pain, and heartache, and He soothes all with love, unconditionally. I am so glad. And that is the message I hope every young person (and older ones as well) has the opportunity to learn.

Donette James

He Is Interested in the Small Stuff, Too!

Be careful for nothing; but in every thing by prayer and supplication with thanksgiving let your requests be made known unto God. And the peace of God, which passeth all understanding, shall keep your hearts and minds through Christ Jesus. Phil. 4:6, 7.

I SAT STARING AT THE BROKEN JUMP DRIVE. I had tried everything and nothing had worked. As a last resort, I decided to split it open and put it back together, hoping that would trigger it to work when I plugged it back into my USB port. *Lord,* I prayed silently, *You know that I need the information on this disk.* All my lesson plans for the school term, a children's story I was working on, my end-of-term examinations, and a host of other invaluable files were all on this one jump drive. I snapped it shut and placed it in my laptop's USB port. I held my breath for the miracle—and nothing happened. My heart sank. Then a thought came to try one of the computers in the computer lab. I'd already tried that option but felt compelled to try again. I slowly pushed the jump drive into the lab computer USB and the same message, "Unrecognized device," came up. I was about to turn away in defeat when the miracle happened: all the files from my jump drive appeared on the screen. I screamed, "Thank You, Jesus!" and ran for another jump drive to backup the files.

This experience taught me two very important lessons. A couple of days before I had lent my jump drive to a student. I had been impressed I should save the files on another jump drive and on my computer, but I figured I'd do it at the end of the term, which was only a few days away. Lesson 1: when the Spirit speaks, don't delay; act right away. Lesson 2: God answers all prayers, and He is interested in every aspect of our lives. I was trusting in God to take care of so many issues in my life during this time, and I felt that somehow He wasn't paying attention to what I considered great needs. When I decided to give up and ask God for a miracle in recovering my files, my faith was as a mustard seed, but I knew there was no other way. I needed to depend on God. After the miracle a refreshing peace came over me. I realized that if God had answered my prayer for the recovery of the files, how much more would He answer prayers for even greater needs and requests. Let us rest assured that God is able and, in everything with prayer and thanksgiving, make our requests known to God.

Tracey-Ann Trail

In Praise of My Scars

The Lord your God is with you, he is mighty to save. He will take great delight
in you, he will quiet you with his love, he will rejoice over you with singing.
Zeph. 3:17, NIV.

LET ME SHOW YOU MY SCARS. (Please don't let my readiness to undress shock you.) These scars represent love and caring—visible proof that my brother and sister-in-law, whose faith I once dared to question, believed and cared enough to help me regain the mobility I had lost.

It all started when I struggled out of the library, clutching the walls. That night I came to grips with reality: I could no longer walk. Someone brought me a wheelchair, and somehow I got home. That was the beginning of my sorrows. As my osteoporosis worsened, so did my gait. Eventually I became fully dependent on crutches. My hips no longer supported my slender frame. What else could I do? The money for the surgery didn't seem to be available. It had been blessing enough to come to the point of retirement with full pension. I knew my Lord owned the cattle on a thousand hills, but why should I be different from other people who couldn't afford surgery? What had I done to merit a miracle when others had to live with their pain and were confined to bed, or worse?

Little did I know that since "He delighted in me" (Ps. 18:19, NIV) and I was just as special as any of His children, my God had a series of miracles waiting for me. Little did I know that my vacation with my California relatives would return me to a new, mobile life. Nor did I know how the miracles would blossom. I did know that God was with me.

Somehow my brother found a doctor and a hospital who would replace both my degenerated hips with cobalt titanium ones. And the blessings continued. I spent four days post surgery in the hospital, with no complications or even pain. My brother and sister-in-law converted their family room into my bedroom so that I could have more room for rehabilitation. Even though I couldn't afford the rehabilitation hospital, a friend skillfully guided me through the path to regain strength in my wasted muscles.

Every time I see the scars I thank God for ordering my steps. I know I can never repay Him. While some of the monetary debt to the hospital still remains in dollars and cents, this privilege of walking again has placed me at His feet in total submission. I have a real debt to pay.

Jean Annette Brice

Giving Thanks Before Thanksgiving

*Giving thanks always for all things unto God and
the Father in the name of our Lord Jesus Christ.
Eph. 5:20.*

GROWING UP, I HEARD ABOUT IT for weeks, and as an adult I'm still hearing about Thanksgiving Day, whether by radio, television, friends, or family members. I find myself reminiscing about one special Thanksgiving, recalling my mother planning for that big Thanksgiving dinner. A number of relatives and one longtime friend would be with us. Mother was a great cook, and even though it required planning, time, and tiring work, she loved to cook and make others happy. Our enjoyment of what she prepared was rewarding for her. I wasn't as happy as she, for I was always given small chores to do when I would have liked to be doing my own thing.

Everyone had started to eat when this long-time friend began saying how thankful she was to be there and still be a friend of the family. When she concluded her remarks, amazingly everyone at the table had flashbacks of a blessing, too. Each person began naming blessings received at some point in their lives.

With the passing of the years and the arrival of children and grandchildren, I find myself thanking God daily for blessings past and present, and I ask the question: "Should one give thanks only on Thanksgiving Day?" I realize the answer is "Of course not!" I agree with the songwriter who tells us to "count your blessings, name them one by one, count your many blessings, see what God has done." Whatever the circumstances, I know that if I counted my blessings the list would be endless. They would include lines from a very expressive poem that says: "With feet to take me where I'd go, With eyes to see the sunset's glow, With ears to hear what I should know: I'm blessed indeed, The world is mine; Oh, God, forgive me when I whine" (Red Foley, "Forgive Me When I Whine").

Thank You, dear Jesus, for countless blessings, seen and unseen. May each day continue to be one of giving thanks as I journey along life's pathway. May I never let the hurried life syndrome cause me to forget from whom all blessings come. I look forward to rejoicing and celebrating with You at the best and most glorious Thanksgiving Day ever.

Annie B. Best

Thanksgiving in Diversity

Let us come before him with thanksgiving and extol him with music and song.
Ps. 95:2, NIV.

THERE WAS A BROAD RANGE of four generations of related characters who gathered at the matriarch's home on Thanksgiving Day. There were daughters with their sons and daughters, and some of those with their children. Some who came were still single, some came with their fiancés. One son came alone. Although he was older than the others (but just as handsome), he had never married. I was a guest there, related to one of the in-laws and a grandmother to some.

The daughters brought pies, casseroles, cakes, salads, appetizers, and snacks. The oldest daughter worked in the kitchen all day, supervising the preparations, making the mashed potatoes, gravy, yams, and setting up the buffet. And the others helped her. It was a yearly ritual, I was told.

One grandson brought a turkey all ready for the oven. There were two kinds of gravy, a choice for the different lifestyles. The family, made up of those who had chosen different pathways, was very happy to be together again in this way on this holiday as they did each year, at their mother's, or grandmother's, home. And she was very happy to have them all there.

The TV featured the usual holiday parade and football game, entertaining old and young alike as they wished. Some just sat and visited with each other. Photos were taken of each group, especially the tiny tots, playing together with toys brought out for the occasion.

What impressed me the most was how well they got along. What love was expressed between them, so diverse in their ways! However, this one day a year they came together in thanksgiving to lay aside their differences and join together in prayer, demonstrated when they all joined hands as the prayer was said to bless the day and the food. Once again we could say, "For the Lord is good and His love endures forever; His faithfulness continues through all generations" (Ps. 100:5, NIV).

Lord, help us all to "be one" in love as You prayed for us to be in Your prayer given to us so beautifully in John 17. Jesus prayed for Himself, for His disciples, and for all believers in the generations to come. May we join together in love and diversity.

Bessie Siemens Lobsien

Heartfelt Thanks

In every thing give thanks.
1 Thess. 5:18.

WHEN MY FAMILY ASKED ME what I wanted for my birthday last year, I asked for a block-of-the-month quilt. Each month I'd be sent all the fabric and patterns I'd need to create one pattern block for the quilt. The quilt they purchased for me is called "Heartfelt Thanks." There are 10 squares of different sizes, and each one is appliquéd with a different thing to be thankful for, such as plentiful harvests, homes, friends and family, angels, peace and harmony, and, of course, cozy old quilts!

The year has been very busy, but I've managed to squeeze in the time to cut fabric, piece border blocks, appliqué designs, and backstitch the wording. The quilt will be finished just in time for my next birthday. When life felt very crazy, when I was sick for three months, when I had a dissertation to finish, when our teenage daughter became ill, when work threatened to overwhelm me, I could take time out and relax in the fragments of my life with the "thankful quilt" and remember that there was much to be thankful for, even in the chaotic darkness of some of those moments.

Now, as I am hand-quilting around the appliquéd images, I have more time to reflect. I had followed the pattern created by the designer, but what if I had designed my own "thankful quilt"? How would I have changed the designs? What would I have wanted to thank God for? Yes, I'm glad for all the things the designer included on her quilt, but I would have added some other things: health, my church community, the fun of creativity, laughter, a good night's sleep, God's protection of us, His forgiveness, His amazing love, hope of a future in heaven, a life full of meaning and purpose. Although they haven't been included in the project, those things are there, appliquéd on the quilt of my heart, and I'm thankful for them.

What are you thankful for? How do those things bring quilt-like warmth, color, and comfort to your life? If you made a thankful quilt, what would be on your 10 blocks? Even if you're not a quilter you can take a basket and find things that represent what you're thankful for—a photo of a friend, a model of a tiny house, a Bible verse that encourages you—and offer up heartfelt thanks to God, who has extravagantly given us all these gifts.

Karen Holford

A Bag Filled With Skittles

The earth is the Lord's, and the fullness thereof; the world, and they that dwell therein. Ps. 24:1.

I THOUGHT I'D SHARE A LITTLE STORY WITH YOU, simple but quite profound. My friend Petula and her 4-year-old son Bronson went out for a walk. On their way back she took out a bag of Skittles candy and put four in his little hand. Of course he immediately put two in his mouth, and two fell to the ground. Petula reported that he cried as if there were no tomorrow, even though he could see the bag she was holding and knew that it was still filled with Skittles. For a moment she thought, *Why is he crying when he knows his mommy has a whole bagful?*

Now for the moral of this story. Isn't it amazing how the Lord uses our experiences to let us know of His immeasurable love? He has said that He will supply all our needs according to His riches in glory (Phil. 4:19). The question is Do we really take God at His word? I was once like that little boy, grieving for what I had lost. I had forgotten that our heavenly Father has a vast supply of whatever I need. It's not locked up, or even hidden. It is available to me. Philippians 4:6 says, "Be careful for nothing; but in every thing by prayer and supplication with thanksgiving let your requests be made known unto God." Whether it's a small loss or a great one, the Lord will come through for you.

Petula's little son reminds me that our Father always has something better in store for us than that which we may have lost. I no longer worry about what I've lost because God has blessed me more than I could ever imagine. Let's not worry about those things but focus instead on what we will gain because of God's grace toward us. There are many Bible promises about this, but one I like is found in Psalm 37:4, 5: "Delight thyself also in the Lord: and he shall give thee the desires of thine heart. Commit thy way unto the Lord; trust also in him; and he shall bring it to pass."

Let's stop placing limits on the Lord and trust Him. Know that His plan for us is far superior to what we could ever think or dream. Remember, our Father is the Creator of this vast universe, and His blessings are endless. Just as Petula held a bag full of Skittles, our Lord owns "the cattle upon a thousand hills. . . . For the world is mine, and the fulness thereof" (Ps. 50:10-12). I thank Petula for sharing this lesson.

Annabell Hall

Be Yourself

I the Lord search the heart, I try the reins, even to give every man according to his ways, and according to the fruit of his doings. Jer. 17:10.

I'VE GROWN UP FEELING VERY "DIFFERENT" and often not accepted by others. I am tall and large-framed. When I was young I couldn't mix with my peers. If I were in a crowd and they'd all be talking away, I'd think, *What on earth do they talk about?* I had a few friends, but I felt I was very poor at socializing, and I felt this very keenly. However, I was always comfortable in the company of old people and could talk to them.

Years went by, and I married and had four children, and all along I found myself "collecting" old ladies. I'd visit them, phone them, write to them, and encourage them to eat nourishing food to keep strong. I was needed; I was making a difference. I began to realize that this is a part of my life, and the fact that I couldn't mix with my peers when young didn't matter at all. I think back and realize that the company of my parents at home was much better than young company anyway. I'm now in my 60s and heading into my own old age. I have friends who are in their late 90s from whom I've learned so much. I treasure the talks I had with my Spanish grandmother, who is long gone now.

We are all diverse. We cannot mirror other people. As one women's camp speaker said, "You are unique—no one can do the work that God has appointed you to do." So I say have confidence in the character God gave you and use it for Him. Take an interest in your own talents and gifts. Over the years I've tried to encourage old people in their faith. I'm looking forward to seeing many of them in heaven. I really hope I will. It's amazing how people can get to be so old and haven't yet found Jesus.

You are here on this earth for a purpose. There is no duplicate of you in the whole wide world—never has been or ever will be. You were brought here for a purpose, to fill a certain need. Don't try to surrender your individuality; it is your greatest agent of power. God has given each of us a gift (Rom. 12:6-8; 1 Cor. 12:27-30). What is your gift? You can be a power in the world by being yourself and concentrating on using what God has given you.

Beryl O'Hare

One Extra Sunday, Please

*To every thing there is a season, and a time to every purpose under the heaven.
Eccl. 3:1.*

I SAT AT MY DESK, head in my cupped hands, and stared at my daily planner. I looked at the long list of items and sighed. I had done nothing I set out to do. There had been so many interruptions, all important but very time-consuming. I looked at my watch. It was nearly lunchtime, and I hadn't started on the list yet. Where would I find the time to do all that I needed to do? What I need is an extra Sunday for this week, I mused. Sundays were days when the office was closed, and I could work uninterrupted at difficult tasks that needed concentration.

"Hoihnu!" I called to my assistant. "Do you have one of those books that we use to requisition supplies from the stockroom?"

"Yes," she said cheerfully. "I'll bring it right there." In a moment she was beside me, order book and pen in hand. "What can I get for you?" she asked.

"Please order me one extra Sunday for this week."

She looked at me with a puzzled expression on her face. "What was it you needed? I didn't quite get it."

"I really need one extra Sunday for this week," I repeated. "Please order one."

Suddenly she realized the joke and replied, "For that I guess you'll need to talk to the office manager. There's none available in the stockroom."

Ah, yes. If only we could order more time when we need it! I longed for chunks of uninterrupted time.

That night I wrote in my prayer journal: "Lord, for You time is not important. You have all of eternity, but I have only now. For me time is a source of frustration because I don't have enough of it. I feel as though time is running away from me." I drew a clock with legs racing along the page with a stick figure of a woman (me) racing after it. Under it I wrote, "If only I could catch time and make it stand still until I get my work all caught up! What a dream!"

Yet God has given us all the time we need to do whatever is important. I need to bring my to-do lists to Him each day for His direction. There will be time enough for everything that really needs doing. No extra Sundays needed.

Dorothy Eaton Watts

Taste Test

O taste and see that the Lord is good.
Ps. 34:8.

THANKSGIVING DAY HAS COME AND GONE, which means it's time to make fruit-cake! Now, I've heard all the fruitcake jokes, such as using them as doorstops, but we like that special once-a-year Christmas treat. We always had it when I was growing up, and I've kept the tradition going. Over the years I developed my own recipe, but there's a problem with it—the cake falls apart when it's cut. Perhaps I put too many nuts and too much fruit in it, but that's what makes it special.

Years ago I was at a social gathering in a private home, and fruitcake was served. I thought it was delicious. It didn't crumble, and made nice slices. Learning that the hostess had made it, I asked if I could have her recipe. There was no reply. Thinking she hadn't heard me—after all, there was quite a crowd in the room—I asked again, with the same result. Embarrassed, I realized that she had heard me but was unwilling to share, even though I wouldn't have been making it for the same people she did.

I have a friend whose mother-in-law would give her a recipe but always leave out a key ingredient! I've always considered it a compliment to be asked for my recipes and have gladly given them. In return, I've received good ones from others.

I love collecting recipes and have many books, boxes, and clippings of them. It may whet the appetite to look at the pictures, read the directions, and imagine what the item would be like. But it's the tasting of a good finished product that brings satisfaction. After we've tested a recipe and found that it meets expectations, we feel comfortable in passing it on to others.

In the same way, it is through personal experience that we "taste and see that the Lord is good." Do you get hungry or thirsty? Jesus said, "I am the bread of life: he that cometh to me shall never hunger, and he that believeth on me shall never thirst" (John 6:35). Now, that's a recipe worth sharing!

In the days before Christmas we plan the gifts we'll give to our neighbors, usually including something homemade. One year it was pecan pralines that made a real hit with one neighbor. He asked if I had made them. I assured him I had—and gladly gave him the recipe!

Mary Jane Graves

Please Trust Me 100 Percent

*And he hath put a new song in my mouth, even praise unto
our God: many shall see it, and fear, and shall trust in the Lord.
Ps. 40:3.*

WE CHRISTIANS SOMETIMES use sentences and phrases that are easy to say but harder to live by. I know I need to ask God, *Am I really living what I'm saying, and do I know what the words really mean?*

I've said phrases such as these: "I'll pray for you," "You are saved by Jesus' blood," "Jesus loves you." Here's one I've heard—and even said: "Trust in the Lord." "Trust in the Lord 100 percent" has been hard for me to live up to.

When all is sunshiny and going my way, it's easy to say that I'm trusting in Him. But when my life is not the way I planned, when my life is upside down with my spouse, children, family, friends, and church, do I trust?

God has promised to be there for me 100 percent. I need to rest in Him (another one of those phrases), but how do I do what He's asked me to do? I sometimes need concrete pictures and ways to see and follow what Jesus asks me to do. I hope that some of the ways I've found will help you also to make your walk with Jesus authentic.

1. Find a place where you can be quiet and alone, even if it is in the bathroom. Turn off the lights, and listen. I know, you may think that's funny, but really listen. What do you hear? If you are in the bathroom you may want to turn on the water, as the sound of water can be a relaxing sound. Silence is also a very wonderful thing.

2. Go outside. I love to climb mountains, sit on top, and see God's amazing world. The sound of wind and the view will still your heart, and He can speak to you.

3. Christian music has been a blessing to me. Many times there's been no church near where we've been stationed, so music has been important to me. I have a little music in my blood, and I play and sing at the piano. Pay special attention to the words of hymns.

Dear Lord Jesus, please teach me each day to trust in You. Hold on to me and never let me go. Help me to believe You and not listen to Satan's lies. Thank You for Your faithfulness to me each day, 100 percent.

Susen Mattison Molé

The Verse

You will not have to fight this battle. Take up your positions;
stand firm and see the deliverance the Lord will give you.
2 Chron. 20:17, NIV.

ONE MORNING DURING MY DEVOTIONS I read today's text. It took me back a few months to a time I faced some of the most difficult situations I'd ever had to endure in my lifetime—a miscarriage, getting fired from my job, the death of a close friend, all within an eight-month period of time. I had clung to Habakkuk 3:17, 18: "Though the fig tree does not bud and there are no grapes on the vines, though the olive crop fails and the fields produce no food, though there are no sheep in the pen and no cattle in the stalls, yet I will rejoice in the Lord, I will be joyful in God my Savior" (NIV). I had deliberately chosen to praise God in spite of everything. It hadn't been easy. Now I wondered if God was trying to tell me something with today's verse.

Just then Jay came online. We'd been close friends some years before; then she got married and moved to the United States. Every so often we'd chat on the Internet, and she'd tell me about her projects. She also requested prayers because of the situation she was facing at home. Jay had spent the past few weeks in South America on a missionary trip and was now packing up, but she was terrified of going back to her husband of eight years, who was emotionally and physically abusive. How was he going to react when she told him that she was leaving him? Would she be safe? I didn't have any answers.

Then I remembered the verse. Excitedly I typed it out for her, encouraging her to be strong and to trust God. "A few minutes ago God gave me this verse for you. Write it out, learn it, and claim it!" We couldn't believe how amazing our God is. He knew that this very morning Jay and I would meet online. He knew she would be confused and in anguish, and He had already prepared a promise for her to cling to. His faithfulness is indeed great!

As we said goodbye, I thanked God for using me. I'm sure He had a million other ways to get that verse to Jay, but He allowed me to witness to His goodness. I whispered a prayer for her and for the thousands of women around the world who are hurting at the hands of those who promised to love and cherish them, and I prayed that God would have mercy on them and fight their battles too.

Dinorah Blackman

Bumps in the Road

In all thy ways acknowledge him, and he shall direct thy paths.
Prov. 3:6.

MANY YEARS HAVE PASSED since I learned to drive, and I'm still driving with Jesus as the unseen passenger directing my path. Over the years my priority to drive safely hasn't changed. I recall riding with my late husband and being called the backseat driver because I'd often give him unsolicited advice until he informed me that he didn't need a backseat driver. That eventually became my second name whenever we went riding.

I'm not being called a backseat driver anymore, but I am still a vigilant observer when riding with my children, grandchildren, or whenever I'm a passenger. When I am driving I frequently see signs along the way reminding motorists that men are working, that lanes are closed, or that there are potholes and bumps caused by rain, snow, or mass transportation.

One lovely spring morning I was driving down the Baltimore-Washington Parkway, listening to a favorite song on the radio. Traffic was moving at a fast speed, and I saw cars changing lanes but didn't know why. Suddenly I saw a large pothole ahead of me. I wasn't able to change lanes and thought of the damage it would cause to my new tires—and perhaps more—but those thoughts were replaced by this thought: *Keep driving; it's better driving over bumps than changing lanes and striking someone's car, causing hurt to a person.* I slowed down and kept driving without any damage to my new tires.

Just as there are bumps in the human-made roads we travel daily, there are bumps in the roads of life that God gives us to travel daily. In 1 Peter 5:8 God reminds us that Satan is a roaring lion, walking about and seeking whom he may devour, making potholes and bumps in the roads of life.

I thank You so much, dear Jesus, for Your road map, the Bible, that You have given me to follow while traveling along the roads of life. May I live worthy of Your calling, for I picture the day when there will be no signs needed to notify me of work being done. Revelation 21:2 tells me that there is a city called heaven where the streets are paved with gold—no holes or bumps.

Annie B. Best

Shelter in the Time of Storm

*He calms the storm, so that its waves are still. Then they are glad
because they are quiet; so He guides them to their desired haven.
Ps. 107:29, 30, NKJV.*

RECENTLY MY HUSBAND AND I were vacationing in our motor home at one of our favorite parks by the sea. There were many empty spaces around us that allowed an unrestricted view of the sea in all directions. What a bonus!

I selfishly groaned when a couple pulled their trailer beside us. Conscience promptly told me that this attitude was wrong, so the next day I went over to make conversation and welcome our neighbors. With a tone of relief they told me how they had parked close to us for shelter from the wind that had been lashing their tent at their previous location.

This started me thinking about those times I fall short when opportunity stares me in the face. I'm sobered when I contemplate how I respond to those about me. Because I profess to love my Savior I need to remember to practice what I preach by sharing, caring, and being alert to those in need.

Others should be able to see strength and safety in my life that may not be found in their own lives. When I think I'm being inconvenienced, I need to remember that Jesus has His arms open for me whenever I approach Him. He is my helper and is ever near, so surely I can offer the same to my brother or sister.

When a friend or neighbor shares a concern that's burdening their heart or my child comes to me because her world is falling apart, I should offer a Christlike attitude that will help them find some comfort and shelter from their storm.

Jesus tells us in Matthew 25:40 that "whatever you did for one of the least of these brothers [and sisters] of mine, you did for me" (NIV). This text gently counsels that to serve others without reservations is to demonstrate true love in action for Jesus. By visiting the sick, feeding the hungry, clothing the poor, and yes, even sheltering the folk by our van, we are surely providing shelter in a time of storm.

This is God's example left for all. When we choose to faithfully reach out to others, we are serving as a lighthouse that guides to the safest harbor of all—Jesus.

Lyn Welk-Sandy

Blow the Horn

Trust in the Lord with all thine heart; and lean not unto thine own understanding.
In all thy ways acknowledge him, and he shall direct thy paths.
Prov. 3:5, 6.

I WOKE UP THIS MORNING with the memory of a past story on my mind. A voice said, "Write it."

My sons, Eric and Randy, were 12 and 10 years of age, respectively. Charles Miller had brought three boys from the city to our home in the country. The boys wanted to walk in the woods behind our house that go more than a mile east and about three fourths of a mile south. I had never let my boys go into the woods without me because I feared they would get lost.

The boys pleaded their case so hard, however, that I gave in. I had read in *Guide* magazine about kids going into the woods and marking their way on the trees, so I instructed the boys to mark their way on the trees so that they wouldn't get lost. I also told them that I would blow the car horn in a half hour; when they heard it, they were to come home. I knew that when the boys got to playing they'd forget to mark the trees. Confidently the boys marched into the woods with enthusiasm and jubilation in spite of my apprehension.

I drove the car up close to the trees. After a half hour had passed (more like 25 minutes), I blew the horn again and again until I saw the boys appear out of the woods.

Eric said, "Thanks, Mom." He then told me that the boys had in fact gotten lost. They followed the sound of the horn, and it directed them to the familiar landmark of a neighbor's fence, surrounding his sheds and dogs. They followed the fence until the fence ran out, then followed the sound of the car horn until they were out of the woods.

We parents send our adult children out into the woods of life. So many times they go out confidently wearing rose-colored glasses, oblivious to the dangers that the world has to offer them. We can't be with them; we must let them go, trusting in the instructions we've taught them all their lives. However, we do have a resource: the "horn." We sound the horn of intercessory prayers for our children again and again, day after day, hour after hour, so that should they become lost, they may be able to find their way straight home to Jesus. Blow the horn, parents!

Ruth Cantrell

A Perfect Change

And that ye put on the new man, which after God is created in righteousness and true holiness.
Eph. 4:24.

"WHAT IS YOUR NAME?" Can you count the number of times you've been asked this question by teachers, doctors, nurses, politicians, police officers, pastors, and especially children? I believe every living person, from early childhood to senior citizen, has been asked to reveal this important mark of identification. For most of us, the reply is fairly simple.

A precious 5-year-old once told me the name her mother gave her. Then with a quizzical expression she asked, "What name did your mother give you?" When I replied, she demanded, "Why didn't she just call you Elizabeth?" And you know, I agree. Life would have been much simpler for me. I've often been bypassed, overlooked, or delayed because some people refused to try to pronounce my name.

Mine is not a name one might find on a common class roll. In fact, when my name was missing from the report of the results of a public examination I'd taken, everyone who knew me was surprised and disappointed. My name *was* on the report, but it was the one that my mother had reserved for official business, not Urceline, the name used by my family, my neighbors, my teachers, and my friends.

Much later in life I was in the process of making a lifelong commitment to a young man with whom I'd been associated for several years. During a conference with the pastor who would conduct the marriage ceremony, I was asked what name I would like to have appear on the marriage certificate. Pronouncing every syllable as clearly and distinctly as I could, I responded with pride, "Quilvie Galethia Green." Can you imagine my shock when my husband-to-be shot back in perfect Jamaican patois (here translated in English), "I do not know anybody by that name!"

My name has been made fun of, misspelled, and mispronounced. It has elicited comments ranging from "strange," "unusual," "unique," to "queenly." I've learned to appreciate and like my name, but I'm especially looking forward to the new name God is going to give to each of us when we get to heaven (Rev. 2:17), aren't you?

Quilvie G. Mills

Safe From Harm

The angel of the Lord encampeth round about them that fear him, and delivereth them. Ps. 34:7.

CAROLE AND I HAD JUST MADE IT to the other side of the crosswalk when we heard the sound of screeching tires, followed by the involuntary melding of metal in an awful, tinny crunch.

"What in the world?" I exclaimed as I turned around. To my astonishment, I saw the twisted, metal entanglement of a car crash where seconds before my friend and I had stood. The accident resulted in the death of one person and the wounding of two passengers. Had the accident happened only 10 seconds earlier, my friend and I could have been counted among the victims of this disaster.

As the tragedy of the situation dawned on us, we began to sob, not only for the unfortunate victims of the wreck but in the realization that we were safe and sound. It could just as well have been us on a stretcher being transported to the nearest emergency room in the back of an ambulance.

When we reached our destination (which, incidentally, was a prayer meeting at a church sister's home), we praised God for His loving-kindness and His protection. We believed it was more than a simple coincidence that we were safe. We interceded in fervent prayer on behalf of the crash victims and their families.

We are called to pray without ceasing and to make intercession for the saints, for we do not know the day nor the hour of our final moments on this earth. We are ignorant of what the future may hold, for God, and God alone, is the master of time and space. Therefore, we must always be ready. Let's practice doing what's right. The devil is busy, inciting men and women to violence, intemperance, and all manner of depravity. But if we are believers and followers of Jesus, our only safeguard is in the name of our God. He is our shield and buckler; all we need to do is to trust and obey. "The name of the Lord is a strong tower: the righteous runneth into it, and is safe" (Prov. 18:10). We had just experienced that!

As we come into the Christmas season, let's praise God for His daily protection, as well as the ultimate gift of His Son who gives us hope for today and each day.

Jeannette Belot

A Loose Connection

He that hath the Son hath life; and he that hath not the Son of God hath not life.
1 John 5:12.

I FEEL IMPRESSED that I should share a vivid dream that woke me this morning. I've always had dreams, usually meaningless. Until a few years ago I could always remember them when I woke up. Then they started to fade as soon as I opened my eyes. *I'm growing old,* I thought, *and my memory isn't what it used to be.* But lately some dreams have been very clear and have left a lasting impression. Last night's was one of those. In it, Jesus came to take His faithful children home—and He didn't take me.

In case you should wonder about my sinful life, perhaps a brief explanation is in order. I've been a happy, practicing Christian for more than 50 years, most of them as a pastor's wife. My family grew up in the church, married in the church, and are bringing up their children in the church. My role has always been a busy one, juggling family responsibilities with a variety of church-related activities. But today I'm doing some serious soul-searching—Jesus came and didn't take me home.

Am I like the Pharisee who went up to the Temple to pray, and God didn't accept his prayer because he was so self-righteous? I don't think so (not consciously, anyway), though I wonder about the subconscious depths of my being.

Am I like one of the foolish virgins of Matthew 25? It could be; it really could be. They were faithful church members, waiting for the coming of Jesus. They had their lamps (God's Word), and they were full of oil (the Holy Spirit) since the lamps were alight and burning. So what went wrong? As time passed their supply of oil ran low, and eventually, when the crucial moment arrived, their lamps went out. By the time they realized their predicament, it was too late to rectify it. The door was shut, and they were left outside.

According to our Bible verse, Jesus is willing to live in our hearts by faith, the power for a victorious life. We cannot afford to have a loose connection.

Dear Father, I am deeply grateful that You shook this foolish virgin awake this morning. Keep me continually aware that a life of service has no merit of its own. It must always be firmly connected to You through Your indwelling Spirit.

Revel Papaioannou

A Penny for Your Thoughts

And when she finds it, she calls her friends and neighbors together
and says, "Rejoice with me; I have found my lost coin."
Luke 15:9, NIV.

HAVE YOU EVER THOUGHT of the worth of a penny? When I was a child, I really thought I was rich if I were given five pennies to spend. I'd take a long time at the candy counter, mulling over which 10-for-a-penny pieces I really wanted before handing over my precious five pennies. When you were little did you ever sing "Hear the pennies dropping,/ Listen to them fall,/ Every one for Jesus,/ He will get them all" as you slowly dropped your 10 pennies, one at a time, into the basket? I outgrew my "penny" days, but I never forgot the worth of a penny. Now I often spot pennies on the street and pick them up—they seem to be the coins dropped most often. I seldom miss a day when I don't find at least one. I find them in gutters, in mudholes, stuck tight in the asphalt, or just thrown in the grass. I find all kinds of copper pennies—real old ones, shiny new ones, bent or flattened ones, painted ones, and some almost unrecognizable they are so chewed up. Some are silver-colored, made during World War II. Regardless of their condition, they're always engraved with "In God We Trust" on the front and "United States of America" on the back.

One day as I counted and wrapped pennies, I thought, *Why don't people care anything about pennies? Why are they so easily discarded?* I've gotten dollars from collecting and turning them in to the bank. The bank doesn't care what shape they are in. They sort them and put the unusable ones into a melting pot and make new pennies. An allegory ran through my brain.

We're all like these pennies— abandoned, lost, and often discarded. God created us, and stamped each with His character, to be used for His service. Satan decided to mar God's plan by abusing us, defacing us, and tossing us in the gutter of sin, as though we were useless. But God sees us when we're run over in the streets, smashed into the asphalt of life, or kicked into the gutter. He sees us abandoned, tainted with the paint of drugs and alcohol or other sin, so that we are unrecognizable. He sees our value even when we're bent in sin. But we can't pick ourselves up. Some of us don't even know we are lost. So God picks us up and cleans, polishes, and restores us to His original plan so that we shine like new again.

Frances Osborne Morford

Be Ready to Be Surprised!

Do not conform any longer to the pattern of this world, but be transformed
by the renewing of your mind. Then you will be able to test and approve
what God's will is—his good, pleasing and perfect will.
Rom. 12:2, NIV.

EACH SABBATH MY YOUNGEST GRANDSON, Clay, slides up next to me on the church pew and produces something meant to occupy him during what seems like an eternity for a young child to sit still. One Sabbath not long ago, as he sat next to me, he cautiously opened his hand to reveal what I thought was a matchbox-sized green pickup truck. I picked it up, looked it over, ran it back and forth on my lap, and returned it to its rightful owner.

And that's when I became witness to a transformation. With nimble fingers he quickly twisted and turned the small truck parts, producing legs, arms, and body out of what had clearly been a small truck. Right in front of my eyes the truck had been transformed into a strong man, standing confidently with hands on hips and chest out. If I hadn't already been spoofed by another transformer of his, I wouldn't have believed my eyes. I've watched Clay take a variety of his transformers and quickly turn them into something totally different from what they had been before.

These new transformers are very clever toys. In their original packaging they bear little resemblance to what they're capable of becoming, and that's the challenge! There's an analogy here . . . Think about a brand-new baby. When we took our first newborn home from the hospital, I had little comprehension of all that mothering our little bundle would require. But what I carried home in my arms that day in fact had far greater potential than I comprehended. When he was lying in his tiny hospital bed beside all the other babies in the nursery, I had to look for his name tag to be sure I was looking at my little "bundle of joy." But believe me—he came with his own unique DNA, smile, personality, and temperament. Put these little bundles of love in a variety of different environments and watch them transform. Unfortunately, not all will receive advantages to transform under the guidance of God's Holy Spirit. The Great Transformer loves all His children. He desires to see each of us grow and experience life changes that makes us all that He would have us to be. Take hold of His transforming power today!

Rose Otis

Teapot Therapy

It was you who created my inmost self, and put me together in my mother's womb;
for all these mysteries I thank you: for the wonder of myself, for the wonder of your works.
Ps. 139:13, 14, Jerusalem.

IF YOU MET ME, you'd think I was a bit odd—I have scabs on the tips of my ears, and I carry a cast-iron teapot as I walk around the lake. If you could read my mind, you'd say I'd been thinking a lot about elbows. The scabs, the teapot, and my interest in elbows are all related.

Four weeks ago I dislocated my right elbow and smashed the head of the radius, a bone in the forearm. "Oh, Mom," my physical therapist son said when I told him over the phone, "that's so painful—and you're right-handed. You'll need lots of therapy." The next day an orthopedic surgeon seconded his opinion: "This is a serious injury. Even after surgery you may never regain full range of motion."

I thought about elbows for 11 days while I wore a cast, typing slowly, singeing the tips of my ears as I tried to wield a curling iron with my nondominant hand, feeling grateful to a friend who served a Thanksgiving dinner I could eat with a spoon.

If I had thought of elbows previously, I saw them only as ungainly joints. When my cast was removed, though, I realized that elbows are amazing. When I couldn't bring a spoon to my mouth, I realized that the elbow is made to bend. When I unloaded the dishwasher and painfully placed the plates, one at a time, in the cupboard, I realized how the elbow is designed to stretch. When I tried in vain to use a can opener, I realized that the elbow helps turn the wrist. Bending, stretching, rotating, washing my hair, pushing the garage door opener, turning a key—almost every motion reminded me that our bodies function in wonderful ways.

And the teapot? The physical therapist has told me that I need to exercise "obsessively." In church I force my hand to rotate; at home I exercise and massage away scar tissue. And as I walk I carry a weight—currently a teapot is ideal—to assist gravity in straightening my arm.

Already I can do much more. I'm thankful for physicians and therapists, but I'm awestruck at the fact that our bodies heal, that scabs come off our ears, that painful incisions become mild irritations, that some range of motion returns. Yes, we are wonderfully made.

Denise Dick Herr

Call Unto Me and I Will Answer Thee

Call unto me, and I will answer thee, and show thee
great and mighty things, which thou knowest not.
Jer. 33:3.

THE SNOW FELL THICK AND FAST, covering the earth with beauty. But alas, it began to melt, leaving messy cleanup and parking problems. The blasting cold winds froze the melted residue as darkness fell. Easing home, I prayed for a parking place. Yes! There were two women shoveling their way out of a parking spot—and they were leaving! They gladly accepted my offer of help and soon were on their way, taking the building-owned snow shovels with them.

Cold and numb, I went inside. But what would happen in the morning? My right rear wheel perched on a mound of ice, while my right rear fender all but touched the next car. The ice and snow would surely freeze, and my car would slide into the next car. What was I to do?

Trudging wearily into my apartment, I went into my bedroom and fell on my knees. "Lord," I cried, "what shall I do? I have no one to help me, and I must get to work on time tomorrow morning. But how will I make it? The slush will freeze tonight, and then how will I ever get the patch of ice from under that wheel? The ice will be hard, and I'm not strong enough to dig it out. Besides, it's too cold!"

I felt impressed to go out right then and get over the mound of ice. *But Lord,* I protested, *the women took the shovels with them, and I don't have another.*

Had the shovels been returned? No. However, a quick peek out the front door revealed that other residents were shoveling out, using similar shovels. Greatly encouraged, I noticed that a man had just finished, so I asked if I might use the shovel, and immediately proceeded to try to chip off some of the ice under the wheel. As I worked, a man offered to help me and set to work.

Then my benefactor got into my car and backed it right out of the spot, free and clear of the other car. To my amazement, another man came out and headed for his car that occupied a spot I had completely cleared the day before—the cleanest spot on the lot! It was beautiful! I quickly got my car into position and glided into the spot.

I drove out the next morning on time and with breathtaking ease. Has not our heavenly Father promised, "Call unto me, and I will answer thee"?

Audre B. Taylor

Together We Stay Warm

And let us not neglect our meeting together, as some people do, but encourage one another, especially now that the day of his return is drawing near. Heb. 10:25, NLT.

TWO WEEKS AGO an enormous winter windstorm roared through our valley. Before the winds had even peaked, a 78-mile-per-hour [125-kilometer-per-hour] gust knocked out power all over town, even to our weather recording station. So we'll never know how high the winds became as they howled unmercifully, tearing at anything they touched. Shingles flew everywhere. Dust from our vineyards and wheat fields billowed in great clouds, obliterating the sun's light at noon. Sadly, many of our lovely old trees toppled like toothpicks in the storm.

When the dust had finally cleared, my neighbor, a city councilman, returned misty-eyed with grief after a tour to survey the damage. For several days crews had to work around the clock clearing streets, power lines, and buildings of the mess the storm had left behind. Now a local park contains all that remains of some beloved neighborhood trees, a pile of wood chips the size of a large house. The fragrance is rich of pine, spruce, and maple blended together.

The most amazing thing about the pile of wood chips is the steam pouring out of its top. Evidently the life yet remaining in the wood is generating heat. While the ground around is covered with several inches of snow, that giant heap of wood chips is bare, refusing to give in to winter's cold.

What a picture this is of the church as Christ designed it! All of us go through storms. Sometimes we teeter, or maybe we are toppled by trials. Life tears at us and shreds us. Yet even when Satan roars in with his worst, the church remains. The world may throw us aside in a heap, yet we survive because we have one another. As we huddle together, encouraging each other in the faith, a wonderful fragrance wafts not only upward toward heaven but also outward to those around us. The warmth is obvious to the passing world. The life of the Spirit of God keeps us cozy, even through the coldest of times.

Storms are gathering on the horizon. Chilling winds are on the way. But inside Christ's church we are meant to find the comforting security of His own body on earth. Together we stay warm.

Laura L. Bradford

Stand Firm

God our Father loves us. He is kind and has given us eternal comfort and a wonderful hope. We pray that our Lord Jesus Christ and God our Father will encourage you and help you always to do and say the right thing. 2 Thess. 2:16, 17, CEV.

AS I WORK AT THE KITCHEN SINK I love to view the birds from my window. I'm always amazed by the many different varieties of these feathered creatures that mingle peacefully together in their busy hunt for food or building material for nests. Some birds are larger, such as the pigeons, doves, and blackbirds; and some are smaller—the honeyeaters, blue wrens, and sparrows. Often scores of galahs, corellas, or parrots visit; they chatter noisily as they line up along the power lines. There are two old pottery kitchen sinks that we fill with water where they can drink and bathe, which encourages the birds into the yard. Watching them gives much pleasure to my husband, Murray, and me.

One day I noticed a strange bird fly in. It was something like a magpie, but I couldn't identify it. The other birds didn't like this intruder, and attacked until it flew off to safer grounds.

A few days later I watched this same bird fly down to our old unused dairy and land on the high roof. Again a number of birds attacked him. However, while still being pursued, he just hopped along the ridge until he came to the end. This time he stood his ground, and eventually the other birds gave up; he was left alone and victorious. He had overcome his attackers.

I've been troubled of late by some folk attacking my character. There's been a difference of opinion regarding doctrine and personnel. I've prayed earnestly that God would give me some direction and guidance as to how to handle this problem in a proper manner.

I shared my story about the bird and its actions with a woman in our small group meeting. She knew of my situation and suggested that with God's truth we should always stand our ground. I immediately pictured the bird at the end of the ridge, standing firm. Was God trying to tell me something?

Dear God, thank You for the wonderful way You direct our thinking, and for using the actions of Your little creatures we are so privileged to observe. May I stand my ground and honor Your name, remembering the lesson the strange bird taught.

Joan D. L. Jaensch

It's Not About You

A new heart also will I give you, and a new spirit will I put within you: and I will take away the stony heart out of your flesh, and I will give you an heart of flesh. Eze. 36:26.

WE HAD JUST RETURNED from a wonderful weekend with friends some 90 miles (145 kilometers) away. When we came back, rejoicing that God had taken us there and back safely, I discovered that I had accidentally left my purse behind. Unfortunately, I had to go back to retrieve it; there were too many important papers in it.

On the way a car came at me unexpectedly from a side road. I swerved, slammed on the brakes, and managed to avoid an accident. I wanted to blow my horn loudly or yell at him, but the ease of allowing an incident like this to spawn a road rage encounter kept me quiet. It was almost as if God had whispered in the frenzy of the moment, "It's not about you." Prayerfully I realized that it was neither about me nor the careless driver. It was, as it has always been, about Him, and how we can reflect His glory in everything we do.

I found myself asking a simple question: What happened to common courtesy, to respect? It wasn't practiced on the highway moments before, and it's often absent from everyday life.

Often we can be so demanding, so selfish, so controlling that we forget about basic politeness in the self-centered rush to get ahead. I realize how much nicer it would be to use the almost-forgotten word "please" and follow it with a grateful "thank you." I know it would be more respectful to say, "Please, would you do something?" rather than demanding that it be done.

I know that while some of our requests are not burdensome, our tone can be so grievous that it sparks a chord of irritation instead of a chord of helpfulness. Just the tone can make such a difference. We have a wily foe to meet and to conquer. He will use the simplest tool to attack. But we can win in the name of the Almighty One.

We must forget about self because it really is not about us. It is rather about the effort of humility we put forth with His help. The evil one is seeking to use anything—a near-accident, a honking horn, an impatient tone—to get us sidetracked from the important things.

Father God, please give me a new heart. Thank You for helping me to realize that it's not about me. It's about You, dear God, and displaying Your glory in everything I do.

G. G. (Geneva Gwendolyn) Taylor

Genevieve

Keep His commandments and do those things that are pleasing in His sight.
1 John 3:22, NKJV.

AS A NURSING HOME VOLUNTEER I was asked to become a friend to a new patient at the nursing home who didn't have any relatives or friends in our area. Upon entering the patient's room, I found a frail, aged woman huddled beneath her bedcovers. Her name was Genevieve.

Each week as we conversed we found more subjects of common interest. Little by little, she became more animated and outgoing. She blossomed like a rare rose.

Because of her crippling ailments, Genevieve uses a wheelchair, and one day she allowed me to push her into the craft room so that she could participate in the sessions. She soon started designing and making bookmarks for the book cart. She became interested in the home's discussion groups and was chosen to be a group leader. She began decorating her wall bulletin board, which she changes regularly, with articles and pictures cut from magazines.

After winning a three-foot-tall Snoopy dog in a raffle held at the home, she immediately donated it to their lounge for the patients and visitors to enjoy. Many pictures have been taken of Snoopy and Gen, with children admiring them both.

She dresses in brightly colored pantsuits and wears a colorful scarf tied around her "ponytail" hairdo. She is cheerful and has a delightful sense of humor.

In spite of arthritis in her hands and limited eyesight, she began writing articles that she sent to the local newspaper. These were accepted and printed. She began a project to solicit community people as weekly volunteers who would be willing to become listeners to the patients and their problems and ideas, and it worked! She prays every day that God will enable her to be helpful to someone that day, and He does. She drinks at the well of knowledge every day by reading her cherished Bible and large-print educational and religious books.

Her philosophy for living is "Always put on clean clothes every day, and don't forget to wear your red shoes!" Translation: don't lose your love of life! She has shown me, by example, that where love abounds it is possible to grow older with grace and to retain a lively interest in the world and in others. She is 88 and "holding." That's Genevieve!

I love her, and every day I try to remember to put on my red shoes! Will you also?

Rosemary Baker

No Postage Due

The free gift of God is eternal life through Christ Jesus our Lord.
Rom. 6:23, NLT.

CHRISTMAS WAS COMING SOON. I eagerly checked the mailbox every day. I love receiving messages from friends and family in this once-a-year greetings exchange. Cards and letters usually contain summaries of blessings and challenges of the past year. Of course, there are always wishes for God's blessings through the new year. These ritual mailings serve as connecting links with friends and distant family.

One day as I walked back from the mailbox I eagerly flipped through the envelopes. A small envelope caught my attention. It was addressed to me, all right, but there was no return address and no stamp. A handwritten note, which I assumed was from the postal service, read: "postage due, 41 cents."

I smiled. In the Christmas rush someone had remembered me but had forgotten the return address and, most important, the postage stamp. When I opened the card and saw who had sent it, I smiled even more. I knew that Jennie had had a busy year that had included a mission trip, an unexpected new grandchild, extra work hours, and more. At first I was tempted to tease her but knowing Jennie would be embarrassed, I decided I'd just pay the postage. Given all that Jennie had on her mind, I was honored just to be remembered.

As I thought about this little experience, my mind went to the meaning and focus of Christmas. Jesus' birth is certainly more significant than a seasonal celebration. He sends greetings all year long in the form of letters through the Bible, through other people, through circumstances, and through the impressions of His Holy Spirit. Have you noticed? We never get a "postage due" with any of His messages. He paid the price long ago.

December 25, so widely celebrated as the birthday of the Christ child, isn't the exact date of His birth, yet we sing the age-old carols. Children dress up in their father's bathrobes to represent shepherds and Wise Men in Christmas pageants. We write "Peace and goodwill" on greeting cards and send them to friends. We celebrate His birth, and we worship Him. This holiday let's thank Him for the free gift of His saving grace that He offers every season and for an eternal lifetime. No postage due!

Beulah Fern Stevens

Of Donkeys, Love, and Christmas

In this was manifested the love of God toward us, because that God sent his only begotten Son into the world, that we might live through him. Herein is love, not that we loved God, but that he loved us, and sent his Son to be the propitiation for our sins. Beloved, if God so loved us, we ought also to love one another.
1 John 4:9-11.

WHILE DOING SOME HOLIDAY DECORATING, I came upon a porcelain figurine of a donkey being led by Joseph and carrying Mary and the baby Jesus. As I lifted it out of the box, some long-forgotten memories took me back in time.

The year I turned 13 my beloved grandmother passed away in April, leaving a great void in our family. Most holidays and lots of free time had been spent at Grandma and Grandpa Morgan's house because Grandma was the cement that held our extended family together. Now another holiday was approaching, and to my siblings and me the thought of Christmas without Grandma made things feel pretty bleak. Our dear grandpa, ever a lover of children, knew he somehow had to keep up the traditions. Not being a shopper, he came up with a great plan to give Dad and Mom some cash and let them do the shopping. We kids were consulted and asked what we would like. The standard answer to that type of question was "A horse."

What a surprise we got several days later! By lowering our standards a bit, we became the proud owners of a donkey. He was several years old, and came pre-named Austin Pepper.

What fun! We rode him all the time and were the envy of all the neighbor kids. Austin soon became a landmark figure. Anyone giving directions in the area might say, "It's just a half mile west of where the donkey lives," or "Turn south just before you get to the donkey's house." If you've ever heard a donkey bray, you can appreciate the thought of his daily greeting. It was Austin Pepper's early-morning ritual, and on a clear day, he could be heard several miles away. He was a well-loved addition to our menagerie and gave many great memories.

Because of Grandma's death and the subsequent wonderful gifts from Grandpa, our family had many years of enjoyment with our pet. Because of Jesus' life and death, a wonderful gift from our heavenly family, we can enjoy eternity together. Let's remember the reason for the season.

Diana Inman

The Jesus I Love

But his mother treasured all these things in her heart.
Luke 2:51, NIV.

When I think about Jesus, in my imagination I see a humble manger, rugged and plainly made, filled with straw. No woolly baby blankets such as cribs usually have. Surely mangers were not meant for young human babies.

I can distinctly hear the mother animal calling her calf, I see the donkey chasing away a fly with its tail, and a cow casting an inquisitive look into the manger, gazing at the strange-looking little fellow lying there. And then I spot a darling little mother looking tenderly at her firstborn, making sure that in spite of His holiness He doesn't have a need for anything.

As she touches the tiny fingers, a sudden thought slips into my mind. Could she believe that in the future He would ever heal so many sick, make so many lame to walk again, and the blind to see? Could she ever imagine how much wisdom would flow from His holy lips, and how many lives He would bless?

But another thought really makes me tremble. If somebody could tell Mary, would she believe that those same delicate hands would one day be pierced by cruel nails? And pressing a kiss on the innocent forehead, would she believe a crown of thorns would be squeezed onto His head while blood streamed over His body?

Kissing the baby lips, could she ever believe that sometime in the future He would cry out in agony, "My God, My God, why have You forsaken Me?"

As Mary caressed the tiny feet in her hands never would it go through her mind that one day blood would drip from those feet in order to save His children from eternal death. And looking down into those innocent eyes, did she ever think how many sinners He would grant forgiveness to in His short lifetime?

When I see those hands in my mind, I feel His arms embracing me, and while He gives me a hug He says, "Come to Me, My child, and I will give you rest!"

This is the Jesus I love. This is the God I worship, the Lord who led me through many trials and tribulations, the Jesus who will be coming soon to take us home.

Charlotte de Beer

God's Surprises

Every good gift and every perfect gift is from above.
James 1:17.

AS THE SEASONS CHANGE and we come into the fall of the year, our thoughts often turn to gifts we are looking to purchase for the special people on our Christmas gift list. We keep our eyes open in each store we enter, just in case we see the right gift. The giving of gifts is a way for us to express our love to each other. Although we usually give gifts only on special occasions, God is always giving us gifts year-round that show His love to us. As I look out my window I see beautifully colored leaves in the sunshine. I hear birds singing and see my granddaughter playing in the yard. Just a few of my gifts from God.

I remember a very special gift that was actually a miracle. Our annual women's ministries Christmas party is always a highlight of the year for our church women. When we gather at Melanie's home, each of us brings special goodies to share for a meal. After the meal we gather together to open presents. For those who have had a secret sister throughout the year, they reveal their identity with their final gift of the year. The other women each bring a gift to exchange.

As the women's leader I know that there's usually a need for an extra gift or two to ensure that everyone has a gift. So that year I brought two extra gifts. As we began the process of opening the gifts I realized we needed them. So I quickly retrieved them and put them under the tree. As the two gifts were given out and opened, I realized how each gift was perfect. The first gift, bath and body items, was happily accepted by a teenage girl. The second gift was a little figurine of forest animals saying "I'll miss you." As Tania received this gift she knew it was special because she was moving away and leaving her church family behind. She felt the special message came from us to her. God certainly put that special gift into her hands that night!

It is humbling to think how God chooses to use each one of us in His service. If we allow Him, He helps us to make life easier for each other along the pathway of life. As we go about our busy lives we must always keep in mind that God is planning to use us. We should be ready to supply one of God's surprises.

Sharon Follett

The Christmas Light

If I am lifted up from the earth, I will draw all peoples to Myself. . . .
While you have the light, believe in the light, that you may become sons of light.
John 12:32, 36, NKJV.

MY FAVORITE THING of the Christmas season is the lights. I like to drive around the neighborhood and enjoy the festive look the neighbors have added to their houses and yards. Every December I hang a string of colored lights around the mirror in our dining room. I delight in gazing at our Christmas tree with its colored lights sparkling on the silver tinsel.

One morning during my quiet time I asked Jesus to speak His message to my heart. This is what He told me: "If I be lifted up I will draw all men unto Me. I am the Light of the world. I am the Lamp set up on a lampstand in the midst of a dark world. I search hearts, and in My presence shadows disappear. Secrets are dispelled. Because I bring light into the darkened corners, the truth will be revealed. Many walk in darkness and some desire light. Lift Me up!

"That's why I chose to come. This earth was so dark with a misunderstanding about God. To the shepherds and the Magi I was Light. As a child and during My public ministry I was Light to many lives. Even on the cross, surrounded with darkness, I was the Light. Lift Me up!

"I light everyone born into this world. Where I am allowed to burn in the hearts of women, I illuminate their communities with beacons of inviting light. Lift Me up in your soul temple! Don't hide under a basket of insecurity or fear. Lift Me up! Don't crawl under a bed of discouragement or doubt. Put Me in Your heart, and My light will fill your life with light. The smile on your face, the words you speak, the way you live, will shine because I am lifted up as the light of your life. You are not the light—I am. My Word is. I want you to understand that as you lift Me up, I will shine through you. I will become brighter and brighter until My light shines in glorious brilliance and this earth is lighted with My glory. Lift Me up today!"

This season, as I light the red and green candles, plug in the strings of lights, and enjoy the soft glow of Christmas I remember that Jesus is my Light. I need never live in darkness. My prayer is that I may lift up Jesus, and like a little candle burning in the dark, I can make a difference. It is Jesus who lights my life with His love. This is what Christmas is all about—His love, His light.

Barbara Ann Kay

Was It an Angel?

Are not all angels ministering spirits sent to serve those who will inherit salvation?
Heb. 1:14, NIV.

WHEN I ANSWERED THE PHONE, my grandson excitedly told me that my husband and I were to be great-grandparents for the very first time. His baby girl was due in November, and he wanted all of her grandparents and great-grandparents to come and meet her at Christmastime.

This sounded like fun, but I realized that Christmas in Hawaii is something that people plan on long before September. I knew it was going to take some prayers to make it happen. We belong to a time-share travel club, but they had nothing available for Christmas and said the best they could do would be to put us on a waiting list. I let our son and grandson know that we were sorry, but there was no way we would be able to come, and let it go at that.

Sometime later I received a call from a man who identified himself as a representative of our travel club. He called to inform me about some new properties our club had purchased and how rapidly it was growing. Suddenly I was impressed to ask him if any of these were in Honolulu. "Yes, there are several there." Then I poured out my story of how we had tried to make reservations to go there for Christmas and wondered if this would make a difference. Immediately he said he was going to check it out, and he would call me again the next morning.

Sure enough, he called to say that I was probably not going to believe it, but there was actually a one-bedroom condo available just two blocks from Waikiki beach. If I would call the reservations department right away, we might be able to reserve it. As soon as I hung up I called reservations. The woman I spoke with said that no one had made any kind of calls regarding the new properties, and that since we were on a waiting list they'd have called us if anything was available. It took a while, but I finally convinced her to check on it anyway. When she returned to the phone she was amazed. A one-bedroom condo was available from Christmas Eve till the following Thursday.

We have many friends who are also members of our travel club, and not one of them ever received a call from anyone about the new properties. I believe that God provided a way for us to go and meet our new little great-granddaughter by having an angel call just when he did.

Anna May Radke Waters

Words Fitly Spoken

And be ye kind one to another.
Eph. 4:32.

A word fitly spoken is like apples of gold in pictures of silver.
Prov. 25:11.

HAVE YOU EVER SEEN the Charlie Brown TV special about the tiny tree he chose to use for Christmas? You may have felt a bit sorry for him when his friends made fun of him and his tree so mercilessly. Happily, his friends do finally help him reinforce the tree and fix it up.

My Charlie Brown Christmas tree experience happened in eighth grade. I had promised I'd provide a Christmas tree for our two-room schoolhouse. Being an apartment dweller, I thought a small table-top tree would be appropriate. When everyone saw what I'd brought, most of them scoffed, "You call that a tree?" One of the seventh graders offered to bring a much bigger tree the next day.

Disappointed and embarrassed, I told our teacher, Mrs. Fisch, "I'll just take this back home with me, and we'll use it in our living room."

"Please don't do that just yet," Mrs. Fisch advised. "Let's see what Allan's tree will be like first."

The next day Allan brought a seven-foot tree. "What a fine tree!" everybody chorused. Then they saw that the tree had a large area that had no branches or needles. "Oh dear!" they groaned. "Is that the best you could do?"

"Sorry. I tried. But the trees were so picked over that there weren't any perfect ones," Allan apologized.

Ideas ranged from getting rid of the tree to getting another one from elsewhere, or sticking the tree in the corner with the ugly part to the wall. Allan blushed deeply.

Sometimes it takes the wisdom of a Solomon to calm down a roomful of disgruntled pupils. Mrs. Fisch listened patiently before suggesting, "Why don't we just use what's already here? Bonnie's would be just right to fill in the bare place on Allan's tree if we wired them together." After it was decorated and the presents placed underneath, the blended tree looked really nice. All of us were happy with Mrs. Fisch's solution. Are we always kind and thoughtful in our dealings with others? If we're not, God can help us become so.

Bonnie Moyers

The Twice-given Christmas Tree

When they saw the star, they were overjoyed. On coming to the house, they saw the child with his mother Mary, and they bowed down and worshiped him. Then they opened their treasures and presented him with gifts of gold and of incense and of myrrh. Matt. 2:10, 11, NIV.

WHEN MY SONS WERE YOUNG, we moved in across the street from two brothers who lived alone. Every once in a while I was able to talk with one of them. They were always friendly and open but very private. I was surprised one winter when one of them came to me and offered their four-foot, fully decorated artificial Christmas tree to give to any family my church might find needy. I was pleased they had associated me with a giving church and was delighted to have the tree. I asked around and found a friend who worked with needy families. She knew of a family she thought would be a great candidate for the tree. I gave the tree with all its dangling decorations to her, and she delivered it to the delighted family. The mother and children were very happy to have a Christmas tree as they hadn't had one in years. Her husband, however, wasn't happy when he arrived home that evening. He said that the tree must go and couldn't stay in the house. The Christmas tree was in their home for a few days before my friend could pick it up and give it to a second family.

The second family was happy to have the tree, and the tree found a very happy home with all members who were glad to have a bright tree for their Christmas celebrations.

A few days later my friend excitedly told me the rest of the story of the twice-given Christmas tree. The father in the first family had silently enjoyed having the tree in his home for a few days, and when it was gone, he turned to his wife and said that he wanted to get a Christmas tree. The entire family went out and bought a small tree and decorations.

The second family enjoyed the original tree as their own, so this twice-given tree brought joy and blessings to both families. When I told the story of the twice-given tree to my neighbors, they were very pleased that their gift had brought happiness to two families.

The thing I have enjoyed most about this twice-given Christmas tree is that a gift given with love is a blessing. Even if that gift is not accepted, the seed of love is planted, and God can produce many blessings from the act itself.

Marilyn Riley

No Room in the Inn

And she brought forth her firstborn son, and wrapped him in swaddling clothes, and laid him in a manger; because there was no room for them in the inn. Luke 2:7.

WE WERE ON OUR WAY HOME from Ukraine. We had crossed the Polish border and wanted to find hotel rooms so that we could easily reach the airport the next morning. We stopped at a hotel whose parking lot was well filled, but the young friend who was driving us decided to ask if they had rooms anyway. They had one room, but we needed more. In the next hotel the parking lot was packed full, and there was a big wedding going on. They had no rooms for us. And so we drove on again.

The first weekend in August must have been a good date for weddings because the next four hotels were booked for weddings. It was very late, and we were getting anxious. We arrived at yet another wedding hotel. Yes, they had vacant rooms. The party was rather loud, but we thought maybe we could still get some sleep, as we were very tired. As we took our luggage out of the car the orchestra began again with full force after their break. That convinced us that we wouldn't be able to get a wink of sleep, and we put our bags back in the car.

We were discouraged. I wondered what it would be like for four people to spend the night in the car. We thought about Joseph and Mary in Bethlehem, who went from one inn to the next, asking for a room. At least nobody in our group was pregnant! We finally found a peaceful hotel and we fell into bed. Only in the morning did we notice how bad the mattresses were. But we had found a bed and a roof.

Joseph and Mary finally found a place to stay as well. The cowshed certainly wasn't comfortable, but they probably didn't get any sleep anyway. Being her first baby, Mary would have been in labor long before they found shelter for the night, the night when the Savior of the world was born so that our redemption would be possible.

Do we have room in our lives for the Savior, or do we turn Him away from our doors as did the innkeepers in Bethlehem? Jesus is asking to be let in. "Behold, I stand at the door, and knock: if any man hear my voice, and open the door, I will come in to him, and will sup with him, and he with me" (Rev. 3:20). Let Him come in—make room for Him in your life.

Hannele Ottschofski

A "Juwa" or a "Mahohoma"?

Finally, brethren, whatsoever things are true, whatsoever things are honest, whatsoever things are just, whatsoever things are pure, whatsoever things are lovely, whatsoever things are of good report; if there be any virtue, and if there be any praise, think on these things. Phil. 4:8.

COLOSSIANS 4:7-18 makes very interesting reading. In this passage the apostle Paul highlights the likes of Tychicus, "a dear brother, a faithful minister and fellow servant" (NIV). This Tychicus must have been something to earn such accolades of praise and commendation.

There is also Onesimus, the "faithful and dear brother." You also find Aristarchus, the "fellow prisoner." Of course, there is Epaphras, who is so down to earth that he is referred to as "one of you." Another of his outstanding characteristics is that he is "always wrestling in prayer for you." What a life! There is also Justus, a fellow worker, who is of comfort to Paul.

Mention is made of "our dear friend Luke, the doctor." It's interesting to note that something good is mentioned about each one except for Demas. It looks as if the apostle had nothing to say about him except that he "send[s] greetings." That's all!

This is what brings me to my experience regarding two people. Our paths never crossed, but when I got to my mission station in Zimbabwe to study, I heard a lot about Mahohoma and Juwa.

In the local language *Mahohoma* means one who is loud and quick, one with a harsh temperament. Although the people spoke about him, I never heard his real name. All that was remembered of him after many years of hard work was Mahohoma!

On the other hand, every time people spoke about Juwa, their faces lit up. I learned later that his name was "Jewel," and not Juwa. There was fondness in their voices as they related story after story of Juwa's simplicity and kindness. An old pastor who had worked with Juwa once remarked in my hearing, "If heaven is not for the likes of Juwa, then I do not know who will enter there."

I asked myself, "When I am long gone, what will I be remembered for? Like Demas, or the other names in Colossians 4? Like Mahohoma, or Juwa?"

Savie Maphosa

A Lost Passport in God's Plan

For I am the Lord, your God, who takes hold of your
right hand and says to you, Do not fear; I will help you.
Isa. 41:13, NIV.

I don't think the way you think. The way you work isn't the way I work. . . .
  For as the sky soars high above earth, so the way I work surpasses the
    way you work, and the way I think is beyond the way you think.
      Isa. 55:8, 9, Message.

ERIKO'S STOMACH TIGHTENED into a knot as the truth hit home. Right in church someone had stolen her bag with her passport and other important documents. Here she was in Mongolia, thousands of miles from home, on a mission to sing at an evangelistic meeting. She was one of eight members of a singing group.

The Golden Angels had been helping out at the largest church in the capital of Mongolia. The meetings had drawn a large group of young people, and at the end of the meeting it was customary for the Golden Angels to greet the people. Eriko was not feeling well that evening and in the rush to get to the back she had left her bag lying on a chair. By the time she had shaken the last hand, the bag had disappeared.

Eriko felt very anxious; however, her mother's words came to mind: "Always be thankful, no matter what happens." She was able to talk faith when her friends sympathized.

Early the next morning Eriko was taken to the Japanese embassy, where she was instructed to make a police report. She was ignored at the local police station because she couldn't speak Mongolian. As she wondered what to do, a kind woman walked up to her and began speaking Japanese. She helped Eriko fill out the necessary forms that were all in Mongolian.

She tried to get help from Mr. Yadomi, a new convert, but he was busy. The next day Eriko picked up her new passport. Since Mr. Yadomi was not around, she was impressed to write him a thank-you note. She was very surprised when Yadomi showed up at church as he hadn't been attending because of language problems. He explained how Eriko's thank-you card with the picture of the Tokyo Adventist Hospital had jolted his memory and spoken to his conscience to return to church again. Now Eriko understood why she had lost her passport.

Eriko Suzuki

The Starling

Fear ye not therefore, ye are of more value than many sparrows.
Matt. 10:31.

MANY YEARS AGO as I was leaving work with a coworker I found a baby bird that had fallen out of its nest. A plump, well-fed little starling was on the ground and couldn't fly as it didn't have all of its feathers yet. Everyone at work thought it wouldn't survive the weekend, but I decided to pick it up and take it home. This little bird was full of energy, squawking and making a fuss. So it was no surprise that it not only survived but really thrived under my family's care. But the bird still couldn't fly, and walked with a decided limp. Maybe it was because of his fall, or maybe something else was wrong. Nevertheless, the bird we now named Junior was full of life and loved to eat and take baths.

Our cat Cookie was much tempted to snatch this little bird and eat it. My dad fixed that problem by throwing a slipper at Cookie. From then on she knew the bird was off limits, and every time the bird sat on the grass Cookie quickly ran off, not wanting another slipper sent her way. The bird had a vigilant protector.

Thinking about all the things the little bird went through made me think about the trials and situations that we go through. This bird was so unaware and so innocent of the dangers surrounding it. First, it was away from the protection of its nest, away from Mom and Dad. Alone, on the cold concrete floor of the parking garage, it was unable to fly. Anyone could have hurt it. Then it was almost snatched by a cat. This young bird faced these unbelievable perils yet was protected.

We too can be taken from a place of safety, and bad things can happen to us. Yet, just as this little bird was helped, God is also there helping us.

The Bible says that God knows when one sparrow falls to the ground. Luke adds, "Are not five sparrows sold for two farthings, and not one of them is forgotten before God? But even the very hairs of your head are all numbered. Fear not therefore: ye are of more value than many sparrows" (Matt. 12:6, 7). So God knows exactly what's happening to each one of us. Not only does He have His eye on the sparrow—He has His eye on us, too. May we always know that God is there for us, and that He is our help in trouble.

Rosemarie Clardy

Our Prayers Reach God

And the smoke of the incense, which came with the prayers
of the saints, ascended up before God out of the angel's hand.
Rev. 8:4.

THE COMMUNIST REGIME in Bulgaria had fallen six or seven years before. There was huge inflation and terrible unemployment. I had just married and was still in the university. My husband worked for the church, and his salary was four times less than what he had made at his previous job. The future was vague, and to my melancholy nature it seemed a little hopeless as well. I was constantly asking my God, *Will I find a decent job after I graduate? Shall we ever have a home of our own? Shall we have a place and enough money to raise our unborn child?* How could I know the answers? It was as if I was expecting a voice from heaven to give me knowledge about my future. I repeated my problems again and again in my mind, but there was no answer. I wanted to talk to God for a while as Job did. I was no longer seeking to find an answer but assurance that God heard me. Oh, if only I could climb up to heaven to where God was sitting, silent and unresponsive.

Then I read the majestic scene described in today's text. It wasn't that I hadn't read this text before, but now it deeply impressed me. There, upon the golden altar before the throne of God, were my prayers with the prayers of all the saints (verse 3). Paying special attention to their prayers, the angel offers them before God as a smell of incense. I felt as if I really had climbed to heaven. Did it matter if I was physically present there, or just my words and thoughts? I was ashamed of my disbelief.

From that moment, whenever I pray I imagine that solemn atmosphere: the throne room of the universe, full of angels, God Himself on the majestic throne, the golden altar, and my prayers ascending up to God.

This innovation was a cure both for my fears and my distrust and my dull thoughts and wandering mind while I prayed. The peace in my heart was restored, and my womanly self-esteem came back. God had answered my questions in a miraculous way through His own Word. Years later He carried out real miracles in my life, showing that there was in fact nothing to worry about.

Pettya Nackova

Recognized Properly

His lord said unto him, Well done, thou good and faithful servant.
Matt. 25:21.

THERE ARE SPIRITUAL APPLICATIONS we can derive from any experience if we look carefully enough. I work in an elder-care facility as an assessment nurse. Total assessment includes evaluating the memory status of the customer (the term we now use when we refer to patients). About 90 percent of the customers are memory-impaired, so it is very refreshing when one of them recognizes a staff member. On the other hand, it can also break your heart when you take care of an Alzheimer/dementia person whose memory is completely wiped clean. They're like little children again. All their needs have to be anticipated and met by the staff.

Among our customers was a petite, elderly woman with striking blue eyes and a soft-spoken manner. We called her Mrs. B. She sat in a wheelchair and was dependent on others to get from one place to the next. She was very friendly and appreciative, though she often got anxious about losing her memory totally.

As I walked by her several times a day I'd give her a smile. Each time, as I got closer to her, she'd ask my name. I would always tell her, but she'd promptly forget it. Sometimes she'd remember that it started with a G, and she'd say, "Ga," or "Ge," then I'd complete it for her: "It's Gloria." This went on for several weeks. Then one day as I walked up to her she said, "You are Gloria. I recognize you properly now, even if I haven't seen you for a few days." I was as delighted as she was. All she needed was a little prodding.

Mrs. B. had cataracts in both eyes, which impaired her vision. When she had them removed, she saw me clearly for the first time without wearing glasses, and she was overjoyed. "I can see you clearly now, even from far away," she stated happily.

As I thought about these experiences with Mrs. B, I praised God as I unraveled some spiritual allusions. How wonderful it is that I have a blessed Savior who knew me by name—before I was even born—and will never forget it. How marvelous it is to know that when He lifts the clouds from my eyes I can see my way clearly. God's eyes are always on me. He sees me clearly. I know He will recognize me "properly" on that day when He comes back to claim His own, if I remain faithful to Him.

Gloria P. Hutchinson

His Shining Face

The Lord bless you and keep you; the Lord make his face shine upon you and
be gracious to you; the Lord turn his face toward you and give you peace.
Num. 6:24-26, NIV.

"LIGHTS! CAMERA! ACTION!" The tape rolled as I confidently fired away in glowing tones, passionately expressing my concepts on positive thinking. Then I was interrupted by the cold words of the director: "Cut! Her face is shining!" The makeup crew rushed onto the set, powdering and wiping my face to rid me of the shine. I learned that a shining face is not a welcome attribute when you're on camera.

As I sat in church on New Year's Eve, being inspired by the sermon of my favorite pastor, the concept of a shining face took on a new and positive flare. In his closing remarks the pastor challenged us with the same wish that Moses proclaimed to the children of Israel, encouraging us to "keep God's face shining," as described in today's text. It took a few moments for the enormity of that challenge to sink in. The realization that God's face was always on me wasn't very comfortable. Worse, it was shining on me, illuminating my being.

It's all right to have God's undivided attention when you're in need of His provisions, protection, and assistance, but what about the "off" times? Repeatedly being on camera made me acutely aware of how careful one needs to be when the lights are on you. At such times you must project your best words, actions, and bearing.

However, with God the lights never stop shining. There is no off time. Herein lies the challenge: can I constantly be on my best behavior? The challenge intensifies when I recall that not even my thoughts are hidden from Him. "Worship and serve Him with a clean heart and a willing mind, for the Lord sees every heart and understands and knows every thought" (1 Chron. 28:9, TLB). It's not only what I do that is on display to Him but more so who I am at the core. I was almost washed away in despair until I pondered the remaining portion of the wish: that the "Lord turn his face toward you and give you peace."

As we face a new year and its challenges, we can all say confidently, "Lights, camera, action. Let the show begin!"

Patrice Williams-Gordon

2010 Author Biographies

BETTY J. ADAMS, a retired teacher, is a mother, grandmother, and great-grandmother. She has written for *Guide* magazine and her church newsletter, and is active in community service. She enjoys writing, her grandchildren, scrapbooking, and traveling—especially on mission trips. **Jan. 13.**

PRISCILLA ADONIS has been women's ministries coordinator for her local church and chaplain for the federation of women's ministries. She likes collecting poems, articles, quotes, and stories, and sharing them with women who need uplifting. She loves sharing recipes, some of which have been published. She enjoys reading good books and studying the Bible. **Jan. 26, Feb. 19, July 14.**

MINERVA M. ALINAYA writes from Cavite, Philippines. She is a former senior lecturer at Bethel College in South Africa, and now serves as the school principal of Patnubay Academy, a nonsectarian school. She sees school as a mission field in which young people need to be won for Christ. **June 12, Sept. 14.**

FLÁVIA TIBURTINO DE ANDRADE, a biologist, was born in Juru, Paraíba, Brazil, and currently lives in Boqueirão, Paraíba, Brazil. She is married to Pastor Edilson Sales. She enjoys presenting seminars at churches, reading books, traveling, and spending time with her family and friends. **Sept. 21.**

JUDETE SOARES DE ANDRADE writes from Brazil, where she sells Christian literature. She considers her three children and one grandchild the best gifts heaven could offer. She owes her joy of living to her friends, who have a special place in her heart. She enjoys photography and reading. **Mar. 17.**

JEBA ANDREWS, a secretary in the retirement plan department, serves with her husband in the Southern Asia Division of Seventh-day Adventists in India. She enjoys life with her son, Alsten. Her hobbies include reading and listening to music. **Feb. 15.**

ANA ANGELOVA, a mother and grandmother, was born in 1934 in Bourgas, a town on the bank of the Black Sea, Bulgaria. She was baptized in 1990, and says that her granddaughter was saved because of the prayers of our brothers and sisters in the church of Sofia. In her free time she likes to knit. **May 17.**

RAQUEL COSTA ARRAIS is a minister's wife who has developed her ministry as an educator for 20 years. Currently she works as associate director of the General Conference of Seventh-day Adventists Women's Ministries Department. She has two sons and one daughter-in-law, Paula. Her greatest pleasure is to be with people, sing, play the piano, and travel. **Feb. 3, Apr. 16.**

LIZANDRA NEVES DE AZEVEDO, who writes from Brazil, has a degree in law. She enjoys preaching, helping people, and, in her free time she aspires to be an athlete. **Jan. 22.**

CARLA BAKER is women's ministries director for the North American Division of Seventh-day Adventists. She has served as a teacher, administrative assistant, copy editor, and magazine advertising manager. She is active in her home church in Maryland, where she is an elder. Carla enjoys traveling, reading, cooking, walking, and spending time with her two toddler granddaughters. **Jan. 9.**

ROSEMARY BAKER is a freelance writer living in Iowa. She is author of the children's book *What Am I?* and has been published in magazines. She is a member of the Iowa Poetry Association, is active in her church, does volunteer work, and enjoys working with children. Arts, crafts, poetry, and painting are her hobbies. **Dec. 16.**

JENNIFER M. BALDWIN writes from Australia, where she works in risk management at Sydney Adventist Hospital. She enjoys church involvement, travel, crossword puzzles, and writing, and has contributed to a number of church publications. **Jan. 25.**

DANA M. BEAN is a third-grade teacher who lives in Bermuda with her husband. Her two young children give her much joy. Dana loves telling children's stories and working as a church clerk. Her hobbies include photography, traveling, writing, reading, and swimming. **Oct. 10.**

JEANNETTE BELOT was born in Haiti, but now lives in Quebec, Canada. She holds the head clerical position in her local church and is active in various ministries, with a special emphasis on health and women's ministries. She's the mother of three grown children, and her interests include Scripture-based reading and music. **Feb. 26, Oct. 4, Dec. 7.**

SYLVIA GILES BENNETT is a fiscal accountant for a local health department. A member of the Portsmouth Seventh-day Adventist Church, Portsmouth, Virginia, she serves as deaconess and communications secretary. She enjoys reading, piano, writing, bowling, and witnessing. **Jan. 27.**

ANNIE B. BEST, a retired teacher in Washington, D.C., is a widow, mother of two adult children, and grandmother of three. She enjoys reading and listening to music. Working as a leader in the beginner and kindergarten departments of her church inspired her to compose a song that was published in *Let's Sing Sabbath Songs.* **Nov. 24, Dec. 3.**

DINORAH BLACKMAN, a teacher, writes from the beautiful country of Panama, where she lives with her husband and daughter, Imani. **Oct. 18, Dec. 2.**

FULORI BOLA writes from Papua New Guinea, where she was director for student services at Pacific Adventist University until 2006, when she became a lecturer in the school of education. A single mother to two teenagers, she loves writing, preparing scripts, and topics on prayer, and working with women and helping students to find Jesus. **Mar. 12, Apr. 19.**

EVELYN GREENWADE BOLTWOOD lives in Rochester, New York, and is a mother of two grown children. She is the Pathfinder and Adventurer coordinator for western New

York, and is a member of Akoma, an African-American women's community gospel choir, which raises scholarship money for young women to attend college. Her passions are writing, camping, and traveling. **Apr. 30, June 10, Aug. 12.**

LAURA L. BRADFORD lives in Walla Walla, Washington, where she seeks to encourage others by writing of the countless ways God has touched her life. Her stories have been published in such books as *A Cup of Comfort for Families Touched by Alzheimer's* and *Life Savors for Women.* **Nov. 18, Dec. 13.**

JEAN ANNETTE BRICE is a second-generation Seventh-day Adventist who retired as a probation officer after 24 years of service. Though she now lives in St. Lucia with her aging father, she's lived in Trinidad for most of her life, where she was active in the disability movement in Trinidad and Tobago. Playing Scrabble is one of her hobbies. **Nov. 23.**

DONNA BROWN, an associate professor at the Northern Caribbean University in Jamaica, is a sought-after motivational speaker and preacher who has inspired audiences nationally and internationally. She has a passion for youth and has served extensively in youth ministry in her church. She is single and counts it a joy to visit the shut-in members of her local church. **Aug. 20.**

DARLENE YTREDAL BURGESON, a retired sales manager, is a caregiver for herself and her husband. Although they aren't well, they spend much time with their great-grandchildren and take them to many interesting places. She enjoys her family and also loves to write. **May 22, Nov. 11.**

JULIANE P. DE OLIVEIRA CAETANO, a minister's wife and teacher, likes to embroider, cook, and write. She writes from her home in Brazil. **Nov. 9.**

ELIZABETH IDA CAIN served as associate dean of women at Northern Caribbean University, Manchester, Jamaica. She attends the St. John's Seventh-day Adventist Church, where she is a member of the women's ministries association, and also serves as a Sabbath school teacher. She enjoys writing and is a designer of floral art. **Apr. 25, Aug. 30, Sept. 27.**

RUTH CANTRELL lives in Belleville, Michigan, with her husband, Ronald, where she is a high school counselor and teacher in the Detroit public schools. They have two adult sons. Her hobbies include reading, telling children's stories, playing the piano, organizing programs, gospel music, working in the church, and encouraging the members. **Dec. 5.**

DOROTHY WAINWRIGHT CAREY is learning to adjust to life without Jim after 48 great years of marriage. God, family, and friends have continued to make life pleasant. Her grandson, Alex, adds much joy. Traveling with a buddy adds enrichment to her life. **Sept. 20.**

HO YI CHAN is from Hong Kong and is now in her first year of premedicine at Union College, Lincoln, Nebraska, where she is preparing for her future as a physician. The Bay View church, Hong Kong, is her home church. She enjoys reading and writing about God's love. **Mar. 16.**

IRISDEANE HENLEY CHARLES is a nurse consultant working in Washington, D.C. She and her husband, Oscar, have three children. She has been involved in many areas of the church over the years and enjoys serving the Lord. Her hobbies include arts and crafts projects, sewing, playing the guitar, and reading. **Mar. 25, Sept. 28.**

MARIA CHÈVRE, who writes from Switzerland, is married and has four children and five grandchildren who live in her native Brazil. She is a technician in medical radiology and a science teacher who holds a master's degree in education in public health. Maria works with ADRA and family ministries. Her hobbies include giving Bible studies, traveling, and lecturing on health. **Feb. 24, Aug. 24.**

CAROLINE CHOLA is the women's and children's ministries director for the South Africa-Indian Ocean Division of Seventh-day Adventists. Previously Caroline served as a volunteer director in Zambia and as a personal secretary, human resources practitioner, and a licensed lay evangelist. She is married to Habson Chola, an entrepreneur. They have five sons. In her spare time she enjoys gardening and singing. **Nov. 19.**

BIROL CHARLOTTE CHRISTO lives with her husband in Hosur, India. Beginning her church employment career as a schoolteacher, she also worked as office secretary, statistician, and Shepherdess coordinator. She is the mother of five adult children, and enjoys gardening, sewing, knitting, and making craft items to finance her projects for homeless children. **Sept. 30, Nov. 15.**

ROSEMARIE CLARDY'S roots are in Queens, New York, though she now lives in the mountains of North Carolina and loves it. She has three amazing boys, two lovable cats, and one silly dog. She loves to garden, take walks, and write little stories to share with others. **Dec. 28.**

ARLENE CLARKE is a wife, mother, and social worker who still has a passion for dramatic presentations that lift up the name of the Lord. She writes from Palm Bay, Florida, where she is a church clerk, Adventist Youth Society sponsor, assistant Sabbath school secretary, and school board member. This is her first submission. **Aug. 19.**

PATRICIA COVE retired after 28 years as a church school teacher and celebrated her fiftieth wedding anniversary in 2008. She is a mother, grandmother, and great-grandmother who has written a newspaper column for some years and has had several articles published in other magazines. She enjoys sailing with her husband, outdoor pursuits, and reading. **Aug. 26, Oct. 3.**

BECKY DADA writes from Nigeria, where she is a retired principal of a secondary school in Ibadan, Oyo State, Nigeria. Currently she is dean of the school of nursing in Ile-Ife. Women's ministries and Revelation seminars are still a priority in her daily schedule. Her hobbies include writing, speaking, and reading. **Mar. 29, Sept. 10, Nov. 14.**

OMOLADE AJIKE DADA is a graduate in mass communication from Babcock University, Ilishan Remo, Nigeria. She is secretary of the postgraduate medical education program in Ile-Ife, Nigeria. The second girl of four children born to a Seventh-day Adventist pastor's family, she loves reading, writing, and knitting. **Feb. 13, Mar. 15, Aug. 17.**

CHARLOTTE DE BEER writes from Hartenbos, South Africa, and is a member of the Hartenbos congregation. She is the mother of two grown children and has five grandchildren. A published author, she loves traveling the world, gardening, reading, writing, walking, and classical music. **Aug. 13, Dec. 19.**

FAUNA RANKIN DEAN lives with her husband, Bill, on a quiet country hillside in eastern Kansas. They have three children, two of whom are college students, and they enjoy sharing their home with several golden retrievers. As a writer/photographer, she spends her days looking for joy in the simple things of life. **Jan. 12, May 27.**

WINIFRED DEVARAJ is a retired teacher and women's ministries director from Bangalore, India. Her only son is studying at Loma Linda University in California in the dental department and has given her twin grandsons. Her hobbies include reading, listening to religious music, telling stories, and helping her pastor-husband visit homes and give Bible studies. **Mar. 26, June 11, Aug. 10.**

LINDA DOMENY is a pastor's wife, has been married to Roger for 16 years, and works as a physical therapist. Her hobbies include gardening, baking, and sharing time with friends. **May 20.**

LEONIE DONALD thanks God every day for the beauty of Queen Charlotte Sound, New Zealand, where she lives. She enjoys long walks, "devours" books, and admits to spending more time in her garden than doing housework. Leonie and her husband of 40 years attend the Blenheim Adventist Church. **Apr. 17, June 5.**

LOUISE DRIVER, now retired, lives in Idaho near three sons and four grandchildren. She works several days a week at a Christian bookstore and enjoys the opportunities to help others in their walk with the Lord through Bibles, books, and music. Her hobbies include singing, music, reading, gardening, and traveling to historical places. **Mar. 30.**

GERTRUDE DUMITRESCU, a pastor's daughter, is from Romania, where she has worked for the Romanian Adventist Radio (Voice of Hope) since 2001 and has had a local weekly biblical broadcasting program since 2004. Gertrude, who has worked in women's ministries for more than 10 years, is a nurse. She graduated from the Adventist Theological University in Bucharest. **Mar. 24.**

MARGARET C. DURAN is a writer of Christian material and has published four books. Although she grew up in a strict Christian home, she says God allowed her to "wander in the desert" for many years to bring her to a total submission to His will. She is 74 years old, but has been an Adventist for only 10 short months—and loves it! **Apr. 9.**

JOY DUSTOW, with her husband, Ted, live in a retirement village near Brisbane, Australia. She participates in the spiritual and social activities of the village and hostel. **Apr. 14.**

RUBY H. ENNISS-ALLEYNE writes from Guyana, South America, where she is a mother of three: Ashton Miguel, Jr.; Rhobyn Hydi; and Rhondell Huann. She enjoys team ministry with her pastor-husband, Ashton, and is the assistant treasurer of the Guyana Conference of Seventh-day Adventists. Her hobbies include working with young people, reading, and athletics (all of her children are national athletes). **Apr. 21, May 13.**

MARIA DE LOURDES FERREIRA writes from Brazil. At 80 years of age she enjoys living in the community surrounding Brazil Adventist University. She is the proud grandmother of Andre, Sara, Tiago, and Pedro. **May 26.**

KAREN FETTIG is the director of the Wyoming women's ministries. She has a personal health ministry called Window of Hope Ministry and is a trained lifestyle counselor and a certified massage technician. Sexual abuse prevention strategies are now a part of her ministry. She is married, with two grown children and four awesome grandchildren. **Jan. 8.**

EDITH FITCH is a retired teacher living in Lacombe, Alberta, Canada. She volunteers in the archives at Canadian University College, and enjoys doing research for schools and churches, as well as individual histories. Her hobbies include writing, traveling, needlework, sudokus, and cryptograms. **Jan. 2, Mar. 10.**

LANA FLETCHER lives in Chehalis, Washington, with her husband. They have one adult daughter. Her younger daughter was killed in a car accident in 1993. Lana does the bookkeeping for her husband's business, is involved in a loss-of-a-child support group, and coleads a Regeneration group. **Feb. 14, Apr. 3, June 24.**

SHARON FOLLETT writes from the beautiful Sequatchie Valley in Dunlap, Tennessee, where she and her husband, Ron, pastor three churches. She enjoys walking in the woods with her husband and their pets, as well as singing, leading church choirs, teaching children to play the piano, and spending time with her granddaughter, Savannah. **July 29, Dec. 20.**

GREICE MARQUES FONSECA is a high school student on the Brazil Adventist College campus in Engenheiro Coelho, São Paulo, Brazil. Her favorite hobby is music—singing and playing the flute and piano. She enjoys traveling to discover new places and making new friends. **Mar. 8.**

VINITA GAIKWAD, the mother of 5-year-old twins, is an English teacher from India who has served in India and Africa in various capacities. She was a missionary to Uganda, and currently works in Saudi Arabia. She has written for the devotional books and had an article, "Stung by Faith," published in the July 2007 *Adventist World.* **Jan. 23.**

EDNA MAYE GALLINGTON, now retired, was part of the communication team in the Southeastern California Conference of Seventh-day Adventists, and is a graduate of La Sierra University, with public relations certification from the University of California. She is a member of Toastmasters International, and enjoys writing, music, entertaining, cooking gourmet meals with her husband, and walking their two dogs. **Feb. 22.**

MARYBETH GESSELE is a pastor's wife who lives in Oregon. She enjoys country living, her grandchildren, and her sewing room. Currently she provides elderly and hospice care. **Mar. 7.**

YAN SIEW GHIANG has served as a youth and church pastor-Bible teacher, as well as acting principal and part-time contract Taoism project researcher. Since 2006 she's been jobless. Her achievements include a handbook on ministering to Taoists and an introductory Bible study for Taoists that she wrote with Daniel Walter. Her hobbies include reading, research, and preaching sermons. **Aug. 29.**

CAROL WIGGINS GIGANTE is a former day-care provider who is a teacher at heart. An avid reader, photographer, and flower and bird lover, Carol resides in Beltsville, Maryland, with her husband, Joe, their dog, Buddy, and new kitten, Suzannah. They have two grown sons, Jeff and James. **Oct. 27.**

ALEXIS A. GORING is a writer who recently graduated from Columbia Union College. She holds a degree in print journalism and a minor in media production. Alexis loves to write stories, read magazines and biographical books, watch good-quality movies, shop, and spend time with her family and friends. **July 17.**

CECELIA GRANT, M.D., is a medical doctor who retired from government service and now works part-time at the Andrews Memorial Hospital in Kingston, Jamaica. She enjoys traveling, gardening, and listening to good music, and also has a passion for young people. **Feb. 11, Mar. 28.**

MARY JANE GRAVES worked at many jobs before retiring with her husband, Ted, in North Carolina. As a part of women's ministries, she started—and maintains—the church library. She also enjoys gardening and sharing the results with friends and neighbors. **Nov. 30.**

SHIRLEY KIMBROUGH GREAR is a systems analyst who enjoys writing, speaking, and teaching God's Word. She and her husband, Carl, are the parents of C. J. and Michelle, and enjoy their five grandchildren. She lives in Philadelphia, Pennsylvania. **Mar. 14.**

JOAN GREEN works as a secretary and receptionist in Boise, Idaho. She has a heart for women's ministries, which is newly established in the Idaho Conference of Seventh-day Adventists. She loves spending time with her two adult daughters and two grandchildren. In her free time she enjoys traveling, short-term mission work, scrapbooking, reading, trying new foods, and building friendships. **May 12.**

CAROL J. GREENE is retired and lives in Florida, where she is active in ministry at her church. **Sept. 11.**

CHRISTINE A. GREENE hails from Alberta, Canada, where she has just completed an undergraduate degree in secondary education. Her interests include writing, reading, playing the piano, and health issues. **May 24.**

GLENDA-MAE GREENE, a retired educator, writes from her wheelchair in Palm Bay, Florida, where she is an educational consultant and delightfully dependent on her charming mother. Together they host prayer circles, teach Sabbath school classes, and do whatever it takes to make their house a home by the side of the road. Her three nieces and nephew continue to bring her joy. **Jan. 21, Aug. 18, Oct. 5.**

ANNABELL HALL lives in Toronto, Canada, where she attends the Toronto West Seventh-day Adventist Church. She is a registered nurse and certified diabetes educator, and has a son and a daughter. She loves reading God's promises and listening to gospel music. **Nov. 27.**

DIANTHA HALL-SMITH is a daughter of God. She's married to a devoted Christian husband, who serves in the United States Air Force. They have two beautiful children. Born in New York, she has lived in interesting places, domestically and globally. She enjoys writing, traveling, and spending time with her family. **Mar. 3, Apr. 12.**

DESSA WEISZ HARDIN lives with her husband, in Maine, where she can enjoy the ocean. She's interested in traveling, writing, art, and music, and is busy teaching herself the piano. An added dimension to her life is grandparenting. She enjoys the devotional book and her friends who have been blessed through it. **Sept. 17, Oct. 29.**

GLENISE HARDY writes from Australia, where she is women's ministries director for the South New South Wales Conference. She is one among five generations of Adventist missionaries. Encouraging women in personal Bible discovery is a passion, and inspiring her five grandchildren with a wonderful heritage is a pleasure. She enjoys measuring rainfall and gardening. **Sept. 12.**

DAWN HARGRAVE, who writes from Australia, has been married for 41 years and has two daughters and two grandchildren. Before retiring, she worked in clerical and financial positions, but now plans to travel. She has just discovered she has talent for writing, particularly poetry. **May 10.**

MARIAN M. HART, a retired elementary teacher and nursing home administrator, works with her husband doing property management. A member of the Battle Creek Seventh-day Adventist Tabernacle for 33 years, she has served in many capacities. Six grandchildren make her a proud grandmother. She enjoys knitting, reading, growing flowers, mission trips, and winter in Florida. **May 11, July 1.**

TERESA (PROCTOR) HEBARD and her husband, Jim, live in Loveland, Colorado, with their children, Daniel and Michelle. They recently returned from mission service in Penang, Malaysia. Teresa worked as a nurse before "retiring" to raise a family. Her passions include sharing God's love through music and creating tasty vegetarian recipes. **Jan. 15, June 27.**

LAURA HENRY-STUMP lives in Ontario, Canada. She's an elder in her church and works in youth ministries. Laura enjoys sharing God's transforming power through preaching, writing, and encouraging others. **July 2, Aug. 31.**

DENISE DICK HERR teaches English at Canadian University College in Alberta, Canada, and loves to travel with her family. She rejoices in the power of words! **Dec. 11.**

KAREN HOLFORD works with her husband in family and children's ministries in southern England. She has authored more than seven books, and is especially interested in creative approaches to prayer and worship. The Holfords have three teenage children. She is also a family therapist, and enjoys quilting and walking in the English countryside. **Nov. 26.**

JACQUELINE HOPE HOSHING-CLARKE has been an educator since 1979, serving as principal, assistant principal, and teacher. She is now director for the precollege department, Northern Caribbean University (NCU), Jamaica, and is currently reading for a

Ph.D. She is married to a pastor; they have two adult children, Deidre and Deneil. Jackie enjoys writing and gardening. **Feb. 25, July 5, Nov. 2.**

LORRAINE HUDGINS-HIRSCH lives in a delightful retirement community in Loma Linda, California. She has worked at Faith for Today, the Voice of Prophecy, and at the General Conference of Seventh-day Adventists. Her articles and poems have appeared frequently in various publications. She is the mother of five grown children. **June 4.**

GLORIA P. HUTCHINSON, a registered nurse with an Associate of Science degree in computer network administration, is the single mother of an "adopted" son, who is also her nephew. She is a member of the Palm Bay Seventh-day Adventist Church in Florida, serving as Sabbath school superintendent. Her hobbies are sewing and reading. **Mar. 4, Dec. 30.**

SHIRLEY C. IHEANACHO and her husband, Morris, are enjoying retirement. They spend a lot of time visiting family and traveling to faraway places; however, she still finds time to write, speak at various church and school gatherings, sing in the church choir, play handbells, and encourage fellow travelers. They have three daughters, Ngozi, Chioma, and Akunna, and two grandsons. **Mar. 5, Aug. 3, Oct. 6.**

DIANA INMAN was born and raised in a family of nine siblings. She is the mother of two adult children and grandmother of five, and lives with her husband on a farm in Michigan. She enjoys antiques, growing herbs and flowers, reading, and writing (sometimes). She is working toward certification as a master herbalist, and coauthored *Eden's Bounty,* a vegetarian cookbook. **July 4, Sept. 5, Dec. 18.**

MARILENA IORGULESCU, living with her son in Romania, is a nurse. She loves to read, garden, and write poem blessings for her friends. "With God's help" she has won a fight with cancer. She received the women's devotional as a gift from a friend, and when she saw its impact on herself, she decided to contribute to it, writing about her experience in knowing God. **Sept. 23.**

CONSUELO RODA JACKSON is a nature lover, conservationist, and environmentalist all rolled into one, and is a veteran church greeter. She has regularly contributed to this devotional book series. Consuelo has a doctorate in wholistic nutrition and has written her first book, *The Gift of Choice.* **June 20.**

JOAN D. L. JAENSCH lives with her husband in South Australia. They have two married sons, two granddaughters, and two grandsons. She is a retired factory purchasing officer and has served 31 years with Saint John Ambulance. She has filled many roles at church and enjoys leadlighting, card making, cooking, gardening, and reading. **Dec. 14.**

DONETTE JAMES is a registered alumnus of Northern Caribbean University, Jamaica, and resides in the United Kingdom. She enjoys reading, traveling, and ensuring that others are comfortable. Her motto is "I do my best (as long as ever I can), and the Lord will do the rest." **Nov. 21.**

KALAISELVI JEBAMONY writes from India, where she works as women's and shepherdess ministries coordinator for the Pudukottai-Thirumayam Region, where her husband is the director. She has a son, who is a nurse, and a daughter, who is a physical therapist. **Aug. 7.**

JUNE JEPTHAS lives in Cape Town, South Africa. She is married and has two sons, and she serves in the health and temperance department of her church area headquarters. **Mar. 27.**

VINODHINI JOHN is a wife, mother, and grandmother. She was an educator for 25 years and now works as women's ministries director for the East Central India Union. She finds joy in organizing women's meetings, conducting adult literacy classes, and preaching. She says her husband is an inspiration to her ministry. **Aug. 4.**

NADINE A. JOSEPH, a student at the University of the Southern Caribbean, is from the island of St. Lucia. She has published a number of devotionals in Merite-Newsletter of the Society of Honors Students at USC, and has been in various leadership roles at the university and church. Her greatest personal accomplishment is her personal and loving relationship with God. **Jan. 1.**

ANA MARIA CALCIDONI KÄFLER writes from Brazil and has a degree in theology from the Latin-American Adventist Theological Seminary. She is a minister's wife and the mother of three daughters and works as a hospital chaplain at the São Vicente Hospital in Curitiba, Brazil. She enjoys preaching, giving Bible studies, and presenting lectures and stop-smoking courses. **Mar. 31.**

BARBARA ANN KAY is involved in women's ministries and is a leader in her home church. Her ministry is writing encouraging letters to women. She assists her husband with farming, growing tube roses, a big garden, blueberries, and ivy year-round in greenhouses. She likes to read, write, hike, swim, and travel to visit her children. **Dec. 21.**

IRIS L. KITCHING is a wife, mother, and grandmother, and with husband, Will, enjoys their blended families: five sons, one daughter, four daughters-in-law, and 10 grandchildren. She works in the presidential section of the General Conference of Seventh-day Adventists, and is communications leader and editor and designer of *Church Matters*, the newsletter at her local church. **Apr. 20.**

KÊNIA KOPITAR is from Brazil but was living in New York City when she wrote this devotional. She loves God's creations: people, kids, animals, and flowers. She likes writing, camping, and being close to nature. **Apr. 13.**

HEPZIBAH KORE writes from Hosur, India, where she is the women's ministries director and shepherdess coordinator of the Southern Asia Division of Seventh-day Adventists. Her husband, Gnanaraj, a minister, is a director in the same division. Her passion is to open the eyes of the women in her country to read the Word and see the world through adult literacy programs. **Mar. 6.**

PATRICIA MULRANEY KOVALSKI is a retired teacher and widow who gets great joy from traveling and visiting her children and grandchildren. Reading and giving English teas are the fun things she likes to do. **Jan. 7, Feb. 12.**

ESTHER KUJUR writes from India. At present she is a teacher in the Ranchi high school and takes care of the women's ministries department of the Jharkhand Bihar Section, Ranchi, India. She has three children. Her hobbies are cooking, gardening, and reading. **Apr. 22.**

RAMANI KURIAN has been an educator in India for the past 32 years, serving as the principal of a higher secondary school. Now she assists in the women's ministries department of the Southern Asia Division of Seventh-day Adventists. She enjoys reading and writing articles for journals. She has a Ph.D. in educational administration. **Apr. 11.**

MABEL KWEI, a retired university/college lecturer, did missionary work in Africa for many years with her pastor-husband and their three children. Now living in New Jersey, she reads a lot, loves to paint, write, and spend time with little children. **Mar. 18, June 3, Oct. 14.**

SALLY LAM-PHOON serves the Northern Asia-Pacific Division of Seventh-day Adventists as children's, family, and women's ministries director, as well as shepherdess coordinator. Her passion is to help children, young people, and especially women unleash their potential. Married for 36 years to Chek-Yat, a gospel minister, she has two grown daughters. **Apr. 24.**

IANI DIAS LAUER-LEITE writes from Brazil, where she is a college professor and is currently on a leave of absence to finish her doctorate in psychology. She is involved in prayer ministry in her church and enjoys reading many topics, but especially relating to prayer. **Jan. 14, Feb. 16, June 14.**

GINA LEE published more than 800 stories, articles, and poems. She enjoyed working at the public library and caring for her family of cats. Gina died in June 2007 from cancer. She has had one or more devotionals in every devotional book since this series began in 1992. She will be missed! **Apr. 27.**

RUTH LENNOX retired as women's ministries director for the British Columbia Conference of Seventh-day Adventists. She and her husband have three adult children and four lovely granddaughters. In 2007 Ruth returned to her homeland of England for the fiftieth-year reunion of those who graduated from medical school with her and her husband. **Apr. 29, May 18.**

NAIR COSTA LESSA is a retired educational counselor who dedicates herself to her family and social causes, and helps to coordinate a children's home for 14 girls. She participates in various church departments and enjoys reading, writing, traveling, visiting family members, and spending time with her children and grandchildren. **Mar. 13, July 12, Oct. 12.**

CORDELL LIEBRANDT lives in Cape Town, South Africa. She serves as an elder at her church and is a paralegal by profession. Cordell loves working with young people and in women's ministries, and has a passion for prayer. She enjoys reading, music, traveling, and being out in nature. **Jan. 10.**

HEPSY LINCOLN writes from India, where she is a teacher. She and her pastor-husband have three children, one son and two daughters. Two of her children are married, and the third is taking nursing. Hepsy's hobbies include reading and communicating with people. **Sept. 29.**

OLGA CORBIN DE LINDO, a retired church school teacher and a retiree of the United States Air Force, writes from Panama. Since the death of her husband, she shares experiences of the love and power of God as a means to alleviate her grief. Her hobbies include reading, writing, playing the piano, and visiting her daughter and grandchildren in Orlando, Florida. **June 16.**

BESSIE SIEMENS LOBSIEN is a retired missionary librarian who served for 21 years overseas as well as in the United States. She has been published in church papers throughout her adult life and is now enjoying her fast-growing great-grandchildren as well as sewing for outreach concerns and volunteering in church work. Her hobbies include relaxing! **Feb. 18, Sept. 9, Nov. 25.**

HATTIE R. LOGAN is employed with the United States Internal Revenue Service and holds a master's degree in human resources administration. She has two sons, David, who is married to Andrea; and Darnell; as well as a granddaughter, Carmen. She loves to sing, exercise, write, read, and meet new people. Hattie has published two devotional books and a four-song CD. **July 20.**

SHARON LONG (BROWN), born in Trinidad, West Indies, has been a social worker for 28 years and is now senior manager with Alberta Children's Services. Sharon has four adult children and two teenage granddaughters. She lives in Edmonton, Alberta, Canada, and is married to Miguel. She enjoys writing, singing, entertaining, cooking and baking, and sewing. **Apr. 2, July 18, Sept. 22.**

TERRIE (RUFF) LONG is an associate professor and social work field director at Southern Adventist University. She enjoys gardening, bargain shopping, public speaking, and inspirational writing. Her desire is to be a beneficial presence in the lives of others; her life motto continues to be "I'm too blessed to be stressed and too anointed to be disappointed." **Sept. 2.**

RHODI ALERS DE LÓPEZ is a bilingual writer residing in Massachusetts. In her ministry as a singer, speaker, and songwriter, she aims to inspire others in their walk with the Lord. Her bilingual Web site is ExpresSion Publishing Ministries. Rhodi is the author of "Suspiros del Alma," and has a CD featuring 12 of her original songs. She is a wife, mother, and church leader. **Sept. 25.**

ADRIANA DE OLIVEIRA LOTÉRIO has recorded two CDs. She lives in Porto Velho, Rondônia, Brazil, and her husband and daughter, Adryelle, accompany her to all of her singing engagements. She will continue putting her ideal into practice: preach the gospel through music. **Oct. 21.**

SAVIE MAPHOSA comes from the beautiful country of Zimbabwe. She and her husband, Solomon, live in Pretoria, South Africa, have two daughters and one son, and are the proud grandparents of three. Savie is an accountant who has worked in the private sector for more than 23 years. Her hobbies are cooking and reading. **Dec. 26.**

DINAH A. MAQUILAN, who writes from the Philippines, has served Seventh-day Adventist institutions in different capacities for 38 years. She is now retired and lives with her 13-year-old adopted daughter in Iligan City. She loves teaching and working with small children. Presently she is acting as secretary-treasurer of her home church. **Oct. 25.**

TAMARA MARQUEZ DE SMITH, a former New Yorker, writes from Ocala, Florida, where she lives with her husband, Steven, and their two daughters, Lillian and Cassandra. Although Tamara doesn't currently hold an office in her local church, she assists with the Adventist Youth program as well as the nursing home Sunshine program. **June 7, Aug. 25.**

MARION V. CLARKE MARTIN, a physician, is immediate past dean of the faculty of medicine of the University of Panama and full professor of medical microbiology. She enjoys reading, playing the piano, and interior decorating, and considers herself greatly blessed with two adult sons and one granddaughter. **Oct. 23.**

JULIENNE LUMIÈRE NGO MASSOCK writes from the University of Consendai in Cameroon, where she is studying nursing. She is the fourth of five children, and is one of the scholarship recipients from the royalties from these devotional books. This is her first submission to the devotional book project. **July 26.**

RETHA MCCARTY has been the treasurer of her church for the past 30 years. She enjoys writing poetry, crocheting, sewing, quilting, and bird-watching. She organized the women's ministries group of her church to write a monthly newsletter as a ministry for the church. **Feb. 6, Apr. 10, Oct. 20.**

RASCHELLE MCLEAN-JONES writes from Palm Bay, Florida, where she teaches language arts and social studies to fourth graders. She and her husband, John, have two young sons, Aaron and Josiah. Working with children's ministries, the choir, and a praise team are her passions. This is her first submission. **Nov. 20.**

VIVEEN MCLEARY is an ordained elder, Sabbath school superintendent, and active member of the women's ministries of Toronto East church. She is also involved with the Women in Mission committee of the Ontario Conference. Viveen is a graduate of West Indies College and taught for many years in Jamaica before emigrating to Canada in 1989. She is single and happy. **May 31.**

PATSY MURDOCH MEEKER is grateful she can still drive and get out and about. While she misses California, she's found that Virginia is a pretty nice state. She enjoys reading and listening to instrumental music. **July 30.**

GAY MENTES does her artwork, Heavenly Reflections, and writes from Kelowna, British Columbia, Canada. Her husband, Alex, is also an artist, and they have two adult children, A. J. and Sharlet, and a son-in-law, Brad Tataryn. Gay enjoys journaling, photography, and floral design. She is a published author, and knits blankets for developing countries. **Aug. 16, Oct. 28.**

ANNETTE WALWYN MICHAEL is a former English teacher who, along with her pastor-husband, Reginald, has recently retired. She loves to write, work in her garden, and read good books. She is the mother of three grown daughters and the grandmother of four. **May 29, June 28, Aug. 2.**

SHARON MICHAEL, M.D., is a family physician in Pennsylvania who enjoys scrapbooking, reading, writing, and traveling. She enjoys teaching lifestyle change to her patients and spending time with her parents, nieces, and nephews. **Feb. 9, May 4.**

QUILVIE G. MILLS is a retired community college professor. She lives with her husband, Herman, in Port Saint Lucie, Florida. She serves her church as a Bible class teacher, board member, minister of music, and member of the floral committee. She enjoys traveling, reading, music, gardening, word games, and teaching piano. **Oct. 2, Dec. 6.**

FALADE DORCAS MODUPE is a professional counselor and is secretary for women's ministries of the South West Conference in Nigeria. She is a soul winner, and a church was established through her evangelistic efforts in Akure, Ondo State, Nigeria. She is married to Kunle, and is blessed with four children, two boys and two girls. **Sept. 19, Oct. 9.**

SUSEN MATTISON MOLÉ grew up as a missionary child in India and enjoyed moving around. She has two girls, both in college, and enjoys hiking, writing, reading, painting, playing her cello, and eating food from different cultures. She still travels around with her Navy doctor husband, as she has for the past 28 years. **Mar. 11, July 28, Dec. 1.**

MARCIA MOLLENKOPF is a retired teacher who lives in Klamath Falls, Oregon. She enjoys church involvement and has served in both adult and children's divisions. Her hobbies include reading, writing, music, and bird-watching. **Nov. 3.**

NATACHA MOOROOVEN was born on the island of Mauritius. In 2000 she completed a B.A. degree in information management and theology in Cameroon. After graduating, she was employed as a pastoral intern and went to Korea as an English and Bible teacher for five years. After working in Maryland, in March 2008 she went back to Korea, where she is working on a Ph.D. **May 15, June 9.**

ESPERANZA AQUINO MOPERA is the mother of four adults and grandmother of five. She enjoys gardening and being a traveling nurse. **July 27.**

ALESSANDRA CHOLET MOREIRA has a degree in architecture and has also studied at Southwestern Adventist University in Texas. She enjoys reading, listening to music, and talking to friends. She actively participates in her church's program by singing, preaching, and teaching Bible studies. **June 23.**

FRANCES OSBORNE MORFORD married her high school sweetheart 60 years ago and spent 30 of those years in South Africa, Uganda, Ethiopia, Lebanon, Egypt, and South Sudan. She taught English and Bible beside her math-instructor husband. They have now retired to beautiful Eden Valley, Colorado. They have two children, three grandchildren, and one great-grandson. **Jan. 20, July 3, Dec. 9.**

YER MOUA was born in Laos and lived there until she was 13 years old, when she came to America. She and her husband, Thomas, have six children, ranging in age from 4 to 21. Her hobbies include hiking, gardening, and raising animals. She enjoys working as a carton-former operator for McKee Foods in Gentry, Arkansas. **Apr. 5.**

BONNIE MOYERS lives with her husband and three cats in Staunton, Virginia. She has two adult children and two granddaughters. She is a musician in her local church and plays for a Methodist church and a Presbyterian church on Sundays. She writes freelance and has been published in many magazines and books. **Jan. 19, Oct. 22, Dec. 23.**

SYNTHIA MURALI is a physical therapist in Pune, India, where she lives with her pastor-husband. Her hobbies include singing and playing guitar. She enjoys serving the Lord beside her husband and conducts prayer ministry in her workplace. **May 9.**

LILLIAN MUSGRAVE and her family continue to enjoy the beauty and uniqueness of northern California, close to family and friends. She belongs to Sierra Christian Writers and enjoys writing stories, poems, songs, and music, as well as being involved in church responsibilities and family activities. **Oct. 26.**

JEGATHA JOHNSON MUTHURAJ is a teacher in an Adventist school and serves as shepherdess and women's ministries coordinator in the Chengalpat-Kanchipuram region in India, where her husband is the region director. She has two young and energetic sons. **Aug. 28.**

PETTYA NACKOVA is an engineer who has a Ph.D. in machine science. She served as an editor in chief for the Bulgarian Adventist newspaper for nine years. **Mar. 23, Dec. 29.**

MARGARET NATHANIEL writes from Hosur, India. In 2000 she retired as the Southern Asia Division family and children's ministries director, having served the church for 46 years in various capacities. Her hobbies are working with children, reading, music, and doing crafts. **May 8.**

ANNE ELAINE NELSON, a retired teacher, has written the book *Puzzled Parents*. Ann is a widow who lives in Michigan. Her four children have blessed her with 11 grandchildren and three great-grandchildren. She is active at church as the women's ministries leader. Favorite activities include making tie blankets, music, photography, and creative memories with her grandchildren. **Jan. 24, Apr. 28, Aug. 22.**

ROSÂNGELA FERREIRA NERY, a nurse's aid, is a children's class teacher in Botafogo, Rio de Janeiro, Brazil, and the mother of two children. She likes to be with friends, listen to music, and practice volleyball and athletics. **June 25.**

CAROL NICKS writes from Canada. She is a librarian at Canadian University College. Her family spent five and a half years as missionaries in Pakistan. She enjoys nature—identifying flowers, hiking, canoeing, and gardening. **June 21.**

MARIA SINHARINHA DE OLIVEIRA NOGUEIRA is a retired teacher who lives in Icó-Ceará, Brazil. She is married and has two adult daughters and four grandchildren. She is active in her church as a deaconess and has written a book of poetry entitled *Folhas Sussurrantes* (Whispering Leaves). She enjoys writing poetry, reading, crocheting, and exercising. **July 11, Sept. 1.**

RUTH H. NYACHURU-MUZE, an assistant professor of nursing in North Carolina, lives with her retired husband. She has served as Sabbath school teacher, leader for health ministries, women's ministries, and family life ministries, and leads prayer bands in her local church. She enjoys entertaining and traveling with her husband. **Oct. 11.**

ELIZABETH VERSTEEGH ODIYAR lives in Kelowna, British Columbia, and manages the family chimney sweep business. She has twin sons and a daughter. Beth enjoys mission trips and road trips across North America, being creative, sewing, cooking vegan, home decorating, organizing, leading Pathfinders and Vacation Bible School, and writing. **July 21, Sept. 26.**

MAI-RHEA ODIYAR graduated from Canadian University College in Alberta, Canada, in the spring of 2006, with a bachelor's degree in elementary education. After graduation she headed straight to the mission field, where she is currently teaching third and fourth grade in Saipan, in the Northern Mariana Islands. She is confident the Lord will continue to lead her. **Aug. 8, Oct. 8, Nov. 16.**

JOYCE O'GARRO, a retired laboratory technologist for 20 years, took care of cancer patients. She has taught all levels, from kindergarten to college, and is a pianist who, at 76 years of age, still teaches piano and plays the organ at church. She has two grown daughters, one son-in-law, and two grandchildren. Her mother is still alive at 102 years. **Apr. 18, June 8, Nov. 17.**

BERYL O'HARE, a 61-year-old wife, homemaker (always), and grandmother of three, writes from Australia. She loves to read and write many, many letters, and sometimes writes articles for magazines on mothering topics, grain milling, including one on long lactation in goats. She belongs to a very small Seventh-day Adventist church and attends regularly. **Nov. 28.**

MARINÊS APARECIDA DA SILVA OLIVEIRA works as a teacher in Araraquara, São Paulo, Brazil. She is married and the mother of two children. She is an active member of the Central church in that city, serving as church secretary and helping with women's ministries activities. She enjoys reading, writing, and talking with friends. Her favorite word is "perseverance." **June 13.**

JEMIMA DOLLOSA ORILLOSA, originally from the Philippines, now works as a secretary in Maryland. She and her husband, Danny, have two married daughters and are so excited to have gained two sons-in-law. Jemima loves to witness for Christ and is involved in several ministries, including overseas mission ministry, prayer ministry, visitation, and raising money for scholarships. **May 5, July 13, Oct. 16.**

ROSE OTIS initiated the first six women's devotional books of this series while serving as women's ministries director at the General Conference of Seventh-day Adventists. She is now retired in Maryland with her husband, Bud, and their two children and four grandchildren. They enjoy gardening and travel. **Feb. 10, Nov. 13, Dec. 10.**

BRENDA OTTLEY was born in Guyana, South America. She is married to Ernest, a Trinidadian, and lives in St. Lucia, where she works as a secondary school teacher and etutor in the University of the West Indies distance education program. She and her husband are involved in radio ministry at PrayzFM. **June 26, July 10.**

HANNELE OTTSCHOFSKI lives in southern Germany. She has four adult daughters. She speaks at seminars and evangelistic campaigns and is an ordained elder of her local church. **July 25, Nov. 5, Dec. 25.**

ANA PAULA COSTA TEIXEIRA DE PAIVA was born in Manaus, Amazonas, Brazil, and grew up in João Pessoa, Paraíba. She is married to Pastor Vilberto Jansen Paiva da Silva, who is a pastor in Curitiba, Brazil. Currently, Ana Paula works at the Curitiba Adventist Clinic and participates in a women's group. **July 22, Aug. 15.**

OFELIA A. PANGAN, a retired teacher and missionary, has been married to Abel for 48 years. They both enjoy the simple things in life—gardening, reading, traveling, being with their loved ones, and playing Scrabble. They are parents of three professional children who have given them nine grandchildren. **Mar. 20, Apr. 26, Sept.16.**

REVEL PAPAIOANNOU, from the biblical town of Berea, Greece, works with her retired-but-working pastor-husband of 52 years. They have four sons and 13 grandchildren. She has held almost every local church position, and at present she is Sabbath school superintendent, teaches the adult lesson, cleans the church, and cares for the tiny garden. Free time is filled with visiting, Bible studies, and hiking. **July 6, Dec. 8.**

PERCY FLORENCE EDWIN PAUL writes from India, where she is a teacher. She enjoys teaching the youth and mentoring and nurturing girls. Her husband is the director of the Ramnad-Sivagangi region. She has a son who has finished his master's studies, and a married daughter who is a homeopathic doctor. She enjoys giving Bible studies and loves to be with children. **July 19.**

LOIS RITTENHOUSE PECCE and her husband are "retired" in Centerville, Ohio. She is active with the Dayton Christian Scribes, a writers' group that she cofounded with friend Betty Kossick 31 years ago. Her favorite role is grandma, but she also enjoys gardening, conducting nursing home chapel services, and teaching beginner Sabbath school. **Feb. 17, June 15.**

NATALIA LORENA HOLM DE PÉREZ has been working with her pastor-husband for seven years at the North Argentine Conference. She has three children: Abigail, Nahuel, and Axel. She is an elementary school teacher who enjoys reading and painting. **Nov. 8.**

BETTY G. PERRY lives in Fayetteville, North Carolina, with her semiretired pastor-husband. She was an anesthetist for 32 years and is presently semiretired. She has two adult children, four grandchildren, and one great-grandchild. Hobbies include playing the piano and organ, quilting, arts and crafts, trying new recipes, and yearly contributions to the women's devotional book. **July 24, Nov. 4.**

ANGÈLE PETERSON lives in Ohio, where she works as an administrative assistant and serves her church in several capacities. She enjoys spending time with her family, especially her niece and nephew, and looks forward to Christ's soon return, knowing that in heaven she'll never need a new car. **July 23.**

BIRDIE PODDER is a retiree who comes from northeast India and has settled in south India. She has two adult children, a daughter and a son, and four grandsons. Her hobbies are gardening, cooking, baking, telling stories, writing articles, and composing poems. She is doing a hand-crafted card ministry for those who need comfort and encouragement and to glorify God's name. **July 7, Sept. 13.**

LOVIERE POINTER writes from Whitby, Ontario, Canada, where she's a single mother of two adopted daughters. She is a member of the Apple Creek Seventh-day Adventist Church, where she currently serves as one of the church pianists. Her hobbies are baking, cake decorating, and sewing clothes for her children and herself. She is a first-time writer. **May 1.**

LIDIA POLL has been the leader of women's ministries for 10 years in one of the six conferences in the Romanian Union. Raised in a family dedicated to the ministry, she and her husband work together on her projects. She has a daughter, who is a pastor's wife, a son, and three grandchildren. Her passion is soul winning, for which she uses all her God-given gifts. **Oct. 1.**

VICTORIA JEEVA PONNAPPA works as the women's and shepherdess ministries director in South Tamil Conference, Madurai, India. She has three girls, all of whom are in nursing. Her husband is the president of South Tamil Conference of Seventh-day Adventists. She enjoys sewing, gardening, and cooking. **Sept. 8.**

DARLENEJOAN MCKIBBIN RHINE was born in Nebraska, raised in California, and schooled in Tennessee. She holds a B.A. degree in journalism and worked in the plant at the Los Angeles *Times* for 21 years before retiring in 1995. She now lives on an island in Puget Sound, Washington, spending much of her time writing, and attends the North Cascade Adventist Church. **Jan. 18, June 19, Sept. 3.**

MARILYN RILEY is the mother of two sons, a baptized Christian since 1972, and an executive assistant at Columbia Union College in Maryland. **Dec. 24.**

SUSAN RILEY was born in Trinidad and Tobago; however, she currently lives in England. She is a mental health nurse, working on a child and family unit. She loves corresponding, walking (especially along the river where she lives), and writing poems. Her goal is to be a freelance writer. **Feb. 8, May 28, Aug. 6.**

CAROL ROBINSON, a first-time contributor, is a social worker by profession who enjoys swimming, singing, meeting people, traveling, outdoor activities, and collecting inspirational thoughts. She has a special interest in helping people mend broken relationships. **Apr. 15.**

CHARLOTTE ROBINSON was born and raised in Arkansas, living there for 49 years. She and her husband, David, have three children, the youngest in academy and the oldest ones in college. Charlotte works for the United States Postal Service (cleaning post offices) and for McKee Foods in Gentry. She has written stories for *Our Little Friend* and *Insight.* **Apr. 5, June 1.**

AVIS MAE RODNEY is a justice of the peace for the province of Ontario, Canada, where she resides with her husband, Leon. Avis is the mother of two adult children and has five grandchildren. Her interests include community involvement, long walks, and spending time with family and friends. **Jan. 30, June 18.**

RAYLENE ROSS is a registered nurse who does a really long commute to work: from her home in Spanish Town, Jamaica, to Englewood, New Jersey, where she works as a labor and delivery nurse. She is the wife to Leroy, and the mother of 5-year-old Zachary Sebastian. When she has time, she enjoys sewing and scrapbooking. At church she is family ministries director and a choir leader. **Apr. 1.**

PEGGY RUSIKE grew up in Zimbabwe but now lives in the United Kingdom. She works in a residential home full-time and has a part-time job in the hospital. Divorced, she is the mother of two young men and a teenage daughter. **Apr. 6.**

QUETAH SACKIE-OSBORNE is an educator who has taught all levels, prekindergarten to eighth grade. She enjoys reading, singing, writing, and traveling. She also enjoys the adventures of being married to Pastor Charles Ray Osborne III, and nurturing their children Queanna and Charles IV. They are all hoping to hold evangelistic meetings in Liberia, West Africa. **May 7.**

LEAH A. SALLOMAN writes from the Philippines where she is a pastor's wife and the head teacher at the Ormoc Adventist Elementary School. They have two children, Eunie Glen and Van Shinar. Leah just passed her comprehensive examination for her master's degree. She enjoys women's ministries, tennis, cooking, baking, and eating. **June 30.**

DEBORAH SANDERS lives in Alberta, Canada. In 2007 Deborah and her husband, Ron, "with the help of angels," wrote a book, *Our Journey Through Time With Sonny*, about their son, who has significant developmental disabilities. The book is a collection of sacred memories shared with the hope they will be spiritually encouraging to others in the family of God until Jesus comes. **Mar. 22, July 16.**

THEODORA V. SANDERS lives in Huntsville, Alabama, with her husband, James, and their five adopted children. They attend the Mount Calvary Adventist Church. She has two adult children and six grandchildren. She enjoys reading, writing, singing, and playing Scrabble. **June 2.**

ELZA C. DOS SANTOS, a minister's wife in São Paulo, Brazil, is the mother of three adult children preparing for marriage. She likes to organize special church events and enjoys reading, traveling, crocheting, and helping future mothers. **Jan. 16, Nov. 1.**

SÔNIA MARIA RIGOLI SANTOS is a minister's wife and women's ministries and Shepherdess International leader in the South Paraná Conference in Curitiba, Brazil. She has two children, Carlos Eduardo and Carla Beatriz, and really misses her child who lives in another country. She enjoys reading, writing, preparing and presenting radio programs, and taking care of her home. **July 15.**

DOROTHY D. SAUNDERS is a retired customer account auditor, former committee person for her district, and is now serving as a local elder in her church. She has been published in the *Veteran's Voices*, a national veteran's magazine, and in *The Philadelphia Forum*, the publication for the Philadelphia Association of Paralegals. **May 2.**

SUSANA SCHULZ is from Argentina. She has three adult daughters and three grandchildren. A missionary spouse, she has studied countries and languages, people and cultures. She was the first women's ministry director for the South American Division of Seventh-day Adventists and is a teacher and director of the ACA program at the Adventist River Plate University. She enjoys classical music. **June 22.**

MARIE H. SEARD is a regular writer for this devotional book project. She and her husband are proud that they have joined that elite group called grandparents. She enjoys family, friends, writing, reading, traveling, and shopping. **Aug. 11, Sept. 6.**

VICTORIA SELVARAJ writes from India, where she is working as a nursing superintendent in a government hospital. She has two grown children, a daughter and a son. Her husband is the director for the Thindivanam-Villupuram region of Seventh-day Adventists. **Apr. 23.**

DONNA LEE SHARP enjoys using her musical talent in her home church, in other churches, and at three care homes, as well as the Christian Women's Club. Her hobbies include gardening, flower arranging, bird-watching, and travel—mainly to visit family members scattered across North America. **Apr. 7.**

CARROL JOHNSON SHEWMAKE is a retired pastor's wife, mother of four grown children, and has eight grandchildren and three great-grandsons. She is the author of seven published books and spent years speaking at camp meeting, retreats, and church weekends. She and her husband are prayer leaders in their northern California church and are eagerly awaiting the coming of Jesus in glory. **Apr. 8, May 3.**

JUDY MUSGRAVE SHEWMAKE lives with her husband, Tom, in northern California. They have four children and two grandsons, and a son and daughter still at home. Judy is the editor of *The Adventist Home Educator Handbook* and the Web site for homeschoolers. Another ministry is found at www.ConnectingRelationships.org. **Sept. 4.**

BONITA JOYNER SHIELDS is the editor for youth Bible study guides in the Sabbath School Department of the General Conference of Seventh-day Adventists. She lives in Brookeville, Maryland, with her husband and two cats who live by the adage "Dogs have masters; cats have staff!" **Aug. 23.**

ENY RUELLA SILVA is a retired teacher who has three adult daughters and four grandchildren. She enjoys gardening, reading, and listening to music. She is a women's ministries leader in her church. **Aug. 27, Oct. 7.**

JUDY GOOD SILVER (Jonah and Mary's "Meme") is so grateful the Lord is still blessing the years within her "dash" (1953-2010). She and Phil share 33 years of marriage and friendship. Her joys include family, friends, home, writing, gardening, the replenishing gift of Sabbath, rocking chairs, porches, and a little piece of heaven nestled in the Shenandoah Valley in Virginia. **Feb. 1, Oct. 31.**

FERNANDA PAULA GOMES SIMÃO is the women's ministries director in the President Medici church and lives in Chapecó, Santa Catarina, Brazil. She enjoys handicrafts, vegetarian recipes, and reading books on topics that can be debated in church. She is currently getting her degree in education, and has been married for six years. **Oct. 19.**

REBECCA SINGH is working as an administrative assistant to the president of Roorkee Adventist College, in India, and takes care of the Hindi church. She has been in the workforce for the past 27 years as a secretary and English teacher. She and her husband have two boys. She loves to give Bible studies and work with young children in her church. **Oct. 24.**

HEATHER-DAWN SMALL is director for women's ministries at the General Conference of Seventh-day Adventists. She has been children's and women's ministries director for the Caribbean Union Conference, located in Trinidad and Tobago. She is the wife of Pastor Joseph Small and the mother of Dalonne and Jerard. She loves air travel, reading, and scrapbooking. **Feb. 4, May 16, Sept. 24.**

YVONNE CURRY SMALLWOOD is a wife, mother, and grandmother, who writes from Upper Marlboro, Maryland. Trained as a scientist, she works in science administration. Her stories have appeared in several publications. **Oct. 13.**

THAMER CASSANDRA SMIKLE writes from Jamaica, where she is an auditor at the Jamaica customs department. She has completed a master's degree in business administration (specializing in financing) at the Northern Caribbean University and is an active member of the Portmore church. Her hobbies include reading, singing, relaxing, and laughing. **Jan. 3, Feb. 2.**

ARDIS DICK STENBAKKEN spends her days editing these devotional books, doing things with her husband, Dick, taking care of her 94-year-old father, and playing with her four grandchildren. She enjoys reading, especially about Bible women, and speaking about them. She is also trying to squeeze in a little quilting, and maybe, someday, do oil painting again. **Jan. 4, July 9, Nov. 10.**

BEULAH FERN STEVENS is a retired nurse and chaplain. She enjoys promoting mental and spiritual health through writing and speaking. She works from her home near Walla Walla, Washington, the place of her birth. She continues to keep in touch with health care by volunteering at the local Adventist hospital. She had an important part in producing devotional books for nurses. **Dec. 17.**

SELENE STEWART is a mother of three children and the grandmother of two. She is currently working as a licensed practical nurse. She is active in Sabbath school and youth ministries and enjoys reading, taking care of her grandchildren, and working beside her husband, a city council member in the city of New York. **Aug. 14, Sept. 18.**

ANDREEA STRÂMBU-DIMA, 29, is a pastor's wife and the mother of a 4-year-old. She writes from Romania, and she has a university degree and a Doctor of Business Administration in marketing. More than anything, she wants to reveal God's love through everything she does, love that she experiences with great joy every day. **Mar. 1, June 29.**

BEULAH SUDHAKAR serves as the women's and shepherdess ministries director in the North Tamil Conference of Seventh-day Adventists in India. She has two sons and a daughter who are all in school. Her husband is the president for the North Tamil Conference in Trichy. **Apr. 4.**

RUBYE SUE, a retired secretary, and her husband, Bill, who spent 40 years in colporteur work, live at a small, self-supporting school in Tennessee, where they appreciate fellow-shipping with the students nine months of the year; they then migrate to Florida for the winter. Rubye, 86, and Bill, 93, enjoy traveling and visiting with their children, grand-children, and great-grandchildren. **Jan. 31.**

JEAN SUNDARAM serves as the women's and shepherdess ministries director in the Southeast India Union, Vandalur, Chennai, India. Her pastor-husband is the president of Southeast India Union. She enjoys reading, sewing, gardening, cooking, mentoring women, and sharing the message of His love. She has two grown children who serve the Lord through medical ministry. **Jan. 28.**

ERIKO SUZUKI has served as a missionary teacher in Korea and the United States, as well as one of the Golden Angels, a missionary singing group from the Northern Asia-Pacific Division. Her education includes a bachelor's degree in music as well as elementary education from Japan. She lives with her parents in Korea and is waiting for God's next call for service. **Dec. 27.**

LORAINE F. SWEETLAND is retired in Tennessee. She recently began an Adventist Food Buying Club for her church and community. She enjoys writing, computer surfing, reading, her church, and the deer, woodchucks, and birds in her backyard. She lost her husband of almost 57 years and now lives alone with her three little dogs for companions. **Feb. 21, May 30, Oct. 15.**

ARLENE TAYLOR is risk manager and director of infection control for three Adventist Health hospitals in northern California. A brain-function specialist, she does research through her nonprofit corporation, Realization, Inc., and presents a variety of seminars internationally. Web site: www.arlenetaylor.org. **Jan. 5, May 25, Aug. 21.**

AUDRE B. TAYLOR, a published writer and retired administrative assistant for Adventist Development and Relief Agency International, enjoys choral conducting. In national media competition she has won an Angel Award for one of her choral and orchestral performances. She is also a practicing psychotherapist in the Washington, D.C., area. **Dec. 12.**

G. G. (GENEVA GWENDOLYN) TAYLOR is a very active member of the Palm Bay Seventh-day Adventist Church. Though now officially retired, she often spends her nights at the hospital, sitting with Baker Act patients. **Dec. 15.**

ROSE JOSEPH THOMAS is a native of Haiti. She lives in Altamonte Springs, Florida, with her husband and two children. She teaches at Forest Lake Education Center. **Feb. 20.**

SHARON M. THOMAS, a retired public school teacher, and her husband, Don, a retired social worker, enjoy traveling together. Sharon also enjoys reading, walking, biking, shopping, playing the piano, and quilting. She is still learning quilting from experienced quilters and life lessons from our omniscient God. **Nov. 6.**

STELLA THOMAS works in the Office of Adventist Mission/Presidential of the General Conference of Seventh-day Adventists. Her motto in life is to share God's love with the world. **July 31.**

TRACEY-ANN TRAIL, a native of Jamaica, works as an information technology teacher on the island of Providenciales in the Turks and Caicos Islands. She loves to travel, and to surf the Internet, and is reviving her passion for writing. She is a proud alumna of Northern Caribbean University in Jamaica and Bethune Cookman University in Florida. **Nov. 22.**

NANCY ANN NEUHARTH TROYER and her husband, Don, now live in Sun Lakes, Banning, California, and have retired from the pastorate. They have one daughter, Stephanie. Nancy spent 24 years traveling the globe with her United States Army chaplain husband. Nancy is editor of a picture journal for His Voice men's chorus. (See www.HisVoiceNews.blogspot.com.) **Jan. 11.**

NANCY VAN PELT is a certified family life educator, best-selling author, and internationally known speaker. She has written more than 20 books, and has traversed the globe teaching families how to really love each other. Her hobbies include getting organized, entertaining, having fun, and quilting. Nancy and her husband live in California. They have three adult children. **Feb. 7.**

SOSAMMA VARGHESE is from India, where she has been serving as children's ministries director for the South West India Union, Thrissur, Kerala. Before that she was the women's ministries director for North and South Kerala. She is a B.Sc. graduate from Kerala University and holds an M.Ed. from Mysore University. Carolyn, their daughter, is a nursing student. **Aug. 9.**

CEREATHA J. VAUGHN has lived in Detroit, Michigan, all her life. She is employed by the city of Wayne as a public transportation driver. As a local elder at the Burns Adventist Church, she has a passion and talent for writing sermons, short stories, and poems. She is single, and devotes her time to serving God wherever He leads her. **Aug. 1.**

CARMEM VIRGÍNIA is a community health agent who is getting a degree in literature. She likes to sing and write poems. **Feb. 23.**

CAROLYN VOSS, Ph.D., is a widow and a retired nurse educator. Her hobbies are sewing, quilting, crafts, walking, golf, and studying God's Word. **Oct. 30.**

MARY M. J. WAGONER-ANGELIN lives in Ooltewah, Tennessee, with her husband, Randy, and their daughters, Barbara and Rachel. Mary is a stay-at-home mom and a social worker at a psychiatric hospital. She volunteers with the Make-A-Wish Foundation, at the local library, and as a coach with Kids in Discipleship. She enjoys Mothers of Preschoolers and humor therapy. **June 6, Aug. 5, Nov. 12.**

CORA A. WALKER is a retired nurse, editor, and freelance writer who lives in Fort Washington, Maryland. She is an active member of the church she attends in Charles County, Maryland. She enjoys reading, writing, swimming, classical music, singing, and traveling. She has one son, Andre V. Walker. **Mar. 21, Sept. 15.**

ARLENE WALKER-ADAMS is a professor of nursing at Indian River Community College in Fort Pierce, Florida. At the time of writing, this wife and mother of a teenage son was completing her doctorate. She sings in the praise team, mass choir, and sanctuary choir at her church. She also serves as counselor for the Pathfinder Club. This is her first submission. **Oct. 17.**

ANNA MAY RADKE WATERS is a retired administrative secretary from Columbia Adventist Academy, and served for many years as an elder and a greeter at church. She and Herb, her husband of more than 55 years, are now "snowbirds," wintering in California and spending summers in Washington. They enjoy their children and grandchildren. **Jan. 29, May 19, Dec. 22.**

DOROTHY EATON WATTS has retired from administration for her church headquarters in India. Dorothy is a freelance writer, editor, and speaker. She has been a missionary in India for more than 28 years, founded an orphanage, taught elementary school, and has written more than 26 books. Her hobbies include gardening, hiking, and birding (with more than 1,600 in her world total). **Jan. 17, Sept. 7, Nov. 29.**

DANIELA WEICHHOLD, originally from Germany, works as an administrative assistant at the European Commission Headquarters in Brussels, Belgium. She enjoys the cultural diversity both at her workplace and in her adopted hometown. In her free time she likes cooking, the outdoors, playing the piano, singing, and doing medical missionary work. **May 21, June 17.**

LYN WELK-SANDY lives in Adelaide, South Australia. She works with bereaved children and young offenders attending court. Lyn spent many years as a pipe organist and loves church music, choir work, and helping Sudanese refugee families. She enjoys photography and caravanning around outback Australia with her husband, Keith. Lyn is a mother of four and has 12 grandchildren. **Jan. 6, Mar. 2, Dec. 4.**

SHIRNET WELLINGTON, born in Jamaica, is married to Pastor Leon Wellington. They have two sons, Rohann and Handel. A teacher by profession, Shirnet says her greatest joy has been in teaching, mothering, and encouraging ministers' wives in their role as shepherdesses. She now serves as an administrative assistant. **Feb. 27, May 14, July 8.**

SANDRA WIDULLE is married and has two children. She loves to put her thoughts and experiences down in writing. She is involved in children's ministries and takes care of the church's showcase. **Feb. 28.**

VERA WIEBE writes from Canada, where she is the women's ministries leader for their area. She enjoys playing the keyboard and sewing for her grandchildren. She also enjoys traveling with her husband, a pastor and conference leader. **Nov. 7.**

MILDRED C. WILLIAMS is a widow and retired physical therapist living in southern California. She enjoys studying and teaching the Bible, writing, gardening, public speaking, sewing, and spending time with her grown children and granddaughter. She likes writing for the devotional book, as it gives her a chance to share God's love with others. **Mar. 19.**

PATRICE WILLIAMS-GORDON is a Jamaican motivational speaker and seminar presenter who enjoys writing, speaking, reading, and a good laugh. She shares ministry with her pastor-husband, Danhugh, who currently serves in Nassau, Bahamas. Mother of Ashli and Rhondi, Patrice is excited about reaching anyone for Jesus. **Feb. 5, Dec. 31.**

MELANIE WINKLER writes from Australia, where she is a wife and an unpublished author of novels. She loves to sing and praise God. She is involved in children's ministries and church planting. Melanie loves the opportunity to share things she has learned with others, especially other Christians. **May 6.**

LATOYA V. ZAVALA is a full-time teacher and a full-time seminary student. She enjoys serving her church as pianist, speaker, and correspondence Bible study coordinator. In her spare time she enjoys playing the cello, reading, writing, going on mission trips, and soaking up life with her husband. **Mar. 9, May 23.**

Prayer Requests

_____

_____

_____

_____

_____

_____

_____

_____

_____

_____

"He will cover you with his feathers,
and under his wings you will find refuge."
—*Psalm 91:4, NIV*

Prayer Requests

_____

_____

_____

_____

_____

_____

_____

_____

_____

_____

"Take my yoke upon you and learn from me, for I am gentle
and humble in heart, and you will find rest for your souls.
For my yoke is easy and my burden is light."
—Matthew 11:29, 30, NIV

Prayer Requests

_____

_____

_____

_____

_____

_____

_____

_____

_____

_____

"Let the peace of Christ rule in your hearts, since as members
of one body you were called to peace. And be thankful."
—*Colossians 3:15, NIV*